UTTAM KUMAR

UTTAM KUMAR

A LIFE IN CINEMA

Sayandeb Chowdhury

B L O O M S B U R Y

NEW DELHI • LONDON • OXFORD • NEW YORK • SYDNEY

BLOOMSBURY INDIA
Bloomsbury Publishing India Pvt. Ltd
Second Floor, LSC Building No. 4, DDA Complex, Pocket C – 6 & 7,
Vasant Kunj, New Delhi, 110070

BLOOMSBURY, BLOOMSBURY ACADEMIC INDIA and the Diana logo
are trademarks of Bloomsbury Publishing Plc

First published in India 2021
This export edition published 2021

Bloomsbury Academic
An imprint of Bloomsbury Publishing Plc

ISBN: PB: 978-93-90358-93-9 ; eBook: 978-93-90358-01-4
2 4 6 8 10 9 7 5 3 1

Typeset in Minion Pro by Manipal Technologies Limited
Printed and bound in India by Replika Press Pvt. Ltd.

To find out more about our authors and books visit www.bloomsbury.com and sign
up for our newsletters

To the everlasting charms of a unique film star,
the heroic laughter behind that stardom,
and the genial man behind that laughter.

The universe has its only language of gesture,
It talks in the voice of pictures and dance.
—Rabindranath Tagore, *On Art and Aesthetics*

CONTENTS

ACKNOWLEDGEMENTS

UTTAM Kumar is a public obsession in Bengal. He coaxes a mix of ebullience and awe from everyone who I have had the occasion of mentioning the book. Moreover, stardom is a slippery idea. I have taken rounds around it, meeting people from various walks who have made it even more elusive. So, my gratitude and exasperation is wide and all-encompassing.

It was in 2004 that I first thought of a project of this nature and have since hung on to it, albeit piecemeal. Personal and professional vacillations aside, the delay is also because I could barely manage to hoard anything more than a steady supply of eagerness. Actual work began only in 2017. At the same time, I have realised—more to my relief than my disappointment—that everything has a time; and that the current shape, tone and temperament of the book would have been unachievable, if it were written even three years ago. Not that it is anything close to being perfect now, but it would have been much worse otherwise. Part of the reason is my own stake in it, which has consolidated over time; part of it because it was always an ambitious project needing research, reflection and reconnaissance in equal measure; and partly because a lot of material I have accessed became available only recently.

A first book carries the imprint of growing up into a kind of individuality and here I cannot miss mentioning my teachers in school, Amit Dasgupta and Rajat Bhattacharya. Unless they had taught me to be confident with a tongue not as native as it now seems, I would not have found the courage to make teaching literature a profession and this book the first public pronouncement of my having been betrothed to a language. The formidable scholars and the freethinking ecosystem at both the Jawaharlal Nehru University, New Delhi, and Jadavpur University, Kolkata, have also played a very enabling role during my university days.

I also owe it to my grandfather Jyotiprasad Banerjee, a professor at the University of Calcutta, for having made me attentive to history in a way a teenager should be, with pleasure and animation rather than with the pencilled sincerity of a textbook student. So did my grandmother Tripti, whose keen eye for history made her read about far-flung countries till well into her 70s. I have not studied either history or film as a professional undertaking. So, the errors here are my own and the joys, if any, belong to such gentlemen and women to whose thirst for life I would want to be an heir. I miss them terribly.

In the same breath, I must mention Professor Moinak Biswas, who has long been a silent support for this project. Now my doctoral supervisor, he has allowed me to take away two years from my doctoral years to concentrate exclusively on the book. I am not sure any other advisor would have done the same. I profusely thank him to be able to secure temporary amnesty from the grinds of research. He also gave me permission to use images from the archive of the Media Lab at Jadavpur University.

My parents Saswati and Tapas have survived my many indecisions and errors, mostly because they hardly had a choice but also because they are extremely nice people. Both have also read various drafts of the chapters with all the parental indulgence they could muster. So has my sister Raina (Debdatta), who took the additional responsibility of keeping me warned about my ritual lapse into lethargy. Can't thank them enough.

Long-time friends Jagori Bandyopadhyay, Nayna Chatterjee, Baidik Bhattacharya and Mallarika Sinha Roy adjusted to my pesky habit of diverting any *adda* towards Uttam with all the kindness that befits helpless comrades. They have also doubled as readers of bits, having signed up for the ordeal under the threat that not one bad word was allowed about the star. Jagori deserves a special mention for also being a film critic of public standing. I have spent many evenings conversing with her, over phone or in person, about the direction the book might be taking. I am especially thankful to her. I am also extremely thankful to Mousumi Dasgupta and Rajendran Narayanan, dear friends and Uttam co-fans, who kept my writing life warm with their gung-ho vocality. So did Sarnath Banerjee, who often surprised me with his thoughtful curiosity about the fate of the book.

I also had readers in friends Rituparno Basu, Arpita Kuila and Anshuman Chakraborty. I have had meaningful conversations with friends Rajat Sur, Sangbida Lahiri, Sandeep Banerjee and Atreyee Majumdar, Gautam Basuthakur, Sreshtha and Abhijit Banerjee, and passingly, with several others—cousins, colleagues, kin. Friends Supriyo Ghosh and Sanjukta Roy, Ishita Dey, Sanjeet Chowdhury, Anirban Biswas, Abeer Gupta, Anirban Das, Kalyan S., Shilpi Goswami, and my oldest buddies Anirban Banerjee and Shamik Chatterjee have played invigorating parts in this saga. I am thankful to Kaushik Bhowmik, a historian of cinema, for copiously advising me on an early draft of a chapter. Nilanjan Dasgupta, Sudipta Mitra, Amitav Sen, Amitabha Bhattacharya, Debashish Mukhopadhyay, Shantanu Chatterjee, Subhojit Chatterjee, Anurag Samuel, Sunalini Kumar and especially

Vikram Thakur have been very supportive of the project. So was Zehra Mehdi, who was almost convinced of Uttam's greatness before she escaped to the United States. This book would have had a longer gestation period unless film writer and editor Shantanu Roychowdhury had nudged or friend and former publisher Saugata Mukherjee hadn't prodded. In recent years, I have had the privilege of the warm company of Professor Shyam B. Menon, Professor Alok Bhalla and Professor Salil Mishra, who have taught me a lot. I have also received earnest support from a younger collective of cinema enthusiasts who have read my occasional pieces on Uttam over the years and kept me going with their kind appreciation. If I am guilty of forgetting anyone here, it is thanks to an unreliable narrator housed in my brain.

I have had the opportunity to write three longish essays on Uttam. I am grateful to former arts editor at *Caravan Magazine* Snigdha Poonam, *Film International* editor Daniel Lindvall and *The Wire's* Sidharth Bhatia for making their publication possible. Writing two academic essays were also part of my preparation for the book. For one of them I thank scholars Madhuja Mukherjee and Kaustav Bakshi—who invited me to contribute to a special issue of the Routledge journal *South Asian History and Culture*. The other essay received the keen attention of Professor Stephanos Stephanides, who, along with Professor G.J.V. Prasad, edited an issue on Partition for Routledge's *European Journal of English Studies*. I am also thankful to opinion editors at *The Hindu* and *Anandabazar Patrika* for publishing two recent pieces by me on Uttam; and to Gayatri Sinha and her team for inviting me to write a two-part essay on Uttam for *Critical Collective*—a learned digital resource and journal.

Among all the professional help I received, I must mention the owners of Angel Video, who have made many hitherto unavailable films accessible on YouTube. I do not know them but I am nevertheless very grateful to them. I must mention Shaktidas Roy, under whose eminent supervision the library at the *Anandabazar Patrika* thrives, as well as Professor Amlan Dasgupta, who gave me access to Jadavpur University's School of Cultural Texts and Records. With over 1,400 booklets, the Rudrajit Mookherjee Collection of Cinema and Theatre Booklets (1932–2005) at the British Library is a wonderland of popular cinema publicity. Gopal Biswas and Chandranath Chattopadhyay, reputed collectors and keen custodians of intangible film heritage, informed and listened equally. They also introduced me to ace collector Parimal Ray, whose lavish reproduction of Uttam Kumar's posters were a ready reckoner. He also gave me permission to use the bulk of the images in I have included in the book. Sandip Ray, son of Satyajit Ray, gave me permission to use one image. And I cannot miss mentioning

Suranjan Roy, who fleshed out a most exclusive image from his late father Sukumar Roy's collection for use on the cover. My immense gratitude to all of them.

I also very thankful to Mr Satchin of India Habitat Centre in New Delhi for inviting me to speak at the Habitat Film Appreciation Forum in August 2018; and to Professor Awadhendra Sharan of the Centre for Developing Societies, Delhi, for hosting a talk on the idea of the book on a rainy evening in March 2020, days before the world stopped on its tracks.

I am in debt of my old friend Pinaki De for his help in procuring some images and his most gracious and creative contribution to the design of the book. Without him, the cover would not have looked half as good as it does.

Publishers Bloomsbury and particularly Chandra Sekhar have earned my highest regard due to the alacrity and professionalism with which he proceeded with the book from the days when a nervous manuscript was aspiring to become a monograph. This book would have wallowed in uncertainty had not Chandra stepped in and given it the shape it now has. My deepest gratitude is to him, to Editorial Manager Shreya Chakraborti, the editorial board at Bloomsbury and to the anonymous peer reviewer who bowled me over with his/her endearing feedback.

Finally, in the later years of the making of the book, Nupur Samuel has been a steady source of fortitude, counsel and endearment in equal measure. I owe a lot to her natural scepticism about the ways of the world.

This is the first definitive book on the life and cinema of Uttam Kumar, or so is what I have conceived it as. If it finds success, I would owe it to Uttam's endless spell, which would have then extended from the lighted screen to the book. If the book fails, it is my doing entirely.

New Delhi
January 2021

A NOTE, OR TWO, ON THE BOOK

UTTAM Kumar would have been ninety-five this year if he lived. He died forty-one years ago, having lived a life much larger than most. And yet, there is little readable literature on Uttam Kumar's life and work beyond the yearly supply of brief cultural reporting. Recollections, anecdotes, gossip—often hagiographic—are repeated ad nauseam in Bengali; but there is little to no assessment, or interrogation, or engagement. There is not one definitive biography in Bengali and barely a book or two in English.

The question is, why?

For years, serious cinema or only those demonstratively inviting in critical attention were taken up for 'studies'. Gradually, critical attention grew to include popular cinema too. In recent years, Bombay (now Mumbai) as a site of silent and studio cinema and Bollywood—as a protean term of cultural and economic transportability—has attracted insightful studies, using materialist, space, reception and even affect theory. But work on vernacular cinema remains pitifully less. Even within that small number, studies by formidable scholars on Tamil, Telugu and Kannada cinema have tapped into the complex network of cinema-meets-politics-meets-mythology. Bengali cinema has remained comparatively untapped. Even when Bengali film scholarship crawled outside the sovereignty of Satyajit Ray, Ritwik Ghatak or Mrinal Sen, it has occupied itself with early cinema—an engagement that has recently produced rather good work. But still, not much on Uttam. Has the star's glaring ubiquity deterred serious studies?

There are just three books in English on Uttam. Nipabithi Ghosh's *Uttam Kumar: The Ultimate Hero* is a bare-bones biography. Veteran film critic Swapan Mullik's *Mahanayak Revisited* is a quickly rendered review of Uttam's work with five of his co-actors, with an additional chapter on Uttam and Ray. The book is less about Uttam than about Mr Mullick's misgivings about popular cinema. The last, Maitreyee Chowdhury's *Bengali Cinema's First Couple* is a gushing homage to Uttam and Suchitra Sen. These works provide scant insight into Uttam beyond what is known. Sharmistha Gooptu's *Bengali Cinema: An Other Nation* is notable, but covers much wider ground than just Uttam or his cinema. So, there continues to be precious little on Uttam in the learned circles: his range of style and performance; the attractions and problems of his cinema; his roles as director, actor and producer; or his persona, stardom, and talismanic legacy.

To encompass the range and scale of Uttam's standing and stardom, adoration and impact, a cultural biography of Uttam Kumar's cinema seems fitting. An abecedarian biography—the necessary framing of life–work–death progression of an actor—runs the danger of underestimating his reach beyond his orbit; while an iconography will overestimate them. This book embodies both these endowments, and abandons them equally. Moreover, this book tracks the moving image in Bengal for almost a century, of which three decades and over 100 films receive close attention. To that end, the book eschews any constricted film theory that would consign cinema practice to pattern. Moreover, one cannot talk about any one set of films in Uttam's oeuvre without taking into account a complex screen persona and the contextual basis of a unique stardom.

Hence, the book moves through a series of queries that are spread, in no necessary order, across the span of the subject. What exactly accounts for Uttam's undying popularity? How could Uttam be a product of a quicksilver world and yet so effortlessly be beyond its power of erasure? To what extent did his cinema typify the imagination of a community in a postcolonial state that was under tremendous social, ethical and historical flux? To what extent did his cinema embody its people, who were mutating with mordant anger at one moment and waiting with cultured hope the next? Is Uttam's cinema a template of collective aspiration or an escape from it? Did his stardom hurt Bengali cinema's intellectual ambitions or did it add to it? How could he give himself such a long afterlife? Is Uttam's stardom a major asset for Bengali cinema or was it, in the final assessment, a massive liability? To answer these questions, the book, among other things, tries to engage meaningfully with Uttam's life, harps back to his cultural importance as 'matinee idol' and pushes forth the social and cultural figuration in his cinema.

With Uttam as the chief protagonist, this book tells the story of Bengali cinema between the 1950s and 1970s, with a galloping run-up to those decades, adding in the end a comprehensive enquiry into the legacy that Uttam has left behind. If the book foregrounds anything, it is a robust discussion of his films, which is unfortunately, a rarity. I have also tried to bring into focus his early and lost films, material about which has been collated from public and personal archives. Of similar import are the small voices of the industry, who have kept the memory of Uttam alive but hardly find mention otherwise. To realise these intentions, the book abandons an exclusive academic template to include anecdotal prattle, industry chatter, urban legends, incipient filmy folklore and so on, because those are important channels of appreciation, appraisal and comprehension of a star figure. At the same time, the book stays clear of flippant gossip about Uttam's personal life, this being a matter of endless speculation and drawing-room chatter for decades, which, I think, should be left there.

The primary conceptual aim of the book is to be able to encompass the importance of the *figure*—to try to locate a celluloid life within a larger historical, political and cultural context. A complimentary métier of the book was to explore why and how a star-persona could reconstitute the bhadralok Bengali visual cultural world in the post-Partition period. The book hence resolutely stays within the domain of cultural history and star studies. This approach, I hope, would not only reveal the star, hero and actor from various competing vantages and claims of having embodied symptoms of the public imagination; but also show how a towering image could be mobilised for an ever-greater pursuit of wholesome, popular, sometimes even radical, progressive entertainment.

But this kind of study is far from easy. Among the basic problems is the proliferation of information on Uttam Kumar in countless magazines, periodicals and broadsheets which have penned down his *greatness*, without bothering to go beyond. They contain a dizzying cycle of repetition of his virtues and value as a star—garnered from colleagues and co-actors, directors, technicians, distributors and theatre-owners. Prima facie, one is bound to read them with fascination, wondering about the extent of Uttam's reach and how many lives he had directly been able to touch, if not also transform. There is, in fact, enough material to write a straightforward, quick and anecdotal biography if one puts together the existing literature, a good part of which comes from Uttam's own memoirs and one written by a friend. But the surplus of familiarity adds lapidary glitter to the bouquet of lore around a star; but the idea itself tends to remain elusive. A large part of my task was to write the book without being carried away by the volumes of homage to his name. As an author, one remains anxious about the possibility of having *too much* of a public figure as his subject of inquiry, not only because there is a good possibility of being overwhelmed by it but also because a subject much taller—in scope and scale—than the author's goal is likely to remain, in good measure, outside the author's reach. Moreover, in the din of laudatory testaments, one has to stay vigilant of the silences, gaps and lapses that simplistic evaluations often smoothen out, not to mention the heavy cross of being a singular, 'infallible' star that Uttam was compelled to bear for most of his working life.

If there is over-familiarity on one side, there is a profound lack of awareness the moment one steps outside the familiar demography; even among those who have kept a close watch over cinemas in India. Whatever little idea there is, it is limited to Uttam's sad retinue of films in Hindi. Even there, the comparatively better ones such as *Dooriyan* or *Kitaab* are forgotten and a quick recall would lead to either the schmaltzy *Amanush* or the deplorable *Desh Premee*. No one even comprehends that some of Hindi cinema's milestones: *Sahib Bibi Aur Ghulam* (*Saheb Bibi Golam*), *Hum Dono* (*Uttarayan*), *Kala Pani* (*Sobar Opore*), *Hum Hindustani* (*Bosu Poribar*), *Lal Patthar* (*Lal Pathor*), *Angoor* (*Bhrantibilash*), *Jibanmrityu* (*Jibonmrityu*), *Chupke Chupke* (*Chhoddobeshi*), *Kati Patang* (*Surjotopa*), *Amar Prem* (*Nishipodmo*), *Anurodh* (*Deya Neya*), *Abhiman* (*Bilombito Loy*), *Bemisal* (*Ami, She O Shokha*) and *Ijaazat* (*Jotugriha*) were all remakes of Uttam's films. This is to say that at least nine of Hindi cinema's biggest names—Guru Dutt, Dev Anand, Sunil Dutt, Rajkumar, Sanjeev Kumar, Rajesh Khanna, Dharmendra, Amitabh Bachchan and even Naseeruddin Shah—have together brought to screen myriad characters which in their original belonged to just one actor. What this means is that Uttam Kumar, thanks to two Satyajit Ray films, is perhaps known much better among a global connoisseurship of cinephiles than he is known in all of India. That is a serious oversight.

A major task of this book was to be able to straddle these extremes of overwrought acquaintance and baffling unfamiliarity. It is through Uttam's body of work and his life *within* and *outside* it, that the book hopes to strike this balance between the persona, the figure and the cult of the star/actor. The extensive summation of such a figure and his world is the onus of 'A Heroic Laughter'. It is followed by 'Twenty-Four Frames of Fame', which invokes gripping, magical moments and testaments that make up the life, times, flamboyance and charm of Uttam Kumar, referring to cinema technology being 24 freeze-frames put into motion per second. 'The Big Picture' stretches out to the beginning of movie-making in India, to allow a mandatory retrospection that, in a thrilling tale of invention, suffering and one-upmanship, would invoke the deep historical context up to Uttam's arrival in the early 1950s. 'Flopmaster general', a term coined to mock Uttam's early foibles as a rookie actor, recounts the rebuffs the actor faced and how he managed to survive them to emerge into prominence. Uttam's stardom reshaped Hollywood-inspired popular melodramas into a specifically Bengali melodrama, producing a matinee idol and the romantic star for every reason and every season, which is what 'Hour of the Star' is about. 'Hard Times in Soft City' is about *the city* in Uttam's cinema—the long and under-appreciated association that his stardom and Calcutta has had with each other under conditions that were exerting themselves on the city as much they were on his films. 'To the Top, to the Top, to the Top' celebrates Uttam's best films, making it a laudatory testament to a fabled actor, idol and star; while 'A Gallery of Portraits' sequesters a series of films that broke away from either the grain of regular romance or offered an interesting or unpredictable template for the star-protagonist. The penultimate chapter, 'Autumn of the Patriarch', interrogates the last years of his stardom, his increasing vulnerability to petitions of miserable, tasteless populism and the concomitant shifts in the cinematic narratives, cultural criterion and the overall polity of Bengal. Evidently, 'The Afterlife of the Bhadralok' is about Uttam's posthumous life, the affective relationship between his cinema and his reception as a quintessentially bhadralok icon; and the calibration of a legacy that increasingly exposes the singularity and starkness of a stardom that was in surplus of Bengal's cinema of containment.

TITLES AND PRONUNCIATION

Except a handful, there is hardly any translation of the titles of Uttam Kumar's films. This is not surprising because those who have ever bothered about them have come from the self-referential cultural sphere of the Bengali-speaking native. So, translation was not deemed necessary. The foremost aim of this book is to reach out to general cinema readership who may not have access to the language of Uttam's cinema. I have hence translated, however insufficiently, all the titles of the films I have discussed at some length. Movies of Uttam or otherwise that are referred to only in passing have been left alone. I hope that the translated titles (and the details thereof) invoke enough interest in the reader to further explore the films. Over the years, I have found a handful of translated titles floating in the blogosphere. Some of my final translations may carry those impressions, but there is no easy way to acknowledge that debt. If I have used any of them, I am grateful immensely. I must also point out that in case of multiple mentions of a film, I have provided the translated title only where it has received detailed attention. Elsewhere, I have mentioned only the Bengali title.

Any act of translation, even a phrase as brief as a movie title, involves complex cultural transportation. I have tried to take them into account. Few illustrations might show how. For example, some titles are familiar, like *Nayak* (The Hero); while some require straightforward translations: *Bicharok* (The Judge) and *Harano Sur* (The Lost Tune), for example. Some like *Pothe Holo Deri* (The Delayed Journey), *Sagorika* (The Call of the Sea), *Nishithe* (At the Dead of Night) or *Mayamriga* (The Red Herring) vary a little from the original, even if the word or phrase manages to carry sense of the title or the subject, or both. Some translations demand explanation. The literal translation of a well-known film like *Antony Firingee* would have been 'Antony the Foreigner'. But 'Firingee' was *not* a term denoting *the* colonial foreigner as the abhorred *other* but is, in fact, and surely in this case, one of mixed endearment. Hence, I have used *The Poet from Another Land* to not overemphasise Antony's foreignness but only hint at it. In some cases, a name would not be enough. For example, a title like *Rajlakshi O Srikanto* would be familiar in Bengal for being household literary characters; but would not ring any bells for those outside the language. I have hence translated the title as *The Deviant and the Demi-monde* to hint what the characters, in reverse order of the original, 'stand' for. In a similar vein, I have translated *Morutirtho Hinglaj* as *The Desert Pilgrimage*, choosing to drop the place-name Hinglaj from the title since it is an unfamiliar destination as far as a typical pilgrim's progress is concerned. A similarly complex case is *Sharey Chuattor*, which I have translated as *The Secret Insignia* with adequate explanation. In all such cases I have tried to ensure that contexts are explained, so as not to lose anything in the act of making the translation comprehensive. Again, a title like *Jotugriha* (House of Wax) does not sound unfamiliar, because of the reference to *The Mahabharata*, unlike say *Jodubongsho*, which too has connotations in the epic, referring to a family that slaughters its own kin. The latter title has hence been translated as *The Parricide*. Another such example is *Kal Tumi Aleya*, whose literal English title would be 'The Mirage Called Time', a rather unpoetic phrase. Moreover, *kal* in Bengali has a wider spectrum of meanings than *time*. I have hence preferred *The Survivor* referring to the film's protagonist. As for, say, *Thana Theke Aschi*, which would become the unbefitting 'one who came from the police station', I have retained the title of the J.B. Priestley play *An Inspector Calls* from which the film was faithfully (and terrifically) adapted. Finally, I would have preferred 'The Menagerie' for Satyajit Ray's Byomkesh Bakshi whodunit *Chiriyakhana*. But Ray translated it as 'The Zoo', which is literal surely but not scrupulous to the collective of weird outlaws in the film. But it is too well known a title to tamper with.

It is for the same reason that I have retained the spelling of *Nayak* though in all other cases, I have used vowel 'o' for the corresponding sound in Bengali and not the customary 'a'. So, it is *Harano Sur* and not 'Harana Sur' and *Morutirtho Hinglaj* and not 'Marutirtha Hinglaj'. Only where the title *begins* with the Bengali sound 'o'—as in *Agniporikha* or *Sesh Anko*—I have kept the 'a' because it would be extremely odd otherwise.

1

A HEROIC LAUGHTER

Behold, I bring you the Superman!
—Friedrich Nietzsche

IT was an evening in May 1966. Satyajit Ray, world-feted director of the *Apu Trilogy* and *Charulata* among others, dialled up a number from his four-room, open-terraced 3, Lake Temple Road residence that swiftly passed Sarat Chatterjee Avenue, kissed the leafy Southern Avenue, ran headlong along Lansdowne Road, jumped A.J.C. Bose Road, snaked past Hungerford Street and on hitting Moira Street turned right, entering the second floor of a sprawling apartment, also on plot no. 3, a little more than five kilometres away. Uttam Kumar, Bengal's legendary matinee idol, took the call. "Uttam", Ray's baritone boomed from across the speaker of the rotary dial phone, "*Nayak* premieres tomorrow at Indira Cinema. I hope you will be there." "But Manikda, the press and public will be in attendance. Do you think I should go? There might be pandemonium", the star reasoned. "Uttam, don't forget it's a Satyajit Ray film. Please be there", Ray commanded. For a moment the lines fell silent, then they sprang to life again. "Sure, Manikda", came the reply.

Next day, the news was out quickly. By late afternoon, crowds thronged every bit of road leading to Bhawanipur, south Calcutta's movie haven. Parts of the city's southern neighbourhoods had to be barricaded. Accosted by the volatile crowd, Uttam Kumar's car, a Chevrolet Impala, had to abandon the usual route of three kilometres and was piloted through the by-lanes of Chakraberia and Beltala. As expected, the venue too was chock-a-block, with hundreds guarding the gates for one glimpse of the star. Uttam was cagey, though this kind of raucous fandom had greeted him on every such occasion for over a decade by then.

On reaching the gleaming, newly whitewashed Indira Cinema, Uttam Kumar disembarked sprightly, managing to escape the waiting hundreds and swiftly moved into the confines of the building. He was escorted to his seat inside the hall cloaked in complete darkness. But it was too late to conceal his presence. The cushy theatre was shaking under the weight of uproarious greeting, 'Guru', 'Guru', with demands to see the star in person. Alarmed, the theatre manager rushed to Ray, already seated. "Sir, if we don't bring him up on stage there will be a serious law-and-order issue. Can I?" he asked. Ray nodded quietly. Minutes later, the lights came on and Uttam Kumar was seen standing on the raised platform in front of the screen. He raised his hand. The crowd fell silent, as if at the wave of a magic wand. Uttam looked straight ahead into the expectant eyes of a hundred restless heads seated in front. "I request you to please be silent and watch the film. Don't forget it is a Satyajit Ray film. Please."

This story, a piquant testimonial to two of Bengal's foremost immortals is partly apocryphal. But that takes nothing away from what this tale testifies to—Ray's sway over his cast, the plaint theatre manager; the affianced, vociferous crowd; and the phenomenal stardom of Uttam Kumar. In some ways, this tale, like the film that was premiering that day, encapsulates the fantasy that was Bengali cinema. And it is not Ray who *colonised* that cinema, either as fantasy or as commerce. It was Uttam Kumar. And only Uttam Kumar.

Image 1.1: Uttam near the Colosseum in Rome, 1966
(Photograph by Satyajit Ray)

Source: Ray archives.

There have been splendid actors such as Soumitra Chatterjee who have been feted internationally; there have been leading men such as Pramathesh Barua, who have defined a generation; there have been the ablest of performers such as Chhabi Biswas, whose screen presence can hardly be bettered. But there was (rather is) one who is all of the above: a leading actor, an extraordinary performer, a commercial magnet, a star-persona, an industry behemoth and a Bengali cultural talisman. There is only one icon of Bengali cinema—with all its highs and lows, its reach and range, its potential and its waste included—and that is Uttam Kumar.

INTIMATIONS OF IMMORTALITY

One of the most recognisable verities of Bengali cinema is that Uttam's three-decade career lorded way above others, whether as actor or as star. What is less understood is how we infused his star-making charisma with the ebullient charm of a Cary Grant romance; the keen intelligence of a Humphrey Bogart whodunnit; or the lyrical vulnerability of a Marcello Mastroianni masterwork. And somewhere in between crept in the debonair infallibility of a Gregory Peck; or the alluring magnetism of a Gary Cooper. And every bit of this Hollywood transfusion was layered with affable, dependable, recognisable screen etiquette and a dulcet bhadralok distinctiveness. This was an irresistible combination and irreproducible with anyone else. Moreover, Atlas-like Uttam carried the industry on his shoulders and like Prometheus, gave it the fire of livelihood for three decades. In an industry famous for greasepaint plasticity, Uttam was a bloody original; in an art form full of conforming puppets, Uttam was an insurrectionist. He was no one's marionette, except that of cinema itself. If all this sounds a bit outlandish, then so be it, because the hero has no better bedfellow than the hyperbole.

And yet, in case of Uttam, none of this is hyperbole. Uttam was indeed a star in the textbook sense, commanding and steering an entire popular industry and dominating its commercial and cultural assets between the early 1950s and late 1970s. Uttam was an informal and personal idol and at the same time a distant and collective cultural icon, soliciting fandom, affection, admiration and undying loyalty to his person and persona. He was not a product of the studio era and embodied the star era all by himself, over 200 films, about half of which remain re-collectible in Bengali cultural memory.

Let me illustrate this further. It has been almost seven decades since Uttam was first hailed as a figure of public adulation and four decades since Uttam Kumar passed away. Four long decades! We are in a world radically different from the one in which Uttam was born, attained his stardom and died. Over these seven decades, the life of a citizen of Bengal (or those with broader links with it) have passed through an alarming parade of changes. Technologies of belonging, climates and culture, objects and trinkets, manners and morals, moments and minutia—every other thing that constitutes the theatre of life—have passed into the graveyard of history. As it should be.

Among the handful who have managed to parry the bulldozing effects of time is Uttam. He seems undying, un-ageing, untouched by history, uncorrupted by the clock. His cult is of a rare variety, which not only shows no sign of abatement but has, in fact, increased incrementally since his death in 1980. To that end, Uttam's star persona has managed to attain a distinguished afterlife; having included, over the years of television, a new generation of viewers with all their baggage of new cultural tastes. His cinema continues to draw weight, the umpteen re-runs of his films find a regular audience, his life and work is a perennial topic in *addas*, his departure publicly and secretly mourned. Moreover, Uttam's birth and death anniversaries are still a Bengali annual cultural event—coercing supplements from broadsheets and periodicals; a retrospective or two; television broadcasts of key films; vague seminars and talks; and mostly other sundry acts of remembrance. His name is still a magnet for mass mobilisation used at will for unctuous political ends, as any observer of Bengal would know.

This is the labourious part of it. Uttam Kumar, every now and then, also emerges in spontaneous outbursts of memorialisation, continuing to live outside the bombast of official commemoration. His posthumous home is in fact in the archetypal reminiscence of the quintessential Bengali subject—his effortless omnipresence finding its way into personal memoirs, nostalgic ruminations and casual revisits. In quickly disappearing parlours of single-screen theatres across the city he seems to be ubiquitous. That's expected. But Uttam's smiling portrait also peeps out from sudden nooks and corners—neighbourly salons, dusty tailor-shops, bare-boned photo-studios, rusty sweetshops and grimy eateries—they either in thrall of his everlasting charm or inevitably peddling his visit in their midst many moons ago. The scale of Uttam's easy visibility across Calcutta and towns of Bengal four decades after his death remains a startling case of fandom. The extent of appreciation of his cinema per se among those who deck up their surroundings with the likeness of him, however, remains a conjecture. Much more difficult is to gauge which Uttam this image refers to: the man, the actor, the star or the *undying* icon.

A finale of this fascination with the star is to be found in a series of portraits of Rabindranath Tagore, Satyajit Ray and Uttam Kumar lined one after the other in a meaningful sequence among poster shops and picture-framing vendors squatting across Calcutta's embattled footpaths. This may be an inexplicable, even revolting, assortment for the bona fide Bengali intellectual but this coexistence carries within it a poignant metaphor of the city's unforgettable relationship with the star.

That metaphor is about the inscrutable nature of stardom. In his memoirs, Uttam, then already a star, recalls being huddled into a train compartment from his car at the Howrah Station while on his way to an outdoor shoot. As usual, he waited anxiously, hoping for the train to depart as soon as possible, before there was inevitable chaos. While waiting, he saw a man peeking into his coupe inquiring if Uttam Kumar would be around. Before Uttam could say anything, the man restlessly passed on. He did not return and the train left the terminus. Minutes later another man, portly and affectionate, walked smilingly into Uttam's cabin.

> A young man was scouting for you. He came to our cabin and asked if Uttam Kumar was around. I stood up and said I was Uttam Kumar. He was very pleased and told me he was a big fan of Uttam Kumar but he did not know how he looked and when he heard that the star may be on this train, he was desperate to find him and seek his blessings. So this man took my blessing and walked out rather pleased, having finally *met* his idol whom he had never seen. He did not speak Bangla so he did not see your films but was yet a great fan.[1]

Uttam had only smiled in reply.

This 'fan', whose relationship to his idol is merely in the realm of imagination rather than visibility—something extraordinary for a film star—perhaps captures the apparently baffling assortment of Tagore, Ray and Uttam. It is not in the domain of comparative artistic greatness that one must measure this assortment, but in the individual cultural imagination—separately but powerfully embossed—that one must recall the unmistakable presence of Uttam Kumar in the cultural life of Bengal. In other words, if Tagore signifies a giant who roamed the world of letters and Ray a gifted life in world cinema, Uttam Kumar is the popular 'hero' for all time, the memorable, monumental, in fact, *mythical* matinee idol.

A STORIED LIFE

Uttam Kumar, born in his north Calcutta maternal home at Ahiritola on 3 September 1926 as Arunkumar Chattopadhyay, made a slippery acting debut in an unreleased Hindi film in 1947 and worked ceaselessly for over three decades till a July day in 1980 when he suffered another cardiac arrest on a movie set and passed away the day after.

A clerk at Calcutta Port Commissioners for several years, Uttam's early days in his vocation were full of disappointment and dejection. As he found some work, he restlessly juggled his day job with his fervent moonlighting for studio assignments. His success came slow, often coercing out of him a petulant sigh, an all-too familiar outburst of a sophomore performing aspirant, who could not stake his job at the altar of his fledgling infatuation. He had stayed put, however, working the ledgers during the day and making rounds of the studios in his free hours.

The established templates of Bengali male stardom and screen masculinity were drawn from the high tables set up by Durgadas Banerji, Pramathesh Barua and Chhabi Biswas, all of who were, to quote Hamlet, 'of the manner born'. They were rich, came from the local aristocracy, were professional by choice and romantic by disposition. Uttam was from a very modest, middle-class family, of ordinary schooling and a sketchy undergraduate education. Thinly built and emaciated, with a crop of oiled back-brushed hair, thick lips, a stout nose and small, curious eyes, the raw-boned Arun was lacking not just in degrees and rearing but also, in 'heroic' looks. So, when he at all got a chance to be in front of the camera, it was thanks mostly to the imploring of friends and relatives with connections in the industry. Otherwise, he had a hard time.

A year into the birth of the new Indian state, in 1948, Uttam did manage to make his first appearance on celluloid, but the film, *Drishtidan*, was forgotten. On the sets of films like *Kamona*, *Morjada*, *Ore Jatri* the nervous, emasculated, unobtrusive Uttam was an object of ridicule, taunted and teased by hangers-on in the studios. He soldiered on nervously, braving the roomful of cocky, loud naysayers. His first few films failed to draw any significant attention to his under-confident roles, whether as a side or lead actor, or to cause any box-office ripples. It was almost certain that Uttam was going to eke out a living out of the grinds of his lowly job or find inconsequential employment as a failed actor. Behind his back, they called him a 'flopmaster general'; to his face they reminded him of the pedigree of his predecessors and the inadequacy of his aspiration. There was none to handhold him, none to supervise his talents or unleash his energies. A gawky Uttam continued to lap up the roles he got, improved upon his borderline stammering, read voraciously and trained himself in soccer, swimming, wrestling and music. And his films continued to come a cropper. Till the early 1950s, then, the dream of being a phenomenally popular matinee idol was not remotely in the reckoning, an unprecedented stardom not even a fanciful idea, nor did he imagine that one day he would be Ray's protagonist and walk the red carpet at the Berlin Film Festival.

But the plot changed pattern since the time he found commercial success with *Bosu Poribar* (1952) and *Sharey Chuattor* (1953), the latter launching his fabled pairing with Suchitra Sen. Then, in 1954, a teary melodrama called *Agniporikha* gave him the stellar push. A precocious straggler of about twenty movies by then, Uttam, almost overnight, became a star. Between 1954 and 1957, a string of humongous box-office successes blurred the hardship and ignominy of his past and made him a cinematic attraction. His apparently average looks became a magnet of affection, his gait of imitation, his manners of romance, his smile of idolatry. Sometime in the winter of 1954, months before Ray's *Panther Panchali* stormed the silos of the Western cinephile, a starry celluloid life premiered around the Tollygunge studios of Calcutta.

Uttam Kumar had a miraculous run at the box office for two full decades after he attained stardom. And the popularity he attained, both off and on the screen, is a stuff of lore. As he entered his mid-30s, he made efforts, not always with success, to be comparatively selective with his films, trying roles that suited his age and the temperament of the time. He also produced, directed, scored music and in one film, lent his mellifluous voice to his character. He found an actors' union, endlessly petitioned for development of film infrastructure, funded both popular and crossover films, raised aid for the poor and the unsecured foot soldiers of his fraternity and was the loudest voice of concern in service of the industry that nurtured him.

Uttam's acting fetched him laurels, awards (the first national award for acting to a male performer, six Bengal Film Journalists Association [BFJA] awards, commendations at Berlinale) and a huge and phenomenal fan following that pulverised both his privacy and person, put to interrogation his closely held middle-class upbringing and stalked his free movements till his last day. Given his sway, popularity and posthumous fame, it would be an act of underestimation to call Uttam just another star who reigned during his lifetime and continued to be an attraction after. Rather, for close to *three* decades, the cinematic materiality and imagination of Bengalis—culturally arrogant and historically zealous—were transported almost entirely upon the actor and his repertoire. Like the great acts that made him the iconic actor that he was, Uttam, at 5 feet and 11 inches, also stood much taller in death; whose purported shadow grew bigger and bigger with each passing day. Now, forty years into his afterlife, Uttam Kumar remains what he died as: the greatest icon ever to have graced Bengali cinema and also one among the principal cultural protagonists of the entire post-Tagorean Bengali public life.

Very few, one can argue, would have been able to fulfil this role of a cultural sovereign for so long; and that too with the limited armoury of popular cinema. How did Uttam manage to? One needs to map Uttam's tremendous tenacity, diligence, charm and of course superlative talent; which were no doubt critical actors in making the star he was. One can also, no doubt, underline that Uttam's stardom was at the cusp of collective aspiration, private fantasy and commercial custodianship. His is also a most curious case of an incremental felicity of posthumous value; a case that must be looked at with as much interest as the calibration that goes into celebrating his cinema. But this prolonged hold over popular imagination cannot be reduced to a prosthetic cultural causality. Rather, we must understand that what Uttam brought to Bengali cinema was more than the sum of the parts that constituted him or his body of work. This *gestalt* and its exceptional legacy remains colossal; his case continuing to intrigue any observer of cinema. To that end, the story of Uttam not only forces us to enquire into the unquantifiable genus called stardom but also think anew the riches of cinema in Bengal itself.

In short, from a clerk to an actor, from an actor to a star, from a star to an icon, from an icon to a screen legend—this is a story that must be told.

CINEMA VARIÉTÉ

Uttam's intuitive proficiency as an actor sits uneasy on his proclivity towards signing films left, right and centre. Anything above 200 films in a working life of three decades is a daunting number, considering that except a handful, he was the protagonist in *all* of them. To be more precise, Uttam had 197 Bengali releases; six more films released posthumously. Then, there were twelve Hindi films, including the first unreleased film and the bilingual ones, of which seven had been released in his lifetime. Seven more, across two languages, were either in pre-production or on the floors when he passed away; while he was in advanced talks to be part of about nine more. So, when we are talking about Uttam Kumar, we are talking no less than 230 films. Even accounting for the sparse pre-stardom period and counting only those movies he managed to complete, it comes to an average of over six films annually for thirty-two years. In actual terms, they averaged much more during his peak. Since this is a staggering output, it is neither possible nor advisable to touch upon every film. In fact, a significant share of the roster of the last five years, both in Bengali and Hindi, is in the rank of being avoidable. But even without them, one has to choose wisely from the large output of Bengali films till 1975, which numbers 166; with an additional film called *Nokol Shona* (False Glitter, 1974), where he played a cameo as himself. But why 1975? That would be clear in a while.

The most likely classification of his cinema would have been on a temporal scale: to divide his working life into three phases. In that case, the first, 1954 to 1961, would be considered the high-noon of romance; the second, 1962 to 1969, would be his peak as an actor; and the final one, 1970 to 1975, would be the years that marked a conspicuous, even if only comparative, decline. But such a division runs the risk of turning a frenetic body of work into methodical platitude, making a forceful case for a progressive pattern as essential to a retrospective analysis. Another possible division would have been as per film genres. Here, the populist catalogue would put the black and white romance at the top, followed by other, even if tenuous, generic heads, for example, 'period films' (*Saheb Bibi Golam*, *Chondranath*, *Jhinder Bondi*), 'thrillers' (*Khelaghor*, *Jibonmrityu*, *Kokhono Megh*), 'comedies' (*Haat Baralei Bondhu*, *Bhrantibilash*, *Chhoddobeshi*), 'social crisis films' (*Anupoma*, *Annapurnar Mondir*, *Ekhane Pinjor*) and so on. This division was a teasing proposition but a strict genre-approach is essentially studio-centric. Since in Bengali cinema studios vanished with Uttam's rise, a division of his cinema based on genres would be deceptive. Though the genres were a legacy that his cinema inherited and often improved upon, to stick to it would be to reinforce a traditionalist method. Moreover, such 'classifications' do not help to unravel a story of stardom.

Why not, instead, understand his cinema on the basis of the evolution of the star-actor? Because an opulent, robust and contentious stardom is best revealed when it can be approached or interrogated from various, sometimes even warring, vantages.

Hence, the first would be the overarching romance melodramas. Since Uttam's rise to the summit of stardom is usually monitored through romance, it would be best to see them under one tent-pole. Nothing better reveals the populist reception of Uttam's screen persona than these films. Under this rubric, *Agniporikha* (1954), *Sobar Opore* (1955), *Sagorika* (1956), *Ekti Raat* (1956), *Indrani* (1958), *Chawa Pawa* (1959), *Agnisonskar* (1961), *Deya Neya* (1963) and *Nayika Songbad* (1967) are the usual favourites. One can add another four dozen films to this list, each playing with the many shades of the genre. In these films, Uttam could perfectly embody (to refer to the famous typology of American sociologist Orrin Klapp) the romantic hero, the Good Joe, the Pin-Up and the unrelenting rebel and all of them, often, in a single role. Also, in much of this cinema, new interventions, from young and zealous men and women, resulting from the emergent codes of modernity were contesting the familial domains of privilege and patriarchy.

While remembering this dominant type of cinema, one must also note that even quite early on Uttam had signed on roles that required little screen romance or any prolonged heterosexual participation in bringing to fruition a pre-conjugal couple-hood, which is what would constitute a *romantic* film. Uttam's participation in *parts* other than *romance* were hence simultaneous and not successive to his having reached the summit as a romantic hero. This is not to say that his choices were always impeccable in either sort of films, but what is important is that marquee stardom *did not* throttle his eagerness to go beyond the jugular. So, Uttam periodically subverted the dominance of the romance form and continued to work on atypical films. Moreover, these apparent melodramas could well go beyond the echo chamber of romantic fulfilment and establish a dialogue with the world around. These films, broadly the 'melodrama of the metropolis', continued to thrive even after Uttam peaked in the romances. In fact, it was through the *star text* of Uttam that a transforming modern melodrama form found a *habitas* in postcolonial Calcutta—the latter having changed perceptively under the mark of a historically irreversible event like Partition. So, the star-figure abetted popular cinema to mobilise its own visual language and respond to the cultural and social zeitgeist of the 1950s and 1960s. *Sharey Chuattor, Ora Thake Odhare* (1954), *Saheb Bibi Golam* (1956), *Surjotoron* (1958), *Kanna* (1962), *Kal Tumi Aleya* (1966) and *Chowrongee* (1968) would be some of them.

One should hence unlearn the lore that romance films had exclusive domination over Uttam's early screen life. Like all mythologies, it is historically unfounded. This is because by late 1950s, Uttam was strongly signalling his move away from any overwhelming image of the youthful romantic hero that he may have accrued through the 1950s. In other words, between the early 1950s and early 1960s, Uttam's accentuating stardom helped the melodrama form, with its signature designs, to coalesce into a dependable commercial apparatus. And it was through the same star figure that the form was slowly pressed from within to cause its gradual dismemberment. This eventually signalled a broader change from the motif of the foot-loose, easygoing Uttam persona to an older, more dignified and less adorable kind of a figure. And this trend was only going to get darker and morally ambiguous as the 1960s progressed. These films also displayed how Uttam's persona transcended simple divisions or genres, subverted typical melodramatic set pieces and upended the commercial deployment of star imagery.

If the city films were one way of signifying this dismemberment, the other were what can be called 'crossover' films. The 'crossover genre' was to be found in the neighbourhood of melodrama but avoided its populist trappings, was grounded in a genteel, evolved critique of their contexts, was rich in narrative and production and usually enriched with some stellar performances. Such films allowed Uttam to play a variety of complex, grey and contrarian characters, which stood in opposition to the image of a matinee idol with 'magical' gifts to overcome impediments to love and middle-class safekeeping. This was a radical shift and one which cemented his reputation as an actor of great range and intelligence. For example, he played an alcoholic in *Sanjeebani* (1952), a distressed psychotic in *Hrod* (1955), a literature professor in *Upohar* (1955), a gullible geek in *Bordidi* (1957), a small-time crook in *Obak Prithibi* (1959), an insolent non-conformist in *Morutirtho Hinglaj* (1959), a humble manservant in *Khokababur Protyaborton* (1960), a Nehruvian utopian in *Shiulibari* (1962), a gallant prince and his cowardly doppelganger in *Jhinder Bondi* (1961), a cold-blooded murderer in *Sesh Anko* (1963), an artful aristocrat in *Lal Pathor* (1964), a tormented psychoanalyst in *Momer Alo* (1964), a witty detective in *Chiriyakhana* (1967), a fiendish humbug in *Aparichito* (1969), a decadent dandy in *Stree* (1972), a wretched loser in *Jodubongsho* (1974) and a sinister, Machiavellian anti-hero in *Baghbondi Khela* (1975). These varied, memorable and prodigious character studies need attention.

All these elements found climactic fulfilment in what can be called his keystone films: *Harano Sur* (1957), *Bicharok* (1959), *Soptopodi* (1961), *Jotugriha* (1964), *Antony Firingee* (1967), *Nogor Dorpone* (1975) and *Agniswor* (1975). Above all, Uttam played himself in Satyajit Ray's *Nayak* (1966). At the end of the day, nothing better endears Uttam to the cinephile than his astonishing turn in the film, a film that came at the median of his working life and tapped into the crescendo that his appeal had reached in the mid-1960s. Across these films the star, the actor, the matinee idol had come together in a way that continues to startle both the critic and Uttam's seemingly endless cohort of fans. This broad classification (which the rest of the book more or less adheres to) helps in situating Uttam's cinema productively within their context and in which they can be best revealed as symptomatic of larger turns and twists.

Image 1.2: Romance extraordinaire. Poster of *Soptopodi*
(The Seven Steps, 1961)

Source: Author.

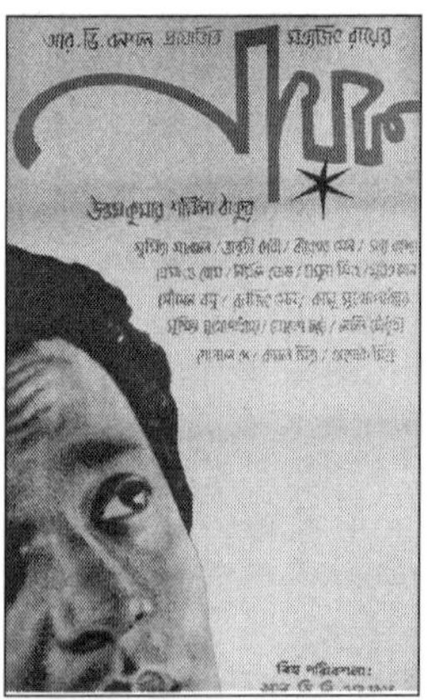

Image 1.3: Ray's observance of the star. Poster of *Nayak* (The Hero, 1966)

Source: Author.

As we will see, Uttam helped reimagine popular cinema, imported a
climate of critique to it, and provided it with intellectual ambition and
an unflinching sense of 20th century modernity. Uttam's best *romances*
were not peddlers of stock expectations; neither were the other dramas
exploding with flimsy set pieces. It goes without saying that his better
films were only nominally star-driven and rightfully make their case to
be among the best of Bengali cinema. To that end, the star-actor and his

cinema are meant to complement each other, instead of the star's image subsuming everything else.

A set of films from his later years reveal the mutations in his star persona, his burning out at the altar of populism and his gradual progress to a kind of decimation. The year that marks the same is 1976, since which the drought of good, even average, roles are too apparent. There is not a single film that stands out and if one counts the dreadful Hindi films, Uttam's downward spiral seems dizzying. His personal appeal remained largely un-corroded but his films started to bomb with a regularity that only his very early films had experienced. His own decisions were largely to be blamed but there were also factors that were extraneous to him, exposing a throng of crises in Bengali social and cultural life. Even if he was planning to walk quietly into the sunset, he couldn't, for he was helplessly chained to the voracity of his industry. His death at work in 1980 fleetingly rescued his box-office performance but that was largely due to a wave of sympathy rather than any appeal of the films.

The story of his filmography does not end here, for there is enough material to deliberate on the many omissions that a long career like Uttam's inevitably divulges. Parimal Ray and Kaji Anirban, who have compiled a gorgeous collection of Uttam's film publicity, have also listed several films which were abandoned or those in which Uttam was replaced. There are other examples mentioned elsewhere. Such things are common in a commercial industry and there is no point ruing every film that did not happen; or which took form with a different cast. At the same time, some of them are bound to pique interest. The case of Satyajit Ray's unmade earlier *Ghare Baire* is referred to later, but one wonders why Chitta Basu's *Jabar Bela Pichu Dake* and Niren Lahiri's *Kantar Konya* in the mid-1950s; Sukumar Dasgupta's *Nodir Namti Anjana* in the early 1960s; and Tapan Sinha's *Kothai Pabo Tare* in the early 1970s did not see light after being formally launched. Of similar instance and the most intriguing was *Anondo Songbad*, which had Uttam and Raj Kapoor in the lead and was to be directed by Hrishikesh Mukherjee. It was announced in the mid-1960s, tickling the possibility that it could have been the Bengali original of Mukherjee's unforgettable *Anand* (1971). Curious too are the cases of *Kinu Gowalar Goli* (1964) and *Chhutir Fande* (1975), both prominent films, in which Soumitra Chatterjee replaced Uttam after his name was made public. Among the unofficial replacements about six stand out: Bikash Roy substituting Uttam in the early comedy *Chhele Kaar* (The Errant Child, 1954); Raj Kapoor reprising his role in *Ekdin Ratre* (1956), the Bengali version of *Jagte Raho*, after Uttam could not come onboard; Kali Banerjee doing the same for Mrinal Sen's *Neel Akasher Niche* (Under the Azure Sky, 1959);

ditto for Dilip Kumar in Tapan Sinha's *Sagina Mahato* (1970); Soumitra coming in as Oghor in Tarun Majumdar's *Sonsar Simante* (On the Edge of the World, 1975) and Dipankar Dey stepping in for Uttam as the irritable father–son duo in Tapan Sinha's much-loved *Banchharamer Bagan* (The Garden of Delights, 1980). These replacements save the last have the usual lore around them; *Banchharamer Bagan* did not come to fruition thanks to an ill-advised legal dispute that Uttam got embroiled in with Sinha. But this one would have no doubt provided a spot of colour and recognition to Uttam's otherwise desolate stretch of duds in the last five years of his life. His death saw several films abandoned and several others that were rebooted later. Saroj De's *Koni* (1984) is the only one worth mentioning that was made later and with an even more suitable cast. Among the movies that were put to sleep along with Uttam the promising were Sabitri Chatterjee's *Sheemarekhar Sheema*, Arundhati Mukherjee's untitled film, Gautam Ghosh's *Srimoti Café* and Tarun Majumdar's adaptation of Utpal Dutt's *Tiner Tolowar*. This last list should also include the film version of *Tiktiki*, an adaptation of Anthony Shaffer's *Sleuth*. It had a long life on stage as one of Soumitra Chatterjee's most remembered plays. It had just two male characters in a tight chamber drama. Both Uttam and Soumitra were keen to adapt it and Soumitra was to direct. But it found no producer, apparently because there was no female presence. Not surprising, given the low standards the industry was setting for itself since the early 1970s. Much later it became a telefilm. In Hindi, Uttam's most famous blunder was to refuse *Sangam*; but there were others too: *Yamuna Ke Teer* and *Woh Din Dur Nehi* were aborted; *Jhankar* with Asha Parekh was abandoned midway; and Uttam walked out of Basu Bhattacharya's *Grihaprabesh* after a few days of shooting. The very early case of the unreleased *Mayador* and Bimal Roy's *Pehla Aadmi* will be recounted later.

THE STAR AND HIS GALAXY

Around Uttam grew a *new* cinematic establishment, complete with a retinue of co-actors, heroines, producers, directors and distributors. He acted with every major popular director and participant actor of his time, while managing a subtle if natural *equation* with all of his leading ladies on screen, notwithstanding the apparently matchless pairing with Suchitra Sen. Like the myriad characters he played, this 'chemistry' with his actresses was also different, in tone and texture, from each other. If with Suchitra Sen the pairing was about tragic-comic romance, with Supriya Choudhury it was a kind of sensual intricacy (if only in a handful of watchable films); and with Arundhati Mukherjee various strands of complex couple-hood. Uttam's most long-lasting screen (and in one case a hugely successful stage) partner was Sabitri Chatterjee, with whom Uttam's work is the most varied, even if there is a tendency to prefer upbeat, genial comedies over others. Among other female leads, Mala Sinha and Aparna Sen were prominent, with whom Uttam had starred in a spate of early and late romances respectively. A roster of close to 200 films meant that there were also several other co-actors: Sondhyarani Chatterjee and Manju Dey in the early period; Sharmila Tagore and Tanuja in the middle period; and Arati Bhattacharjee at the end. There are also short but memorable imprints of Sumitra Debi, Madhabi Mukherjee, Anjana Bhowmik and Nandita Bose. Kaberi Bose bookends Uttam's peak career with two films each at the beginning and at the end. With them, however, there was no single template that was at work and hence 'partnership', if any, is beyond any affective pattern.

But Bengali cinema's rich trajectory was not only about its leading star or the enchanting women. Uttam's cinema (as well as his performances) was bolstered by an august congress of outstanding performers who provided him the support and in some cases, adroit guidance. It is unthinkable to talk about Uttam Kumar's cinema without mentioning Pahari Sanyal, who was a foremost actor in the 1940s and along with Jahar Ganguly, another leading actor, had made a happy transition into playing the benign guardian in countless films in the 1950s and 1960s. Then, there was Bikash Roy, an actor of copious talent, and Uttam's immediate predecessor Asit Baran, who were peers as well as aspirants for leading roles but made an unrepentant shift towards slighter but meaty characters after Uttam became the primary preference for the actor in a leading role. Others, like Nitish Mukherjee, Dhiraj Bhattacharya, Bhanu Bandopadhyay, Nirmal Kumar, Biswajit Chatterjee, Basanta Chowdhury, Kali Banerjee and Anil Chatterjee had been cast in prominent leading roles in films of considerable value but continued to play the supporting cast in Uttam's films. Uttam's sibling Tarun; Jiben Bose, Anup Kumar and Subhendu Chatterjee had ample talent for brief, effective parts that were never jarring in contrast to the charm and élan of Uttam. Then there was Kamal Mitra, Haridhan Mukherjee, Shyam Laha, Sisir Batyabal, Bankim Ghosh, Subhen Mukherjee, Gangapada Basu, Nirmal Ghosh, Shailen Mukherjee, Rabi Ghosh, Dilip Mukherjee, Dilip Roy, Asim Kumar, Nabadwip Halder, Nripati Chattopadhyay, Partha Mukhopadhyay, Dipankar Dey, Victor Banejee, Santosh Dutta; and theatre doyens Ahindra Chaudhuri in early and Utpal Dutt in the later years. There are many others. Jahar Roy and Tulsi Chakraborty deserve doffing a hat or two too, though they were not always cast wisely in spite of their felicity for superlative comedy. Two major figures find detailed mention later: they are Chhabi

Biswas and Soumitra Chatterjee, who were, by all means, Uttam's most formidable predecessor and peer respectively.

But the men, talented and genial as they were, naturally filled only half of Bengali cinema's universe. There were the equally talented female actors—starting from Kanan Debi, often referred to as the 'first lady' of Bengali cinema, to Sunanda Banerjee, Nibhanoni Debi, Prabha Debi, Chandrabati Debi, Molina Debi, Sobha Sen, Aparna Debi, Padma Debi, Rajlakhki Debi, Chobi Roy, Bharati Debi, Smritirekha Biswas, Renuka Roy and the formidable Chhaya Debi—who had ably and effortlessly shouldered the responsibility of the other half of the guardian figures integral to the family melodramas of Uttam's early stardom years. The younger lot—Dipti Roy, Anubha Gupta, Sabita Chatterjee, Namita Sinha, Sumita Sanyal, Basabi Nandy, Sumitra Mukherjee, Sondhya Roy, Lily Chakraborty, Lolita Chatterjee, Kanika Majumdar, Mithu Mukherjee—played the second, or supportive, or wronged, or in a handful cases even the leading woman.

It would be a matter of grave oversight if one does not take into account the directors, the screenwriters, music-makers, vocalists and technical crew that complete the Uttam 'biosphere'. Like any other record of a star *system*, there has been a tendency to invisibilise the crew. But the Uttam story is hollow without Nirmal De, Sukumar Dasgupta, Ajoy Kar, Niren Lahiri, Chitta Basu, Kartik Chattopadhyay, Haridas Bhattacharya, Manu Sen, Subodh Mitra, Sushil Majumdar, Salil Dutta, Arabindu Mukhopadhyay, Parthapratim Chowdhury, Hiren Nag, Pinaki Mukherjee, Sunil Banerjee, Sudhir Mukherjee and Pijush Bose. This list must include the director ensembles Agradoot, Agragami and Yatrik. The older generation of Nitin Bose, Debaki Bose and Naresh Mitra and younger radicals like Satyajit Ray and Tapan Sinha were not among those who got marginalised by the star system. But all of them had a role to play, small and big, in the process that produced a 'phenomenon' called Uttam Kumar. Similarly, littérateurs Premendra Mitra, Tarashankar Bandopadhyay, Subodh Ghosh and Ashutosh Mukhopadhyay came to be major stakeholders in Uttam's success. Then, there were men who shaped the story into a living film—screenwriters Nripendrakrishna Bhattacharya, Bidhayak Bhattacharya, Binoy Chatterjee, Prasanta Deb; cinematographers Anil Gupta, Bishu Chakraborty, Dinen Gupta, Ramananda Sengupta, Bijoy Ghosh; art-director Kartik Basu; sound-recordist Shyamsundor Ghosh; editors Dulal Dutta, Baidyanath Chatterjee, Ardhendu Chattopadhyay, Kali Raha; make-up artistes Bashir Ahmed and Debi Halder; choreographer Bob Das; publicists Panchanan Sarkar, Sudhirendra Sanyal, Bibhubhusan Bandopadhyay; scenarist Kavi Dasgupta; and finally the still photographers Sukumar Roy, Tulu Das, Pahari Roychowdhury and Prabhakar Prabhu. Those who designed the stunning posters and booklets of Uttam's cinema were admired artists in their own right: O.C. Ganguly, Raghunath Goswami, Ranen Ayan Dutta being the most notable of them. Then, there were the influential producers and distributors: MP, HNC, Screen Classics, Delux, Kanan Debi's Srimati Pictures and Chayabani were some of the more prominent ones from the early phase. The list is not exhaustive for sure, but would give an idea about the characters who populated the world of Uttam Kumar. It is unfair to discuss these talents in a span and sweep of a single mention. Needless to say, I would keep going back to their work in the context of the overall scope of our subject.

In the Uttam universe, I reserve the final space for music, for if anything, it was the attraction that followed Uttam in a typical Uttam film. Since the early 1950s, Bengali cinema soundtrack had started to adjust itself to changing public tastes, incorporating an increasingly modern idiom and a noticeable shift in melody. By then, the heydays of spiritual musicals were well over and thanks to Pankaj Mullik, Pramathesh Barua and Bimal Roy, film soundtrack had increasingly attained a smarter, starker, svelte character, which was set to lyrics that were not divorced from the quotidian. K.L. Saigal took with him the preference for nasal base and new vocalists such as Hemanta Mukherjee, Dhananjoy Bhattacharya, Manabendra Mukherjee, Manna Dey, Shyamal Mitra and later Kishore Kumar (Geeta Dutt, Sondhya Mukherjee, Pratima Bandopadhyay and later Lata Mangeshkar, Asha Bhosle and Arati Mukhopadhyay being the counterparts) brought a refreshing clarity and distinction to their voices. The singers were put to remarkable use by Timirbaran Bhattacharya, Anil Bagchi, Rabin Chattopadhyay, Sudhin Dasgupta and Nachiketa Ghosh. Hemanta and Shyamal were also exceptional composers in their own right. They could be popular, melodious and evocative in equal measure and at the same time. Rabindranath Tagore's vast treasure trove of songs were there of course; along with those by Atulprasad Chattopadhyay, Rajnikanta Sen and Nazrul Islam. A band of socialist-minded lyricists emerged too, such as Gauriprassana Majumdar, who, along with the more mainstream Pulak Bandopadhyay, Pranab Roy and Mukul Dutta, gave compelling words to the tunes. Together they have delivered an evergreen and unforgettable roster of songs, many of which have worked their way into being timeless classics from this gilded age of popular film soundtrack.

Finally, there were those who were not really part of the movie production or business but in some way or the other had a role to play in the public reception of Uttam. There is hence a certain perception of Uttam the actor; then there is Uttam of colleagues and industry-insiders; an Uttam known to his minions; the familial, at-home Uttam; the Uttam of his partner Supriya, so on and so forth. Moreover, many people of a certain generation have a personal anecdote to share about the star. It could range from having accosted him during his morning walks around Calcutta's Maidan area; having a glimpse of him at a wedding reception; or at a film premiere, or at a day's shoot; to peeking into his Studebaker. Sometimes there were also more privileged memories: facing him alone with a camera in tow at a suburban function; having a meal at his house; or having a seat beside him in the car. It seems that in Bengal, for everyone born over half a century there is their 'own and personal' Uttam, which no less animated and keep us apprised of his expansive universe.

AN ORDINARY MAN, AN ASSIDUOUS ACTOR, A STARDOM IN SOLITARY CONFINEMENT

Should we see Uttam's body of work in tandem with his expansive stardom or sequestered from it? Was stardom binding or liberating for him? And in all of this, where can we locate the person of Uttam?

If one reads Uttam's interviews; or reads his occasional columns; or manages to extricate an unguarded moment or two in the numerous profiles of him, one is immediately conscious of being in the company of a generous soul. There are also a few moving details to be extracted from remembrances of others—especially about the kind of training, discipline and rigorous improvement that Uttam managed to bring to his work even long after he was safely in the realm of stardom. But we see a more rounded person in his own writings, where Uttam comes across as a man of conscience and empathy; probing the riches of his own success one moment only to stop and reflect on its limits in the next; is cautious about his image and appearance but at the same time tries hard to not be obsessed with it. He never lost sight of his middle-class origins and remained conscious of his many deficiencies—be it his lack of formal education; or his inability to speak English fluently; or even the more personal fact of having publicly strayed away from his legal wife. There was also the usual retinue of annals, anecdotes, popular gossip and industry prattle that perpetually and perilously surrounds a public figure like him. Uttam did have his share of personal controversies, though he was not a man comfortable with lending his name to wanton sleaze and tangle. In fact, the worst of them involved his adopted daughter Shoma, who had an infatuation with him which was not unlike daughters growing up under the shadow of a larger-than-life father (figure). But those nuances were lost to the paparazzi press. A degree of personal overreach though, in the end, accentuated his aura, transcending boundaries of economic, cultural and gender groups within his audience. But that was more in keeping with his outstanding work and the cult that grew around him rather than any sustained dependence on skullduggery.

As a person Uttam never pretended to be anything but cautious and conventional, harbouring an everyday chauvinism that a traditional upbringing and nominal education would implant early into a young man—about family, caste, women, progeny and the predisposed order of things that bind them. But with time and fame, he had also let go of several of his ingrained prejudices. Similarly, he was a believer in the usual sense but not religious. In an interview to Kavita Sinha[2] in the mid-1970s he quipped, not without irony: "Haven't you seen that in my Bhawanipore home there is a great frenzy about religious festivities? Do I participate? Yes. Do I take them seriously? No. I do believe in a powerful force but I would rather I sit alone in the company of that force than make a great frenzy about worshipping him." He also corrected another error. "I do not read the *Gita* because I am religious, as many would think. I do so to become more conversant with Sanskrit. I have taken lessons in Urdu and Hindi. As for Sanskrit, I want to improve it on my own."

Uttam did not realise the transformative effect he had on the history of Bengali cinema. At least, not consciously. He had, therefore, harked on the struggle of his early years and the rejections that had piled on for about six years—between 1947 and 1952—when he was reprimanded if not rejected. But when he mused about them, he did not blame individuals but rather the state of things. "Those days the typical characters were not very real. They were staid, artificial, puppet-like. I felt helpless till Sukhen of *Bosu Poribar* came my way. He was real; tactile."[3] Uttam's real learning perhaps lay in his conscious decision not to attach his success, when it finally came, to the early melodramas or not to even one kind of melodrama.

His conscious dissociation from the prison-house of image is most thoroughly intelligible in Uttam's reflections on acting, something that one barely comes across in the laudatory assessments. But they are revelatory. In his part-autobiography, he says,[4]

> I never took acting loosely, just as a livelihood. It was always a craving, an emotion. I did not have much training and from each of my early directors—Nirmal De, Debaki Basu, Naresh Mitra, Tapan Sinha—I learned a lot. When I worked with Manikda (Satyajit Ray), I saw him from close quarters. He is scientific and methodical. He would never intrude into a scene unless he has to. He gave me, any actor for that matter, a free range.

Uttam noticed Ray's habit of holding his handkerchief between his teeth when he was lost in thought. During *Chiriyakhana*, he rehearsed a scene imitating that gesture. Ray stopped him and asked if he was keeping that in the actual take. "If you permit, I will, I said. Do that. It makes a lot of sense, Manikda assured", Uttam later recalled.[5] But Uttam learnt much more than a gesture or two from the directors he admired. He gradually mastered the art of *silent acting*; of *passive performance*; of pregnant pauses and deliberate delays; of breaking long dialogues into meaningful parts; of importing almost undetectable changes on his facial muscles to indicate a change in mood; of using the cinematographer's lens to his advantage. There are several testimonials to his continuing interest in the craft of cinema: the functionality of anamorphic lenses for example, or the intricacies of production design, the technology of colourisation and projection; the habitual commercial servitude of mainstream cinema; and of course the minutiae of performance: where does the person end and the performer begin. It is to the last query, often philosophical in bent, that he owed his stiff resistance to playing real/historical figures on screen. Otherwise, Uttam cited *Bhrantibilash*, a proficient adaptation of Shakespeare's *Comedy of Errors* as a test case of performance.[6] "Everything about the two brothers were similar, even their dress and gait", said Uttam.

> So, how does one communicate the difference, which will be palpable to the audience and invisible to the characters in the film? It had to be as imperceptible a variation as possible, but variation nevertheless. For example, the married brother would be more confident with women, his taking the nose puff would show that. The bachelor brother—a smoker—would on the other hand smoke nervously in front of women. Slight changes such as these make all the difference. One does not need to be loud in such matters.

This was the performance part, but what about cinema in general? In an interview, he quipped.[7]

> I have come to agree with Ingmar Bergman that cinema is a completely different template. Theatre needs the actor to keep the mood sustained for a given period in front of an observant audience. That is one way. But cinema needs an actor to stay in part through the thick and thin of the general chaos that prevails around. An intense scene needs a light change. That's an hour in between two shots which must come out with the same intensity. So how does one retain the mood? One word: concentration. If during a break an actor gets assailed by stormy debates on politics or sports or general gossip,

he/she is most certainly likely to lose the thread, which I have seen happening to my co-actors.

Uttam had earned the good words of Ray for ruthlessly practising the art of staying insulated through the thick and thin of a typical day at shoot. All his leisure was kept for the hours after pack-up. For Uttam though, the actor's preparation was not just what he did on the sets. He said,[8]

> An actor has to be a life-long learner and an observer of his world. The world is our textbook. He should read—newspapers, books, journals. And he should watch good movies, preferably from Hollywood and the west. Cinema after all is an art with strong roots in the west. So they adapt, change and grow much faster than us.

Uttam, a year before his death, had visited the United States on an invitation from the Bengali diaspora and spoke at length about Hollywood and his deep admiration for Marlon Brando and Peter O'Toole.

As a star Uttam found himself at the summit early and with the unpleasant job of sustaining it for more than the next two decades. Through the 1960s, he managed the same with aplomb, but by the early 1970s, the cracks started to show. Except a set of distinguished performances in 1974/1975, his last hurrah, bad films, as we have seen already, piled on top of each other. They managed to box Uttam's boundless talent into a sort of rusted, stuffy conformity. It was a decline that was inevitable after having reached a summit. It was also a decline that was collateral and conditional to the general degeneration of a vernacular cinema culture which refused to grow with time and technology. Moreover, unlike stars elsewhere, Uttam refused to be drawn to the wages of garrulous politics. In several interviews he had said, repeatedly, that he found politics corruptible and stardom alienating. In his later years Uttam drew attention, again and again, to his being without any support; to the lack of good plots and directors; to the abysmal physical architecture of the industry. He also had a clear sense of seeing his acting life coming to an end.[9]

> I would soon like to move out of acting into directing and then I want to fade out. Before that, I would want to see a Pune-like film school in Calcutta; a board to decide and veto on scripts; a training school for actors; and uninterrupted power supply to the studios.

Ironically, in this late period Uttam not only felt isolated *because* of his stardom but also *from* it, while continuing to act in movie after movie that fell way below his standards. In the same interview with Kavita Sinha he reveals his increasing yearning for spending quiet time with himself and his books, but his public life displayed an entirely obverse sensibility: of being sucked into a clamour of sociability and flattery. And yet, Uttam managed to stay distanced from himself: "Frankly, no one has ever listened to me. The cacophony of silvery adulation and the blank noise of fandom has always drowned my voice", he had rued in another conversation not long before his death.[10] Uttam, then, was the primary witness to the levity of his own stardom, which was both precarious and phenomenal at the same time.

The idea of Uttam Kumar, then, is a complex one—his longevity giving his stardom the multifarious tensions that are found, if ever, in an entire system and rarely in a singular trajectory of an actor's life. The complexity of his stardom also helps to comprehend why Uttam's fame stands distinctly separated from the politics of stardom in Tamil or Telugu cinema; or that of the cyclical and industrial nature of stardom in Bombay. This complexity was beyond the reach of most during his lifetime; when any consensus on his performative range was obfuscated by the sheer quantity of movies and the habitual ubiquity of his presence. But, as Ray has said in Uttam's context, an actor should finally be measured against his best work and in the ensuing years, Uttam's remarkable work has managed to extricate his name from the tyranny of numbers and the muddle of mediocrity.

Over the years, a few other patterns in his body of work and his singular stardom has come to light. Here are three hypotheses.

A HISTORICAL CONDITIONALITY

Indian cinema, as will be revealed in the course of the book, was actually *not* the point of reference for Bengali cinema. Whether as a historical or a cultural project; or whether in art or popular cinema, the better part of Bengali cinema looked beyond the confines and geography of South Asia. There was a curious and sustained correspondence between the history and practice of cinema as a global artistic, cultural and technological tool and cinema in Calcutta (which was dominated by but not interchangeable with Bengali cinema). The moving image arrived very early in Calcutta and responded unfailingly to the ebb and flow of cinema across the world—sometimes tenuously, sometimes rigorously. At least till the mid-1970s. This is important because the object of our study may be a game-changing figure in Bengali cinema but he was by no means a messiah; nor was his rise meteoric. Both assessments are erroneous and hence ruptured from history. And ruptured from history, a work on this star-actor (or any star actor for that matter) that begins in medias res, will carry the danger of deteriorating into pointless mythology rather than develop into a cultural history. It is this lapse into that sort of tacky and frantic allegory that this book would hope to caution against at each stage of its journey.

To that end, Uttam's work cannot be divorced from the historical framework of Bengali culture in general and cinema in particular. We need to see how charged historic moments played out during the high noon of Bengali popular cinema, with Uttam's gigantic footprints determining that trajectory. So, we should take note of how the industry that Uttam eventually made his own was formed and what was its constitution before the years of Uttam's stardom. Bengali cinema was not anchorless, or without a grammar of style or a semiotic of stardom before the mid-1950s. It was, in spite of that period's immense political and historical demands, an industry of repute, if not also one that was thriving. It had developed a deep-seated cultural anchorage among the middle and professorate classes; had found ways to accommodate high literary influences; had a substantive and ready line of production facilities; exquisite theatre halls; a talented crop of actors, makers and technicians; a robust, argumentative, demanding viewership and an influential critical apparatus in the form of the BFJA, which was founded in 1937.

The double moment of renewal in the 1950s—when Satyajit Ray and Uttam Kumar had arrived on the scene—was part of that history and not sequestered from it. Since then, global cinematic concerns, such as the foregrounding of the city, the potency and limit of modernity, class and gender concerns, modes of storytelling, experiments with film form, romance and music, melodrama and stardom, found renewed reverberations. So, from the vantage of retrospect what is clear is that Bengali cinema's advent into the period after the Partition was marked by two narrative and aesthetic practices. If one, symbolised by Satyajit Ray and others, created the practice called 'art-house' cinema, the other saw itself lodging entirely behind the cult of Uttam Kumar. What Ray and company did to Bengali art-house cinema, Uttam, as its star performer and top box-office draw, did to popular Bengali cinema. They could be said to have established two 'schools' of cinema, two celluloid ecosystems around them, which ironically converged in the figure of Uttam (not only but most definitely in Ray's two films with Uttam). At the same time, Uttam represented much more than just being the totem of a purported 'filmmaking' school. As much as he imbibed an organised film tradition, Uttam found himself in a position to redefine it; and he did. His stardom triggered a new cinematic language; produced a new reception circuit for popular cinema; and offered a new definition of stardom, helping Uttam emerge as the singular vanguard of his cinema. More importantly, his cinema re-invigorated the weakened connection between cinematic modernity in the West and cinema in the subcontinent, as some of the global shifts in the appreciation of melodrama found meaningful continuity in Bengali cinema too. Within the architecture of populist melodrama and arcane idyll of his early romances; the progressive chronicles of his middle years; and the un-*heroic*, agonising, flailing middle-age portrayals of his later films, Uttam's cinema powerfully encompassed the seductive tumult of his time again and again, often diffident and lambent in their emphasis but never too absent. To that end, the cinema of Calcutta as an artistic, aesthetic and popular practice and Uttam Kumar as an actor, star, 'matinee attraction' constitute a historic part of each other.

A DULCET NATURALISM

Uttam's popularity, as I have already indicated, was not built on an edifice of feel-good, gratifying romances of various moulds, notwithstanding the popular perception to that effect. His stardom was actually built on his screen persona's consistent ability to *conform* and *contradict*, to understand the melancholic heft of the period while also being able to navigate it gently, without rebellion and rancour. In Uttam's persona, the everyday desire of the 'everyman' found nuanced upliftment; while in Uttam's stardom was found the 'heroic' consummation of survival and love.

And yet, at the heart of his extraordinary acceptability sits a striking, anomalous prospect. Bengali cinema in its formative years was an enterprise that attracted elite and proficient Brahmo men (and women) with a visionary, reformist streak; or, quixotic, passionate men with rich and aristocratic lineage. The third influential social group came from East Bengal, who made up for their lack of landed capital with better education, a more liberal world view and an entrenched cultural zeal. Uttam is the *only* transformative figure who was none of these three. He had neither the class, nor the felicity, nor the intellectual capital of those key, zealous men (and women) before him. Given the antecedents of both Uttam and Bengali cinema, there was no apparent reason why Uttam was the 'chosen one' to have given Bengali popular cinema a historic direction in the decades after Partition. Not only that, Uttam was also the only major Bengali luminary from the western part (most of his co-actors, directors and crew, came from the east) of the partitioned state of Bengal who commanded unqualified, unrestricted admiration from those who came from the eastern side. Few other parts, if any, of

Bengali life have had the privilege of receiving equal adulation from across the cultural divide of the east and the west.

So what caused the insurgency called Uttam Kumar? Was it because Uttam was a product of a historical moment in Bengal, his ascent signifying a new, participatory middle-class in cultural mobilisation? Is his rise to fame symbolic of Bengali cinema's arrival into lived modernity, where class and birth were increasingly a matter of fortuity rather than privilege? Or did Uttam's ascent to phenomenal adulation from a rather ordinary life enmesh his *real* life with that of the persona of the *reel*, constructing a figure who could be both comfortably proximal as well as bewitchingly fantastical? All of these factors had a role to play.

The fact is, Uttam, instead of following his influential peers and predecessors, used his innocuous ordinariness to subvert the predominant style of high, aural theatricality and brought to the fore a self-effacing, idiomatic, free-flowing and an entirely natural style of performance. This is most unambiguously found in Uttam's ability to play variations of the caught-in-the-whirlpool everyman—one who could as easily mingle in the crowd as he could also stand out. So, the changed circumstances of Bengal's chequered years doubtlessly found in the indistinguishable young man the possible successor to the hoary heroes of yesteryear; a young man in whose ordinariness one could trace the hapless new citizen; the displaced refugee; the wandering soul; the conflicted usurper; the troubling aspirations of a young artiste; or the youthful lover hopelessly in love. So, if in his romances Uttam had hypothesised an assertive conjugality, in several other films he had invigorated the founding of a munificent and un-anchored persona, whose bonhomous charm was symptomatic of a dulcet, undemanding but companionable male figure.

This is precisely why Uttam Kumar could not make a successful move to Hindi films. Uttam was not exactly a trained (Stanislavskian) actor or one to follow a punishing methodical manner (read Meyerhold). Apart from being an inseparable, organically constituted part of Bengali cinema, he managed to thrive in the eeriness of his unforced style, having inferred the range and scope of celluloid imagery early on in his career. His acting was hence rehearsed, but not choreographed, practised but not 'performed'. His heuristic learning, intrinsic contemporaneity and natural felicity made him embody the idiomatic nuances of the Bengali diction and language, complete with an unerring sense of poise and movement, gesture and response, animus and reflection. It was not about training to speak Hindi. It was impossible to transport the gestural demands of the language that was fundamental to his performance to anything outside it. It was inevitable that he ended up lending his worst parts to Hindi cinema, looking clueless and out of place; while the range, depth and subtlety of his acting, the cosmopolitanism of his style and the pursuit of brilliance in tens of Bengali films have remained, four decades after his death, outside the gregarious celebration of 'Indian' cinema.

A BHADRALOK DESIRABILITY

When we combine the historical conditions with Uttam's screen naturalism, a certain pattern seems to emerge. It was through Uttam's screen persona that popular cinema announced its having arrived into an unambiguous present. Much of the magnetism of the 1950s melodrama lay in the incorporation of this self-assured figure, which came coupled with an identifiable, flesh and blood world *inside* the films; a credible script and a wonderful soundtrack. But the most significant factor for the appeal of his cinema was the exploration of *resolutions* to the series of crises that could effortlessly interchange between what was *desirable* and what was *realisable*. Viewed closely, hence, a significant body of Uttam's work was never an escape *from* the conditions of existence but a reminder that their *inescapability* was to be embraced with dignity. And what helped in the abutment of this liberal cause was the clever use of star value. Hence, as he became more confident, Uttam started playing roles with a more distinguished sense of belonging, characters with firm if polite conviction, where he could push the boundaries of social and moral one-upmanship. And instead of creating any fissure, his move away from pure romances seemed justifiable and obligatory; even if he made occasional returns to romance throughout his career.

A note of caution. Uttam's cinema wasn't always a template of recording the contemporary. His roster being of a staggering number, there were exceptions. So, the final verdict on the liberal quotient of Bengali cinema under Uttam is open-ended. But it is certainly a fact that several portrayals of Uttam were closer to a broader humanist (and unabashedly middle-class) appreciation of the present than to any reactionary, paternalistic nostalgia for a mythical, pre-modern past. This aspect is highlighted in *The Encyclopaedia of Indian Cinema,* which says that Uttam Kumar's early romances re-invigorated the bhadralok, apolitical humanist literary tradition in cinema while at the same time "abandoning the many conservative tenets of that same tradition".[11] This was the underlying algorithm of the bhadralok figuration. But there was more.

A defined bhadralok aspiration as such was not to be achieved through a tenacious imagination of escapist romances. Instead, the apparently self-sustaining world of Uttam's romances is constantly poked at by hunger, crises of religious and caste identities, anxieties of employment, class conflict, homelessness, conjugal one-upmanship, dignity of labour, threats of social boycott and the uneasy cohabitation in the Bengali milieu between love actually and social sanction of marriage. Resultantly, the films showed significant transgressions from formula to accommodate emancipatory exertions in the meaning of citizenship, identity and couple-hood. This is precisely why there is a need for a corrective, revisionist estimation of Uttam's films, which would help us break away from the comfortable, conventional coupling of romantic drama and stardom.

Uttam's stardom was something that the popular industry had meticulously invested in, partially obscuring these productive tensions. But we must see Uttam's real ascent to stardom as part of this appreciation *of* and complex encounter *with* modernity, something barely visible when an entire system was trying to piggyback on a star's charismatic proficiency. It is hence no accident that even in the apparently formulaic romantic melodramas, where the profession of the leading man is hardly a matter of scrupulous audience deliberation, Uttam plays doctor, scientist, engineer, architect, lawyer, radio singer, industrialist and so much more. All of these professions/livelihoods were entrenched in an appreciation of a thriving urbanity, referring to the broader embrace of modernity in Nehruvian India. So, in spite of romances having cultivated the out-of-reach stardom of Uttam, his persona, was at the same time of an identifiable, omnipresent, next-door variety. Much of this range was visually achieved in letting Uttam's screen persona appear in sartorial codes—from rolled-sleeve formal shirts, ties, pointed shoes, tuxedo and three-piece suits to loosely-worn *kurtas*, homely singlets and light, cotton *dhotis*. To that end, he was not a star whose celluloid allure obscured the demanding environs of the world around but actually made them more bearable.

So, even if he could never completely eschew his mannerisms, so typical of the acting cultures he inherited, he could put all his performances into neatly divided and appreciable identities, which spanned almost every aspect of middle-class life. No single entity in the history of the whole of Bengali culture has so neatly embodied the imagination, anxieties and fetishes of the middle class. It is at this cusp that the unmissable bhadralok sensibility of his cinema aligned itself unequivocally to the transnational star imagery of his persona. Hence, if one part of Uttam—the Hollywood-like stardom—can be gauged through the imported form of the melodramas; the other part—his downright *identifiability*—can be gauged only when one is keyed into the very Bengali reworking of the transnational form. One cannot hence see Uttam as either star *or* a screen bhadralok. He was both of them equally while each constituted much of the other. And this fact alone gives his phenomenal, boisterous stardom a refined and genteel embellishment. One must not think that one film or character individually presents this convergence of the bhadralok and the star. There was, rather, an organic interchangeability between the two, which matured over time and emerged as a cumulative figuration. This was both the genesis and continues to be the best reason behind Uttam's immortal appeal.

We shall see how.

THREE QUESTIONS ABOUT A CINEMATIC ODDITY

But none of it means that there was no trouble with this broad reconfiguration of the star persona and the cultural mobilisation of his cinema. In the din of a robust cultural history, we must hence not be so blind as not consider a set of concerns that taunt and torment this unique position of dominance and this spectacular exceptionalism.

First, Uttam's ascent to stardom marked the end of the studio era, and the authority and sovereignty of cinematic reach and commerce shifted from the industrious nature of the studio system to the individual and intimate charms of the matinee idol. With Uttam's rise, thus, cinema in Bengal shifted from an assembly hall kind of collective film culture to that of a pyramid—with the star being the summit—from whom everything else had to be mobilised. Was this shift entirely benign or did it sideline outlier subjects and borderline experimentation that we see in the 1950s? Within the popular domain, films such as *Hrod, Saheb Bibi Golam, Bicharok* and *Khokababur Protyaborton* with Uttam in the lead; and those like *Neel Akasher Niche* (Under the Azure Sky), *Dakhorkora* (The Messenger, 1958), *Sagor Songome* (The Holy Island, 1959) and *Nirdharito Shilpir Onuposthitite* (In the Absence of the Artist Tonight, 1959) without him, remained exceptions. Otherwise, mainstream cinema largely found refuge in romance melodramas, often at the cost of films that were pushing the envelope. Does this perceived capitulation to romance in the 1950s show an industry in the pink of health—cheeks glowing, eyes sparkling, chest puffed out, and steps sprightly? Or does it show an industry sheepishly surrendering to the safety of stardom, seeking refuge in formula and refusing to think beyond the jugular? This is a more complex matter than it appears to be, because Uttam's romances were not always formula romances and he himself was worried about this tendency. But the propensity to seek submission under stardom cannot be overlooked.

This tendency became all the more apparent in the 1970s when Uttam the actor, the matinee attraction and the immaculate enchanter was slowly consumed by a bulk of his own bad films. He had confessed again and again that he was tiring out both as a star and as a performer in trying to hold aloft the populist demands of the industry for an abysmally long period. *Nayak* partially addressed this concern but in actual life, the stakes were much higher and the strains were all too visible in the kind of films Uttam signed in his later years. So the question is, did he let himself be sucked thoughtlessly into a numbed state of excess, of sycophancy, veneration and fame? Or did he exhaust himself in trying to keep the industry on a supply of wages?

This leads to the third and most unsettling query. Uttam had come to personify *a cinema* that had an urban temperament, an intuitive understanding of human nature, a credulous world of fictional lives and an effortless ease of articulating middle-class concerns. In short, that was the cinema of the essential plenitude of life; the wit and grit of Bengali manners with its own world of longing and love, joy and sorrow, melancholy and melody. With the passing of Uttam, this wholesome, intelligent, enjoyable cinema perished. This was the visible casualty; and an expected outcome of Uttam's early and untimely death.

But why could Bengali cinema never manage to walk out of this sense of fatality? Does it mean that Uttam's long and almighty domination—in surplus of the cinema that he sustained—manufactured a gaping void underneath the gleaming surface? Did his death provoke a desperate and unprepared deviation from the embedded codes of modernity that sustained Bengali cinema? Or did that death unleash an entrenched, subliminal vulgarity that undiscerning populism inevitably nurtures behind the cover of modernity? It could be either. We will see. But whichever it was, Bengali cinema's race for the bottom since the 1980s elicits the fabular image of Uttam and his colleagues guarding the gates with supreme alacrity over the years; which unattended since his death, had let the floods in, sweeping away the very foundation of that cinema.

TO DIE, TO SLEEP; TO SLEEP: PERCHANCE TO DREAM

That day—the day of Uttam Kumar's death, 24 July 1980—was to become marked permanently in the crowded annals of Calcutta, a city not unfamiliar with portentous historical events. And not for once was it meant to be anything else. He was, after all, just fifty-three.

He was surely not the Uttam Kumar of yore, an earnestly and sometimes impossibly handsome man of runaway charm and enchantment. And yet, though not as young as his admirers would have loved him to be forever, our hero seemed to have left the scene too early. He was still a heartthrob, his stature managing to stay unswayed by the string of insipid, uncouth duds he was involved with in the last five years. Nor did his matinee magic stand severely decimated by a handful of compelling films where he had visibly appeared to be ageing and un-heroic. And yet, his death, however devastating for his fans, seemed to have come to him at an opportune time. Death released Uttam Kumar from appearing in further atrocities. Death saved him from having to work tirelessly to keep the industry going. Death cloistered him from further ignominy of being accused of dragging down an industry that he had once almost single-handedly piloted to unprecedented riches.

So, Uttam Kumar died, largely, as Uttam Kumar—Bengali cinema's biggest ever star; the much-thronged, much-remembered procession alongside his mortal remains reinforced and revisited his talismanic stature. The *Nayak*, on death, became the *Mahanayak*. A literal translation of *Mahanayak* into English would be *superhero*, though this is not what the English word would otherwise refer to. And yet, that meaning is not lost to generations that came after Uttam. They would argue that he has indeed proved to be a star with credentials of a superhero (one who rose from his times, as in Nietzsche's Superman), who acted as a custodian of a Gotham-like industry, which, prone to venality, corruption and mediocrity, collapsed after his early death. In the end, then, Uttam's was death by exhaustion rather than death by neglect. Was it merely a coincidence that one of Uttam's dream roles was that of Innokentiy Smokunovsky's eponymous Prince of Denmark in Gregory Kozintsev's dark and derelict Russian *Hamlet*? Perhaps not.

Of all the things his death took away, the one that was most universally adored and missed was Uttam's smile, because he smiled like a benign, guileless, youthful god. And his fans, who were greying with him, were less bothered about his films as long as they saw him smile. What that smile meant and what it conveyed through the historical sweep of time to a besieged populace in a truncated, postcolonial, Bengal continues to haunt. In fact, the death of that beatific smile has hence been bereaved, collectively, many a time since. But there been much less of an effort to interrogate the actor behind that smile, and to appreciate the phenomenon behind that actor. It is time one felt deeply the absence of a genteel and luminous laughter in the culture industry—the heroic laughter of a graceful and keenly imbibed modernity.

At heart, this book is about that laughter.

Hence, by no measure does this book consider itself the last word on its object of study. If at all, it proposes to take the reader, with any amount of interest in cinema, through the sprinkling of diamonds and rust that make the anointed life of a storied, star figure. Uttam Kumar was a hero of a *time—the time* when you would confiscate a few moments out of the daily grind and, enthralled in the embellished darkness, would contemplate the images on the alabaster screen; *the time* which now seems gilded in gold in spite of being writ in black and white; *the time* which was troubled, deficient, famished and yet so fulsome, so humane, so poetic; *the time* when you would yearn, sing and romance your way into the magic of the monochrome moving picture.

Ei Poth Jodi Na Sesh Hoi.
[May we never fall out of that time.]

NOTES

1. Uttamkumar Chattopadhyay, *Nayoker Kolome* (A collection of writings by Uttam), edited byAbhik Chattopadhyay, Saptarshi Prokashon, 2015, p. 59.
2. 'Ontorongo Uttam', *Boisakhi* Journal, edited by Dhrubojyoti Mondol, 23 (2013–2014), pp. 79–87.
3. 'Ontorongo Uttam', p. 84.
4. Uttamkumar Chattopadhyay, *Hariye Jaoa Dinguli Mor* (A memoir of early days), edited by Abhik Chattopadhyay, Saptarshi Prokashon, 2013.
5. 'Ontorongo Uttam', p. 84.
6. 'Ontorongo Uttam', p. 84.
7. 'Ontorongo Uttam', p. 83.
8. 'Ontorongo Uttam', p. 82.
9. 'Ontorongo Uttam', p. 85.
10. Chattopadhyay, *Nayoker Kolome*, p. 33.
11. Ashish Rajadhyaksha and Paul Willemen, *Encyclopedia of Indian Cinema*, Oxford University Press, 1998 [1994], p. 134.

2

TWENTY-FOUR FRAMES OF FAME

Fame is a bee./It has a song—/It has a sting—/Ah, too, it has a wing.
—Emily Dickenson

WITHOUT being philosophical or obdurate, it is worth pondering over the simple but inscrutable idea of *fame*. What is fame and how does one measure it? Does it register itself differently for a movie star? How is fame in that case different from mythification? And does it stalk the star in his or her lifetime? In other words, how are we to be remunerated if we fuse a name and a person with his fame and his persona? This chapter attempts to reflect on the same. Instead of trying to untie the person, the actor and the star that was Uttam Kumar, it mixes them up in a series of historical, cultural and anecdotal recollections. The rest of the book will try unravelling the multiple lives of Uttam, but let us begin by considering all three together, bound in a complex, sinewy patchwork of factuality, fame and fortuity. Here are twenty-four sketches on Uttam Kumar—sketches that try to grasp the nature and scope of his iconicity. Why twenty-four? Because cinema is, after-all, twenty-four image frames pressed into visibility per second. And also because, as that wicked Frenchman Jean-Luc Godard wrote in one of his films: "Photography is truth. The cinema is truth twenty-four times per second."[1]

1

Arathoon Stephen was an Armenian refugee-turned-millionaire real-estate mogul in Calcutta who had built the Grand Hotel in the early 20th century. The hotel supplied food and booze to two of his properties nearby: the wooden Old Opera House (later to become Globe Cinema) and Empire Theatre, both being landmarks of early public entertainment in Calcutta. Built in 1908, the latter was a posh venue for mixed public shows, including boxing. In 1930s, the theatre changed hands, was redesigned and came under the management of Warner Brothers to become New Empire. It continued to host plays, concerts and ballets, its stage having associated itself with Rabindranath Tagore, Yehudi Menuhin and Uday Shankar. Its next-door neighbour, the spacious, W.M. Dudok-designed Lighthouse, built in 1934, was dedicated to Hollywood from the very beginning. This Calcutta neighbourhood—popularly known as Chowringhee—had seen the birth of cinema in the subcontinent with Elphinstone Picture Palace, in 1907. Soon, Elphinstone, Electric (Albion) Theatre and Elite were followed by Lighthouse, Metro, Globe and Paradise; who were soon joined by Roxy, Orient and New Empire. Housed within less than a kilometre in the same neighbourhood, they encircled a colonial geography of leisure, mostly from Hollywood, oozing a debonair air that overawed proximity to projections of stardom potentially released. Madhu Bose and Satyajit Ray have, for example, fondly remembered their days of watching Eddie Polo and Charlie Chaplin, Buster Keaton and Douglas Fairbanks, their large, protuberant posters adorning the walls of these citadels to cinema.

In the Bengali New Year of 1956, something interesting happened. On that day, New Empire opened its doors to Debaki Basu's much loved literary comedy *Chirokumar Sobha*, indicating a historic first in Chowringhee for a Bengali film. Only Paradise cinema, on Bentinck Street nearby, had made such an exception three years ago with *Sharey Chuattor*, something that was made part of the film's publicity.

A more distinguished moment came on 14 November 1957. This time, the site was the 1935-born, Thomas W. Lamb-designed, MGM-backed Metro Cinema, whose art deco edges kissed the neo-Baroque behemoth Whiteaway, Laidlaw & Co., forming the most recognisable skyline of Esplanade. The plush red carpets and gilded interiors of Metro cinema were passport to the charms of MGM's famous line-up of Spencer Tracy, Norma Shearer, Clark Gable and Greta Garbo, the last being one to whose reclusive ways Suchitra Sen would deeply be attracted in the autumn of her life. The list of MGM stars also included the Darjeeling-born Vivian Leigh. The famous musicals of MGM with Fred Astaire, Judy Garland, Frank Sinatra, and others dominated the screen in the 1940s and the early 1950s. Calcutta gentry, after having savoured their film at Metro, usually headed for Firpo's, the Italian restaurant and delicatessen next door, where among other things, they feasted on roast duck, pressed beef, ham pie, pomfret fillet with tartare sauce and gâteaux millefeuille. Chowringhee had always been unapologetically colonial in its bearing and even after a decade since Independence, Metro had strongly remained an exclusive domain of the finest entertainment from Hollywood. It was the centrepiece of the affluent, cosmopolitan climes of Calcutta's downtown, a melting pot that befitted only the well-heeled and the well-versed.

Following Paradise in 1953 and New Empire in 1956, in November 1957, Metro made the historic amendment to their English-film-only policy, when it released *Chondronath*, a luminous old-world literary melodrama, bowing to the irrepressible stardom of its young leading man. The final frontier of Hollywood's marquee moviedom fell that day as Bengali cinema made an exultant entry into the glitter and glamour of *sahebpara*, taking a giant leap from its native provinces of Bhawanipore and Hatibagan. It was the cinematic equivalent of the empire writing resolutely back.

What connected all the three films that broke the exclusivity of Hollywood in high-brow Esplanade? All of them had Uttam Kumar in the lead.

2

But Metro had something more than just MGM charm and plush interiors. The chief projector of Metro Cinema was a corpulent but serious looking man named Satkari Chattopadhyay, who, when he kept his eyes firm on the first reels of *Chondronath* as it unspooled and fell on the alabaster cloth, could not hold his excitement. Uttam Kumar, by then the undisputed star of Bengali cinema, was after all, his eldest-born. Mr Chattopadhyay had projected on screen many a star in Metro; or before that at Elphinstone Picture Palace, where cinema in India began and where he had started as a young projectionist. But even in his wildest imagination he would never have thought that one day he would project a Bengali film sitting in the heart of Chowringhee and that too one that was bowing to the extraordinary stardom of his own son. The father and the son created history that November night in 1957. Born to a projectionist and cameraperson, Uttam Kumar in some sense, was born *behind* the movies—though he had to cross every severe obstacle to *arrive* in front of it. Satkari Chattopadhyay passed away in 1959, but the screens he once lighted continued to reverberate with the charm of his famous ward.

3

It was in Metro that Uttam saw *Random Harvest*—starring Ronald Colman and Greer Garson—a modestly successful MGM film. Though the film was released internationally in 1942, Uttam saw it during one of its reruns. Impressed, he adapted it as his first home production, making elaborate changes to suit local expectations. *Harano Sur*

(The Lost Tune) became a blockbuster romance and continues to be one of Uttam–Suchitra's un-ageing films.

A scene in *Harano Sur* faced odd difficulties. It involved Uttam's character Alok undertaking a shave. As usual, Uttam carried the scene with aplomb and the first 'take' was okayed. But the sound technician realised that he hadn't turned on the sound equipment, so taken was he by the scene. But the 'scene' was done with and the lights were to be dismantled for the next shot. He, distraught and guilty, rushed to Uttam. "I cannot tell this to Ajoy-da (the director). He will be very angry. After all, the scene needs to be shot all over again." Uttam went to the director. "Have you undone the lights?" "No, why?" "I need to do this scene again." "Why? It was fine." "No, no. Something did not go well. I know it." "Are you sure?" "Yes." The scene was lighted and shot again; while the technician went back to his position, overwhelmed.[2]

The next faux pas during the shoot was from the director Ajoy Kar, who was also the co-producer and was on camera. The setting was that of a stormy night, when amidst a torrent of rain and lightning, Alok would flee an asylum where he is held forcefully, thanks to his accident-induced amnesia. It involved extensive lights and sets to create the mood. But this time Kar, so engrossed was he in Uttam's 'uncannily natural acting' that he forgot to unlock the camera lens. Uttam was told of the error. Once again, without any annoyance, Uttam readied himself for one more take. This time too, Kar—stupefied—did not remove the cover. Uttam was confessed to again and he, without raising any heckles, repeated the scene. The third time things went right, without disruption.

In the film, the amnesiac Alok would flee the asylum to land up, accidentally of course, at the house of Roma—his doctor and would-be wife. Outside the film, the director and the sound recordist became life-long admirers of the producer-star's easy generosity. There are such examples galore.

4

Harano Sur won a Certificate of Merit from the Indian government. As co-producer, Uttam Kumar had to travel to Delhi to collect the award. As a debutant producer and lead actor, it was a triumph that was hard for him not to feel very thrilled about.

Excitedly, he was getting ready in the morning to catch the ten o'clock train from Howrah Station, when the local inspector arrived. "Sorry Sir, but you cannot go today", he informed Uttam. "Why? On what crime?"

"Not crime, but because of who you are. There is not a bee that can enter Howrah Station. It is choked to its last breadth. News has broken out that you are expected there on your way to Delhi. Crowds have gone wild in expectation."[3] A hapless Uttam called up a senior police officer pleading for help. After all, it was a national award and this could not be a reason to not attend it. "Do one thing. You reach the exit gate. I will do the rest."[4] So was it done. Uttam's car, reportedly a Studebaker President, was ushered in through the station's exit gate. But there was no way he could get to the train unhindered. Wrestling with the crowd, a couple of policemen managed to huddle him into the train. A harangued but relieved Uttam found himself seated in a first-class cabin. Finally, the star could be assured that he was on his way to collect the producer's award.

This actual event of a railway station filled with delirious fans of a star is 're-enacted' in Ray's *Nayak*. In the film, Uttam's character Arindam Mukherjee is seen travelling to Delhi to collect a prestigious acting award. However, in reality, there was no exclusive national award for actors. But in a curious case of real life following the reel, in 1967, the Government of India did institute the Bharat Award for best male lead in Indian cinema. And unsurprisingly, the inaugural award went to Uttam Kumar. He was judged the best male actor that year for Satyajit Ray's *Chiriyakhana* (made a year after *Nayak*), an award he shared with Uttam Kumar for Sunil Banerjee's *Antony Firingee*.

Image 2.1: The thoughtful sleuth. Film still from *Chiriyakhana* (The Zoo, 1967)

Source: Ray archives.

5

In spite of awards and adulation, our hero, at least in the initial years of this stardom, was not betrothed to it. His memoirs attest to the meaningful distance he had maintained, often scrupulously.[5]

> I am engulfed in darkness; pitch, impenetrable darkness. But I am standing in the middle of bright, hard light, circling a land irradiated by it. But I know this light is ephemeral, it can extinguish itself any moment. It can throw me deep into darkness, into an everlasting night. But beyond the darkness that surrounds me is life aglow, not the fake light I am under, but real radiance. I had come from that darkness one day, crossing on the way realms of shadows. And I know how abysmal that dark period is.

This was how Uttam remembered his days of struggle and trial; a life on lease from a lowly clerical job, a life of putting everything at stake at the altar of the moving image and its salacious seduction.

If these were the dark days of lonely struggle, there was also the rosy public image. A newspaper had once published a description of Uttam's residence. It said that the star had abandoned the last link with his middle-class past by building a wonderland of a mansion, which had so advanced architectonics that among other incredible things, it made possible for Uttam to drive his car straight up three floors and park it close to his living room. Clearly, the scribe, in a moment of mania, gave the otherwise modest star an insurmountable tableau of success, something like Charles Foster Kane's 'Xanadu' in *Citizen Kane*.

Kane's famous last word was the enigmatic 'Rosebud'. Roses were no less enigmatic for our hero too

> My car had stopped at the traffic and I looked around. I could see a roadside flower vendor selling a bunch of roses. My eye fell on a particular one. There was no way I could get out of my car on that midday street in Calcutta. I requested Nyapa [his chauffeur and confidant]. He rushed to get me the anointed flower. But by then, I was noticed. People began to assemble near my car and would press their cheeks against the window, peering inside. One or two were pushing the doors to get in. I tried, in vain, to hide my face with a magazine. Nyapa came back with the flower and started the car. But I realized it was not the one I desired. It was too late to go back. I had been virtually surrounded. I, Uttam Kumar, who, if the grapevine is to be believed, have everything at my disposal. But that day I couldn't even procure a single piece of rose that I had so fancied.

Uttam wrote this too,[6] hinting how abiding stardom was after all, a binding prospect.

On other days, this same star would arrange to have his blockbusters viewed at his home on a movie projector. He would sit on the mattress that was laid out on the floor and watch his films along with family, friends, acquaintances. At key points, Uttam would clap and shout at his own film, simulating the awed excitement of a typical fan: "Guru, what a dialogue", or "Look the way Guru walks", or "Guru, you are great". Then, if someone would whistle in exhilaration, he would turn to him and say in a stern, if mock reprimand, "Who is it that whistles! Please don't", and then promptly go back to clapping and shouting with childlike glee.[7]

6

Uttam was never far from the suspicion that was entrenched in a deeply middle-class conscience for anything that came riding on fame and fortune. But his fans, needless to say, did not share his agnosticism about fame. Crowds would materialise at the mere hint of Uttam Kumar's presence, sniff for his schedule and congregate at key locations to just watch him pass by. They would close in on his car, tear at his shirt, pull his tie or reach for his face. This was not just in the initial days of his stardom but continued throughout his working life, including the day of his funeral congress. He could only book himself a ticket in the night shows and enter only when the theatre was darkened; would arrive at weddings and functions way past midnight; choose the earliest hours at daybreak to complete his daily dose of morning walk. By the time the city woke up, Uttam would be back indoors, stay either at home or be ensconced in the studios during the day, and only when the city was fast asleep would he tiptoe outside under the cover of the nocturnal sky.

People who have grown up in the 1950s and 1960s remember regularly seeing Chhabi Biswas peering from his Bansdroni balcony, Bikash Roy watching the world from his Jodhpur Park verandah, Pahari Sanyal taking a walk near his Hindustan Park home or Kamal Mitra strolling on his first-floor terrace on Sarat Bose Road. No one ever remembers having seen Uttam, relaxed and unguarded, in a moment of domestic candour. There was no way he could *be* without the mob periling the precincts.

Those were not the days of pet bouncers or police protection. A star would be left to himself, largely. Uttam's defence on the face of relentless mob attention was to stay out of the way of harm; or cleverly manoeuvre through fan mayhem; or steer himself through secret exits. There were moments of lapse, panic and pandemonium. Once he was also wounded. But he took them in his stride as a necessary evil resulting from his fabled popularity.

7

But little did he know that his stardom had stretched well beyond the limits of the city. This was in the early 1960s. It was an outdoor shoot at Jiaganj, an ancient riverine town about ten kilometres from Bengal's medieval capital of Murshidabad. As a red herring, it was announced well in advance that Uttam Kumar was indisposed and was not travelling with the crew. Clandestinely, the crew with Uttam arrived by train at the town late in the evening. And defeating all attempts at concealing his arrival, the small, scenic station was already overrun with people. The crew, nervous and caught off guard, sat inside the locked compartment for a long time waiting for help. After much confusion, Uttam was rescued by local men who carried him prostrate (*changdola* in colloquial Bangla) out of the train and into a car.

A key river scene was scheduled to be shot the morning after. The crew, heckled, harangued, exhausted, retired for the day thinking that the ordeal was over. But it was just the beginning.

Next morning, as the team reached the banks of the river they were dumbstruck. On both sides of Bhagirathi, that side being Azimgunj, hundreds were travelling on foot—men, women, old people and children—walking in a line towards the bank with the look of what seemed like a mission. Before the team could fathom what was happening, a local messenger arrived with the news. People had set out at daybreak from the Muslim-majority villages miles away, so that they could have a look at Uttam Kumar. It was not the usual crowd that would gather at shooting sites. There was only a handful of crew members and they were inept to 'attend' to the gathering hordes in any way. Instead, the crew hurried with the boats to the middle of the stout river and proceeded with the shooting. But that had a telling effect. As per Uttam's own version of the story, mounds of sodden earth soon started flying from both sides of the river. The crowd wanted to get close to their idol; nothing less than that would do, and hence the lovelorn vehemence. One big piece was also aimed for the star himself, because he showed no inclination to gratify the demand. That piece, recounted Uttam, landed on the poor director, who was trying to dodge another piece from another end. There was total chaos. But the crew managed to escape to their den largely unhurt.

One can read this episode as a simple case of mob excess that is not unheard of in the annals of cinema. The other reading should consider this episode, which was not unique in case of Uttam, as symbolising a bigger query, which is about Uttam's reach as a star. This was in the 1960s; there was no way that the 'idea' of a cinestar would travel through television or other means of media to distant lands. The only 'carriers' of cinema ephemera, if at all, were city periodicals, while broadsheets, which reached the provinces, rarely carried news from the world of 'entertainment'. Film theatres were few and far between. Cinema was *not* yet the vehicle of mass outreach in the provinces.

So, what was the basis of a stardom of such scale taking shape amidst a people whose physical familiarity with Bengali cinema was, at best, partial? At a more cultural level too, there could not be any feasible explanation. After all, Uttam Kumar did not 'build' his fandom through the more realisable channels of loud mythological or period films. If at all, his cinema was unapologetically middle-class. There were exceptions but they were not enough to create any recognisable template for the provincial viewer. In short, his cinema was deliberately dissociated from the traditional tropes, Hindu or Muslim, that apparently appease the people in the hinterlands. So, there was no palpable reason why Uttam Kumar's body of work would cross the divided territories and attract obsessive mass adulation in a far-flung Bengal village.

Either we have historically misread the gap between 'the country and the city', or Uttam Kumar was that rare thing—a star who could transcend the divisive logic of cultural pattern and taste. Moreover, as Uttam's stardom expanded its geography, it also 'carried' Bengali cinema's reach outside the urban towns and centres in the 1950s. In that case, the fundamental novelty of cinema, its potential as a storytelling medium, and the identifiable and aspirational cultural sphere that Uttam's cinema exemplified merged into the figure of the star-actor. That could explain some of it, if not all of it.

In fact, this link that Uttam's stardom managed to establish was both unprecedented and unsurpassed. Before or after him, no actor has created even a surfeit of that transcendental link between the stiff upper-lipped cinema consumer of Chowringhee and the vast multitudes in the bosom of Bengal. Historically, there was only one man in Bengal who could get thousands spontaneously to march to a river one early morning and shower him with love in the form of mounds of sodden, fresh muck.

8

Image 2.2: The hero, up and close. Film still from *Nayak* (The Hero, 1966)

Source: Author.

If the muck was an act of unmitigated affection from the uninitiated, there was no dearth of admiration from the other side of the spectrum. Satyajit Ray wrote in *Sunday* magazine a month after Uttam's death:[8]

> I must say working with Uttam turned out to be one of the most pleasant experiences of my filmmaking career. I found out early on that he belonged to the breed of instinctive actors … I hardly recall any discussion with Uttam on a serious, analytical level on the character he was playing [for *Nayak*]. And yet he constantly surprised and delighted me with unexpected little details of action and behaviour which came from him and not from me, which was always in character and enhanced the scene. They were so spontaneous that it seemed he produced these out of his sleeve. If there was any cogitation involved, he never spoke about it.… Any artist, however, must always be judged by his best work. On that basis and within the gamut in which his talent was best revealed, Uttam's work shows the rare virtues of grace, spontaneity and confidence. Such a combination is not easy to come by, and it is hard to see anyone taking his place in the cinema of West Bengal in the near future.

At a memorial gathering held later at Technician's Studio, Ray was even more profuse in his praise.[9]

> Some days ago I saw my film *Nayak* after a gap of ten or maybe twelve years. Many of you must have seen it too. I saw the film with rapt attention and have detected few issues with my direction. I doubt

my own volition, aspects of my work and the conditions in which I have to work and I am not surprised that I am yet to make a perfect film. But did you see Uttam Kumar? In a two-hour film that centers around him, he is perfect from every angle, in every scene. The story, the script, the making is mine. But Uttam made it his own with the charisma and effortlessness that only an actor of his caliber could do. Discerning viewers of cinema can identify the difference between good performance extolled by the filmmaker and performance that is endowed with the gifts intrinsic to the performer. And I can vouch for the fact that Uttam excelled in the second. I find no fault with him as an actor.... There is none like him and there will be no one to ever replace him. He was and he is unparalleled in Bengali, even Indian cinema.

9

I am sorry but we can't seem to process your passport application.

Why not?

I know you are Uttam Kumar, you know you are Uttam Kumar and the entire passport office, where most are your diehard fans, know you are Uttam Kumar.

Then?

But sir, your papers say you are Arunkumar Chatterjee and there is no appropriate document to show that Arunkumar Chatterjee and Uttam Kumar are the same. You are, Sir, a star and we love you but your passport, unfortunately, needs documents.

In June 1966, Uttam Kumar and Satyajit Ray were headed to Berlin, invited as guests of the famed festival, for *Nayak*, which was selected for screening. Uttam was as excited as a child. This was his first tour outside India and that too as an invitee to one of the world's leading festivals. But he was born as Arunkumar and had changed his screen name three times in the early years to suit prickly producers or the vagaries of filmic identity. Later, when he prevailed, the screen name Uttam Kumar stabilised. But his *real* name, technically, was still Arunkumar. When recalling the incident above,[10] he wrote, "Fame was not a passport to my passport, after all."[11] Anxious, he began scouting for papers which could show that Uttam Kumar, the supreme matinee idol, and Arunkumar, the port commissioner's clerk, were one and the same after all.

In the end, he did go to Berlin. And also to London, Paris, Zurich and Rome. Berlin, he said, was like a first romance, a love at first sight. He was charmed by the informality of the local people, something that

Germans are not particularly known for. He often stole time from formal meetings and dinners and let go of himself in the city, trying to soak in every bit of it. Every star is tempted to secure a bail from the prison-house of fame. Uttam was no exception. At no danger of being hounded and stalked in that foreign land, Uttam found a new spring in his footsteps. At the festival, it was less breezy. The Golden Bear winner, Roman Polanski's bleak absurdist horror flick *Cul-de-Sac*, or Godard's 1960s dry and droll non-linear satire *Masculin Féminin* could not impress him. He confessed not being too taken up by European cinema's obsession with 'de-dramatisation'. But he liked talking to Italian Marxist auteur Pier Passolini (one among the jury) and could declare to Geraldine Chaplin his admiration for her legendary father. At the press conference someone asked him if he was Soumitra Chatterjee's brother to which he replied just with that radiant smile of his. But what stayed with him are sudden recognitions from people completely alien to Indian cinema.[12]

> Outside the Zoo Palast, I was often stopped by someone shouting 'Der Held' (referring to the international title of Ray's film), approaching to get an autograph. Often I looked up to see who they were. One day a lady, guessing my surprise, said: 'This is the first time I have ever seen an Indian film. This is the first time I have ever come to ask for an autograph of a film star.'

Nayak received a nod of special recognition at the festival.

Uttam dodged an interview at a London television studio during that visit, most likely to avoid drawing attention to his pitiable English, which would appear even starker next to an Englishman. His Rome visit was preserved in several photographs that Ray took of him around the Colosseum—complete in black suit and tie with a white, patchworked, silk pocket square hanging out of his breast pocket and thick-rimmed, squarish goggles guarding against the Italian sun. There has always been some rumour but no actual record that Elizabeth Taylor, on watching *Nayak* in London, wanted to work with Uttam, whom she found charming and versatile. One wishes to lay hands on at least a passing testament to this otherwise improbable story.

10

A scene of a youthful, bespectacled professor checking answer scripts. He is sitting cross-legged on his bed near the open window of a sparse but clean room in a typically middle-income house. His manservant Bhola is completing the usual chores nearby.

Each one is an idiot, rascal, full-fledged monkey!

[Bhola turns around, stands erect] Babu, who are you calling names!

[Professor, still fiddling with scripts] If they write gibberish on answer scripts, how do I mark them?

Aah. So you say. [Bhola comes closer, grins] Babu, do the young these days have any mind for studying? Go and see, they must be busy watching cinema-theatre. Go and you will see, they have lined up attentively; all sizes, all ages are there. [Bhola makes gestures with his hand to indicate sizes]

[Professor looks up] Right you are. They seem to only care about Uttam Kumar. How he cuts his hair, how he dresses, how he walks, they are losing sleep on those things. And they leave the test in unison. What's wrong? [Professor bristles, sits upright and looks straight into the camera] Apparently the questions are difficult! Future treasures of the nation!

This is a scene from Tapan Sinha's 1955 film *Upohar*, in which Ashok Sarkar, the youngish professor, is lamenting the serious lapse in attention that the students seem to be suffering, thanks to an upstart star about whom they seem to be obsessing. This reference to the stardom of Uttam in a contemporary film is a curious interpolation of the *actual* in a work of fiction and all the more so because it comes so early in Uttam's career. But what is striking is that Ashok Sarkar is played by none other than Uttam himself. It is 'he' who dismisses the 'star'. I am aware of no other Indian film, at least not that early, in which an actor disapprovingly refers to the magnetic stardom of his own 'alter ego'. In *Upohar*, Uttam and Manju Dey play a city couple in search of an apartment, which leads them to a caustic, penny-pinching house owner. The film deliberately underplayed the charm of Uttam to provide an authentic glimpse into middle-class anxieties about housing and finance. The scene contrasts the film's middle-class setting with the fanciful premise of a typical melodrama, banking on the newfound stardom of a certain Uttam Kumar. And it does so with Uttam himself doing the favours.

This is the maiden onscreen 'reference' to Uttam Kumar's stardom in a Bengali film but not the only one. Tapan Sinha's 1966 comic fantasy *Golpo Holeo Sotti* (the original of *Bawarchi*) is about a cook who appears from nowhere to mend a family's fractured relationships. One afternoon he reads out an interview of Uttam Kumar in a film magazine to regale the wives of the combative siblings. They listen with rapt attention to the matinee idol and then exhale profound, wide-eyed sighs thinking of the star's capacity to be respectful to his audience.

In *Kokhono Megh* (Shadows of the Cloud, 1968) two women are on a visit to Darjeeling. While painting the beauty of the snow-capped scenery one of them asks her companion sauntering nearby what thoughts she is lost in. "I am thinking about Uttam Kumar", she replies; minutes before Uttam Kumar's character—a dandy intelligence officer in woollens and glares—appears for the first time in the film. In another late romance, *Bikele Bhorer Phool* (Love in Autumn, 1974), Uttam plays the reputed writer and scholar Anish Mitra, a greying and dashing bachelor, who is mistaken as Uttam Kumar on a beach by a group of giggly college girls. In the 1973 comedy *Basanta Bilap*, a reed-thin lover, in a moment alone with his ladylove asks her to call him 'Uttam Kumar' with appropriate bashfulness; so that he can seal that moment with precious and 'romantic' glee.

Bengali cinema is replete with references to its star figure, who is never too far away from the imagined indulgences of the middle class. He is the totem of romance and a talisman of the bounty of life—something, as we will see, was a key factor in the seemingly never-ending reach of his appeal.

11

That Tapan Sinha more than once inscribed his script with a mention of the real-life stardom of Uttam Kumar says a thing or two about his deep admiration for the actor. Apart from Satyajit Ray, he was another director of repute beyond Bengali cinema, who worked and stayed impressed with Uttam. In fact, between 1955 and 1964, Uttam worked thrice with Tapan Sinha—in *Upohar*, *Jhinder Bondi* and *Jotugriha*. The first was a credible social critique laced with moments of nimble comedy; the second was a thrilling period piece; and the third a restrained and refined unfolding of a couple's slow-burning estrangement from each other. In all three cases, the casting of Uttam was somewhat of a coup. No one thought that as early as 1955, a twenty-nine-year-old Uttam, beginning to enjoy the fruits of stardom, would pull off the character of a married, bespectacled professor. In *Jhinder Bondi*, not only was Uttam pitted against Soumitra Chatterjee, but the best part of the script was stored for the villain Mayurvahan, which was to be played by Chatterjee. Unfazed, Uttam put in his best. Tapan Sinha remembered how, unknown to him, Uttam renewed his training in horse riding, which he had picked up during the shooting of *Bou Thakuranir Haat* (The Consort's Tale, 1953) a few years ago. He came to the sets in Udaipur prepared. What also startled both Sinha and the foil fencing trainer whom Sinha had hired for a scene with a crucial duel was Uttam's keen attention during the training schedule. When the American trainer asked him, "Can you really learn this thing so quickly? I have trained many, it takes months if not years." Uttam replied, "I am an actor. I will not be able to learn the art of fencing but I can fake it convincingly. That's my job. That is what I do when I observe patiently."[13] The trainer was much pleased with the final outcome. There was a scene which Sinha remembers particularly. It was one of drunken frolic when Uttam, as the princely wastrel Shankar Singh, would sing a slew of random songs without erring on the intricate tunes based on classical arrangements. Sinha later said,[14]

> Ali Akbar Khan did a magnificent job of creating the impressionistic, drunken medley. Uttam listened carefully, recorded the songs and took them home. On the day of the shoot, he came so prepared that the first take was flawless. I cannot imagine how an actor could be so impeccable and yet so unforced in such a difficult scene where he is both drunk and scrupulously tuneful by habit. I had to pat his back that day.

In *Jotugriha*, which Uttam also produced, Uttam played one half of a couple heading for divorce while Tapan Sinha's wife Arundhati played his wife, Madhuri. *Jotugriha* is easily one of Uttam's tallest performances. Sinha recalled,[15]

> It was what can be called in the mold of 'silent acting'. One has to have a range of expressions and get at the bottom of their rhythm to make this kind of acting meaningful. Uttam and Arundhati did so with aplomb. I could not have had a better producer or set of actors.

In later years, Uttam's many mistakes included a severe misunderstanding with Sinha over *Banchharamer Bagan* (The Garden of Delights), which led to a court case. But that did not stop Tapan Sinha, long after Uttam was gone, from paying him rich tributes. He has repeatedly said that Uttam could be compared to the finest actor that any country has ever produced. Sinha wrote in his memoir *Cholochitro Ajibon* (Cinema Forever)[16] that many were born with talent, but Uttam was born with equal amount of diligence. It was hence impossible to find a better actor anywhere. Sinha was unflinching in his assessment that Uttam was the greatest he knew, much much more than a star or a matinee idol, and should have been known internationally.

One collaboration that should have become a reality but never did was that of Uttam and Ritwik Ghatak. It is not that they were ceremoniously distanced, for unknown to many, Ghatak wrote the story and screenplay of *Rajkanya* (1965), which had Uttam in the lead.

The film is far from being of any note whatsoever. Then, there was the unmade *Choturongo* (The Quartet, 1916), Tagore's demanding novel of ideas, the script of which, written by Ritwik Ghatak, was to be filmed by poet and filmmaker Purnendu Patri. Patri approached Uttam to play Sribilash, the phlegmatic narrator. Uttam refused.

Personally too, they were closer than people know. In more than one occasion Ritwik had gone on record telling Uttam that he was keen to work with him; though given Ritwik's proclivity to scorn everything that sniffed of populism, it is not clear if he meant it. Either way, Uttam was more than willing to oblige Ghatak with anything the latter might bring to the table, even, by one account, willing to finance such a film. In the early 1970s, during a particularly difficult period of Ghatak's long and degenerative battle with alcoholism, tuberculosis and psychological breakdown, Uttam stood by Ghatak, financially and otherwise.

But one account of them has attained the collectability of a fable. Pegged by Uttam to write a script with him in mind, Ghatak, characteristically evasive, promised a reading one evening in the early 1970s only if Uttam bought him his favourite rum. They sat on a park bench and Ghatak read, sipping the raw rum from the bottle. Uttam listened mesmerised. Expectedly, alcohol felled Ghatak before he could finish; and Uttam brought him home. After ensuring that his guest would have a good night's sleep, Uttam, while leaving the room, saw a ream of papers peering out of Ghatak's pocket. Curious to know how the script ended, Uttam took it out, only to discover that not a single word was penned on it. The mercurial director had all through been reading the script from his mind, unaided and undeterred.

There is no truth in this tale. But one wishes there was; and that in a parallel world, an angry, hurt and cornered Ghatak would come to direct his sublime swansong with a post-romance, post-*hero*, post-matinee Uttam.

12

If part of Uttam's performative finesse was, as Ray said, spontaneous, the other part could be traced to his obsessive preparation for the roles. He would not only come prepared, as Tapan Sinha's story tells us, but would be heavily immersed in thinking about them on the sets. He would be so engrossed that he would often fail to recognise people he was otherwise familiar with. For a film called *Kanna*, where he played a musician, he would make arrangements to visit a blind violinist in the dead of the night in Esplanade to silently learn from his ways. He learnt to play tennis for just one scene in *Bicharok*. He prepared in the same way when he was supposed to play a car mechanic in an aborted film or a Sikh man in a revenge thriller. In these cases, he zeroed in on a person who resembled the character and followed him keenly. It has already been noted how he had rapidly learnt horse riding and foil fencing. There are several other testimonials to this effect.

Two incidents among many can illustrate Uttam's immersive ways. In the cult hit *Soptopodi* (The Seven Steps), a couple of the climactic scenes from *Othello* were enacted. The dubbing for the roles of the misunderstood Moor and Desdemona were done by two leading Indian Shakespeareans: Utpal Dutt and Jennifer Kendall (Kapoor). Uttam would visit the dubbing studios so that he could pick up the nuances and then took home the recording. For days, he would practice at home, at night, in front of the mirror, so that he could bring out the urgency, fatalism and drama that Dutt's voice so effectively caught. Sometimes, Uttam's wife Gauri would wake up with a start to find her husband's hand on her throat, he engrossed in 'the murder scene'. She had to plead with him to *act* with some restraint. No wonder, the actual enactment of the scene impressed even the usually dismissive Dutt. Suchitra Sen did a fine job too as Desdemona. The scene remains etched as an unforgettable moment in the entire corpus of Bengali cinema.

The second incident is more telling. During the shooting of *Morutirtho Hinglaj*, the entire crew had camped in Digha, a beach town about 200 kilometres from Calcutta. Heat, sand, the sun and the meticulous schedule took a toll on everyone. But Uttam was completely sucked into the role of Thirumal, a nomadic and rebellious lover. There is a dramatic scene in which Thirumal, out of rage and exhaustion, tries to throttle his lady Kunti. Sabitri Chatterjee, who played Kunti, later recalled that it was an intense scene and at the shoot, she realised that Uttam (as Thirumal) was actually pressing her throat with the full force of his hands, oblivious to the pain he was causing her. Unable to defend or release herself, within moments she retched and lost her consciousness. When her senses were restored, she saw the director Bikash Roy severely reprimanding Uttam for his careless act but Uttam was still so immersed *into* Thirumal that he couldn't figure out what went so wrong! It took some time before he could emerge out of his state of hypnotic absorption to realise the mistake. He rushed to Sabitri and repeatedly asked for her forgiveness.

13

For the regular audience, among all Uttam's felicities, perhaps the most startling was his lip synchronisation to a pre-recorded song, as we saw earlier from Tapan Sinha's quote. And there is little doubt that in all of Bengali cinema, no one did it better than Uttam. A young Uttam had trained with the noted instructor Nidan Bandopadhyay, which aided him as an actor and music director. But the rest was his ear for music and his natural talent for the notes.

Till the late 1940s, it was quite the norm for actors to have a singing voice—K.L. Saigal, Pahari Sanyal, Nitish Mukherjee, Rabin Majumdar and Asit Baran were all singers. It was hence no surprise that the only professional preparation Uttam ever took to be an actor was getting trained in vocals. And by all accounts, he was more than an amateur, coaxing out of both experts and avid listeners a recommendation or two in support of his musical inclination. By the time he came to be an actor of some standing, however, playback music was the settled norm. His first ever lip sync, for 1948's *Drishtidan*, was done by Asit Baran, his immediate predecessor as a leading actor.

The collective talents of that era, dispersed in various directions after the decline of New Theatres, coagulated once more around the stardom of Uttam. The young joined the fray; some of them, like Hemanta and Salil Chowdhury, having come from Indian People's Theatre Association (IPTA). By 1955's *Shapmochon,* Uttam seemed to have found his voice in Hemanta, though their first pairing was in 1952, for a forgotten film called *Sohojatri.* And it was a match like no other. Hemanta gushed about it, saying that Uttam seemed to have been born to give blood and flesh to the timbre in his voice, so exact and so rich was the pairing. And then, there was no stopping. Till the early 1960s, as long as the romances dominated popular reception, the Uttam–Hemanta *jugalbandi* (in films like *Shapmochon, Indrani, Joutuk, Bondhu, Soptopodi, Kuhok, Bibhas, Sathihara, Dui Bhai, Sesh Anko* among others) kept busy Radio Ceylon, Vividh Bharti and Gramophone Company of India in equal measure—spreading a rainbow of moods through melodies—from rhapsodic romances to languorous longings. In between, Uttam also sang six couplets for Debaki Basu's *Nabajanmo* (1956), managing to put into celluloid a brief but memorable imprint of his own talent for singing. After Hemanta and Uttam parted as a regular pair (even if they continued to collaborate sparingly), Shyamal Mitra stepped in (*Deya Neya* being their finest) and soon came Manna Dey (the hard-to-better score of *Antony Firingee* is stuff of lore), both managing to create a niche. Later, Kishore Kumar chipped in too, their coming together remembered for a set of songs for *Rajkumari* and *Amanush.*

But whoever was the singer, Uttam brought an uncanny corporeality to the act of syncing his lips to the voice giving the minutest rhythm and tonal modulations of the song and the situation within the narrative a most realistic and virtuoso treatment on screen. He literally *embodied* the song sequence. And he worked hard for it. He took recordings back home, enacted scenes in front of mirrors, practised alone in his room and often, as Manna Dey recalled, carried a portable record player on his walks, preparing intently. At parties, Uttam sang with abandon—especially songs of Tagore—and regaled many an audience. And they broke into ecstatic applause at the sight of their matinee idol singing to glory under the midnight moon. Among extant recordings available, one is particularly interesting. Here, Uttam sings a Tagore song flamboyantly, even if apologetically, at a function, appearing briefly between two legends of Rabindra Sangeet, Debabrata Biswas and Suchitra Mitra. He also scored music for two films, of which *Kal Tumi Aleya* astonished everyone, including Hemanta and Asha Bhosle, who did the playback.

A sophisticated, musically rich, cinematically congruent and hummable soundtrack in film after film seemed to have completed the tableaux of affirmative endowments that Bengali popular cinema received during its golden period. And there are many such unforgettable moments on screen, some shot on other leading actors—both men and women. But when Uttam sang—as the audacious Krishnendu (*Soptopodi*), as the possessive Utpal (*Dui Bhai*), as the secretive singer Abhijit (*Deya Neya*), as the besotted foreigner Hansman (*Antony Firingee*), as the lonely concierge Syata Bose (*Chowrongee*), or as the frolicking aristocrat Surjo Kishore (*Sonyashi Raja*)—Bengal seemed to have loved and longed, wooed and squandered, laughed and mourned with him.

14

For a heterosexual man with charms that travelled to as far as Germany and England, if not also to the United States, where he attended a month-long tour in end-1970s, it was natural that Uttam was at the centre of a wild female following throughout his life. Like other fan constituencies, whose stern borders he had breached, here too Uttam's élan could easily topple walls, especially of age. His fans included women in their teens to those in their autumn. One cannot but marvel how women born as far between the 1920s and 1950s could, without diffidence or exertion, claim Uttam to be 'their' own romantic fantasy; something that Ray's *Nayak* brought to the fore. In his heyday it would be a regular joke in most Bengali families where the wife would be so besotted by the matinee idol that she would be found sighing deeply in an unguarded moment when thinking about him. And because Uttam attracted no less a fandom from men, such moments would become those of shared fixation and amusement than a crisis of trust. He would receive the usual retinue of letters written in blood; or those urging him to save a young woman caught in a hapless romance; or midnight calls that would pledge, at the other side of the phone, singular loyalty. For his women admirers, Uttam was that *desirable* star who was also a sort of an ideal *lover*, even if not a *possible* one. Uttam had learned to live with these temptations, as he had done with other forms of fan obsession.

In one funny incident, Uttam is said to have received a letter of distress from a collective of men. Their grouse? That Uttam was visiting their neighbourhood in New Alipore to supervise the construction of his new apartment. The men were of course not complaining about that. The problem was that every morning during Uttam's visit the women would be so engrossed in staring at him, that all the men would have to forfeit the morning meal on their way to work. The letter requested if Uttam could make his visit sometime later in the day after they had gone to work so that the women could look at him at leisure without being harangued by hungry men waiting to be fed.

Another man was hungry for something else. At a shoot outside Calcutta, a young man lunged at Uttam and started to rub his head on his chest straightaway. Uttam could not decide if he should be alarmed or annoyed. Pulling away the next instant, the man sheepishly reasoned that he had couldn't stop himself, not because he was attracted to Uttam's bosom but because he wanted the residual whiff of the many female actors who had leaned lovingly on it over the years.

The more colourful stories are about women of course. Considering social protocols of that period, it is a revelation how Uttam's female fandom was unabashed in their obsession. For example, once at a function in a prominent city auditorium, Uttam saw a woman madly waving at him from an unnatural elevation across a large window. Intrigued, he asked her how could she manage to climb up there. The lady without batting eyelids told him that she was standing on the shoulders of her husband to stare at him properly.

But this pales in comparison to other instances of female 'attention'. During one of his outdoor shoots at Bardhaman, Uttam had stayed at the mansion of an aristocratic family native to the region. On his return to the city, he resumed the week's scheduled performances for *Shyamali*, the only stage-play Uttam had ever been professionally a part of. At the greenroom after the day's performance he discovered the wife of his recent host, who confessed to having been sufficiently smitten by the star to have set out on a mission. "I asked her a thing or two, and then she gave me the calamitous news that she had left her house for good and wants to spend her life with me."[17] Uttam had to use every charm and power of persuasion in his disposal that night to convince her not to aim for the impossible.

In another case, the cast involved had consisted of a more unyielding prospect. This was during Uttam's return from Ranchi after a shoot. He was, expectantly, mobbed at the Ranchi station that early evening. His fans continued to hang from the windows of the train compartment long after the first whistle. After another long wait and after many requests some of them disembarked. The rest dispersed as the train slowly left the station, jumping onto the platform, while a tense Uttam looked from his window hoping that no mishap would come their way. It was on settling down thereafter that Uttam realised that three young women had managed to duck all gatekeeping and were sitting opposite him on the moving train. They sat there silently and kept looking at him straight, without any hint of nervous unease. After a while, as the train gained speed, Uttam hesitantly asked what they wanted. "All we ever wanted was to have a good look at you, from close quarters. There was no way we could have given this chance a miss today", they said, unperturbed.[18] After fifteen very tense minutes in which Uttam sat still under the unflinching gaze of those three young women, he noticed some movement. One of them stood up and pulled the chain. As the train came to halt, they said goodbye, got down and disappeared into the darkness with the same unruffled calm with which they had sat and watched their darling star.

15

Not just by corybantic admirers, the darling star, in personal life too, was buttressed by the fullness of women—as progenitor, protector and preserver. He was, through his life, extremely close, in the manner of good Bengali boys, to his mother. As the eldest son, he had the bulk of her attention as a child and there are those usual tales about how she had predicted, long before others, the future greatness of her offspring. But Uttam was not a prodigy and all Bengali mothers think very highly about their sons anyway. So even if those stories bear any value, they are not an exception. But it is a fact that long after he had left his home and wife, Uttam would continue to visit his mother regularly, if he happened to be in Calcutta.

Much more tender are his reminiscences about his elder sister Putul, who was lost to a bout of illness when Uttam was at a raw young age. For years, Uttam could not forget Putul, who was his first companion and also an indulgent keeper of his early and paltry secrets about sporadic attempts at acting.

Gauri, his wife-to-be, came in his life when she was in senior school and Uttam barely out of it. She was certainly his cynosure for a few years, when at every step Gauri's presence and counsel seemed to have had an impact on Uttam's day-to-day care of the self. She doubtlessly stood by him during his faltering and fledgling years as an acting aspirant. When they got married, in 1948, Uttam was balancing acting and a job; after four years he abandoned the latter, putting the onus of running the household on shaky earnings on Gauri. She managed meticulously. But stardom, after all, did take its usual toll. With fame and reputation, Uttam floated away from the confines of a regular, middle-class conjugality. The world of more bountiful embraces awaited him.

The woman most readily to have opened herself to him was Sabitri Chatterjee, who had a lifelong pining for Uttam, which was never fulfilled. But she worked with him the longest and their on-screen partnership was extremely varied and productive. Uttam reserved his best gushes and his most tense moments to open up to Sabitri but they never filled any formal template of companionship. A much-respected and admired actor, Sabitri, still active and single, barely eschews her most earnest but tangled affection for the man she loved all her life.

Uttam shared a rather absorbing relationship with Suchitra Sen, which unlike Sabitri, never veered towards a romance but ticked most of the boxes of an intimate friendship. They had an outstanding on-screen understanding and a deep sense of bonding off it. They mildly flirted in public and were never miserly in their concern for each other. Uttam was the producer of one of Suchitra's more perceptive acting stints in *Uttar Phalguni* and forfeited a day's shoot of his own production to celebrate Suchitra's winning the best actor award at the Moscow Film Festival for *Saat Pake Bandha*. But there was never any romance, however much a bulk of the Bengali film press may have spent reams of paper in the expectation of an exposé throughout the decades that Uttam was alive.

Uttam romanced Supriya Choudhury outside his marriage from the beginning of the 1960s but officially moved in to stay with her at the Moira Street apartment in 1963, after a major and public outbreak of a squabble with his wife Gauri. They apparently also got married in December 1963, but that can only be an idealistic and not legal binding. Given Uttam's fame, his life was an open book, at least by standards of star curiosity in that period. Hence it deserves admiration that both Uttam and Supriya showed abundant balance in trying to fulfil their professional commitments, which they did for the next seventeen years, while being officially in the middle of a legal, if not social, 'scandal'. Unfortunately for Supriya, any official claim on her lover remained fraught with complications for a long time. She was deliberately rebuffed at Uttam's funeral as having no more *claim* to him than anyone else in the impersonal 'crowd'. Unorthodox and unapologetic for her time, she survived him by more than three-and-a-half decades and passed away only recently. To overcome the humiliation she unduly received for being Uttam's live-in partner, she had emphatically and for long gushed about their intimate *romance*, often to the embarrassment of the more learned admirers of either. For peddlers of gossip though, those reminiscences have always been a fistful of saleable sleaze.

In later years, actor Lalita Chatterjee and Miss Shefalli, the famous cabaret performer who had a notable stint in Bengali cinema, is said to have been close to him. But by then, Uttam was way beyond being just a romantic 'interest' of either.

There has always been a concealed if obstinate curiosity to know if Uttam was a womaniser. The answer to that would be a matter of perception and conjecture rather than any serious enquiry. Was he generous to women who showered affection? Certainly yes. Did he return their affection? Yes, again. But only when he felt terribly lonely and sought meaningful female company, especially under the weight of alcohol-induced self-pity. Which was more often than he would be allowed to confess. But on other days and when not under any influence, the insistent glare of stardom and his very ordinary moorings in middle-class habits stopped him from being either audacious or unrestrained. Up to a point.

16

Given his widespread fame and acceptability across the divide of class, gender, and Bengal's east and west, it was natural that Uttam would get drawn into the rigmarole of electoral politics. The organised Left, which was on ascent—first in public sympathy and then electorally since 1967—was shunned by him. "I have read the life of Mao. Unlike him, communists are expensive here. They smoke 555", he had said in an interview. "Frankly, I do not get their idea about living one life and speaking of another", he had added.[19] The Leftist organisations were used to being held in high and somewhat unquestioned esteem by cultural fronts across Bengal and so Uttam's non-committal reproach did not go down well with them. There was hence a campaign since the late 1960s to turn him into a right-wing, reactionary matinee idol, a sort of flaky, bourgeoisie *project*.

Between 1967 and 1972, Bengal experienced unprecedented political turmoil, street violence and surge in armed ultra-Left-wing resistance, thrice thrusting the state under President's Rule. During that time, the embattled Ajoy Mukherjee, who also had three brief and volatile stints as Bengal's chief minister, offered Uttam secret support if he stood as an independent candidate from one of Calcutta's prominent seats. Uttam refused politely, repeating his deep distrust of politics.

Since he eschewed political prominence, perhaps expectedly, politics came knocking at his conscience. One morning, during the peak of Naxal violence and the state's counteroffensive, Uttam, on his usual round of a dawn-time walk in Esplanade's sprawling Maidan, chanced upon an 'encounter killing'. This was no extrajudicial killing of another young student, which was not uncommon in those days. The victim that fateful morning near the Aryan Club was Saroj Dutta, a leading Naxalite intellectual, editor and co-founder of the Communist Party of India (Marxist–Leninist). He was 55, not in any sort of health to make a run for his life and had no defence at his disposal. Though in August 1971 Bengal was under the President's Rule, it was widely believed that the Congress had played a shady role in this heinous act. Dutta was declared 'untraceable' and within days Uttam's presence at the scene of crime became a matter of hushed deliberation. He was pressured by the Naxals to become a witness and by the police who wanted him to stay away by all means. Uttam, in what was something of a shock to the industry, left in huff for Bombay and then to Allahabad and did not come back for over three months, citing personal work. His absence created even more flutter and even caused some damage to the industry, thanks to his unplanned and long leave. He was terrified and deeply troubled but he was left with no choice but to be silent about that morning. This incident has been fictionalised in novels and films, but for all official purposes, Dutta's case still remains unresolved. No amount of persuasion to Jyoti Basu, chief minister through most of the long years of Left governance in Bengal, could make him open an investigation into the death of the Naxal ideologue. Uttam maintained a stoic silence in public though he did give clear hints about his hapless indictment in this grievous murder, in an unguarded moment, under the influence of alcohol.

17

Charity came easily to Uttam. There were numerous names—poor technicians, crew, assistants and under-the-radar studio hands—who would be on the receiving end of Uttam's resources, money and contacts. His wallet would open at almost every request of a daughter's wedding, a mother's illness, a son's training for trade. In 1959, just after his father passed away, an ailing Uttam, on his severe insistence, was put on a truck for a fundraising walk. The collections were historic. This is just one instance. Several times Uttam would be part of protests to make sure that the film crew were paid on time and were treated well in the studios. He had once barricaded theatre hall owners so that Bengali films were given a fair chance, and organised countless events to raise money for ailing or poor comrades in the film industry. Whether for Obhinetro Songho—the collective of film technicians and actors—or then its breakaway Shilpi Sansad, which he headed, Uttam was never found wanting whenever there was a moment of crisis in the collective or personal life of industry personnel—across political, gender or age groups.

There were also fundraising cricket matches that Uttam had organised, of which two stand out. The first one was in the late 1960s, when Eden Gardens witnessed a flurry of actors, crew and industry regulars in starched white clothing, playing each other in what turned out to be a rather interesting match. The other, more prominent one, came in 1979. Bengal was hit by severe flooding across the state; the districts of North Bengal were especially ravaged. To raise funds, Uttam led the Bengali film industry to a heavily-attended and high-profile match at the Eden Gardens. Attended by Dilip Kumar, Rekha, Amitabh Bachchan, Shivaji Ganesan and Satyajit Ray among others, this was as big an affair as could be, most of the participants having responded to a personal invite from Uttam Kumar.

One act of charity, I must recount, went horribly wrong. It concerned a radio programme. Since the early 1930s, a programme called *Mahisasurmardini* was broadcast on radio to inaugurate the fortnight of the Durga Puja, Bengal's biggest festival. A mix of a scripted radio-play, soaring music and rhetorical recitation, the programme recounted the mythical origins of the Durga cult. It was conceived and scripted by Banikumar, was accompanied by the delightfully esoteric score of Pankaj Mullick and a powerfully rendered narrative by Birendrakrishna Bhadra. Since its early years, the programme had secured a cult following, eventually becoming an inviolable tradition. There has been only one exception to this unbroken rendition; in 1976, which fell during the period of Emergency. Eager to showcase their hold over the popular medium of radio, Prasar Bharati's Delhi bosses instructed their counterparts in Calcutta to conceive of a new programme to replace *Mahisasurmardini*. And the orders were carried out dutifully. Titled *Debi Durgatiharini*, D.N. Chakraborty wrote the script for it, Sanskrit scholar Govindalal Mukherjee read from the scriptures, Hemanta Mukherjee scored the music and the indelible voice of Bhadra was replaced by a host of actors, most prominent among them being Uttam. There is another version of this story that contests any wilful intervention from

Delhi and considers the decision to discontinue the original version on routine changes being brought to radio programming.

The behind the scenes events may be foggy but what is indisputable is that the new version, beamed on the anointed date and time in 1976, failed miserably. An avalanche of letters and rants arrived at newspaper offices, there were street protests to that effect and Uttam and Hemanta were on the receiving end of public vilification. Because of their stature, they became synonymous with the 'violence' unleashed on a custom held dearly. To mollify the bad press it had received, All India Radio had to broadcast the original programme within days and the new one was shelved irretrievably.

The negative reaction had long concealed the actual constitution of the new version, because few cared to listen to it carefully. In the new one, Uttam's gift for naturalism and a sensible, authoritative rendition stood in sharp contrast to the highfalutin and operatic version of Bhadra, giving the mythical saga a next-door kind of credibility, which the original was far removed from. The music was no less, eventually becoming the best work that Hemanta had done in his later years. The scripting was deft too. In short, the new one lacked in none of the individual compartments. But the backlash of traditionalists was not to be taken lightly and this misfired adventure on radio—which he blamed on his tendency to agree to all sorts of requests—haunted Uttam for a long time. He was already struggling with a spate of bad films and hostile audience reaction that they had provoked; and had found his name muddied further by the reactions to the radio broadcast. It added one more thorn to the crown of blunders in the last five years of his life.

Uttam's biggest 'charity' in those days, thus, was to let the industry and its ilk exploit the heft of his name for ends beyond his control; or to keep itself on the supply of wages. But that's a story we need to ponder over separately.

18

"Uttam is Uttam. I am delighted to be part of a function to honour him. I have seen most of his Bengali films. They are wonderful. *Such mooch, Uttam Saab lajabab kalakar hai.* (Truly Uttam Saab is an artist without a parallel.)"[20]

As rains lashed the beach outside, the words showered music on the ears of Uttam Kumar, who was in the audience as Dilip Kumar uttered those words. It was one of those monsoon-soaked September Bombay evenings in 1976. Uttam was in attendance at the city's glitzy Sun and

Sand, the premises of which were famously dedicated to the whimsy of Bombay's self-indulgent stardom. Uttam was there to celebrate the blockbuster hit *Amanush*, Sakti Samanta's double-version weepie, which was Uttam's first and only success in Bombay. It was ten years after his *Chhoti Si Mulaqat* disaster, Uttam was fifty and no one knew more than him that he had missed the bus to India's so called cine capital forever. Yet, in that September, if not august, gathering Uttam was delighted to note the appreciation of Dilip Kumar. Dilip Kumar was four years older than Uttam, had preceded the latter in attaining stardom, ruled the 1950s, and had since the mid-1960s bowed out. Uttam had soldiered on, unable to leave or unable to lead, because at fifty, he was still the only asset the Bengali industry could bank upon. But in many other ways Uttam and Dilip Kumar were complementary—being leading men who could gravitate between genres and roles, had led their respective film dominions to maturity, and helmed it in moments of crisis and contemplation.

It was indeed a gathering of Bombay's leading stars, producers and directors, and Dilip Kumar's endorsement clinched the deal. Uttam responded humbly, saying that he had been apprehensive about signing *Amanush* because in his middle age, he thought he may not be the right choice anymore for a leading role in a film. But the film was his biggest success, both in Hindi and, surprisingly in Bengali as well, receiving nine Filmfare nominations and taking home two. It was later remade in Telugu (with N.T. Rama Rao) and Tamil (with Shivaji Ganeshan), among others. What is somewhat surprising is that during the six-day stint in Bombay that week, Uttam signed six new films, both in Hindi and Bengali. Clearly, in his autumn of discontent, Uttam was not a pushover as yet.

19

In the same gathering at Sun and Sand, Samanta's *Ajnabee* was feted too, which had Rajesh Khanna and Zeenat Aman in the lead. Incidentally, before *Ajnabee*, the last film of the hit Samanta–Khanna pairing (after *Aradhana* and *Kati Patang*) was *Amar Prem* (1972), a remake of Uttam Kumar's *Nishipodmo* (The Night Flower, 1970). Impressed by Uttam's splendid performance and the film, Samanta wanted to remake it in Hindi. Samanta's first choice though wasn't Rajesh Khanna. But Khanna was keen to fit into the role of a 'babu' after his eloquent turn in *Anand*. Though Khanna insisted that he himself chose the role, he is on record saying that he failed miserably in comparison to Uttam, though the film fetched him a Filmfare nomination for acting and remains one of his enduring films. Khanna later said,[21]

I insisted that I must see the Bengali version. I am not alien to the language but on viewing it I realized that it would be impossible for me to match up to the range of Uttam *Saab*. I saw the film 18 times and with each viewing it dawned upon me that I cannot even hope to do a film that extracted the best from this extraordinary actor. I had in fact thought of declining the role but it was Hrishida who stepped in to help me prepare. But I must concede that I failed because I could in no way match up to the Himalayan heights of his range. He was in a class by himself.

Khanna, who would often refer to Uttam as 'the greatest living actor of my times' was also a regular at Uttam's Moira Street residence whenever he touched down on Calcutta.

20

Rajesh Khanna or Dilip Kumar were vociferous in their praise but he was no exception. Uttam had a long list of admirers in Bombay—Guru Dutt, Shashi Kapoor, Dharmendra, Amitabh Bachchan. They were part of Hindi remakes of his films; or knew the language. And little did they hide their great admiration. Raj Kapoor for example, as early as 1956, is said to have considered him for the Bengali version (*Ekdin Ratre*) of the bilingual *Jagte Raho*, where Uttam's veteran contemporaries Chhabi Biswas and Pahari Sanyal played key roles. But Uttam was too busy to spare dates and Kapoor came to play the panicky thief who startles mute into middle class corruption and treachery in both the versions. Later, Uttam was seriously considered by Raj Kapoor for *Sangam* (1964), but here too the script played a spoiler. At the height of his stardom, Uttam Kumar did not want to play Gopal, the better but sacrificial guy, as his entry role in Bombay, though he was far from picky about such things in Bengali films. In fact, Dilip Kumar had also refused the role. Uttam is said to have later regretted his decision because *Sangam*, a Technicolor romance epic of three hours, went on to become a blockbuster. The missed bus of *Sangam* hurt him especially after Uttam's own vehicle *Chhoti Si Mulaqat*, which was his Bombay debut in 1967, was a debacle. From its expensive making to the insipid response, the film, in which Uttam had invested his own money, was a mammoth failure, leading not only to a state of despondency and financial ruin but also the first of several cardiac arrests. Uttam was under a deceptive impression, no doubt supplied by his minions in Bombay, that Raj Kapoor had sabotaged *Chhoti Si Mulaqat*. This, he was told, was done to restrict the Bengali actor's chances in Bombay's competitive industry, where Raj's brother Shammi was a rising star. Even if we consider hypothetically that Raj Kapoor had malicious intentions, a look at Uttam's debut Hindi film is enough to convince us that Kapoor did not have to try too hard. Whatever be the truth, Raj Kapoor had repeatedly lamented not being able to work with Uttam Kumar. They met several times in Calcutta and Bombay and shared a more than cordial relationship.

21

On its part, the film in question remains an elephant in the room. *Chhoti Si Mulaqat* repeated the antediluvian story of Uttam's Bengali blockbuster *Agniporikha*, which catapulted him to stardom but which seemed dated even in 1954. In 1967, it was more so and even if the subtleties of the script in the Bengali version made it bearable, the Hindi version, with its over-the-top requirements, seemed hopelessly forged. Also, a film in which Uttam had built expensive sets, signed Vyjayanthimala, Shailendra and Shankar Jaikishen, was ultimately directed by an untested underling called Alo Sarkar. The proponents of the conspiracy theory have never asked on whose advice Uttam, who had signed the top heroine, musician duo, lyricist and crew, settled for an untested, rookie director. It is unlikely that Uttam was unsure of his ability to let good directors helm his projects, because he had repeatedly signed the best of them in Bengali to direct the films he produced. So why Alo Sarkar? Who was he, except being a small-time technician in New Theatres who had a few contacts in Bombay? But he, of all, came to direct Uttam's debut Hindi dud. And Uttam did not learn from the mistakes of his Hindi venture. Sarkar continued to milk Uttam and no amount of advice from others could remove him from Uttam's close group of minions. An outrage called *Bandi* (1978)—one of Uttam's shady films from his sunset years—was also directed, if one can call it direction by any measure, by the same Sarkar. Along with other dreadful massacres such as *Nishan* and *Desh Premee*, *Bandi* signifies the depths of despair that any film can stoop to.

It is also appalling, if not surprising, that Uttam aligned with so calamitous a counsel for a good part of his working life, who slowly but surely thrust him into one debacle after another. Uttam had memorably risen up the ranks, was conscientious of his triumphs; and aware of the easy traps of stardom. Yet, he became enmeshed in a world of spoils, crowded with a retinue of indulgent toadies who would regale him on endless alcohol-fuelled evenings with stories of his greatness. As we progress onwards 1975—by all means the last of Uttam's memorable years—we witness a singular, one-way, careless drive into an abject and delirious misery, whether in his management of personal life or his performances.

Clearly, Uttam let himself be at the beck and call of an industry that risked becoming bankrupt without him. In 1954, when he became a star, Uttam was twenty-eight. And since then it was the same story. At thirty-three, and then at thirty-eight, he was the leading man in Bengal cinema, the chief supplier of its box office and its only hope of subsistence. At forty-three, he was *still* the leading man, the chief supplier and the only hope. At fifty, he was *still*.... In other words, Uttam Kumar was at the top from when early Dilip Kumar was at the helm to a period when Amitabh Bachchan became a star. Those who knew him in person have recounted numerous times how Uttam would often get up in the middle of night, that too after a hard day, to rehearse in solitude. Wasn't he tired? He was indeed but how could be fail his audience? But by the mid-1970s, this involvement with the audience had turned into a desperation to not fail the industry. So, if one part of this absurd longevity is about Uttam's transcendental appeal; the other part, equally startling, is about an industry that shamefully failed to grow beyond the custodianship of its primary breadwinner. It was like one of those profligate families of nincompoops which survived on the goodwill of a renowned, resourceful but ageing patriarch. Uttam could have played a hand in changing that. But in the end, he did not. At least not in a forceful way.

It was destined to end in a moment of shameful heartbreak. And it did. One day in 1980, Uttam accosted Satyajit Ray's longtime assistant Punu Sen on the precincts of a Tollygunge studio. "Punu, ask Manikda (Ray) if he has any roles for me. Even an insignificant, walk-on role would do. I can't continue to do anymore the rot I am doing", Uttam said in an unguarded moment to Sen.[22] The Dantesque descent of the once mighty hero—*Ray's hero*—could not have been more telling. Ironically, within two days of his telling Punu so, Uttam was to suffer his fatal cardiac arrest.

Time Magazine famously wrote[23] for French actor and iconoclast Jeanne Moreau that her case "forcefully demonstrates the verve, style and flamboyant femaleness that makes her the envy of European sex symbols much greener in years.... Too bad that a first-rate actress so often has to squeeze her victories out of second-rate scripts". This description, every bit, would suit Uttam too, except the small change from female to man.

22

Uttam Kumar's death signified a defining moment in 'Bengali' life. It was Thursday, 24 July 1980. By the late hour, Uttam Kumar lay lifeless in

Belle Vue Hospital, adjacent to the park that Uttam would often take his walks in. Even before the doctors could sign the certificate of mortality, his brother, the actor Tarun Kumar signed a bond and brought his deceased elder sibling to their home in Bhawanipore, the home Uttam had left seventeen years ago. Here he was wreathed by family members and a woman named Roma, the actor's famous on-screen partner and the by-then reclusive Suchitra Sen. It was 12.40 a.m. Uttam's partner Supriya, admitted in another clinic for being unwell, was kept totally in the dark.

Only a day earlier, Uttam was busy shooting for a film. He complained of chest pain and got himself hospitalised later that night. The doctors diagnosed yet another cardiac arrest; the fifth on record. Next afternoon, he felt marginally better. But things deteriorated in the early evening and at around 9.30 that night, he was declared dead.

Within hours of Roma having wreathed the man she had romanced so many times on screen, dawn broke. And so did the news. The newspapers bugled the demise of a colossus. 25 July 1980. *Nayak* was dead. The greatest screen legend ever to grace Bengali cinema—the endeared 'Guru' to generations of viewers, admirers, fans and matinee idolaters—was no more. He was only 53. But it seemed he had spent a lifetime or more under the gaze of the public eye.

By late morning, the whole of Calcutta was in a state of shock and eventually, mourning. The city was pulverised; crowds thronged the streets, starved and went sleepless. Calcutta—Uttam's *Madeleine*— which had lined up unfailingly every week for over three decades to see him play an ensemble of characters, congregated to see him one last time. Thousands marched towards his Bhawanipore home, while others waited at key city landmarks to witness the course of his hearse. Still others watched from balconies, balustrades, or from behind Calcutta's famed Venetian window grills. Calcutta literally halted to a stop to bid adieu. As far as one could see, there were countless heads, restive, plaintive. As far as one could see, people were in a state of disorientation. Trains stopped on their tracks and sellers of flowers showered their wares on the hearse. Traffic choked. Few schools and colleges announced a day off to let their wards join the funeral procession. Soon it was apparent that not since the death of Rabindranath Tagore had so many hundreds joined a mourning march. Soon it was apparent that Calcutta's box office draw of the century, had in his death, walked away into the sunset with his final blockbuster.

I, almost four at that time, clearly remember my uncle: a man of about thirty, who seemed to have turned haggardly suddenly. He was returning from the market, distractedly waving a broadsheet and howling from the head of the street, crying out to everyone he could see, *Uttam Kumar mara geche* (Uttam Kumar is dead). Those who heard him, stopped. Stupefied. Others seemed to collapse. This is one of the stories among many others, in which people could remember, with near precision, the events of that morning and in what state he/she was when the news of Uttam's death broke. This was a piece of *breaking news* that shattered most preserves in the city; the strong and sad gust of untimely death broke through every lock on every door, across streets and by-lanes; the covered curtains; the blinded windows; it pierced through every dank attic in old crumbling buildings; every dark corner kept away from the light of the world; every gaunt old man's half-hearing ear.

Sometime in 1980, months before his death, Uttam wrote,[24]

> Some say I am a genius; some say I am a fluke. I am neither. I have worked very hard. I took risks. I entered a small man and was rejected publicly.… I have have heard some say 'the moment I saw him I knew a great actor had arrived'. I cannot but laugh. No one has ever seen me arriving; because I didn't. I pushed myself in.… And then I aimed for the sky. I couldn't stop. I couldn't play the assassin of my own soaring drive. But then, it has been long. I have worked without a holiday. I am tired. Not unwell or ailing, but exhausted, yes. Is there a word for paradox in Bangla? Then let me tell you the biggest paradox of our lives. The public is our best ally and the public is our most punishing nemesis. Uttam is 'great' because of the public and one day Uttam Kumar will be a living dead, because there would be that public too.

Perhaps to avoid the ignominy of being consigned to history while still being alive, Uttam, who didn't arrive overnight, left in a huff.

23

While his hearse was being carried south by a sea of people from his Bhawanipur house to Tollygunge's Technicians' Studio down the choked Ashutosh Mukherjee Road, few kilometres away at Alimuddin Street, in a closed room filled with cigar smoke, sat a few bespectacled men, in starched white *kurta* and *dhoti*. This was the meeting room of the Communist Party of India (Marxist), the governing party of the state of Bengal. Letting a pall of Cuban smoke out of his cigar, Pramode Dasgupta or PDG, the Party Tsar (officially, Party's General Secretary) asked his comrades, "Is our government associating itself with the funeral of a Tollygunge matinee idol?" Without haste, the resounding verdict was no. 'The government of the people' as the CPI(M) had peddled itself to be, was not comfortable in associating itself with the 'commercially propelled' leading figure of a 'conformist, capitalist' practice called popular cinema. Uttam Kumar was the 'indiscreet charm of the bourgeoisie', deserving socialist condescension. Only a year ago Uttam had organised a fundraising cricket match that had raised substantial aid for the same government. And the government bowed and accepted every penny that came its way. But when it was their turn to return to the star some courtesy, the CPI(M) had showed its despicable side.

Later that same day after lunch, PDG thumped, "Tell Buddhadeb [Bhattacharya, then Minister of Culture and Information] that the decision to stay away is right. But Jyoti babu wants a wreath to be sent. Go ahead. I have no objection." 'Rejected' by the government, Uttam could not be laid at Rabindra Sadan, the theatre auditorium and the centre of CPI(M)'s cultural activity, where before and since Uttam, many a public soul, with varying degrees of closeness to the Party, rested after death to let citizens pay their last respects. Instead, Uttam's hearse, wreathed in a mountain of white flowers, was briefly halted in front of Purna Theatre near his Bhawanipore home, where thirty-two years ago his first ever film had released, a film in which he had been, like Marcello Mastroianni, little more than a junior artiste. But no Trevi Fountain was cloaked in dark cloth by the government that day in Calcutta as was done on the death of the Italian heartthrob in 1996.

24

Years after his death, in 2009, the Department of Posts released a ₹5 postage stamp honouring Uttam Kumar. This came on the heels of the Indian Railways naming the Tollygunge station, then the south terminus for the south–north Calcutta metro railway corridor, Mahanayak Uttam Kumar station. In 2017, Calcutta Port's new museum unveiled a framed cheque signed by its young clerk Arunkumar Chattopadhyay as one of its prime exhibits. Uttam's make-up room in New Theatres 1 studio has been kept untouched, as a memorial, since the day he died. A lofty statue of the Mahanayak, better than most other stony mortifications of cultural mascots that Calcutta harbours, stands at the crossing of the studios in Calcutta's 'film district' of Tollygunge.

One does not know how to react to the fact that Uttam did not receive even a Padmasree, leave alone Phalke and other weighty proclamations of *greatness* from the aphasic officialdom. But was that ever a problem? After four decades of his death, Uttam remains omnipresent in

Bengali life. Land in Calcutta and you will see broadsheets, hoardings, shops, posters, books everywhere with his face on them. Forty years after his death. Bring a few talkative Bengalis together and in a while they will be in an immersive *adda* about Uttam Kumar and his films; humming a song or two, replaying a scene here and there, momentarily lost in those languorous silver screen hours that seem to be ever so redolent, ever so haunting.

Only the other day a metro commuter journeying south told the man at the Esplanade station ticket counter, pointing to his companion, "Can I have two Uttam Kumars please?", referring to their destination. A man, standing behind in the queue, quipped, "Dada, how can there be two Uttam Kumars? There was only one. There can never be another one, never", with humour that is intrinsic to Calcutta streets. Uttam, with his irresistible, impossibly radiant smile, lives in that humour, as much as he lives on those streets.

NOTES

1. Jean-Luc Godard, *Le Petit Soldat* (1960 film). Available at https://www.oxfordreference.com/view/10.1093/acref/9780191826719.001.0001/q-oro-ed4-00004889.
2. 'Mahanayak Uttam Kumar', *Boisakhi* Journal, edited by Dhrubojyoti Mondol, 23 (2013–2014): 159–160.
3. Uttamkumar Chattopadhyay, *Nayoker Kolome* (A collection of writings by Uttam), edited by Abhik Chattopadhyay, Saptarshi Prokashon, 2015, p. 20.
4. Chattopadhyay, *Nayoker Kolome*, p. 20.
5. Chattopadhyay, *Nayoker Kolome*, p. 71.
6. Chattopadhyay, *Nayoker Kolome*, pp. 23–24.
7. Asishtoru Mukhopadhyay, *Ojana Uttam*, Dey's Publishing, 2006, p. 12.
8. Sandip Ray (ed.), *Satyajit Ray on Cinema*, Columbia University Press, 2013, pp. 107–108.
9. Satyajit Ray, *Probondho Songroho* (Collection of Essays), edited by Sandip Ray, Ananda Publishers, Kolkata, 2015, pp. 331–336.
10. Chattopadhyay, *Nayoker Kolome*, p. 19.
11. Chattopadhyay, *Nayoker Kolome*, p. 19.
12. Chattopadhyay, *Nayoker Kolome*, p. 113.
13. Tapan Sinha, *Chalachitra Ajibon*, Dey's Publishing, 2009, p. 216.
14. Sinha, *Chalachitra Ajibon*, p. 218.
15. 'Uttam Kumar', *Tehai* Journal, edited by Saptarshi Bhattacharya, 2:1 (January 2010): 291.
16. Sinha, *Chalachitra Ajibon*, pp. 214–219.
17. Chattopadhyay, *Nayoker Kolome*, p. 21.
18. Chattopadhyay, *Nayoker Kolome*, p. 58.
19. 'Mahanayak Uttam Kumar': 81.

20. Uttamkumar Chattopadhyay, *Amar Ami* (An unfinished autobiography), Dey's Publishing, 1980, p. 171.
21. Amio Sanyal (ed.), *Uttom Sorbottomo*, Ritwick Publication, 2008, p. 138.
22. Jagori Bandopadhyay, 'Chiriayakhanar Tumi Ki Jano', *Anandabazar Patrika*, 24 September 2017.
23. Available at http://content.time.com/time/subscriber/article/0,33009, 871437,00.html.
24. Chattopadhyay, *Nayoker Kolome*, pp. 32–33.

3

THE BIG PICTURE

History never really says goodbye. History says, 'See you later'.

—Eduardo Galeano

TO understand how Uttam Kumar's stardom was transformative, a short history of the coming of the movies to Bengal is a necessary rite of passage we must undertake. It is a fascinating story full of memorable moments and whimsical characters. Moreover, there are these often-overlooked links and surreptitious continuities between the dawn of cinema in Bengal and its high noon under Uttam Kumar. As we approach that high noon, we see that cinema, like everything else in Bengali life, started to unravel in the 1940s, when a series of crises and an ill-advised surgery left the province wounded to the bones. But that same decade, ironically, came to be historically and culturally decisive. Hence, if we are to consider Uttam's rise to stardom as a landmark moment in Bengali cinema, then on one side of it was the *studio era* while on the other was the *star era*; if one was characterised by socials, the other was dominated by romances; if one had a theatrical bent, the other was unmistakably more cinematic. So, if we have to understand Uttam, we must cover this ground before we can find ourselves within gazing distance of the architecture of his stardom.

BEFORE LIGHTS AND SOUND, THE CAMERA

The story of cinema in Bengal, like everywhere else across the world, begins with the first techno-modern apparatus of representation anywhere in the industrial world. And that was photography. The pre-cinematic landscape had a proliferation of 'optical toys'—magic lanterns, panorama, diorama, phantasmagoria, Fantascope, Zoetrope and so on. But it was photography, which, like most modern nations, mirrored colonial India's arrival into modernity. Photography in the Indian subcontinent was tied to the global circuit of technology, capital and goods in the mid-19th century. And like most such explorative technologies that announced the arrival of modernity in

67

colonial South Asia, photography too first arrived in Calcutta, within a year of public pronouncement of Louis Daguerre's daguerreotype in Paris in 1839. Calcutta's legendary stationer Thacker, Spink and Co. was advertising the new magical invention called the daguerreotype in 1840. In a decade or so, a number of commercial establishments had set up shop and soon studio and carte de visite photography became a rage. Calcutta's elite English neighbourhoods had calotype pioneers such as F. Schranzhofer, while J.W. Newland's daguerreotype studio was being advertised in local Bengali journals, indicating the increasing acceptability of this new practice. Soon, individuals such as Frederick Fiebig and studios of Bourne and Shepherd and Johnston and Hoffman or those like Fritz Kapp and Edward Sache captured the city and the imagination of the middle classes. Histories of photography[1] in the subcontinent hint at the extent of popularity that photography enjoyed in the colonial cities. Photography continued to appall, intrigue and tease, eventually becoming part of regular diversion, self-reflection and the chief mode of memorialising. By the 1880s, photography—emboldened by collodion process and albumin prints; then stereoscopic technology; and then the game-changing Kodak camera—had become a part of public life in Calcutta. The enthusiasm to embrace photography by the Indian elite and middle-classes hints at their rapidly changing relationship with technology, which, along with the railways, the telegraph, gaslight and electricity, trams and omnibuses, industries, ports, and so on were part of a broader and increasingly complex network of modernisation. Perhaps the most distinguished moment of this negotiation would be cinema, to whose attractions we will soon arrive.

Photography's parentage of cinema is even more striking when we discover that all the earliest names in Indian cinema—Hiralal Sen, Dhirendranath Ganguly, Debi Ghosh, Dadasaheb Phalke, Harishchandra Bhatavadekar—were photographers of repute (the only exception perhaps being Baburao Painter) and had run successful photographic enterprises before they were seduced by the moving image (just like the Lumière Brothers). To that end, the lives of Sen, Ganguly and Ghosh in Bengal stand testament to a fascinating continuity that connected the middle years of the 19th century to the beginning of the twentieth—from the awed amazement at the photographic image to the irresistible fascination with the 'bioscope'. The best example of this continuity is however the Rays, the first being Upendrakishore, whose fame in mustering the intricate nuances of halftone photography went much beyond the confines of India. His grandson, Satyajit, heir to his grandfather's scientific temper and his father Sukumar's wondrous imagination, took to cinema instead.

THE IMAGE STARTS TO MOVE

Just like photography, cinema too wasn't an invention of one man or one clime but involved multiple inventors—explorers of science, laboratory romantics, go-getter entrepreneurs. The unique visual and optical language exclusive to the new technology of photography expectantly led to the desire to capture movement within the image. Just after Eadweard Muybridge's *The Horse in Motion* successfully experimented in the locomotion of the image, Étienne-Jules Marey's chronophotographe and the 'motion' caméras of William Friese-Green made news, while Thomas Edison's Kinetograph and Charles-Émile Reynaud's Praxinoscope brought the world on the verge of cinema. By the mid-1890s, Auguste and Louis Lumière's cinematographe signalled the firm arrival of motion pictures. After their iconic screening in Paris in December 1895, the Lumières dispatched travelling ambassadors across lands. It was only a matter of time till cinema arrived in India, much like photography did, almost exactly at the time of its circulation across the world. In July 1896, Lumière emissary Maurice Sestier organised the first recorded public screening of cinema in India at Bombay's Watson Hotel.

While Bombay's claim is part of celluloid history, cinema's arrival in Calcutta is a thrilling whodunnit! There is fleeting evidence that there were private screenings in Calcutta predating the official cinematographe event in Bombay. The date to which the earliest of them could be ascribed is July 1896, when in an issue dated to this month an article in the *Journal of the Photographic Society of India* gave an account of having witnessed Edison's kinetograph. Then, in January 1897, travelling salesman Thomas G. Hudson exhibited films at Calcutta's Minerva Theatre with his Animatograph. At the same time, Rev. Eugène Lafont of Calcutta's St Xavier's College is known to have shown film clippings to his students and colleagues. Famous for his astronomical experiments and for a large spectro-telescopic observatory he had built atop the dome at St Xavier's, the Jesuit Lafont was also a pioneering teacher of science. Records reveal his famous weekend public lectures on latest science instruments (like phonograph), shipped from Europe. Hence it is likely that he had access to a Kinetograph before others did. Later, in September 1897, first at the Minerva Theatre with Mr Sullivan as exhibitor and then in March 1898 at Classic Theatre film shows were said to have been organised. But one had to wait till October 1898, for cinema to officially burst onto the Calcutta scene. This event, quite a pageantry as it was, is best recorded in the version that cultural historian Samik Bandobadhyay gives us. He writes:

On 29 October, 1898, Amritlal Basu ... 'player, playwright and actor-manager' ... screened a package of actualities and 'fakes' that included the Death of Nelson, Queen Victoria's Diamond Jubilee, and Gladstone's Funeral Procession, at the Star Theatre at 75/3 Cornwallis Street. The screening was sandwiched between a performance of the play *Babu* and Miss Nelly Mountcastle dancing her snake number, followed by a rainbow number.[2]

The man behind these shows was one J.J. Stevenson, another travelling showman. As cinema historian Ranita Chatterjee says,

Several screen technologies arrived in Calcutta around the same time. In these years, newspaper advertisements refer to at least four different technological apparatuses showing moving pictures in Calcutta—the Cinematograph, the Animatograph, the Bioscope and the Kinetoscope (in winter 1895–96)—all brought in by different itinerant exhibitors. Significantly, these technologies arrived in the city independent of Bombay.[3]

From the anonymous exhibitor of Kinetograph and Hudson and Lafont to Sullivan and Stevenson; one or more of them could be entrusted with the distinction of having brought the moving image to Calcutta. But whoever may have imported it, cinema persuasively declared its intention to make a living in Calcutta, much sooner than expected.

THE CONTENTIOUS COMRADESHIP OF THEATRE

It was at the theatre that cinema found its first address. But why did the prominent stages of Calcutta, Star, Minerva or Classic, get involved in the history of cinema? To understand this, we must look at the collaboration between theatre and the moving image—as spaces of performance, vehicles of spectacle and schools of talent—that was established at the dawn of cinema. In *Frontline* magazine's commemorative volume on Indian cinema's centenary, film scholar Moinak Biswas wrote:

This was the common context—theatre houses incorporating the moving picture in a variety menu, often by inviting the itinerant showman to add the novel item of moving pictures. These were meant to win back, according to some commentators, audiences who were turning away from the stage. These showmen would be touring the whole imperial region in the East—Burma (now Myanmar), Ceylon (now Sri Lanka) and India—with motley troupes and second-hand film packages. The machines they brought were mostly of British,

French, American and German make. 'Cinematographe' being the pioneering Lumiere invention, the name gained wide currency everywhere, including Bombay and Calcutta. The generic name for cinema, 'Bioscope', lodged in the Bengali vocabulary for many years to come, seems to have come from the apparatus used by J.J. Stevenson to show films at the prestigious Star Theatre in October 1898.[4]

This propitious link between theatre and cinema was going to stay so for a long time to come. This is because theatre and cinema, even with their fundamental differences, were more than willing bedfellows in Calcutta's burgeoning relationship with both dramaturgic and cinematic modernity. Public theatre was the first public culture in the colonial city's life, eventually giving rise to cultural properties, both tangible and intangible, that were leased to cinema.

The recorded history of modern theatre in Calcutta dates back to 1753, when The Playhouse was set up by early European itinerants with active support from the renowned British Shakespearean David Garrick. It was sacked in 1756 along with the city a year before Bengal decisively fell to East India Company. Then, in 1775, the Calcutta Theatre was built, with Garrick again as donor and advisor, and had a comparatively long life of thirty years producing memorable plays, including *The Merchant of Venice*. Another important figure in the 18th century public theatre in Calcutta was the Russian scholar-adventurer Gerasim Lebedeff, who adapted Richard Joderrell's *The Disguise* and Moliere's *Love Is the Best Doctor* into 'Bengallee style' performances. In the next hundred years, a long line of theatres, mostly British, kept the colonial settlers busy with Shakespeare, Sheridan and Congreve. Among the more notable theatres were The Chowringhee Theatre (1813–1839) and Sans Souci (1839–1849). Both theatres were lost to fire: the first was gutted; in the case of the second, its chief patron Mrs Leach's dress caught fire during a performance, and she later succumbed to injuries sustained from that accident. After her, Sans Sauci declined quickly, letting seven Belgian Jesuits buy the land and the remnant of the theatre building to build St Xavier's College in 1860, which still stands on the same plot. But before closure, Sans Souci created history and controversy with what else but *Othello*, where one Baishnav Charan Addy, a 'native', played the tragic moor doomed to self-loathing and destruction amidst an otherwise white European cast.

Bengali theatre began diffidently in the 1830s but took long strides in the second-half of the 19th century, with the founding of the National Theatre in 1873. Together with Bengal Theatre, Manmohan Theatre, Emerald and Corinthian, it signified a shifting consciousness towards indigenous, rousing matter while the more cosmopolitan Minerva (that National Theatre morphed into) and Star Theatre were more openly supportive of mixed content. Despite the pulls and pushes of change and continuity that stalks any public culture, what held theatre together was that the public stage created the early notions of what will later become constitutive of public stardom. Theatre stalwarts Girish Ghosh, Ardhendusekhar Mustafi, Noti Binodini, Danibabu, Amarendranath Dutta, Aparesh Mukhopadhyay became major attractions for the city's crowd between the last three decades of the 19th and the first two of the 20th century.

But public theatre could never position itself as a rich ground for formidable middle-class (bhadralok) cultural activity. In spite of fine actors, large-scale productions, well-anointed venues and staple audience interest, Bengal theatre, well into the early 1940s was producing an endless catalogue of mythologicals or historicals that were gaudy, loud and populist. In the early 1920s though, an influx of new talent gave public theatre some traction. Figures like Sisir Bhaduri, Naresh Mitra, Radhikananda Mukherjee, Jogesh Chaudhuri, Tulsi Lahiri, Nirmalendu Lahiri, Ahindra Chaudhuri and Sotu Sen brought bhadralok 'respectability' to theatre. It also attracted talents such as Durgadas Banerji, Pahari Sanyal, Tulsi Chakraborty and Chhabi Biswas in the ensuing decades. But by then, public theatre was being regularly poached by cinema's voracious appetite for both content and talent. Most of the stars on stage became renowned on screen as well.[5]

Still, cinema's vulnerable beginnings were shouldered by theatres as venues for screenings. Cinema, for a while, brought in the crowds to the theatre. For a much longer period the theatre provided the schooling needed for actors and directors, technicians and often the germ of a film script. In fact, in many cases, the movies were a vehicle to repeat, ad infinitum, a play, with all the stifling constraints of the stage. The interdependence came under tension only as late as the 1940s. The cultural axis of popular entertainment was by the early 1950s shifting to cinema, while serious theatre came to be dominated by Leftist groups after IPTA's landmark production *Nabanno*. With Uttam's stardom, cinema would upstage commercial theatre irreversibly and send it into a state of stupor. One must note, with unfailing irony, that one of the last hurrahs of the popular stage, *Shyamali*, had Uttam in the lead. Clearly, of all things theatre finally abrogated to cinema, the idea of a public star was the most treasured, which by the 1950s had started to belong entirely to cinema.

There were significant other factors behind the decline of Bengali commercial theatre, which is outside the scope of this story. But that was still half a century into the future from their initial and intuitive comradeship.

THE GENESIS GENERATION

Just like Harishchandra Bhatavadekar was a witness to the initial few screenings in Bombay,[6] a young man called Hiralal Sen was among the starry-eyed witnesses to the 'Bioscope' in Star Theatre in 1898. Till he was won over by the movies, Sen was a photographer of repute, winning a number of competitions, including the most prestigious one managed by the studio Bourne & Shepherd. But cinema not only caught Sen's attention but also seemed to have caught him by his throat. He went straight to Stevenson to learn the art of projecting movies. When Stevenson played truant, Sen went ahead and ordered the entire Bioscope equipment from a London firm (by some accounts it was John Range & Sons). Apart from the cinematograph machine, the paraphernalia included an oxygen gas bag, an ether saturator and a limelight set, since much of Calcutta was still without electricity and Sen had planned to exhibit his films in tents, using the limelight. Incidentally, Sen received considerable advice in his new venture from the same Eugene Lafont. Sen was already running a photo studio called HL Sen & Brothers. On getting his movie equipment, he renamed his concern Royal Bioscope Company. It got formally registered in 1902. The Royal Bioscope Company started creating indigenous content and made at least forty odd shorts—actuality films, filmed theatres, advertisements and those resembling a moving version of variety tricks. Sen is also said to have shot scenes of everyday life in Calcutta: moving trams, bathing ghats, cock fights and so on. They were shown in makeshift tents and at wealthy Calcutta houses such as the Tagore Castle; or at Dalhousie Institute; or at the Indian National Congress-backed All India Industrial and Agricultural Exhibition of 1901. Among the ones known to have been shot by Sen are the dance sequences of *Flower of Persia* in Star Theatre. The companionship of renowned stage actor Amarendranath Dutta bolstered Sen's ambitions. Dutta ran the Classic Theatre, giving Sen unhindered access to the plays. Sen's film of Dutta riding a real horse in *Sitaram* created a stir. The clip was advertised as 'superfine pictures from our world-renowned plays'. But the most memorable partnership was the popular play *Alibaba and the Forty Thieves* in the filming of which Sen is said to have introduced trick photographic techniques. The film version was a major and thumping success, but instead of bolstering the partnership, it brought it under strain. The play's lead actress Kusumkumari, who found herself at the receiving end of competitive affection from both Sen and Dutta, further complicated matters. After this setback, Hiralal moved out of the staged film domain. He retained close contact with the Pathe Frere Company and later also shot the first commercials for Jabakusum Hair Oil and

Edward Tonic, a malaria drug. The high point of Sen's work[7] was a film made in the wake of the first Partition of Bengal in 1905. The anti-Partition lectures of nationalist leader Surendranath Banerjee were pre-recorded and played along with his actual lecture at Calcutta's Treasury House, which was shot by Sen. This feat gave the film an impression of a talkie. Apparently, the Library of Congress had considered this film a benchmark till at least 1912. Sen's final triumph was his film on the Delhi Durbar of 1911.

Sen was an innovator and he was invested in production, equipment and later, in setting up of an exhibition theatre (Show House). He had also started training local actors for cinema. But eventually, having run out of resources, enthusiasm and support, he sold his life's work to his brother in 1913 and heartbroken and dejected, took refuge to care for his own flailing health. And no sooner had he retired that Bengali cinema took a turn towards narrative cinema, virtually erasing Sen's single-handed efforts to create a pool of indigenous, non-narrative content that gestured to the arrival of moving images in India. Later, a fire at a godown in Calcutta's Roybagan destroyed the entire corpus of Sen, which is now considered a colossal loss for Indian cinema.

The diminution of Sen is usually attributed to the accident of fate, itinerant legal troubles with his brother Motilal, protean technology, constant requirement of investment and to the rise of his astute competitor Jamshedji Madan's Elphinstone Bioscope Company. But it is also true that Sen was a cinema romantic, a man of vision but without the industry and perseverance of an entrepreneur. Moreover, he was undone again and again by his own kin, who used his name and resources to build, unsuccessfully, their own careers in the fledgling movie business. The successful careers of Bhatavadekar[8] and Jamshedji Madan (as we shall see) reveal a streak of cleverness and skill of trade inherent to the climate of Bombay, while Sen's life betrayed the capacity for myopic decisions, family intrigue and self-destruction, not atypical of Bengali efforts in building a life in commerce.

In spite of every obstacle he encountered, Sen has not been forgotten. *The Guardian*, while reporting about Indian cinema's 'centenary' in 2013, argued that the history of cinema in India must be pushed a few years prior to Dadasaheb Phalke's *Raja Harishchandra* of 1913.

In October 1917, Hiralal Sen was sick, bankrupt and just a few days away from death when he received some cruel news. His brother's warehouse was on fire and, as it burned, Sen's career as a film-maker went up in flames. The warehouse contained the entire stock of the Royal Bioscope Company, the Sen brothers' firm, which showed and produced films in the Kolkata area in the early years of the 20th century. The blaze destroyed Sen's films, and with them much of the proof of India's early cinema history.[9]

Hiralal Sen, along with Aurora's Anadi Basu, could well be called the genesis generation of Indian cinema. His work partly resembles that of Hollywood's proto-studios such as Edison Manufacturing Company and American Vitagraph.[10] The fate of Sen also mirrors that of cinema pioneer Edwin S. Porter (*The Great Train Robbery*, 1903), both having been lost to obscurity after their trailblazing success in the earliest hours of movie history.

If Sen was a romantic, Dhirendranath Ganguly (1893–1978), commemorated as DG, was a maverick. His long association with the poet Rabindranath Tagore notwithstanding, DG's real hero was Charlie Chaplin. Being trained in both fine art and photography, DG was a master of the art of concealment. He produced, in 1915, two volumes of photography and performance stills, where he modelled a range of inter-sexual facial movements on himself. He soon founded The Indo-British Film Company with its office at 34, Mohun Bagan Row. With ex-Madan helmsman N.C. Lahiri and painter Jyotish Sarkar in tow, DG produced the rousingly successful silent film *Bilet Ferot*. Though the Madans had already released the first full-length Bengali silent *Bilwamangal* (1919), *Bilet Ferot*, which had a delayed release in 1921, was the first film to have involved a full 'Bengali cast and crew'. The cast included the rare exception of the heroine coming from the Bengali gentry. Shusheela Devi was not only the first bhadralok heroine but had also mastered horse riding and driving the motor car, both of which were advertised as 'attractions' of the movie. *Bilet Ferot* was also the first comedy in Bengal, providing a welcome exception to the growing preponderance of mythologicals in 1920s cinema. But DG was a fidgety sort and his cinema was full of slapstick clichés. After two more films, the Indo-British Film Company winded up and DG left for Hyderabad. There he established the Lotus Film Company, attracted the ire of the Nizam when he showed Razia Sultan falling in love with a Hindu man in an eponymous movie, came back to Calcutta and co-founded British Dominion Films with investment from princely elites. The first film they planned was Rabindranath's *Tapati*, which the poet had also scripted. But *Tapati* remained incomplete and what got made was *Flames of Flesh* (1930) a film based on the legend of Padmavati. Among seven other films that this company produced, *Panchashar* (1930) deserves mention as it was remarkable for its time because DG's wife Premlatika Debi (screen name Romola) acted with him in it. Romola's death the month after the release of the film left DG inconsolable. He was further undone by the coming of sound and closed down his studio to become part of Barua Pictures. During the 1930s and

1940s, DG was associated with films having original titles (not content though) as risqué as *Money Makes What Not* (1931), *Excuse Me Sir* (1934), *Night Girl* (1934), *Blood and Beauty* (1935), *Country Girl* (1936) and so on. He also had two stints with New Theatres. By the mid-1940s, he made a living as a freelancer and briefly flirted once more with his own company DG Talkies. More than producer, director or actor, DG was a showman—the first in a line of mavericks only cinema can manufacture. Throughout his active life, he wanted to bring to Bengali cinema an air of respectability, especially around the thorny issue of female actors. DG was one of those impatient individuals no establishment could pin down; neither could he create anything substantial for posterity. But his career and person mirrors the fascinating, mercurial and a most amusing trajectory of early Bengali cinema; a feat celebrated when he became the seventh awardee of the Dadasaheb Phalke Award in 1975. What is unknown to many is that in a 1951 film called *Ore Jatri* DG acted with a scrawny newcomer named in the cast as Uttam Chatterjee, signalling a riveting, fabular link between the earliest 'persona' of the Bengali screen with its most enduring.

Several other companies vied for a slice of the cinema pie during the years of the Great War and after: such as Filmcraft International, Taj Mahal Film Company, Kohinoor Film Company, Photo-Play Syndicate and Kali Films; but except Aurora Film Corporation none could really hope to come close to the wealth, reach and domination of the Madans' Elphinstone. Ranita Chatterjee, who has exclusively worked with the Aurora archives, gives us a glimpse into the company's early history. She writes,

> Aurora's co-owner Anadi Bose had a longer history of involvement in the arts and entertainment business in Calcutta: he had made investments in the Bengali Public Theatre (in Manmohan Theatre) in the 1900s. Following on from the trend set by Hiralal Sen and A.N. Dutt (Amarendranth Dutta), Bose held regular film screenings in Manmohan Theatre.[11]

Aurora's retinue, including the magician Charu Ghosh, travelled across Bengal and showed a curious mix of imported films, tricks and stage-magic—a sustainable and cheap entertainment model which was, literally, up their sleeve. When the initial delight of the 'fantastic' moving images began to wane, the Auroras won a government contract to shoot movies for the amusement of British soldiers stationed in India during years of WWI. Bose hired Debi Ghosh and started to film theatrical shows, Bankim Chandra Chattopadhyay's *Bishbrikha* being one. But it was with the home production of the second 'Bengali' film *Dasyu*

Ratnakar (1921) that they arrived into the domain of narrative cinema. Aurora also pioneered the shoot, editing and exhibition of newsreels prior to film shows.

Aurora not only survived the Madan onslaught of the 1920s and New Theatres' blitz of the 1930s but was doing well enough to nurture film aspirants of the early 1950s, their youthful catalogue having included the very young Uttam. Among their most celebrated achievements was to have distributed Satyajit Ray's *Pather Panchali* (1955) and to have produced his *Jalsaghar* (1958). But they were also active in the popular cinema ecosystem, having produced several of Uttam's early films (*Shodanonder Mela, Raikamal*). Aurora ensured a singular continuity of production between the earliest decades of cinema and Uttam's arrival into the scene five decades later. The company, though long past actively producing or distributing films, is still in operation. It rents out its studio space in Calcutta's Salt Lake though its original studio at Narkelbagan, like many of Calcutta's properties of historical repute, fell to the kiss of a raging fire a long time ago.

Incidentally, both *Bilet Ferot* and *Dasyu Ratnakar* were released in Russa Theatre in south Calcutta's Bhawanipur, signalling the first tentative steps of Bengali cinema out of the confines of the north and central districts and the distribution stranglehold of the Madans. Russa, later renamed Purna, was owned by Paris Cinema and Varieties Limited, which was, in fact, a completely Bengali firm. This historic hall was a leading, independent and elegant theatre till late into the 1980s and has been a key character in Bengali cinema history, including that of Uttam's. Now, it stands on a patch of land on S.P. Mukherjee Road, shut, darkened and forlorn, its bare bones exposed to the elements.

THE ARTLESS MADANS

Whatever be the achievement of these early houses and their commanders, the history of bioscope in Calcutta for the decade that followed the end of the Great War doubtlessly belonged to Parsee magnate Jamshedji Framji Madan's firm. In fact, so total was the domination of the Madans of the period's celluloid produce that silent narrative cinema in Bengal has come to be synonymous with them. Jamshedji Madan, who rose to prominence in the world of commerce from being a prop boy in Bombay's Parsi theatre circuit, made his fortunes as a supplier of goods to the British Army. In 1883, he moved to Calcutta and around 1902, having registered his company, took to the new-fangled technology of cinema with the gusto of a wealthy trade baron. When Hiralal's firm faulted, Jamshedji's Elphinstone Bioscope Company acquired exclusive rights to the films produced by Pathé. Having ensured a regular supply of films, the Madans intended to move the business from theatre halls and makeshift tents around the Maidan to a permanent venue. In 1907, just a year after the nickelodeons were built in the United States, the Madans established the fancy Elphinstone Picture Palace. It entered the record books as India's first permanent movie theatre, built as a focal building near Calcutta's Victorian Gothic arcade, the Stuart Hogg Market, and right opposite the imposing headquarters of the Calcutta Municipal Corporation. The Madans not only had a venue of their own but also monopolised the distribution business. By 1915, the Madans were showing a retinue of mostly swashbuckling, imported films in the Palace of Variety, the Crown and Electric Theatre, all owned by them. Their fortunes improved considerably after the Great War and soon Madan had the rights of distribution to the entire corpus of films from both Metro Goldwyn Mayer and United Artists. In its heyday, Madan's firm is said to have controlled over 170 screens across the subcontinent. Madan's theatres not only edged out all local competition but for the next decade or so made Calcutta the centre of India's burgeoning film production culture that included Ceylon and Burma. The house of Madan made a seamless transition under Jamsedji's son Jeejeebhoy on the death of the founder in 1923.

Eventually, as the need for indigenous content started being felt ever more strongly, the Madans developed a sophisticated production and distribution line, introduced salaried actors and technicians and were fully invested in the business of cinema. But Jamshedji's astute business sense told him not to flirt with 'egotistic' artistes, at least in the department of direction. As a principle, he employed his manager, typist and accountant, among others, to direct movies for him. His manager and son-in-law Rustamji Dotiwala is credited with directing the first full-length Bengali (as indicated by the intertitles) film *Bilwamangal* in 1919, which advertised itself as the 'greatest play India has known' and its heroine Miss Gohar 'as the most emotional and well-known actress of the Indian stage'.

Though it built an entrenched production and distribution set-up in Calcutta, Madan's firm never wanted to become a particularly Bengali concern, nor was it desirable to be one. The silent genre ensured that one film could be released across the subcontinent, helping the Madans stick to a predominantly Parsi theatre ecosystem of extensive props, glamorous sets and glitzy costumes. They also enrolled a bevy of Anglo-Indian actors such as Patience Cooper, Renee Smith and Effie Hippollet and directors such as Eugenio De Liguoro, Camille Le Grand and Georgio Mannini. A typical Madan concoction would be a film like *Savitri* (1923), a Hindu mythological, sartorially close to Parsi theatre, starring an Anglo-Indian actress with an Indian name and directed by the Italian Mannini. Like this film, *Bishnu Avatar* and *Dhruba Charitra* (both in 1921) or more famously Jyotish Banerjee and Eugenio de Liguoro's *Nal Damayanti* (1921) were quintessential cosmopolitan kitsch that made the Madans famous. Naturally, contemporary reception of the Madans' endless exotica was far from satisfactory.

While the preference for kitsch in content and a streamlined factory-line production and distribution is all too obvious, what is often overlooked is that it was the house of Madan which had introduced Sisirkumar Bhaduri to cinema. Madan also nurtured talents like the director Madhu Bose and the actor Durgadas Banerji, both becoming formidable figures of cinema in the next decade. Even Kanan Devi, who rose to fame in the talkie period, was a Madan discovery. The first Bengali talkie, Amar Choudhury's *Jamaibabu* (1931), was from the house of the Madans too, having fallen forty-two days short of the release of the first Indian talkie, *Alam Ara*. Talkies also strengthened the routine use of song-and-dance interjections in movies, which was epitomised by the Madans' 1932 film *Indrasabha*, which had a whopping sixty-nine songs, a record that is yet to be bettered.

But the real importance of the Madans far outwits native concerns. First, the Madans' consolidation as a major filmmaking firm signalled the gradual but irreversible move away from the earthy, noisy, amateurish fairground entertainments towards the ticketed and plush environs of early narrative cinema, which contributed heavily in cinema becoming part of city's consumptive habits. Second, as Sharmishta Gooptu writes,

> The Madan Company, which dominated Bengal's nascent film industry in the 1920, embodied Calcutta's competitiveness in relation to Bombay. Madan's distribution network and theatre chain and their control of the best of Hollywood's productions established crucial links with Bombay at the same time making for a substantial leverage in Bombay's film circles.[12]

Third, the Madans, notwithstanding their tacky preferences, introduced directors and actors who would provide new blood to Bengali cinema for the decade to come. They also bought rights to produce elite Bengali literary classics such as *Bishabriksha* (1922 and 1928), *Durgeshnandini* (1927) and *Radharani* (1930) all based on Bankim Chandra Chattopadhyay's works. They also produced *Giribala* (directed by Madhu Bose, 1929) based on a Tagore novel.

So, by early 1930s, cinema in Bengal had an established production ethos, technicians, actors, a chain of theatres and an evolving relationship with classic literature, all bequests from the Madans. Though often pilloried for its penchant for monopoly and vilified for its lack of understanding of cinema's artistic nuances, it is undeniable that the Madans left behind an evolved cultural and technological groundwork for a Bengali bhadralok cinema to evolve in the 1930s. Moreover, their particular, even if skewed, streak of cultural and technological cosmopolitanism undercuts the more heavily nationalist political rhetoric of those years. This was perhaps their most remarkable feat. Nothing survives of their work except *Jamaibabu*, which is no less a loss than that of Hiralal's oeuvre. And that is precisely why there cannot be a history of 'Bengali' cinema without the 'artless' Madans.

The story of the demise of the Madans is a classic cinematic parable. Here was a firm in control of their trade till the dying days of silent cinema and not uninformed of the distant roars that talkies were making in late-1920s. Once talkies stormed in, the Madans were quick to adapt to the new technology. But they soon lost out, unable to comprehend the specificity of the newfound cultural codes and unprepared to part ways with the methods they had perfected during the silent period. Movies now came loaded with language, music and culture-specific demands— locations, spaces, costumes, stories and even actors, who were tied to the tongues native to them. All these proved, in the long run, alien to the Madans. Gradually, from the mid-1930s, as their deal with Columbia Pictures collapsed, Madans suffered a meltdown: the theatres changed hands, film production dropped significantly, actors and crew left and the large studio space near Tollygunge in Calcutta was sold. The new owners, Indra Movietone, renamed the Madan Studio as Indrapuri Studio, which still stands, with a lambent memory that goes back to Madan's halcyon, 'silent' days. Elphinstone Picture Palace changed hands too and thrived as Minerva (not to be confused with the theatre) through the better part of the century; and then survived as Chaplin towards the end of it. But in a display of shocking myopia, the earliest movie theatre in Indian history was demolished in 2013 after it was left to rot for decades in a state of agonising neglect. The Cornwallis (later Sree) has shut too. Electric (or Albion) Theatre (now the seedy Regal), Crown (later Uttara Cinema) and Palace of Variety (Elite) still stand in solemn gloom, devoid of any real patronage, be it commercial, or for them being makers of cinema history.

Thankfully, the story of the Madans is commemorated in a wonderful impressionist painting by Gaganendranath Tagore called *Madan Theatre by Night*. The painting shows the colossal façade of one of Madan's picture palaces, washed in the yellow glow of electric light dominating a throng of assembled crowds, waiting for a 'bioscope' exhibition.

TAGORE AND OTHER CUSTODIANS OF BENGALI CINEMA

The Madans may have roamed the landscape of Calcutta cinema of the 1920s like a colossus but elsewhere in the Bengali public life there was significant transformation. The local Bengali theatre continued to be a major addiction and new vernacular dailies and periodicals catered to a progressively demanding readership; in literature and music there was new blood and public discourse was increasingly taking a nationalist shape. It is hence pertinent that much of the debate around the reception of cinema grew around it being a product of both mass consumption and as constituent of a specifically Bengali idiom. Though demand for 'nationalist' content in cinema was yet to gain any significant weight, there were already considerable efforts from the British administration to keep an eye on the medium given its formidable reach. The first decisive step towards that possibility came just after the Great War. As scholar of early cinema Manishita Dass points out,

> The Indian Cinematograph Act of 1918 and the subsequent constitution of censor boards at Bombay, Calcutta, Madras, and Rangoon set up a basic machinery of censorship. These boards' primary aim was to target cinematic representations of sensitive political issues—anything that might be interpreted as a reflection of or a reference to the nationalist struggle, seditious sentiments, revolutionary uprisings, communist ideas, or anything deemed offensive to Hindu or Muslim religious sensibilities.[13]

The next major step came in the mid-1920s in the form of a definitive policy. After a visit of a team from the tellingly 'Victorian' body called British Social Hygiene Council in 1926–1927, in October 1927, the colonial government announced the formation of the Indian Cinematograph Committee (ICC). ICC's subsequent report presents an unmatched account of early cinema anywhere in the non-Western world. After ICC's recommendations, an increasing demand was made of cinema industries across India to 'organise' their business and avoid seditious content. Understandably, the cinema of the coming decade developed under the shadow of this officious postulation.

If colonial anxiety sought to influence cinematic storytelling in the 1930s, in the case of Bengali cinema, another set of anxieties, which can be broadly called aesthetic, came to take hold. This was a natural corollary to the increasing acceptability of cinema outside its early domain of attraction as cheap thrills and swashbuckling entertainment. As cinema became increasingly acceptable to the educated classes, it received more attention from the intellectual vanguards of that class.

While 'concerns' about cinema in Bengali print date back to at least 1913 (adverts and briefs of film as 'spectacle' or 'event' can be traced much earlier) on the pages of periodicals like *Bharatbarsha* and *Prabasi*, it was Saurindramohan Mukhopadhyay and his *Bharati* magazine that gave shape to early film criticism in Bengali in the mid-1920s. Film historians Dass and Gooptu mention how early commentaries engage in the newfangled technology of cinema, the nature of Hollywood imports and how the new form is to be best appreciated in the Indian context. Soon, the 'appreciation' of cinema turned to local productions and offered detailed notes on their strengths and limitations. As a result, in the late 1920s, a series of what Dass calls 'middlebrow film periodicals'—*Nachghar, Deepali, Bioscope, Chitralekha*—came to the market to whet the appetite of a readership increasingly interested in cinema. Needless to affirm, the advent of sound furthered the intellectual climate necessary to engage in cinema's artistic potential, while gradually a search for a more Bengali context took root. No wonder, we see the emergence of significant debates about film form and technology as well as critical classifications of film content. A bhadralok code of what is taste and how cinema *must* reflect the same is quite evident in these discussions.[14]

That the late 1920s was progressively putting Bengali cinema under the weight of artistic expectation was nowhere more apparent than in the words of Rabindranath Tagore. In a well-known letter written to Murari Bhaduri in 1929, Tagore wrote:

> Moving image has been till now blandishing literature. The reason for this is that no artiste by the sheer power of his/her creativity has been able to salvage it from slavery.... The main component of the moving image is a scenic progression. The beauty and charm of scenic progression should be such that it is able to captivate the audience without speech. If the language of a medium is encroached upon by another language, it expresses the disabled nature of the medium.[15]

Remarkably, Tagore had comprehended early that the future of an 'independent' moving image was in realising its visual potential and to not let it wither under its perceived addiction to literature. Tagore's endorsement of cinema and his plea to unchain it from literary dependence should be seen as a marker of the broader intellectual shift in the perception of cinema as a new, potentially radical, art form.

Rabindranath himself got involved with cinema in several ways, in India, the United States and the erstwhile Soviet Union. He titled the silent *Giribala*, scripted the silent (unmade) *Tapati*, and was involved in the production, direction and casting of *Notir Puja* for New Theatres. Tagore's most interesting involvement with cinema was in 1930, when at the invitation of Himanshu Rai and Universum Film AG (UFA Studios) in Munich, he wrote a script based on the Bavarian folk practice of Oberammergau Passion Play, which recounted Christ's last days.

Tagore's prose script, 'A Play in the New Technique for Film', humanised the life of Christ. But the film was never made. The script was reborn later as the long poem *The Child*, the only one the Nobel Laureate ever wrote in English.

In spite of his caution against literary dependence, it is ironic that Tagore has ended up being the chief 'purveyor' of literary content in Bengali cinema. Beginning in 1923, his work has been filmed on stage, filmed separately, adapted to both *silent* and *voiced* screens, adapted by Ray and others, or that by Uttam Kumar, found colour and in recent years, has been spiced up with experimental visual/sonic language and in-your-face sexuality. This is apart from the fact, as claimed recently, that in about 250 Bengali films about 450 Tagore songs have been used so far. Incidentally, Tagore's death in 1941 saw thousands of mourners in a procession that was filmed by Niranjan Pal, Himangshu Rai's friend and guide in Europe, co-founder of Bombay Talkies, son of Congress leader Bipin Pal and a theatrician and librettist in his own right. He had shot it on behalf of Aurora Film Corporation.

What Rabindranath and other like-minded, globetrotting individuals were hoping for was that cinema in general would stop being a minion to literature; and that Bengali cinema should start looking for a room of its own, instead of being slavishly dependent on the over-the-top spectacle of Hollywood or the stagey, high-octane parochialism of commercial theatre. This was precisely why intellectuals and artists began to collect towards the medium of moving images. In fact, if one looks at the ancestry of Bengali cinema, one is struck by the obvious traffic that it had with the larger project of modernity—partaking in reformism, social change and cultural mobilisation. As Chandak Sengoopta writes:

> It is one of the paradoxes of the Brahmo history that the community was rather less opposed to the cinema than to the stage. Apart from Satyajit Ray himself and his uncle Nitin Bose, such cinematic pioneers as Himanshu Rai, Niranjan Pal, Dhirendranath Gangopadhyay, and Madhu Bose were all Brahmos and the list would grow longer if it included technical personnel.[16]

And this is not to include the litterateurs, poets and writers. Even in the case where the pioneers were not Brahmos, such as Birendranath Sarkar, Hiralal Sen or Pramathesh Barua, the kind of schooling—acquired in India or abroad—that they brought to cinema was conspicuously emancipatory. Whether their august assembly ushered a new age for Bengali cinema in the 1930s or it had to wait for another two decades is a matter of debate and even degree, but what was certain was that the introduction of *sound* brought Bengali cinema, like cinema everywhere else, on the brink of an irrevocable change.

MOVIES LEARN TO TALK

There was more than one claimant for the title of the first talkie. Three films, Warner Bros' *Don Juan* (1926) and *The Jazz Singer* (1927) and crime drama *Lights of New York* (1928), have laid claim to that distinction, which altered popular tastes in cinema forever. The film that did the same in Calcutta was Universal Pictures' *Melody of Love,* released at the Elphinstone Picture Palace in late 1928. The Madans spared no effort to include *sound* in their cinematic architecture. In the early 1930s, Madan's firm was still producing three-fourths of the released films, mostly talkies. Yet, in less than two years after that, almost as confidently as it had ruled, the Madans walked into cinematic oblivion.

The Madans' state of decline propelled New Theatres to pick up the baton of cinema. New Theatres was a liberal house with an extraordinary man at the helm. Buttressed by sound, a new enthusiasm for more 'artistic' content and a congress of undeniable talent, New Theatres broke Madan's stranglehold and Bengali cinema's long association with bhadralok ethos began. In the historical progression of cinema this phase is full of turning points in visual, aesthetic and narrative forms as well as in the production of stardom. Not only did New Theatres inherit Madan's areas of influence across the subcontinent but it continued to produce (Urdu) or influence (Tamil) cinemas in multiple languages with their cultivated sensibility, organisational discipline and commercial acumen. This was a significantly more difficult a task than what Madan's language-neutral silents could achieve before. As Sharmistha Gooptu notes:

> For New Theatres, the elitist Bengali vision of film art co-existed with parallel production strategies, which allowed it to address a wider cross section of cinema audiences. It was a balance that derived from a twin agenda of making films more acceptable as a middle-class entertainment, and of making the most of the commercial possibilities of the talkie era.[17]

Like several other institutions of the period that bore a strongly Bengali stamp, New Theatres was propelled by a streak towards social benefaction. Pearycharan Sarkar was one of leading reformists in mid-19th-century Bengal. Among his many achievements was introducing schoolgoing children in Bengal to the new elements of English grammar. Birendranath (B.N.) Sarkar (often spelt Sircar), who founded New Theatres eighty years later, introduced the finer elements of cinema to the moviegoing public of Bengal. He was, after all, Pearycharan's great-grandson. In between, B.N.'s grandfather J.N. went to Balliol College Oxford and was a bar-at-law while B.N.'s father N.N. was Advocate-General of Bengal. BN was educated at the University College London and was a civil engineer by training. Whatever he may have lacked, pedigree wasn't one of them.

On his return, Birendranath got involved with *Buker Bojha* (A Weight on the Chest, 1930) which was the directorial debut of noted silent era cameraman Nitin Bose. The film fared poorly but BN, like Hiralal Sen in another time, got addicted to cinema. But unlike Sen, Sarkar was attracted to the business of cinema rather than its creative agitation, a weight he clearly did not want on his chest. He leased land near Tollygunge to establish a studio and started to build a theatre fitted with talkie technology in the north of the city. Both were inaugurated in December 1930. The theatre at Shyambazar, called Chitra, was inaugurated by a young Congress leader called Subhash Chandra Bose who was then the Mayor of Calcutta. Eighteen years later, in 1948, by which time Bose was a legend and was forever on leave from history, Chitra saw the premiere of a film called *Drishtidan* (The Gift of Sight), directed by the same Nitin Bose, in which a young man of twenty-two called Arunkumar Chattopadhyay, a die-hard fan of Subhash Bose, emerged under the gaze of the public for the first time. He later earned fame as Uttam Kumar.

Chitra was more than just a phase in the cultural evolution of cinema. It pointed towards the shift of moviemaking from Madan's kitsch to New Theatres' conscientious bhadralok values. In the early 1930s, a couple of exquisitely designed theatre halls were set up. Next to Chitra, in December 1932, came up Rupabani and near Sealdah Station came up Chhabighar. Referring to Rupabani, Madhuja Mukherjee writes:

> The Nan brothers of Screen Corporation, headed by BC Nan, were collaborating with European companies, distinguished artists and Bengali engineers trained in England, to build [Rupabani's] structure … Rupabani also installed a state-of-art ventilation system and mechanism to control temperature. Needless to say, it was producing a social space for the 'respectable' classes, and the inaugural brochure presented Rabindranath Tagore, Bengal's literary and cultural icon, as the 'chief organizer'.[18]

In some ways, this expanding sphere of film circulation paved the road for a period of unsurpassed success and reach for Bengali popular cinema in the 1950s and 1960s. Like north Calcutta's Shyambazar, Bhawanipur in the south too had acquired a series of movie theatres, dotting the south–north link of S.P. Mukherjee Road. Uttam's house on 46A Girish Mukherjee Road was a street on the east of the cluster of movie halls in Bhowanipore. Hence for about a decade, till he shifted his base elsewhere, the euphoria that Uttam's films provoked—garlanded posters, jostling crowds, gregarious ticketers, ear-splitting whistles and 'flash mob' exuberance—was something that was unfolding less than a mile from his house. A short walk separated the at-home Uttam Kumar from the sites of raucous fandom that constituted his public stardom.

THE ELEPHANTINE NEW THEATRES

B.N. Sarkar had meant to do much more than just setting up a studio and a movie hall, which had already been done, at least the studio part, by the Madans, or DG or Pramathesh Barua. That Sarkar meant business was indicated when he employed Wilford Deming, Jr, an American sound engineer who had overseen the production of Imperial Film Company's *Alam Ara*, India's first talkie. Sarkar hired Deming for a whopping monthly fee of 250 dollars to supervise the sound ecosystem that he was building in Calcutta. Deming left Calcutta a few months later much impressed. He wrote: "Calcutta provided a complete surprise, contrasting with the rushing, haphazard methods of Bombay. Here, I was presented with the nucleus of what has become a real production unit, well-financed and with an ambitious programme of producing pictures for India comparable to those of independent Hollywood companies."[19] In less than five years, when, making best use of the training and topped with indigenous imagination, Nitin Bose managed to introduce playback singing in Indian cinema in New Theatres' *Bhagya Chakra* (1935), Deming's prophecy proved incontestable. In between, Sarat Chandra Chattopadhyay's *Dena Paona* (1931), directed by litterateur Premankur Atorthi had established New Theatres as an institution of reckoning. This reputation was cemented through Debakikumar Bose's *Chandidas* (1932), a film which turned a story from the Vaishnav folklore into a musical about class archetypes and romantic yearning. It gave Bengali cinema the first *romantic* pair in Durgadas Banerji and Umashashi; a singer of tall standing (K.C. Dey); a cinematographer (Nitin Bose); and a composer (R.C. Boral), the labour of each becoming something finally worthy of cinema's distinctive format.

The primary objective of New Theatres—with its iconic logo of a pair of trumpeting elephants facing each other—was to make sure that the achievements of the Bengali cultural sphere in literature, music and other arts were extended to cinema, without compromising on the commerce. One way to do that was to contemporise literary fiction and it was no surprise that New Theatres banked on Sarat Chandra Chattopadhyay's immense acceptability among the literate classes. The climax of this engagement was *Devdas* (1936), a film that made New Theatres a crucible of the new kind of cinema of the talkie period. *Devdas* naturalised the performances, while the scenography, sets and costumes were thoroughly identifiable—a far cry from the otherworldly excesses of the Madan repertoire. The Pramathesh Barua-directed Bengali language *Devdas* became a prototype of good, wholesome cinema that was also culturally verifiable as Bengali, if not also Indian. It was also less stagey and visibly less theatrical than most of its peers, letting the audience empathise with the doomed lover, his capacity for sacrifice as well as his weakness for an extreme sense of self-worth. But *Devdas* was not an exception. There were a few dozen films in Bengali, Hindi and even Urdu that were to gain currency across India. Among the notable Bengali films were Pramathesh Barua's *Grihadaha* (1936) and *Mukti* (1937), Debaki Bose's *Bidyapati* (1938), Nitin Bose's *Desher Mati* (1938) and *Porichoy* (1941), Prafulla Roy's *Abhagi* (1938), Amar Mullik's *Bardidi* (1939), Phoney Majumdar's *Daktar* (1940) and Soumen Mukhopadhyay's *Priyo Bandhobi* (1943), ensuring that New Theatres continued to define Bengali cinema's maturity into adulthood. Then, in 1944 Nitin Basu's protégée Bimal Roy came to the fore with *Udayer Pathe*, a path-breaking melodrama empathetic to the emerging ethos of the period. The film, inspired by IPTA's socialist moorings, is now renowned for introducing powerful setpieces that would dominate Bengali cinema's style for years to come. Roy followed *Udayer Pathe* with *Anjangarh* (1948), adapted from Subodh Ghosh's cult realist story *Fossil*. The film was based on land conflict in mineral-rich tribal belts and ought to have (but did not) have a major impact on cinema's evolving romance with Marxist sentiments. In some ways, these two films paved the way for the more direct 'New Wave' social realism that was ushered in in the early 1950s by Nemai Ghosh and Ritwik Ghatak. By that time, Roy had also found his own Vittorio de Sica in *Do Bigha Zameen* (1953), a film that received wide international acclaim.

New Theatres was in great shape through the 1930s but was dealt a heavy blow by a fire that broke out at its storeroom in 1940. Comparable in scale to the conflagaration that destroyed the entire legacy of Hiralal, New Theatres and Bengali cinema lost much of its treasures in that fire—which seems to be a kind of a catastrophic Calcutta leitmotif. But B.N. Sarkar, characteristically, recuperated and continued to pursue his business, which, Ranita Chatterjee's research indicates, not only tapped into an expanding market for Calcutta studios, but also the transnational circulation of film from the Indian subcontinent in the interwar period. Chatterjee also notes that except for two years, the rest of the 1930s saw New Theatres producing more films in languages other than Bengali. This means that notwithstanding its leadership position in the Bengali market, New Theatres was eyeing the domestic (colonial Indian) and 'international' market with equal élan.

But Sarkar's proclivity towards utilising all the available talents and not letting a domineering style rule over his business proved a matter of tribulation at the end. Too many egos clashed, too many talents battled for the trophy that was New Theatres, while Sarkar himself remained stoically uninvolved with any whiff of the personality cult. By the mid-1940s, a number of its legendary cast of talents left. B.N. Sarkar, forever the munificent do-gooder, soldiered on, but with increasingly less ammunition. Much of what New Theatres pioneered in terms of narrative and production continued well into the early years of Uttam Kumar, with two of his earliest films, *Nobin Jatra* (1953) and *Bokul* (1954), being produced by the studio. But as Uttam became an embodiment of Bengali cinema's popular potential, B.N. Sarkar sold what is still the most renowned studio ever in Bengal and retreated into solitude. He was still to live twenty-four more years; but he never came back to make one more movie.

In spite of New Theatres' runaway domination, other firms too had their share under the arc lights, not least being the 'undying' Aurora and the rookie Sri Bharat Lakshmi Pictures (SBLP), whose founder Babulall Chowkhani made money distributing Madan's repertory during its decline and then found his own studio (1934). SBLP also imitated the New Theatres logo; except that in case of SBLP, a diaphanously dressed buxom woman was sandwiched between the pair of upstretched elephantine snouts. SBLP often referenced the New Theatres style in its films but interjected them with slapdash humour, spectacle and an ingrained boisterousness that provided an appeal beyond the literate audience that New Theatres largely targeted. Uttam's first stint in front of a movie camera was inside the sprawling studio of SBLP on south Calcutta's Anwar Shah Road, on whose gates the nervous twenty-one-year-old appeared one day for a miniscule part of a bridegroom in a Hindi film called *Mayador*.

In less than ten years, however, half of the studios were gone. New Theatres and SBLP closed down in 1956, while Rupasree was burnt down in 1951 and by which time Film Corporation Limited had been liquidated. Priyonath Ganguly's East India Film Company, The Indo-British Film Company and Barua Film Unit were long gone anyway. Priyonath's second venture Kali Films changed hands to become

Technicians' Studio and was run as a collective; while Aurora marched on, so did MP Productions, Calcutta Movietone and Indrapuri (erstwhile Madan) Studio. Except MP Productions, the rest largely became space-on-rent, including the two studios of New Theatres. Uttam's exceptional stardom from the mid-1950s onwards meant that the 'need' for the old and grand studio system was over. Why that was so is integral to our story and we will come back to it soon.

RETHINKING A MIXED LEGACY

In spite of the strides taken in cinematic form and taste and the presence of towering figures, the legacy of the period is mixed. This had to do with the incapacity to record an identifiable contemporary imagery, that eventually held back cinema of that period from emerging into a viable idiom of the times. As Manishita Dass writes: "From its very inception, Indian cinema['s] … development is marked by a double movement—simultaneously toward and away from the modern—on a thematic as well as on a stylistic level, and by a preoccupation with tradition."[20] This evaluation held true for decades to come, mostly from Leftist cultural historians. A sweeping overview would reveal that Bengali cinema was caught in a time warp that provided limited escape from an embedded bondage to the socio-mythical in content and the theatrical in style. At the same time, one need not get too carried away by hard-fisted Leftist critics who found little merit in any cinematic form that has not fitted into their constricted idea of purposeful cinema. The fact that IPTA turned to cinema without delay (mid-1940s) is an ironic rebuff to the facetious suspicion of the medium harboured by Leftist writers. There are many instances when Leftist judgements considered celluloid a doomed and dreadful prospect, with many continuously denouncing Uttam's cinema as reeking of greasepaint-aided bourgeois escapism.

Rather, one is likely to be much better rewarded if one looks closely at individual films during that period. Instead of wallowing in what cinema of the 1930s and 1940s couldn't *be*, younger scholars have interrogated them as what they are: probing into their cinematic strengths, their populist postures, their mixed genres and their ambiguous relation to Bengali culture's assimilated arrogance. Subhajit Chatterjee[21] refers to variations in theme and format of conjugality in films like *Abhinaya* (1938), *Garmil* (1942), *Samadhan* (1943), *Dui Purush* (1945) and *Gnayer Meye* (1951), seeing them as participants in larger debates around colonial modernity. Madhuja Mukherjee[22] pays close attention to *Devdas*, *Daktar* and *Chandidas* before moving to films like *Alibaba* (1936) and *Avatar* (1941), both revealing multiple historical trajectories of Bengali cinema. Bhaskar Sarkar[23] mentions *Bhuli Nai* (1948), *Diner Pore Din* (1949) and *Beyallish* (1951) as unabashedly reflecting a stimulating moment in the history of the emerging Indian nation-state. Scholars have also pointed out that a spate of ghostly thrillers—*Kalochaya, Bhairab Mantra, Jighangsha, Kankal, Sanket, Adrishya Manush, Chupi Chupi Ashe* and *Hanabari*—made between 1948 and 1953 hints towards a time of indeterminate productivity in Bengali cinema. To this list of exceptions one should add films like Pramathesh Barua's bank-breaking futurist comedy *Bengal 1983* (1932), Charu Roy's *Bengalee* (1936), Sisirkumar Bhaduri's *Talkie of Talkies* (1937)—a sardonic film where he played a professor of 'Hegelian dialectics'—and DG's oddly but characteristically titled *Cartoon* (1949). The final example would be Uday Shankar's *Kalpana* (1948), though it was not a Bengali-language film per se. Whatever these films were, they cannot be abandoned to the alleged gallery of pansy mythologicals and staid socials. Hence, any effort to ghettoise Bengali cinema would be to forcefully go against the nuances of its actual practice.

In fact, the claim of a new scholarship goes beyond pointing out the limitations of Leftist prejudice. They ask us to question what has been entrenched as an elemental binary in Bengali cinema: the merry division of its long history into *before* Ray and *after* Ray. This division has been the bequest of socialist dominance in film criticism, which has often claimed that the Film Society movements from the late 1940s onwards signified the 'true' emergence of film consciousness in Bengal. This has led the socialist critics to draw a simplistic equivalence between historical and cinematic production, turning them blind to the tensions embodied within the film form itself. In other words, by wrongly trying to see cinema history as a prototype of historical materialism, they have often remained oblivious to cinema's potential to disrupt the obvious. This inherent radical potential of cinema was something to which Tagore so early wanted to draw attention. And no other cinematic moment achieved this disruption with more transformative effect in Bengali cinema than Uttam Kumar's stardom.

OF MANNER BORN

But there is more to this period than just a mixed legacy of film craft. For example, if imperial interest, lively public debate, sophistication in cinematic environs and breakthrough in art and sound of cinema technology signified irrevocable changes, there were also compelling continuities, embodied by men rather than machines. In other words, there were a number of actors, technicians and directors who had made a mark in the silent period and continued to work, successfully, into the talkie period, each marking for them a legacy that was impossible to deny. Durgadas Banerji, Kanan Debi, Pramathesh Barua were key figures in the sound era after having started in the 'silent' years. Sisirkumar Bhaduri, Naresh Mitra, Ahindra Chaudhuri were also products of the pre-talkie period but made successful transitions. So did directors Madhu Bose and Nitin Bose. Debaki Bose and Phani Majumdar belonged largely to the talkie era and continued to work well into the 1950s. So did actors Dhiraj Bhattacharjee, Radhamohan Bhattacharjee, Tulsi Chakraborty, Rabin Majumdar, Chhabi Biswas, Pahari Sanyal, Jahar Ganguly, Sadhana Bose, Yamuna Barua, Bharati Debi, Malina Debi, Chandrabati Debi, Chhaya Debi, all of them having found degrees of success in the 1940s. Bengali cinema of the 1930s and 1940s is an elaborate compendium of their collective talents. They often directed each other, collaborated and acted in the same film, many of which have managed to overcome the ravages of time and taste. Many of them also continued to be revered thespians till well past Uttam's attainment of stardom. The 'sound era' stars and actors were joined by litterateurs Premankur Atorthi, Shailajananda Mukhopadhyay, Premendra Mitra and Nazrul Islam in scripting and direction while singers and musicians Pankaj Mallik, Kundanlal Saigal, R.C. Boral, Timirbaran Bhattacharya and K.C. Dey secularised cinema soundtrack. In terms of its own goals (and not critical reception) Bengali cinema in those decades was a robust affair with a new-found soundscape, dramatic socials, lures of longing and romantic pursuits; while its temperamental actors were beginning to taste the spoils of fame.

No actor represents cinema between the early 1920s and mid-1930s more temperamentally than Durgadas Banerji. Born to a rich landowning family in 1893, Durgadas grew up obsessed with acting, even though he came to Calcutta to study painting. Later, he took up the job of a title-writer and scenario painter at Madan's company. A chance meeting with Naresh Mitra, actor and director, opened the doors to acting. Mitra brought the young man, suave and handsome, to meet Sisirkumar Bhaduri, his co-founder in Taj Mahal Film Company. They signed Durgadas for *Chondronath*, a film that made the actor's stellar career. Durgadas, a trained oil painter, was said to be averse to the use of harsh colours for his palette. In his acting, he seemed to prefer the same. Having seen Hollywood films in his sophomore years and not yet corrupted by the loud styles of theatre, Durgadas tried a more natural style, largely unknown to either the industry or the audience. Though the silent films had little by way of subtlety, Durgadas continued to impress. He found success with Madan's Bankim Chandra adaptations as well as hits such as *Rajani* and *Kanthahar*. The Bankim adaptation

Durgeshnandini, where he played Osman, was reportedly the first Indian film to have a formal exhibition in Europe and the delighted audiences named him 'Douglas Fairbanks of the East'. At the time he entered cinema, Durgadas was also called to the theatre. This was much more difficult terrain because Bengali stage had Sisir Bhaduri, Anindra Chaudhuri, Indu Mukhopadhyay and Jogesh Chowdhury, all of whom could give, during their time, the finest of stage actors anywhere a run for their money. Durgadas stood his ground and created a counter-style, reserved and dignified, that would stand in sharp contrast to the larger than life theatricality of the quartet. Between the mid-1920s and at least the mid-1930s, Durgadas dominated the screen and shared the stage with equal ease, creating a 'box office' that was unmatched till Uttam's. John Barrymore-like, he made a successful transition from silent films to talkies, making best use of his voice and his maturing style. His New Theatres musicals *Chondidas* and *Vidyapati* were milestones; while *Thikadar* (1940) and his swansong *Priyo Bandhobi*—released days before he died in 1943 of cirrhosis of the liver—are considered fine testaments to his virtuoso style.

Elegant, handsome, full of the pride of his birth and a stentorian voice that could stun the air, Durgadas signalled a shift in performative tradition. He was the first Bengali matinee idol—a generous, temperamental, authoritative figure—who counted Prithviraj Kapoor among his dear friends. In his short life, in his success across both stage and film and in his immense popularity with women, he reminded the cinema literate of Hollywood actor Rudolph Valentino. He was also among the first to have succumbed to abject alcoholism—a trap of fame and fortuity that later engulfed, among many others, K.L. Saigal, Pramathesh Barua, Geeta Dutt, Riwik Ghatak and even, to an extent, Uttam himself. Uttam's success reminded old-timers of Durgadas because for them, Durgadas' baton, in spite of him having a very dissimilar background, had successfully passed on to Uttam. While this is not entirely erroneous, closer scrutiny will reveal that Uttam's natural felicity and sophistication was as much an improvement over Durgadas', erect, high-collared stuffiness as was that of Durgadas' over his peers. It is indeed ironic that naysayers taunted Uttam with the sarcastic 'here comes the new Durgadas' when the young clerk faced the harsh lights of the studio in his salad days. That the taunt would one day become a banner of success for Bengal's biggest ever star was not for the studio hangers-on to foretell.

If Durgadas was a stylist, Pramathesh Barua was a romantic, who regaled in merging his real life with his over the top screen portraits. He was a populist and mannerist and was keen to infuse certain artistry in Bengali cinema, though not always with success.

He was, like Banerji, moody and sentimental but unlike the actor, Barua was a man of many faculties—actor, producer, director, and, most importantly, a maker of cultural taste and prototype. Born in 1903 into a tiny royal estate in Assam's Gouripur, Barua grew up as a big-game hunting royal heir but soon came to study in Calcutta's Presidency College, where he learnt about films and also the freedom struggle. Soon he found himself in Europe, and with a letter of recommendation from Tagore, stopped to learn the craft of cinema, first from Ernst Lubitsch and then Rene Clair. Among other things, he imported 'artificial lighting' to Bengali cinema with his first production *Aporadhi* (1931). He also directed the futuristic comedy *Bengal 1983*, whose audacity did not go down well with the audience. He was close friends with both DG and Debaki Bose. And because he was not from the professional stage, he could often break free, both as director and actor, from the fatal embrace of theatre on the moving image. The films he made in the early 1930s for his own firm, Barua Pictures, fared poorly but at New Theatres he created a new aesthetics of cinema, a new cultural prototype and a memorable screen persona; while managing—in *Mukti*—to use a Tagore song for the first time in a film. Apparently, on watching *Devdas*, Sarat Chandra Chattopadhyay walked up to Barua, held his hand and said: "If I was born to write *Devdas*, you were born to play it."

But more than any technology or being chic, Barua most memorably imported the stately temperament that he inherited to a notoriously perfidious domain of mass entertainment. Naturally, he was doomed. Like his peers, he left New Theatres in the late 1930s but unlike them, who were called to better opportunities, Barua simply walked away one fine morning. That was vintage Barua. Among his last endeavours, *Sesh Uttor* (1942) is in good measure a highly watchable film. He died in 1951, when he was forty-eight, even younger than Durgadas, mostly thanks to drinking but he was sickly of health too. Even though Durgadas was a bigger star, Barua was the first Bengali performer to have created a cult around him. An entire era in the late 1930s to early 1940s has come to be known as the 'age of Barua'. In a notable essay, sociologist Ashish Nandy wrote: "Few public figures epitomized so neatly in their personalities the transition from the relatively self-contained world of the traditional landed gentry to the world of modern, monetized, mass entertainment and the demands of urban, impersonal, cosmopolitan living."[24] Barua embodied this change, most visibly in the figure and person of the protagonist. It was thanks to Barua's bequest that from the 1940s onwards better Bengali films almost inevitably have an urbane, enlightened protagonist who is at heart a would-be cosmopolitan or is already one. Uttam brought this figuration to its most robust and effortless climax, though in ways very different from what Barua's effeminate, maudlin exertions would have otherwise recommended.

But in spite of their persuasive legacies, neither Durgadas nor Pramathesh was the veritable predecessor of Uttam Kumar. If there was one figure who was the genuine pioneer of the new performative 'style' that Uttam had made his own, it was Chhabi Biswas. Born in 1900 to an aristocratic family on Beadon Street, Sachindranath De Biswas breathed theatre in what was the most histrionic of neighbourhoods in Calcutta's north. His sharp features earned him the name Chhabi, which means 'picture', and stayed with him when he joined the pictures in his 30s. He debuted in 1936 with *Annapurnar Mondir*. By 1940, when Durgadas was ageing, Biswas was the younger Turk (along with Jahar Ganguly). But he did not fall for the heavily mannered style of either Durgadas or Barua. In fact, notwithstanding the customary theatre training, Biswas gradually liberated screen acting by infusing a distinct individuality, a character-specific body language and a next-door credulity that were never the forte of any of his illustrious precursors.

In the 1950s Biswas managed, with considerable ease, to shift to playing figures of authority, empathy and reverence in many films with Uttam in the lead. But that was the lesser part of his accomplishment. The better part was reserved for Satyajit Ray. Before his active life was tragically cut short by a fatal car accident in 1962 he had starred in three leading roles with Ray (*Jalsaghar*, *Devi* and *Kanchenjunga*). All the three roles were written with Biswas in mind, something not common with Ray. Biswambhar Roy, the egotistic, feudal, antiquated zamindar in *Jalsaghar*, is indeed an exceptional study of a man who stood, tragically, against the currents of his time. But Ray was not his only call to greatness. Chhabi Biswas appeared in Tapan Sinha's *Khoniker Otithi* (The Guest, 1959), *Khudito Pashan* (The Hungry Stone, 1960) and most memorably in *Kabuliwala* (The Man from Kabul, 1957); or in stellar roles in *Headmaster* (1958), *Shashibabur Sansar* (The World of Shashibabu, 1959) and the national award-winning *Dada Thakur* (The Humorist, 1962). There was also Rajen Tarafdar's powerful study of a stubborn provincial landlord in *Antariksha* (The Space beyond the Sky, 1957). There are many other impressive roles as the ageing father, the enabling guardian, the unimpeachable orthodox, and often as an embodiment of a stern, formidable but in the end 'empathisable' patrician of a generation past. His sudden death robbed Bengali cinema of one of its paramount figures.

Often together on screen, Uttam and Chhabi were as good as it gets, as assuring of greatness as would be fitting to either. Suffice to say, if there had been no Chhabi-da, perhaps there would have been no Uttam either. Uttam has recalled time and again his sense of awe and wonder at watching Chhabi-da on the sets and on screen. Biswas's sudden death left him distraught. Perhaps as a tribute to the thespian who virtually taught him to act, he confessed imitating, unsuccessfully, Biswas's stellar turn in *Jalsaghar* in *Stree*, where Uttam played a floundering aristocrat unable to live up to the demands of modernity. But otherwise, Uttam was the most obliging inheritor of Biswas' legacy. Chhabi Biswas signalled a distinctive turn in performative art with his endearing fidelity to effortless naturalism while importing for the protagonist an undeniable weight of persona. In Uttam, that turn found its most delightful fulfilment. Apart from Uttam and Soumitra Chatterjee no male actor in the second half of the 20th century signifies so richly and so thickly the cultural heights that Bengali cinema's performative practice could reach.

BOYS TO MEN

The post-Barua phase in Bengali cinema—the mid-1940s to be precise—had a number of good actors and many of them were claimants to the so-called trophy of a matinee idol. But the foremost among them, Pahari Sanyal and Jahar Ganguly, were both late-comers to cinema and hence were already reaching their forties when Durgadas and Pramathesh vacated the screen. They appeared in a number of leading roles and with aplomb but with each passing year the need for younger lead actors was felt. This was a need that could not be filled by actors such as Dhiraj Bhattacharya or Nitish Mukhejee who, in spite of their formidable screen presence, never really had any claims to the leading man's mantle, either in the 1940s or later.

In fact, there was no dearth of young aspirants too, even though talent was not necessarily in abundance. The most promising of the younger lot was Rabin Majumdar, Radhamohan Bhattacharya and Asit Baran, all of whom debuted in the early 1940s. A protégé of Barua, Majumdar succumbed to alcoholism no sooner had success come his way in *Shapmukti* (1940) and *Garmil*. He could never find his feet again. Radhamohan Bhattacharya, who had a stiff, taciturn style, never took cinema to be more than an avocation. Neither was he a box-office draw. Even after the much-noted debut in *Udayer Pathe*, he refused to be affianced to cinema, preferring a life of scholarly pursuits and was, in fact, agnostic to fame. Asit Baran, a thorough gentleman, was of considerable likeability but no charm. A top draw before Uttam's rise, he had a conspicuous career for over ten years, starting from 1941's *Pratisruti*. Thirteen years Uttam's senior, by the mid-1950s he quietly made way for the rising star. He would shift gears, from being the lead actor in early Uttam canon to playing a friend, romance-rival, brother and eventually a father-like figure in the mid-1970s.

Both Radhamohan and Asit Baran were introduced by New Theatres, along with Ratin Banerjee (*Shodhbodh*, 1942), who vanished, Jyotiprakash Bhattacharya (*Minakkhee*, 1942), who committed suicide, Raja Gangopadhyay (*Anjangarh*), who died young in a car accident, and the obscure Debi Mukhopadhyay (*Pratibad*, 1948). Samar Kumar (*Nobin Jatra*) and Prabirkumar (*Antariksha*) were two other young debutants who melted into oblivion after their initial promise. An intriguing case was the Lucknow-born Talat Mahmood, who learnt Bengali when he found a foothold in Calcutta for the tremolo in his voice. But his handsome looks beckoned him to the screen and he appeared against Kanan Debi (*Rajlakshmi*, 1945). He took the name Tapan Kumar and continued to sing and act in both Bengali and Hindi films till he left Calcutta for good in 1949.

One actor with whom Uttam had limited traffic despite being a contemporary was Utpal Dutt, much of whose life was spent in theatres, Shakespearean and otherwise. Dutt was not strictly a professional actor, using his earnings from films, whether in Bombay or in Calcutta, to fund his radical and outspoken plays. He was a man of letters and of strong political views. His early screen outings are mostly innocuous and way below his talent. It was only from the 1970s onwards that Satyajit Ray repeatedly cast Dutt in a slew of dazzling roles. Dutt and Uttam together have few moments of spark—one being *Soptopodi*'s iconic *Othello* scene (where Uttam lip-synced to Dutt's unfogettable rendition of the Moor), while *Chowrongee* was another one. But they starred together in several other films, almost none of which recommends itself to remembrance, *Amanush* included. That's an awful lapse indeed.

Like Utpal Dutt, Soumitra Chatterjee—Ray's favourite actor and an iconic figure in his own right—was never part of Uttam's so-called circle that took shape around his stardom. In fact, he was long considered a rival and a political adversary of Uttam. Satyajit Rays' later conviction about Uttam being the actor nonpareil was not an uncontested certification for many of Ray's own admirers. In Uttam's posthumous attainment of stature of legendary collective affection, Ray's conviction now seems natural, but it would have been very different in the 1960s, when Ray was the touchstone of cinema's intellectual authority, and Ray's staple Soumitra was considered an embodiment of the former's vision. Hence, given Soumitra's debut success with Ray in 1959's *Apur Sansar* (The World of Apu), younger critics and cinephiles began to hail Soumitra as the perfect counterfoil to the allegedly easy charm of Uttam. In person too, the two were very different. Soumitra had a good university education, had worked in radio broadcasting, was a talented young elocutionist, edited a literary magazine, was tutored by thespian Sisirkumar Bhaduri, and to top it all, had found lavish favour with the tall man who became Indian's ambassador to world cinema. Uttam had none of the above. Uttam's fame came not because of his background, but in spite of it; and he allegedly possessed the aura of the distant star, far away from the probing eyes of art cinema. Hence a somewhat allegorical but calibrated 'rivalry' between them became a savoured pastime for a generation, notwithstanding the fact that in real life, neither of them, friends and colleagues as they were, ever endorsed any sense of professional one-upmanship. In fact, as Soumitra has revealed, they often met clandestinely at Great Eastern Hotel and had a good laugh over a few pegs of their preferred scotch about the apparent existence of rival gangs crying hoarse to compare the 'greatness' of one against the other.

But in 'reel' life, when the two favourites of the two 'warring' camps came to be part of a film, it whetted popular appetite. And it happened quite early. Soumitra and Uttam were pitted against each other, for the first time and most memorably, in Tapan Sinha's *Jhinder Bondi*. In this film, Soumitra not only matched steps with Uttam in a famous sword-fighting scene, but even surpassed him in places as the wily villain Mayurvahan. Even with a double role, Uttam looked comparatively defensive in this costume drama. Later in that decade, they came together in *Aparichito* (The Stranger), an erratic adaptation of Dostoevsky's *The Idiot*. This film had a complex script with Uttam's pompous Rogozhin pitted against the innocence of Soumitra's Prince Myshkin. In this film too, both of them rose to the occasion, even though Uttam took long strides in the latter half of the film as his character molds into an obsessive rogue. In both these films, Soumitra benefited from being pitted against the charisma and power of Uttam rather than the other way around. And why this was so was to become clear in the next decade. In the 1970s, they came together in *Stree* (The Wife), but here Uttam ran away with the accolades as a whimsical, moody, decadent Calcutta aristocrat. Soumitra's role as an inquisitorial photographer was unconvincing. Two years later, Soumitra suffered another coup in *Jodi Jantem*, a film loosely based on a Perry Mason thriller. The film itself is nothing to write home about but Uttam's P.K. Basu—the pipe-smoking retired advocate turned detective—is an absolute treat. In the late 1970s, they were cast in forgettable outings such as *Dorpochurna*, *Pankhiraj* and finally *Pratisodh*, the last atrocity having been released after Uttam's death. But nothing was nearly as appalling as an awful adaptation of *Devdas* (1979). Both of them were well past their prime and were severely miscast, but somehow, here too, Uttam's Chunilal was borderline believable, especially when pitted against an ageing

Soumitra's pathetic 'young' protagonist. It goes to show the lack in both imagination and industry of the Bengali cinema establishment that it could not exploit the combined talents of these two actors, their appeal to their respective constituencies and their (imagined) rivalry for creating more substantive cinematic material.

In one case, however, the possibility of cinematic history was squandered by Uttam himself. In the mid-1950s, while recovering from a fracture, Satyajit Ray went back to the script of *Ghare Baire* (Tagore's *Home and the World*), which he had formalised some years prior. This time, he informally offered the role of Sandip to Uttam. Uttam, after having considered it, turned the role down, reasoning that it was too early in his career to play the crafty nationalist. Ray pursued for a while and in fact, wrote a more detailed treatment with Soumitra in mind for Nikhilesh and Suchitra Sen for Bimala. But problems persisted and the film got stalled. When revived decades later with a different cast (Soumitra played Sandip), Ray's film failed to carry the genius of his earlier films. The unmade *Ghare Baire* is one of those *if* films and would have been the original cast's big triumph. Uttam, of course, had more than made up for his foolish refusal to play Sandip by signing for *Nayak* ten years later. But that triangle of Uttam–Suchitra–Soumitra never ever materialised on Bengali screen. Uttam is also said to have given a pass to the role of the Sikh truckdriver in Ray's *Abhijan* (The Expedition, 1962), which was also later played by Soumitra. But this claim, however interesting, remains unsubstantiated.

Their respective dominions notwithstanding, until the time Uttam was in command, none of Soumitra's non-Ray films, in spite of some them being decent cinema, could barely hope to match Uttam's in either box-office appeal or general impact. In comparison to Uttam's undisputed stardom, Soumitra was a talented Ray actor and, in some cases, an occasional visitor into Uttam's terrain. On the other hand, Ray's *Nayak*, in time, took away from Soumitra any exclusive claim to having been the more insightful of the two actors. That equity remained intact till Uttam's death. Uttam lived and died the star that he was (and an actor of no less talent), and it was only with his death that the comparison, fragile as it always was, collapsed.

Interestingly, Soumitra, unburdened by any comparison with Uttam and unhinged from Ray's overwhelming shadow, managed to come into his own in the 1980s. If a handful of cinemagoers did come to fill in the seats in the gaping darkness that was Bengali cinema, it was because of some of Soumitra's extraordinary roles (specially, *Atonko*, 1986; *Koni*, 1984 and *Ekti Jibon*, 1988). He could comfortably sidestep the grand idiocy of the cinema of that decade and could hoard for posterity a series of brilliant portrayals that came his way. Some more characters he played in the ensuing years are now proving to be the only takeaway from the vacuous inheritance of Bengali cinema from the last three decades.

Incidentally, it was Uttam who was to play the passionate, protective swimming coach Khitish-da in Saroj De's *Koni*, an uplifting film about a swimming aspirant's relentless struggle to overcome poverty, nepotism and apathy to emerge as a champion. Uttam had given word to the film's writers that he would lose weight and take to swimming again. It was to be the film that would belatedly be his declaration of stepping down from the insufferable mantle of the hero that Uttam found himself chained to. Two months after his commitment, Uttam passed away. Initially stalled, *Koni* was revived with Soumitra as Khitish-da. Jayanta Bhattacharya, the script-writer, has claimed in his book on Uttam that not long after shooting began, he saw Uttam in his dreams. And he seemed to be saying, "Do not worry about the fate of *Koni*. Pulu (Soumitra) is doing it after all. He would give it his best." Call it fortune or fortitude, Soumitra's brilliant portrayal in the film, recalls Bhattacharya, made Ray call Khitish-da his peak as an actor. In *Koni*, hence, met a posthumous legacy, and also perhaps an imaginary friendship between two of the tallest male actors in all of Bengali cinema.

There were others too, contemporaries of both. Kali Banerjee and Basanta Choudhury, who appeared in the late 1940s and early 1950s respectively; and had long and parallel careers with that of Uttam, never could or did make any claim to his position. Exceptions aside, neither of them were anywhere near the prodigious talents of Bikash Roy, Bhanu Banerjee and Tarun Kumar. They were not really star material, though they were integral, in fact imperative, to Uttam's sweeping success. One must not forget the very genial Anil Chatterjee, who has the distinction of having worked with the quartet of Ray, Ghatak, Sinha and Sen, and was also one of Uttam's most capable co-actors. There were also actors such as Dilip Mukherjee, Nirmal Kumar, Ashim Kumar, Prasanta Kumar and others who had appeared in supporting roles. In the 1960s, Biswajit and Subhendu, both Chatterjees, and in the end 1970s, Victor Banerjee, Dipankar Dey and Mithun Chakraborty shared the screen with Uttam, who was by then a bit of a mentor for them. There were also other younger actors—Samit Bhanja, Sontu Mukherjee, Swarup Dutta, for example—who came to enjoy some renown from the late 1960s onwards.

Each of these men, across generations and decades, had more than a thing or two going for them, but none could bring to the table talent, charm and aura in equal measure; or carried that artful and evasive gene of stardom. Uttam did. Moreover, he was aided, doubtlessly, by a number of conditions, chances, fortuities while managing to avoid the inevitable booby traps of fame in his early days. That mattered. We have to wait a little more to know how.

DAYS OF DISQUIET

Whatever be the tensions *inside* the form of cinema and the function of its leading actors (till the early 1950s), one could not hope to understand that decade in Bengal unless one was out on the streets. Calcutta was not unused to public protests, at least since the early years of the 20th century. From the first, eventually annulled, proposal to partition Bengal in 1905 to the ill-willed bills and laws, to deaths of nationalist leaders, Calcutta had achieved notoriety for being able to summon to quick congress agitating crowds. But nothing had prepared the city for what was to come in the 1940s. A succession of monumental tragedies not only undid the city's recompenses and charms but also had it bloodied to the bones.

Colonial Calcutta's fate was tied to the world and the world, by the early 1940s, was spinning out of control. No one recorded it better than Rabindranath Tagore. In May 1941, Tagore gave a powerful lecture at Viswa Bharati, later christened *Crisis of Civilization*. Here, he lamented how Europe's barbarity was "tearing up humanity in an orgy of devastation. From one end of the world to the other the poisonous fumes of hatred darken the atmosphere". Tagore went on to proclaim that the "the spirit of violence which perhaps lay dormant in the psychology of the West, has at last roused itself and desecrates the spirit of Man".[25] Tagore's observation was characteristically acute and prophetic. But little did Tagore know that the Empire would also bring in its wake bombing, arson, bloodshed, famine and an unprecedented scale of mass migration to his own people; little did he know that the Empire, on its final demise would leave behind a state deep in self-loathing; a nation truncated; a people pulverised; and a city on the verge of collapse. And all of this, within less than a decade after his death.

Tagore's own death three months from the day of that prophetic speech was the first of many public tragedies. His passing away signified the passing of an era and the beginning of what would be the last great period of Bengal's long romance with progressive ideas. Calcutta had congregated in thousands for Tagore's final journey to a crematorium in north Calcutta. Fifteen-year-old Uttam was among that crowd, wondering in his adolescent mind about the extent of loss that could bring a multitude into a conspicuous display of collective mourning.

With Tagore's death, the tortuous decade of the 1940s unveiled itself. What blighted Calcutta cannot be explained in terms of its own doing. Throughout its history, Calcutta had been a steady receptor of the Empire's boom, strapped to colonial circuits of mobility, technology, power and capital. No wonder then that with the advent of the 1940s, Calcutta was to become the inevitable first casualty of the Empire's approaching doom. Twice in 1942 and then more heavily in 1943, Japanese planes bombed Calcutta, adding extreme paranoia to already debilitating wartime exigencies, uprooting scores of people from their home and hearth. Then came the Bengal Famine, orchestrated by the colonial state at Churchill's insistence, when they stubbornly refused to stop the diversion of grains to feed its forces abroad. The catastrophe claimed thousands of lives and had put the rural economy in peril for years to come. Historians now count the 1943 Bengal Famine as an act of genocide and the most grievous price that India paid for WWII. The violent, visceral impact of the famine haunted a generation, especially those who were close to Left organisations. In August 1946, communal violence broke out in Calcutta on a scale hitherto inconceivable, leading to eventual ghettoisation and a new kind of spatial apartheid. Before the scars of that conflagration were to be healed came the Partition and the deluge of refugees to the city from East Pakistan, the scale of which was, again, extraordinarily daunting. Nothing had prepared the new Indian civic bodies for this massive offensive on the city's infrastructure. The fact that planning was minimal, execution dismal and corruption ubiquitous made any hope of purposeful rehabilitation a matter of indefinite prospect.

Calcutta was in shambles, seeing its daily life sink pervasively into an endless perpetuation of dread. When the British Empire finally collapsed, it left in its wake a Calcutta, once its gilded 'Second City', in a state of wounded paralysis. A range of crises—homelessness, displacement, hunger and alienation—brought the city under siege. In 1947, there was new hope, yes, but it had to be dragged to its full prospect over the mayhem that was laid down on the streets of Calcutta. In a recent anthology, leading historian Sekhar Bandyopadhyay, after cataloguing the long list of devastations, says:

> These were the best and the worst of time, occurring in crowded sequence, churning up catastrophe and exhilaration in equal measure and ruthlessly compressing vast, unprecedented, indeed, unimaginable changes in urban landscape and demography within a span of little more than ten years. The city that was forged in and by these years was a very different Calcutta.[26]

For years after the 1940s and Partition, Calcutta (also Bengal) was bound to that moment of convulsion that was still in near and nervous memory; while Calcutta's air was still haunted by the surgery, a new kind of perception of life and objects came to be formed.

FOR A NEW CULTURE TO COME

The disquiet of the decade had no precedent. The scale of mass mobility, malady, death and disenfranchisement necessitated a new kind of *understanding* of the present. But there was no artistic prototype which could satisfactorily provide a method to comprehend the scale of that convulsion. By the mid-1930s, artists, writers and intellectuals in Bengal were coming under Leftist influence, decisively moving away from the broadly romantic-liberal ethos of which Tagore had been the archetype. As the vehemence of the 1940s unveiled itself, there was an even greater need to push for radical rethinking, which locally found voice in the Kallol group of poets; and nationally in the IPTA, formed in 1943. With committed young artists under its banner, IPTA systematically sought to develop a new critical–cultural practice where art and activism would coexist.

There was no way cinema could refuse to embrace this restive period. While Bengali popular cinema was searching for new possibilities, a different kind of cinema gradually took shape: for lack of a better word which came to be known as *art-house* cinema. A product of film society movements, European influences and critical realist turns in literature and the arts, Bengali art-house cinema imported a humanist aesthetic and politically charged narrative, while turning away from the excesses of social dramas of the studio era. Heralded by a group of zealous and learned men and women, this kind of films was unseen and unfelt in not just Bengali but Indian cinema before.

It was inevitable that this new turn in cinema was to be led by the IPTA. Two principle protégées of IPTA, Nemai Ghosh and Ritwik Ghatak, brought the organisation's political angst, formal experimentation and radical aesthetics to Bengali cinema, though in Hindi there were already a couple of near-instances to that effect. What Ghosh and Ghatak brought to fore was cinema's capacity to correspond *with* and respond *to* the present through its own language, something at which the studio socials would baulk. The particular power of moving images to convert the accuracy of embattled space and time into an appropriate cinematic language was certainly not lost to them. As scholar Moinak Biswas says:

> It can be argued that the first moment when the city–cinema encounter produces a proper transition from enumerable to elaborated space was the early 1950s, the moment of post-independence planning and reconstruction, when the cinematic institution itself underwent a major transformation. Realism is the predominant category through which we have understood the changes, but it is instructive to see the specific relations that emerged between the new social realist content and film form.[27]

A number of films made between the mid-1940s and the early 1950s did, however, provide a template for the breakthrough works of Ghosh and Ghatak. Films such as *Udayer Pathe* (Towards the Dawn, 1944), *Dharti Ke Lal* (The Son of the Soil, 1946), *Neecha Nagar* (The Fallen City, 1946), *Diner Pore Din* (Days on End), *Babla* (The Schoolboy, 1951) and *Beyallish* ('42) show a movement away from the studio-produced dramas of the earlier decade. The films range from being about working-class desolation to the possibility of change and upliftment through collective action. Apart from the possibilities that these movies showed and the history that was unfolding around, three things had substantially altered the perception of cinema in those years. First, European art-house cinema opened itself to discerning viewers, most effectively through the inaugural International Film Festival of India in Calcutta in 1952. However, the Calcutta Film Society, founded by Satyajit Ray and others in 1947, had already made available a retinue of landmark films to cinephiles in the city. Second, cinema technology improved. Till well into the 1930s, the predominant camera was the Super Parvo. Then, the standard cinematographic equipment, especially for outdoors, was the impossibly stilted Mitchell. The WWII years made possible the access to the Cineflex, the cheap American remake of Arriflex 35 II, the first mass-produced 35 mm camera. Interestingly, the turn in Bengali cinema that propounded a new aesthetic had been undertaken through astonishing improvisations of the Mitchell; though by the mid-1950s cinematographer Subrata Mitra had bought an Arriflex II.[28] Third, the Indian Cinematograph Act of 1918, after a full three decades, was amended to set up the Central Board of Film Censors (CBFC) under Cinematograph Rules, 1951. The new board immediately found itself at war with the clause of 'freedom of speech and expression' enshrined in 19(1) of the Indian Constitution. Soon, the existing parameters of Article 19(2) were amended. As historian of film censorship Someswar Bhowmik says: "While by transference and selective adoption, the inherent philosophy of film censorship thus remained distinctly similar to that enunciated during the colonial period, important changes were wrought in the operative principles."[29] All these changes played a part in cinema of the 1950s.

The film that managed to tap into the zeitgeist better than others was Nemai Ghosh's only Bengali film *Chhinnamul* (The Rootless, 1951). As Samik Banerji recalls: "It was left to Nimai Ghosh in *Chhinnamul* (1951) to capture the essence of the *Nabanna*[30] experience for the cinema, with his ruthlessly authentic documentation of the migration from eastern Bengal to Calcutta after 1947."[31] Moinak Biswas echoes. He writes:

> *Chhinamul* is one of the first Indian films to show a political consciousness of the reality of the metropolis.... As we are invited by the film to witness the city of Calcutta, we are made aware in a quite unfamiliar and urgent way that we are in the midst of an intractable present, a present that cannot be escaped from because it has a special status of reality validated in the film, validated by cinema as a new political practice.[32]

Even more than Nemai Ghosh, Ritwik Ghatak saw cinema as a potent medium to bring into fruition the uncompromising, radical mission of art. In spite of his copious talent, reckless disorderliness, financial troubles and surrender to alcoholism militated against his desire for a more fulsome career in cinema. Ghatak could complete only eight full-length films, three of which—*Meghe Dhaka Tara* (The Cloud-Capped Star, 1960), *Komal Gandhar* (E-Flat, 1961) and *Subarnarekha* (The Golden Thread, 1965)—deal with Partition and constitute the basis of his international fame. It is impossible to see his cinema without its sociopolitical triggers, dominated by his Marxist leanings. Ghatak's formidable trilogy invests the Partition with the moral weight and irretrievability of the apocalypse. But the work that complemented *Chhinnomul* was *Nagorik* (The Citizen), Ghatak's first, unreleased film. *Nagarik* explores a middle-class family's descent into poverty while desperately trying to hold on to bhadralok mores. As littérateur and critic Sibaji Bandyopadhyay wrote: "It is undeniable that *Nagarik's* characters, like those of the trilogy, try to grapple with the problem of instantaneous switch in the substantive meaning of belonging."[33]

But the pioneering efforts and the exultant evaluation in learned circles cannot hide the fact that *Chhinnomul* and *Nagorik* were stilted and tacky in practice and pedantic and ponderous in content. They had neither the emotional connect of *Do Bigha Zameen* nor the moving lyricism of *Pather Panchali*. They are, in fact, highly revered samples of poorly made cinema. At the same time, their importance is undeniable as the prototype of a particularly charged moment in the cinema history of Bengal (and India).

THE MASTER OF EVERYDAY LIFE

The push to formal realism, political critique and radical aesthetics, given by Ghosh and Ghatak, did not remain exceptions. On the contrary, they became a sort of drive for new and young filmmakers. In fact, in three years, the arrival of Satyajit Ray amplified, several times, the appeal and intellectual authority of this new kind of cinema. Ray's case was different from IPTA's men. Along with the usual European influences, Ray was also a keen observer of Hollywood. He also developed a profound sense of the *visual* that he partly nurtured in Santiniketan and partly inherited, among others, from his father Sukumar Ray, a poet, illustrator and editor of consummate virtuosity. In fact, Ray came from a larger family of artistic talents who had given him a culturally rich and cosmopolitan upbringing and education that was more Tagorean than off-the-cuff Marxist.[34]

Ray had burst onto the scene with *Pather Panchali* (Song of the Road), a deeply etched human drama that changed the perception of Indian cinema forever, while also rebooting Bengali cinema. Listing a line of films from the 1930s to 1950s as precursors, Moinak Biswas has rightly claimed that *Pather Panchali*

> consolidated a great deal of their [Bengali cinema's] realist aspiration, while at the same time negating some basic attitudes underlying them. Their naturalistic tendencies were now shaped into an organic wholeness of perception; life was captured not only in its dramatic polarities but its effervescence, its unguarded moments.[35]

In another article Biswas expands on this idea. He writes:

> A great density and beauty of description suffuses the narrative as it moves freely between plants and animals, the human world and the natural cycle. The tapestry of sounds, colours and shapes is woven through a narrative voice which, as Apu grows up, shifts imperceptibility between outside and inside him.[36]

Ray's vision was so wholesome and yet so unique, so full of a breathing attachment to and empathy for his subject and yet so timeless, that it caused tumult. There are few experiences in cinema that can match up to the warmth, understated humour and sheer generosity of Ray's visual imagination. If there was ever a master of quotidian life, it was him. Naturally, a substantive segment of urban, educated viewership, unmoved by the studio era socials and longing for a more astute cinematic experience started to warm up to these films. It was soon conspicuous that the foundation of this new art cinema was not in its volubility, but its essence; not its saleability but its aesthetic; not its social acceptability but in its liberation of imagery. Bengali art cinema could now stake a claim to the red-carpet respectability of European cinema. Ray's emergence has hence been considered, rightly, a groundbreaking event.

Unlike many other practitioners of the craft, Ray was immaculately systematic and recondite in the pursuit of his art rather than being one drawn easily into the rigmarole of political and social upheavals unfolding around him. And that is precisely why he never directly dealt with the Partition. Moreover, Ray's body of work follows a well-anointed intellectual project. This project was to recount/retell the entire story of Bengali modernity all over again, through cinema. With the *Apu Trilogy* (1955, 1956, 1959) Ray explored the original theme of the decline of the rural idyll and the coming to the city of the orphaned teenager. The famous scene of the train's entry into the undisturbed landscape and its intrusion throughout the trilogy symptomises it as the enchanter-in-chief of modernity. *Jalsaghar* (The Music Room), *Devi* (The Goddess, 1960) and *Charulata* (The Lonely Wife, 1963) present three sovereign tensions in the flight to modernity: feudalism, Hindu orthodoxy and the question of women. They remain constitutive of Ray's overall trust in the incontestable but quiet, interrogative progress. *Tin Kanya* (Three Daughters, 1961), *Kanchenjunga* (Kanchenjunga, 1962), and even the double-bill *Kapurush O Mahapurush* (The Coward and the Holy Man, 1965) are part of this schema. The only exceptions were the comic fantasy *Parash Pathar* (The Philosopher's Stone, 1958) and the road movie *Abhijaan* (The Expedition, 1962). Ray did not find it fit to deal with the 'contemporary' at least till *Mahanagar* (The Big City, 1963). Here, for the first time, as Chandak Sengoopta[37] says, Nehruvian themes were put under the scanner of critical re-evaluation. Ray then undertakes two extended studies of exceptional individuals: that of a sensitive but fallible star (*Nayak*, 1966) and of an infallible and incisive detective of keen intelligence (*Chiriyakhana*, 1967). It was no surprise that in both, Uttam Kumar led an ensemble cast. Ray continued to expand into newer territories of concern and craft in the 1970s, not only through his grim Calcutta trilogy of *Pratidwandi* (The Adversary, 1970), *Seemabaddha* (Company Limited, 1971) and *Jana Aranya* (The Middleman, 1976) but also through his fabulous musical parables, detective stories and a historical, while going back to his uncompromising forte of realism from time to time. Ray is often incomparably thorough, brilliant, insightful and witty at the same time. He has given Indian cinema (and world cinema too) a body of exceptional films which remain embedded in cinematic memory.

AUTEURS AND INDIES

Mrinal Sen, who has often let his Marxist convictions overrun his artistic instincts, took a long time to find his oeuvre. He began with the Uttam-starrer *Raatbhor* (1955), a film which he has disowned ever since. He had a life-long distaste for greasepaint populism and more so for Uttam, about whom he never had a good word to say, not even at the memorial after the actors' death. That's of course a personal choice, but had he been less prudish and more accepting of the star's talents, Bengali cinema would have gained immensely. But Sen—a thorough gentleman and a man of liberal views otherwise—was trapped in a self-perpetuating echo chamber when it came to cinema. He made seven more films before his *Bhuban Shome* (1969) struck the right chord: between a wry narrator, a dry landscape and an amusing set of wily protagonists. Sen followed this piquant film with his Calcutta trilogy: *Interview* (1971), *Calcutta '71* (1972) and *Podatik* (The Guerilla Fighter, 1973). Sen, unlike Ray, is much less concerned with telling a story; or to probe a crisis through the turmoil of an individual. Sen's *city films* are about the ensemble, sometimes the crowd itself, which charge into the camera, fade in and out without notice, sink into chaos and corruption, creating a vortex of dysfunction that threatens to spill out of the screen. Or so was Sen's aim. Like Ghatak's early films, they are difficult to appreciate as cinema. Among the films that followed, *Mrigoya* (The Hunt, 1976), *Ekdin Protidin* (One Ordinary Day, 1979), *Kharij* (The Closed Case, 1982) and *Khondohor* (The Ruins, 1983) show a mellower, more judicious and matured Sen.

Among Bengali cinema's great quartet of auteurs (Ray, Ghatak, Sen and Sinha), Tapan Sinha was the cheeriest. Sinha, who had trained in sound engineering from London's Pinewood Studios, entered the scene in the 1950s and found a niche for his kind of *middle of the road* cinema soon. About his Uttam admiration we already know but Sinha was much more. In the language native to him, no one straddled the range of cinematic genres as he did; and no one had consistently been able to bring together a lyrical union of populist delights and critical overtures. Among his best are *Khudito Pashan* (The Hungry Stone), *Kabuliwala* (The Man from Kabul), *Nirjon Soikote* (The Lonely Beach, 1963), *Jotugriha* (House of Wax), *Atithi* (The Runaway, 1965), *Banchharamer Bagan* (The Garden of Delights), *Adalot o Ekti Meye* (A Woman at the Court, 1982) and *Ek Doctor Ki Maut* (1990). His three sequentially meaningful Calcutta films—*Aponjon* (The Kin, 1968), *Ekhoni* (The Present Moment, 1971) and *Harmonium* (1976)—are ingenuous and powerful urban documents told in a range of styles, including a portmanteau form in *Harmonium*, where the protagonist is the instrument itself.

The range, longevity and influence of these auteurs notwithstanding, there were several filmmakers who were staunchly independent, trying to develop a style of their own, even if they may not have covered enough ground to be called *auteurs*. And most of them remained disaffected by populism as such and Uttam's stardom in particular. A list like that should include the trio of Tarun Majumdar (*Polatok, Sonsar Simante, Sriman Prithwiraj*), Rajen Tarafder (*Antarikhho, Gonga, Palonko*) and Purnendu Patri (*Swopna Niye, Strir Potro, Chhera Tomsuk*). Then, there was that one distinguished film and its maker(s): Sambhu Mitra and Amit Maitra's *Ekdin Ratre*, Toru Mukhopadhyay's *Ingit* (1961), Parthapratim Chowdhury's *Chhaya Surjo* (1963), O.C. Ganguly's *Kinu Goalar Goli* (1964), Amar Ganguly's *Kanchonrongo* (1964), Utpal Dutt's *Ghoom Bhangar Gaan* (1965), Harisadhan Dasgupta's *Eki Onge Eto Roop* (1965), Barin Saha's *Tero Nodir Pare* (1966), Bhupendranath Sanyal's *Dheuer Por Dheu* (1966), Manju Dey's *Obhishopta Chambal* (1967), Nabyendu Chattopadhyay's *Adwitiya* (1968), Arundhati Mukherjee's *Podi Pishir Bormi Baksho* (1972), Ajit Gangopadhyay's *Muktisnan* (1977), Utpalendu Chakraborty's *Chokh* (1983), Raja Mitra's *Ekti Jibon* and others.

It must be noted that Tarun Majumdar directed Uttam as part of the ensemble directors' group *Yatrik*; O.C. Ganguly had originally cast Uttam in *Kinu Goalar Goli*; Harisadhan Dasgupta made the middling Uttam–Suchitra starrer *Komollota*; Parthapratim cast Uttam as Gana-da in *Jodubongsho*; and the cinema literate Purnendu Patri desperately wanted and failed to cast Uttam in Tagore's *Chaturango* and Premendra Mitra's *Telenapota Abishkar*, neither of which he eventually made.

Till the 1980s, many of the more talented makers, irrespective of the span of their career, avoided Uttam or ended up doing a poor film with him. Had they been more open to try him out, or if Uttam would have been less waspish about committing himself to intellectual cinema—especially in his later years—the shelf of Bengali cinema could have been very different. In the end, everyone lost out, thanks to the pointless disputes that art and popular cinema imagined between them. In an industry as modest as Bengali cinema, the two kinds of cinema should have more productively partnered with each other. But they did not; at least not widely. Thankfully Tapan Sinha and Satyajit Ray stayed away from this partisan entrapment, giving fine films, borrowing talents from both dispositions.

Moreover, there is also a problem of perception. Art cinema's insistent claims on critical attention and cinematic authority has caused three interconnected consequences. First, it obscured much of the assets of Bengali cinema before the 1950s, some of which I have tried to retrieve. Second, it managed to divide the previously monolithic world of Bengali cinema into two halves, the art house and the popular, which would stay in tense cohabitation for years to come. Third, so enormous was the intellectual authority of this kind of neo-realist cinema that it sought to overwhelm everything that did not measure up to its standards. Bengali popular cinema of the 1950s could have been the 'natural' casualty of art-cinema's self-glorifying solipsism.

But in actuality popular cinema thrived many times over. They were often accused of being populist, escapist, contrite or disingenuous; and yet they drew people to the halls, paid wages to cinema's working class, sustained an informed viewership and kept the industry solvent, in spite of several deterrents, till the early 1980s. In other words, the so-called 'low-brow' popular cinema subsidised art-house cinema's 'high-brow' ambitions. And that it did, and that it could go on doing it, is essentially because of Uttam Kumar.

Why and how did that happen? That's the tale that we are here to tell.

NOTES

1. Siddhartha Ghosh, 'Early Photography in Calcutta', in *Calcutta: Changing Visions, Lasting Images*, edited by Pratapaditya Pal, Mumbai: Marg Publications, 1990, pp. 143–158; Christopher Pinney, *The Coming of Photography in India*, New Delhi: Oxford University Press, 2008.
2. Samik Banerji, 'The Early Years of Calcutta Cinema', in *Calcutta: The Living City*, Vol. 2, *The Present and Future*, edited by Sukanta Chaudhuri, Oxford University Press, 2013 [1990], pp. 293–301.
3. Ranita Chatterjee, 'Journeys in and beyond the City: Cinema in Calcutta 1897–1939', Unpublished PhD thesis, University of Westminster, 2011, p. 60.
4. Moinak Biswas, 'Rich Tradition', *Frontline* 30:20 (18 October 2013), pp. 81–94.
5. For further discussion on theatre, see Parimal Ghosh, *What Happened to the Bhadralok*, Primus, 2016, and the adjoined references thereof.
6. For a detailed history of early cinema in Bombay, see Kaushik Bhaumik, 'The Emergence of the Bombay Film Industry', Unpublished PhD thesis, Oxford University, 2011.
7. Jayanta Kumar Ghosh, *Bratyojoner Bioscope*, Calcutta: Dey's Publishing, 2008.
8. Available at https://theprint.in/theprint-profile/hs-bhatavdekar-the-indian-who-created-a-motion-picture-14-years-before-dadasaheb-phalke/205710/.
9. Available at https://www.theguardian.com/film/2013/jul/25/birth-indias-film-industry-movies-mumbai.
10. For an elaborate discussion on early proto-studios, see Brian R. Jacobson, *Studios before the System: Architecture, Technology, and the Emergence of Cinematic Space*, Columbia University Press, 2015.
11. Chatterjee, 'Journeys in and Beyond the City', p. 69.
12. Sharmistha Gooptu, *Bengali Cinema: The Other Nation*, Delhi: Roli Books, 2010, p. 32.

13. Manishita Dass, *Outside the Lettered City: Cinema, Modernity, and the Public Sphere in Late Colonial India*, Oxford: Oxford University Press, 2016, p. 76.

14. See Madhuja Mukherjee (ed.), *Aural Films, Oral Cultures: Essays on Cinema the Early Sound Era*, Kolkata: Jadavpur University Press, 2012.

15. Rabindranath Tagore, 'A Letter Concerning the Moving Image', addressed to Murari Bhaduri, November 1929, translated by Madhurima Mukhopadhyay, in Mukherjee, *Aural films, Oral Cultures*, p. 86.

16. Chandak Sengoopta, *The Rays before Satyajit: Creativity and Modernity in Colonial India*, Oxford University Press, 2016, p. 382.

17. Gooptu, *Bengali Cinema*, pp. 65–66.

18. Madhuja Mukherjee, 'Inside a Dark Hall: Space, Place, and Accounts of Some Single-Theatres in Kolkata', *South Asian History and Culture* 8:2 (2017): 269–282, 272.

19. Quoted in Banerji, 'The Early Years of Calcutta Cinema', p. 298.

20. Dass, *Outside the Lettered City*, p. 31.

21. Subhojit Chatterjee, 'Remapping Transitions of Bengali Cinema into the 50s', *Journal of the Moving Image* 9 (2010): 117–146, 124.

22. Madhuja Mukherjee, 'Rethinking Popular Cinema in Bengal (1930s–1950s): Of Literariness, Comic Mode, Mythological and Other Avatars', *South Asian History and Culture* 8:2 (2017): 122–142.

23. Bhaskar Sarkar, *Mourning the Nation: Indian Cinema in the Wake of Partition*, New Delhi: Orient Blackswan, 2010, p. 137.

24. Ashish Nandy, *The Ambiguous Journey to the City: The Village and Other Odd Ruins of the Self in the Indian Imagination*, Oxford University Press, 2007 [2001], p. 59.

25. There are several sources for this speech. See, for example, Dr Dian Rahmani Putri, 'Critical Discourse Analysis Approach (CDA) in Rabindranath Tagore's Speech "Crisis in Civilization"', *Bali International Journal of Arts Humanities and Social Sciences Studies* 3:2 (February 2018): 19–25, 24.

26. Sekhar Bandyopadhyay, 'Introduction: Calcutta in History and Historiography', in *Calcutta: The Stormy Decades*, edited by Tanika Sarkar and Sekhar Bandyopadhyay, Delhi: Social Science Press, 2015, p. 4.

27. Moinak Biswas, 'From Space to Location', *Positions: East-Asia Cultures Critique* 25:1 (2017): 9–28, 14.

28. Madhuja Mukherjee, 'The Story of Arri: Imagined Landscapes, Emergent Technologies and Bengali Cinema', *Journal of the Moving Image* (2011): 61–80.

29. Someswar Bhowmik, 'Film Censorship in India: Deconstructing an Incongruity', in *Routledge Handbook of Indian Cinemas*, edited by K. Moti Gokulsing and Wimal Dissanayake, London and New York: Routledge Taylor and Francis, 2013, pp. 297–310, 299.

30. Landmark Bengali play that signalled the climactic cultural reach of All India Progressive Writers' Association.

31. Banerji, 'The Early Years of Calcutta Cinema', p. 299.

32. Moinak Biswas, 'The City and the Real: *Chhinnamul* and the Left Cultural Movement in the 1940s', in *City Flicks: Indian Cinema and the Urban Experience*, edited by Preben Kaarsholm, Calcutta: Seagull Books, 2007, pp. 40–59.

33. Sibaji Bandyopadhyay, *Sibaji Bandyopadhyay Reader*, New Delhi: Worldview Publications, 2012, p. 233.

34. For an excellent analysis of the bequests of Ray from his family, see Sengoopta, *The Rays Before Satyajit*.

35. Moinak Biswas, 'Modern Calcutta Cinema', in *Calcutta: The Living City*, Vol. 2, *The Present and Future*, edited by Sukanta Chaudhuri, Oxford University Press, 1990, pp. 302–315.

36. Moinak Biswas, 'Early Films: The Novel and Other Horizons', in *Apu and after: Re-visiting Ray's Cinema*, edited by Moinak Biswas, Calcutta: Seagull Books, 2005, pp. 37–79, 47.

37. Chandak Sengoopta, 'Satyajit Ray: Liberalism and Its Vicissitudes', *Cinéaste* 34:4 (2009): 16–22, 18.

4

FLOPMASTER GENERAL

Ever tried. Ever failed. No matter.
Try again. Fail again. Fail better.

—Samuel Beckett

IN 1951, a cartoon titled *Bengal's Hero,* appeared in the periodical *Acholpotro,* edited by the intractable Dipten Sanyal, whose pen was infamous for its caustic critique on matters of culture. The cartoon showed Uttam Kumar as an infant lying on the lap of a woman who is sitting, bent forward, in a cross-legged posture. They are in the manner of a mother cuddling her child; except that the waddling Uttam is holding within his embrace the neck of his (much-older) beloved, while uttering, with saccharine smugness, "Dear, do you love me?"

For the lampooner, Uttam—with his lack of credentials, or training in acting, or exposure to good education—had bared his vulnerability by staking his claim on a tall ambition. But his vulnerability wasn't only his own. This cartoon, for example, also hinted at the paucity of young new actors to play the female lead, the lack of which forced filmmakers to cast the youthful Uttam against actors who were all past his age. And this was just one of the problems that Bengali cinema found itself mired in. There were tensions that were far starker; tensions way beyond the concerns of cinema; or even the arts in general, as we have seen. In fact, it would not be an exaggeration to claim that the vast changes that the 1940s ushered in threatened to strip the prior decades of any sense of affirmation. But for Uttam, ensconced in his own tussles, the big picture was unavailable. Hence, among all the rants, rebuffs, asides and assorted projections of failure, the cartoon was a snub that had hurt him the most. It not only made fun of his debacles, but also infantilised him, hinting at the oedipal nature of his misplaced drive to be a leading man of celluloid. It was the unkindest cut of all.

Nevertheless, Uttam's early failures were not just a catalogue of his deficiencies but also bring to light a popular industry in churn. There could not have been a more fraught time than the end 1940s, when Uttam knocked on the door of the studios. The industry overlooked Uttam's arrival because he had nothing to offer that could provide major

112

relief from its entrenched difficulties. Hence, the apparent impossibility of Uttam's tall ambition and the difficulty of its appreciation do not sit uneasy on those beleaguered years. His failures seem natural and in keeping with the zeitgeist.

THUS CAME THE STRAGGLER

Except for the early death of his elder sister Putul, Uttam's childhood was largely uneventful. More than one large house in the winding Girish Mukherjee Road was occupied by the extended family of the Chatterjees. There was not much of financial comfort but there was plenty of company on indolent afternoons and balmy evenings. Most such large families had a strong paternalistic bent built on clearly defined structures of authority. So was the case here, which meant that there was little in the way of reckless adventure. Much of Uttam's reminiscences about his childhood refer to his innocent efforts to steal some time and chance to observe the elders during theatre rehearsals and secretly practice them on his own. Studies were important so far as not to fail a class. Otherwise, Uttam's attention was distributed between football and a secret pining to be on a public stage one day. Cinema was nowhere in the vicinity of his juvenile aspiration. It was theatre, if at all.

Between his leaving school in the early 1940s and his first, abortive entry into cinema in 1947, Uttam, or rather Arunkumar, seemed to have grown up through the restlessness of the period. As part of the populous, prominent, participatory neighbourhood of Bhawanipore, he was drawn to the protestations against the country's captivity; to the veneration for Subhash Bose; to rallies and processions to garner funds for the Indian National Army (INA); to collect aid for feeding the famished; or to functions where young men in tight-fitted clothes would sing full-throated peans about nationalist pride and blithely hope for a more just world. None of it, except a febrile and fragile sovereignty of a bifurcated nation-state actually materialised; and a partitioned Bengal, butchered repeatedly through the 1940s, was brought to its bruised knees.

Through the thick and thin of those wounded years, Uttam clutched to his love for acting. And help was at hand. The largish collective of the Chatterjees, like most middle-class joint households, nurtured an amateur group who regularly staged plays or the folk form *jatra*, for extended family, kin and the neighbourhood. Intermittently during his school years, Uttam would be part of amateur productions at home or at school. He later co-founded the Lunar Club that did what many Bengali cultural organisations did: staged plays, published a periodical and occasionally doubled as a social-service enterprise. Through his adolescence and teen years, Uttam took to the stage with the readiness of a fish taking to a pond. Lunar Club, Morsumi Club, Surid Samaj, and the Hilary Institute of Calcutta Port—these groups or platforms nurtured the young Uttam's amateur efforts at acting. He was not unsuccessful in making an impact among his friends, colleagues and relations. But there was nothing startling in his talent, either then or in his early years in the industry. When not called upon to duties to a long-suffering nation, he learnt singing, played soccer, trained in wrestling and mastered swimming. He was good in all of them, especially swimming, even if he saw them as preparation for a stint as an actor. But till his early 20s, Uttam did not show any marked willingness to be a professional performer. He adored acting and wanted to pursue it as long as the contrarian demands of livelihood allowed him to.

It was only after he got a job, found himself in a relationship with Gaurirani Ganguly and was called to a miniscule cameo in an unreleased film in 1947 that he gathered the courage to think about acting as a profession. At the same time, no one more than him was aware of the hazards of his ambition. The apparently innocent aspiration, he knew only too well, was an overreach for the eldest son of a limited-income family. Rather than something as obviously erratic as acting, it was inevitable that even before he finished graduation, in 1944, the teenager got sucked into a job. In his case, it was that of a clerk in the cash department of the office of the Port Commissioner. Nothing could have been farther for a dreamy-eyed young man than a stuffy port office smelling of dry currency, where he would mostly count cash and update the ledger book.

In popular Bengali accounts, a lot has been made of Uttam's job as a clerk and his indomitable will to escape. As if, he was the only one with the dreamy-eyed ambition to make a mark in acting. But it was less daunting than it is made out to be. He was neither the first nor the last to have dreamt of a life significantly removed from the dust and drudgery of a rathole. There have been many. Charlie Chaplin and Carry Grant served in the vaudeville; Clark Gable served as an acting *extra* for two years; Michael Caine grew up a homeless cockney and a drifter; Johnny Depp, Harrison Ford and Tom Cruise were telemarketer, carpenter and porter respectively. Closer home, among Uttam's contemporaries, Dilip Kumar was in the canteen business and Dev Anand was a lowly attendant at the Censor Board office. We know that Amitabh Bachchan was a clerk in a brokerage firm, Sunil Dutt worked for BEST in Bombay and Rajnikant was a bus conductor. In our time, the case of supremely talented Nawazuddin Siddiqui weltering in the shadows for fifteen years before his spectacular rise to international fame is close to being lore.

Uttam was aiming high not because he was an exemption but because others before him had done it. After all, Durgadas, in spite of his lineage, was a scenarist in Madan's company, while Jahar Ganguly (Sulal-da), a leading actor when Uttam was warming the benches, was a lower division clerk in the Bengal Telephone Company. Ganguly, who later steered Uttam with the unfailing attention of an older brother, was in destitution with a paltry salary since he arrived in Calcutta in the second decade of the last century. It took Ganguly more than a decade before he could find some foothold in Star Theatre in 1930. It took another decade to become a top actor, which he was when Uttam arrived on the scene. Ditto for Pahari Sanyal or for that matter Tulsi Chakraborty, who was part of a circus troupe that toured Burma throughout his youth. Unless one was a prince like Pramathes Barua, struggling to establish oneself in movies was a natural rite of passage rather than an insufferable torment. To that end, Uttam was part of a legacy rather than being an exception to it.

During these years, the young Arun would often steal some hours out of his grind and sit in the darkness of a movie theatre, watching men and women straddle the screen. He could catch the last of Durgadas in *Thikadar* and *Priyo Bandhobi*. He clearly remembered the impressive turns of Tulsi Lahiri, Santosh Singha and specially Pramathesh Barua, Chhabi Biswas and Dhiraj Bhattacharjee. On stage too, he saw, wide-eyed, the domination exercised by the likes of Ahindra Chaudhuri and Sisirkumar Bhaduri. Much like Durgadas who did the same about three decades ago, Uttam would often go home engrossed in replaying a performance in his head. But he was not an uncritical receptacle of their commanding presence, as would be expected from one with no training in arts. Uttam often found himself contradicting what he saw on stage, arguing to himself that the overt loudness and histrionic excess of a play like *Sirajud-Daulah*, for example, seemed unnatural. "Did these figures, memorable in history as they may be, talk with such overt theatricality? Why would not they talk like anyone else; why would they scream, shout and be so demonstrative in their expression of otherwise everyday human emotions", he had wondered.[1] This is a compelling observation, because he was right in questioning the high-octane performative canon of the stage. He was, in fact, somewhat ahead of the times in doing so; but no one really took the trouble to tell him so. There was no one to answer his queries, no effort to channelise his enthusiasm or to satisfy his curiosity. He could not follow upon his instincts and throw himself into a full-time acting career, because with his kind of education, the clerk's job, secured thanks to an influential uncle, was the best he could get. There was nothing in his credentials to point to the contrary. The only thing he could do was to wait.

THE FIRST DAYS

Ganesh Mukherjee, who took the twenty-one-year-old Arun to his first film set, came, not surprisingly, from theatre; not stage but radio plays. He was a regular at All India Radio's then Calcutta headquarters at 1, Garstin Place, which since the shift of the radio office has become renowned as a haunt of 'spirits'. On most evenings Ganesh-da was at Bhawanipore, regaling the young in local clubs with stories of the theatre and the studios. Ganesh-da gave in to local lad Arun's persistent request for a cameo in a film he had signed with his producer-friend Bhola Addhyo. Soon, one morning in 1946, Arun, on Ganesh-da's instruction, found himself at Sri Bharat Lakshmi Studio, that same one with the elephants and diaphanous lady 'coat of arms'. Wide-eyed and gawky, Arun stumbled upon a glittering marriage-ready house constructed bang in the middle of a large, vacuous and dark studio-floor. "Your role is that of a young groom who comes to his wedding and is then beaten up. Don't worry. You will not be hurt. This is what we call filmic thrashing. You can now go and get the make-up" were the first words that director Ranjit Bandopadhyay said, after he had measured Arun meticulously. The dutiful Arun spent that day and five more days, obviously bunking work, to get thrashed in *Mayador* (The Embrace of Affection). But that film never found a theatrical release. Whether it was a boon or a setback, whether the spirits were 'conspiring' against or for him, whether it was a good or bad idea to receive some flaying in his debut film is anybody's guess. After all, no one got to know that Uttam was in the reckoning to become an actor. Except Uttam himself. He got enchanted.

1947 was tumultuous. From the depths of despair of a country and province split in two, a Tollygunge dressmaker called Dhirenbabu emerged with an invite to appear for a screen test. The dressmaker's dispatch was not one of acknowledgement from the industry but a solicitation of the endearing local boy to go and try his luck. But the film he was called for—*Drishtidan* (The Gift of Sight, 1948)—was a big one. It was a Tagore novella, and the esteemed Nitin Basu would helm it—the same Nitin Basu who had hand-held Dilip Kumar to stardom. Radhu Karmakar would do the cinematography, Timirbaran would score the music, and it was being backed by none other than Bombay Talkies, and unlike *Mayador, Drishtidan* was in Bengali, the language native to Uttam.

Drishtidan is narrated by Kumudini, a god-fearing woman of singular intelligence whose loss of sight early in her marriage gives her ungainly 'insight' into the life of those around, sometimes pushing her to dangerous assumptions. Uttam, still Arunkumar, played the younger version of Kumudini's (Sunanda Banerjee) husband Abinash, the well-meaning doctor whose misguided experiments as a young medic were partly responsible for her blindness. The older Abinash was played by Asit Baran. After Kanan Debi's retreat from leading roles, Sunanda Banerjee, Anubha Gupta, Sumitra Debi and Sondharani Chatterjee were among the lead actresses who, since the mid-1940s, continued to provide traction to the persona of the leading lady with grace and intelligence. Sunanda Banerjee was particularly impressive in *Dui Purush* (The Two Men), *Dutta* (Dutta, 1951) and *Ulka* (The Meteor, 1957) and was Bengal's first female producer.

In spite of the heavyweight cast and crew, *Drishtidan* flopped. Nitin Basu went back to Bombay; Asit Baran and Sunanda Banerjee moved on. Uttam stayed put, stuck actually. He got ₹27 as fee for the film and found on its release that the posters did not mention his name. They were not supposed to. But the film had an inordinate effect on his personal life. Gauri Ganguly, whom he was covertly and timorously dating, took her grandmother to watch the film and showed her—with less diffidence than expected—that she was in love with *that* man on the screen. The Gangulys were a well-known family from Aston Road in the posh neighbourhood of Lansdowne. Gauri's confession created a commotion. The affair was now known and a decision had to be taken. After much to and fro and some scurrying here and there, the parents of both consented. Uttam and Gauri got married.

The same year, that is 1948, after these two films and without any more ground beneath his feet, Uttam appeared for a screen test for Bimal Roy's *Pehla Aadmi* (The First Man), a tragic love story set against the travails of Subhas Bose's INA. This film, as was expected of Roy, did not flinch from bringing to screen issues that were politically contentious. Released in 1950, it was also Bimal Roy's last film for New Theatres. He left soon after, with his crew, to join Bombay Talkies. For *Pehla Aadmi*, Roy was keen to introduce a new actor, which eventually turned out to be Nazir Hussain. Uttam had a secret desire to be part of New Theatres because it was still the most credible cradle for cinema aspirants. But he does not mention appearing for this screen test, though Arabindu Mukhopadhyay (director of *Nishipodmo*) does. Mukhopadhyay was assistant director to Bimal Roy. In his memoir *Alochayar Dinguli* (Days of Light and Shadow) he remembers that even though Uttam failed the screen test, he managed to leave an impression. Bimal Roy had apparently prophesied that in proper hands, a great future awaited Uttam. Mukhopadhyay wonders what would have happened if Roy had not left New Theatres and had stayed back in Calcutta to nurture or witness Uttam's rise; or if Uttam, pegged by Roy, had left for Bombay. The second is a teasing question.

Two of Uttam's near contemporaries, Abhi Bhattacharya and Shetol Batabyal (Pradeep Kumar), had made a name in Bombay by the early 1950s. In fact, it was Abhi's absence from Calcutta that gave Uttam Kumar his first major hit *Bosu Paribar*, a film to which we will return soon. Similarly, *Morjada*, an early Uttam film, was first vacated by Pradeep Kumar thereby him to step in. In spite of his initial success, Bhattacharya could never become a leading actor. An arrogant Pradeep Kumar, on the other hand, was betrothed to his sudden fame because it was barely deserved. By the late 1950s, Pradeep Kumar was becoming obsolete. Later, in the 1960s, a similar trajectory of initial fame followed by irreparable decline awaited Biswajit too, in spite of his Bombay stint being bankrolled by Hemanta Mukherjee.

So, Uttam's move to Bombay at the very beginning of his career is one of those thorny *if* theorems of Bengali cinema. If he cracked Roy's film and went to Bombay, Bengali cinema would have hardly gained anything; as was the case for the other three actors. If he went and failed, then the loss would have been incalculable. None of these examples and hypotheses still explains why Uttam, already forty, was so keen to stake his fortune on his Bombay debut in the mid-1960s. And his fate in Bombay, incidentally, turned out to be worse than that of his colleagues. Imagine that happening in the early 1950s. There would be no Uttam and no stardom in Bengali cinema to talk about. But Uttam stayed put after being rejected for *Pehla Aadmi*, continuing with his labours. Perhaps he was destined to become the 'first man' of Bengali cinema.

TAUNTS AND REBUFFS

In the next couple of years, Uttam, willy-nilly, became part of the movie industry. After the unreleased *Mayador* and the brief appearance in *Drishtidan*, Uttam had signed *Ore Jatri* (Listen, Traveller, 1951), the producer being a childhood friend of his father. The ambitious film pitched stepbrothers Shankar and Sekhar, who, having moved through several bends in their life, come to face each other on behalf of warring enemies in a INA-like battle in Manipur. The film's model is that of familial separation and reunion, which became one of Hindi cinema's abiding motifs at least since 1965's *Waqt*. But this film was a bit too ambitious than its scope would allow and vanished without creating much flutter. It was in the shoot of this Rajen Chowdhury film that Uttam was continuously sledged by a group of hangers-on at Indrapuri Studios. This was new for him, but it meant that he was rising up the pecking order. After all, he was the 'second hero' in this film, playing, again, a doctor. On the first day of the shoot with the redoubtable

Prabha Devi, Uttam's character had to examine her during a bout of illness. Uttam, young and vulnerable, got affected by the comments that came his way: about him being frail, about tying his feet to the ground to save him from flying away when giant studio fans whirled, the back-handed comparison with Durgadas Banerji and so on. When the camera started rolling, Uttam nervously started to examine Prabha Devi. A little later, a bemused Prabha, without any previous hint, looked straight in the direction of the crew and said, "How will this young man heal me; he has turned cold and is shaking in his pants", causing a wave of loud laughter. Uttam's shoot was cancelled for that day. He went home cloaked in shame and torment. Should he abandon his efforts at acting altogether, he mused. But soon he recuperated and on the following days, over rounds of tea, toast and cigarettes which he sponsored, he literally bought over the naysayers. Soon his detractors turned his most ardent supporters, often rooting for him after even an ordinary scene. The art of diplomacy was clearly not lost on the young man.

Uttam's first film as a leading man was Nabyendushundor Banerjee's *Kamona* (A Plea, 1949). The small-budget film came Uttam's way unexpectedly, and the posters named him as Uttam Chatterjee. The film had a heavily melodramatic storyline and the plot centred around the childless and much maligned Utpala (Chhabi Roy) rather than her husband Rajib (Uttam). It tanked. The next one, Digambar Chatterjee's *Morjada* (The Honourable, 1950) showed initial promise but sank thereafter. The film pitted three sets of adults as stakeholders to Prosanto (Uttam) and Doli's desperation to find togetherness, creating a regular tragi-comic tapestry. Prima facie, the film was par for the course in the early 1950s but could not attract any attention. It was the only film in which, as advised by others, Uttam appeared under the name Arupkumar. It didn't help in any way.

Yet, the story does not end here. This was the film in which Pradeep Kumar, already a recognised actor, was substituted by the rookie Uttam (rather Arun, alias Arup). Though not a success, the film was symbolic of a change of order in Bengali cinema, the decisive impact of which was to be felt in a couple of years. Also, this was the film in which Uttam managed to get the attention of his co-stars, including the heroine, Smritirekha Biswas. The bubbly Biswas was an under-utilised early talent in this period and was shuttling between Bombay and Calcutta. She was, in fact, the female lead in *Pehla Aadmi*. She grew fond of her young co-star and gave Uttam dollops of suggestions on how to conduct oneself in front of the camera. Uttam did not hesitate to hang on to every bit of that tutoring.

Uttam became a father in 1950 to his only child Gautam, who, it has to be mentioned, did not make the mistake of getting into his famous father's shoes. Shepherding one's ward to the movie business by a parent of some renown is now part of an unexceptional cartelism in Bombay. Though less common in the 1970s and even more so in the dominion of Bengali cinema, it was not an unknown idea when Gautam reached his 20s. In fact, his case was unlike, say, Suchitra Sen's daughter Moon Moon Sen or Biswajit's son Prasenjit Chatterjee. They had come to be part of the movie industry because their parents were of influence (and talent), though neither of the two wards could have been really called an actor of any distinction. Uttam saved his son, who looked nothing like his father and is not known to have any talent for the camera, the indignity of being another reluctant, incompetent but thrust-into-the-limelight progeny of a star whose name and fame could not have been bettered. Gautam, instead, ran a small business.

But, back in 1950, all this was in the future and Gautam's birth brought Uttam some much needed joy when otherwise it was all about the airless cash office at Kidderpore or the stifling failures in the industry. The films he had appeared in were not necessarily worse than the norm in those days. But they were commercial embarrassments and frankly, had little by way of challenge for an actor of Uttam's promise. But either way, those backing Uttam till then wanted to retract, unwilling to invest any more on a young aspirant who could not solicit audience acceptability.

But in reality, something surprising happened. Uttam, thanks largely to the recommendation of actors Pahari Sanyal and Jahar Ganguly, secured a three-year contract with MP Productions, a leading production company. The contract guaranteed a monthly salary of ₹400 for the first year, ₹600 for the next and ₹700 for the final year. It was monetarily lucrative for a beginner and did not require him to quit his day job. It is unlikely that MP boss Murlidhar Chattopadhyay was canny enough to invest in this raw talent for the future. The choice to sign him up was out of a need to usher in new faces and to stop further erosion of talent to better offers in Bombay. From the point of view of Uttam, however, this contract came not because of his career till then but in spite of it. Most of his biographers have been awed by Uttam's 'strive and determination' through those years of struggle. But what was natural was the struggle, what was exceptional was the windfall that came Uttam's way. In about four years, without much to show, he was doing better than most of his co-aspirants. This, after all, was a profession that was notoriously perfidious. Uttam, by that standard, was far from being out in the cold.

Thanks to the contract, Uttam came in touch with several key people in the industry. Among them were actor Santosh Singha, known for his training of young aspirants, impresario Bimal Ghosh, who scouted for talent and director Bibhuti Laha, who would go on to play a mentor first and then partook fully in Uttam's rise to stardom. Bimalbabu had seen Uttam in one of his early films and had made up his mind to bring him to MP. On being asked how the new actor was measuring up, Bimalbabu had publicly told everyone that he was not impressed at all with this new guy and there was little hope for him. He did the same to deter others from showing any interest in Uttam. But this hidden admiration continued only till Uttam's films for MP too started to come a cropper.

Uttam was not hired as a leading man but just as a salaried actor. But for his very first film with MP, Agradoot-directed *Sohojatri*, he got the part of the lead because Asit Baran had been lured to Bombay for Bimal Roy's *Parineeta*. Bharati Debi, Uttam's co-star in the film, already had an established pairing with Asit Baran. A leading actor since the later days of New Theatres, Bharati Debi was also a trailblazing figure outside of her roles. Unhappily married to a wrestler and unable to find release, she had converted to Islam to divorce her first husband, then reconverted back and married a second time. Though they co-starred in several other films (only once more as a couple) her best remembered role with Uttam was to come fifteen years later. In Ray's *Nayak*, she played Manorama—the compliant wife of a domineering husband and awed middle-aged fan of the matinee idol who was her immediate co-passenger on a train. In a key scene in the film, she helps the sozzled star put his feet back on the sleeping berth under the gaze of her young, silent daughter. In later years Bharati Debi acted in two memorable Tapan Sinha films (*Nirjon Soikote* and *Golpo Holeo Sotti*) and acted in and produced the national award-winning *Sagor Songome* (The Holy Island) that was directed by Debaki Bose. For years, she also penned a regular newspaper column.

Sohojatri (The Fellow Traveller, 1951), had many of the tropes that later romantic melodramas had marshalled as set pieces—train romance between fugitive souls escaping strict parenting, a series of trite coincidences that keep them apart, bank failures leading to a sudden bout of poverty and an expected but-long delayed union. But Bharati Debi's Sunitilata looked too seasoned next to Uttam's raw-boned and clumsy Sunitikumar, the most possible reason for the film's abject failure. This film, however, is distinguished as one in which Hemanta Mukherjee gave voice to Uttam for the first time, a pairing which attained mythic popularity in less than four years after that.

Uttam's next film, for MP again, was *Nostonir* (The Poisoned Nest, 1951). Sunanda Banerjee was the principal actor of this film by Pashupati Chattopadhyay, which is often mistaken as an adaptation of a famous Tagore story. But it was nowhere close to that and was, in fact, a typically maudlin tale of the ill-fated Sita who is relentlessly abandoned and exploited by the men in her life, including her willowy old father. Uttam's young engineer Monojit had little more screen time than a cameo. This film too fared poorly. In the meantime, *Ore Jatri* released and did no better than the other two.

Except *Kamona* and *Sohojatri* none of the films had Uttam featured in the publicity, neither were the scripts banking on him to deliver any memorable performances. These films were germinal to Uttam's early efforts at finding a foothold but it is difficult to see them as any sort of signpost in his journey towards stardom. Uttam's later stardom consolidated these films as a collective roster of pre-fame failure, but in actuality they hardly carried any promise of what was to come in the next three years.

No wonder, more people started to give up on Uttam as duds hovered over his increasingly deficient prospects, and a title like 'flopmaster general' came to sit uneasily on his nervous head. No one is sure why the term was coined because Uttam worked for the Port Authority and not the Indian Post. So, the pun on postmaster general is an inexplicable honorific. Moreover, Uttam had not yet gained any distinction in the industry to attract a title of that sort. But the name not only circulated widely but also stalked Uttam for years. "The distributor offices at Dharamtolla are increasingly unprepared to part with their funds the moment they know that you are in the lead", Uttam was told by the same Bimalbabu,[2] virtually sealing his prospects. It was also at this time that the 'Oedipal' cartoon appeared.

THE SAVIOUR

1952 arrived, like years previous to it—without any major hope for change in popular Bengali cinema. Amidst the retinue of usual uncertainties, there was one certain fact. This was going to be Uttam's last year of trial and error. He was twenty-six, married for four years, and had a two-year-old son. He had seen all his six films bomb at the box office; his bosses at the port corporation were increasingly reluctant to give him any more leeway; and there was little conviction left among the producers and, more importantly, the distributors that Uttam was worth putting any money into. At home too, he was running out of the subsidy of time and attendance that he was drawing. A couple of more flops and it was certain that Uttam would have had to leave the precincts of the studio *para* forever. Or stay put as an also-ran.

Had not a New Theatres screenwriter called Nirmal Dey come out of self-exile to mould into a script a Japanese short story; had not both Abhi Bhattacharya and Asit Baran been found wanting of dates; had not MP Productions been convinced one last time that their reluctant choice should be that once-promising but now failed young actor, *Bosu Poribar* would not have been made. At least, not with Uttam Kumar in the lead. But the producers banked on Dey to put together a taut, credible script (which he also shot and directed) that did not put the onus of the film on Uttam's shoulders but built the plot around a crisis of trust and family bonding.

Bosu Poribar (The Basu Family), later remade into *Hum Hindustani* (1960), is the story of an upper-class family, whose collapse into dire hardship tests the self-imposed moral framework of good and evil. Set during WWII, it was about a family settled in Calcutta that had seen better days as owners of land in the provinces. The family was a new entrant to the middle-class province, whose links to the older feudal revenue were becoming weak. And yet, they were holding on to an outdated social climate that placed huge importance on respectability and honour. When a contentious court case goes against them, the members of the family are forced to abandon the income from their property and go about town in search of a living. Elder brother Sukhen (Uttam), an insurance agent, is the sacrificial one who takes up the onus to run the family, which includes his four siblings. Sukhen is primarily at odds with Satyen, the younger sibling, a law clerk at a reputed attorney's office. Satyen is the archetype of a loser who would shrink in shame, hide from his fiancée and make trivial adjustments to his new financial reality rather than work harder. Much of the tension of the script erupts out of the two clashing viewpoints of Sukhen and Satyen and to a large extent signifies the film's partaking in the new social order. The tension is brought to a crisis when a theft in Satyen's office bares the hidden rift between the brothers; which is then resolved in a high-pitched climax. By pitting the two ideologies together, the film questions the easy privileges of the landed class, which were being usurped by a confident, if struggling, progeny keen to engage with the emergent possibilities of an expanding modern life. To assert the point, Sukhen, the saviour, also moonlights as a writer, whose debut novel *Madhyabitto* ('The Middle-class') becomes a bestseller, rescuing the family from assured ruin.

Bosu Poribar not only brought Nirmal Dey successfully out of his exile but established him as a director of perceptive cinematic sense. Since he was trained in fine art and photography, the visual image was his natural playground. Among others, he earned the good words of Satyajit Ray, who considered Dey as one of the ablest directors of that turning period of Bengali cinema. This film also brought to fore the immense comic talents of Bhanu Bandopadhyay and Jahar Roy, both playing emphatic moneylenders to Sukhen. The duo would later go on to become major actors in their own right, often starring together in films that made use of their maiden name in film titles. *Bosu Poribar* also saw the debut of Supriya Bandopadhyay, who played Sukhen's sister Sujata. After a couple of more films, she vanished for over seven years to resurface later in the decade with Ritwik Ghatak's cult partition tragedy *Meghe Dhaka Tara*, which remains her *tour de force*.

Bosu Poribar gave Uttam his first bonafide commercial success, buying him some more time to carry on with his fragile ambition. As if it was a sign of better days to come, for he resigned from his job to become a full-time, professional actor. Uttam's performance, sufficiently believable against the stodgy Satyen of Nepal Nag, was appreciated. And so was the film. After *Bosu Poribar*, Uttam started to be known outside the studio *para*, while there was a degree of recognition from peers and seniors. His life did not change dramatically though, except perhaps his long overdue decision of letting go of the clerk in him.

As if to mark this act of forsaking, Uttam was advised by many to make better use of his smile in future films. As is most evident ever since, he more than obliged.

FILMS THAT DARED

Uttam's other two releases of 1952 were stand-out films by some measure, even though they did not make much noise. In later years Uttam's success and stardom wiped these films from public memory, to the extent that like the six flop films, these two films, *Sanjeebani* and *Kar Pape?* cannot be seen anymore. However, these two films were by no means comparable to those that came before. *Sanjeebani* (The Healing Tree) was released in February 1952, two months before *Bosu Poribar*. It is hence to be seen as Uttam's third flop in a row for MP Productions after *Sohojatri* and *Nostonir*.

Sukumar Dasgupta, who started making movies in the 1930s, was a veteran of MP Productions. Dasgupta could think out of the box, was keen to explore cinematic storytelling and could helm a film with an ensemble setting. Over the years he had developed a lightness of touch that gave his movies a firm intelligence without succumbing to the excesses of drama. When he adapted the script of *Sanjeebani*, he was strongly advised against signing Uttam, because it was a risky film and because Uttam was perceived, rightly, as a box-office dud. "I think you should rather choose Chhabi (Biswas) or Dhiraj (Bhattacharjee)", MP's boss Muralidhar Chattopadhyay advised Dasgupta. "Let Uttam get ready. He is not prepared." What Dasgupta said in reply is telling: "If we do not give him a chance to act, then how will he get a chance to prepare?" Chattopadhyay concurred.[3] Dasgupta's confidence in the young actor's ability to pull off a difficult character played a definitive role in the young aspirant's early days. Also, rarely would a studio let an actor *use* its film 'to prepare', risking the success of that film. But both Dasgupta and Chattopadhyay did let Uttam do the same. Uttam never forgot this act of generosity.

Billy Wilder's 1945 noir *The Lost Weekend* about the travails of the dipsomaniac Don Birnam (Ray Milland) was the source film of *Sanjeebani*, though like several other indigenised versions, this one too, remains unacknowledged. The film is about the author Rabindra Bose, who tasted fame after the success of his first book *Charandhani* (The Sound of Steps). But his second book fails miserably. Pegged by his literary associations, Rabi slowly starts to take to alcohol hoping that the magic potion will 'cure' him of his shortcomings as a writer. But soon he finds himself sliding deep into the morass of severe alcoholism, losing any capacity to even write—good or bad. He even spurns his fiancée Reba (Sondharani Chatterjee) when she tries to take away his bottle from him. Hospitalised after an accident, Rabi is detected with pathological, alcohol-induced delusion and is advised long-term treatment. Reba brings him home, where after a severe bout of adamant resistance and struggle, Rabi starts to recover slowly.

Sanjeebani gave Uttam his first complex, meaty role and he did not fail to impress either the director or the critics. Dasgupta was delighted with the outcome and the high-brow *Anandabazar Patrika* noted that Uttam was impressive in parts. The film failed to draw much attention but Dasgupta held that it was his own lack and that of the script; he had no complaints against Uttam. The financial fate of the movie made MP reconsider, till the end, if they wanted to cast Uttam anymore. He was, after all, not the first choice for MP's next venture *Bosu Poribar*. But the film's critical approval and the director's trust in Uttam made this film different from all that had come his way before.

If *Sanjeebani* was distinct, *Kar Pape?* (The Sinner, 1952), which was again from MP and released in August 1952, was audacious. The leading character of the film is Ashim, a debased rich fop, who contracts syphilis thanks to his reprobate lifestyle and is punished accordingly. Written and directed by the reticent veteran Kaliprasad Ghosh, the film is set over five years starting in 1938, roughly during the WWII years, at the end of which the mass production of penicillin provided, for the first time, an effective and reliable cure for syphilis. Halfway through the long cure he is advised, Ashim (Asit Baran) forcefully marries his betrothed beauty (Manju Dey) keeping her in the dark about the state of his malady. But he only manages to infect her as well, resulting in botched pregnancies and a paralytic baby. That child dies too and Ashim, insensitive and reckless in his pursuit of sexual consummation, prepares to marry again. Pushed against the wall by his negligence, the pain of losing her baby and her own torment, Beauty shoots him fatally. Uttam's Shankar is the foil to Ashim, who in the very end takes his fiance, Ashim's sister Geeta, now in the clutches of the disease, to one Dr Bose, and is assured that a new wonder drug is likely to cure her for good.

Clearly, this film was not in the league of congenial, uplifting social dramas and refused to coat the contentious theme with any air of respectability. Instead, Ghosh thrust the ugliness of the disease in-your-face—horrible to look at and excruciating to suffer. But most importantly, he provided a fiercely feminist solution to Ashim's foolhardy egotism. In Bengali cinema, this was an unprecedented theme. No wonder, *Kar Pape?*, ahead of its time and unflinching in its depiction, did not receive an appreciative audience. The critics, however, loved it and called it the best film from the MP stable. Uttam was noted too but the draw of the film was Manju Dey, as intriguing an actor as one can be, about whom we will have occasion to discuss more.

As for Uttam, *Bosu Poribar* had already proved to be a commercial success while the other two gave him traction as an actor, allowing him some cheer after five gloomy years in the industry. Uttam found what he was lacking the most: confidence. But at the same time, had MP Productions not provided him the long rope with five films in a row, defying market predictions and their own hesitations, the story could have been very different.

Sonjiboni and *Kar Pape?*—more experimental and daring than most precursors from the popular stable in those years—have faded, never to have found any rehabilitation in later years. But it is obvious that the films showed a decisive move towards using cinema to showcase socially contentious issues. They, along with *Bosu Poribar*, also displayed the emergence of a popular medium that could deal with precocious and realistic problems of the war years and after. These films show a discernible and discursive change in the direction and temperament of popular cinema. 1952 was also the year that Ghatak's *Nagarik* was made (even if it released twenty-five years later). To that end 1952 proved to be, in more ways than one, a key year in the history of Bengali cinema and a significant one for Uttam.

LEARNING THE ROPES

In his part-autobiography *Hariye Jawa Dinguli* (The Lost Days of Yore) Uttam makes a thoughtful observation about warming up to a career in acting. He writes:[4]

> Acting is not child's play. To look good in a couple of movies, to romance a couple of heroines, to saunter into the streets in an expensive shirt, to drive in a posh car, to have a group of college kids shower frenzy or crowds display spry recognition—that's not acting. Acting is a pursuit, it demands meditation. Those who come under its spell are doomed.

This memoir is largely limited to the pre-stardom period and gives a detailed and sentimental account of his difficult days. This observation, however, stands out because it reflects back at a period when Uttam is unsure of how the medium of cinema will eventually make use of his pursuit of natural acting. His reflection also helps us to identify a brief tension between two forms of performance, when in 1953 Uttam would appear on the professional stage. The play was called *Shyamali,* which proved to be a breakthrough in Uttam's life. It was Star Theatre's biggest blockbuster since its inception in 1883 and ran for a record 484 nights between 15 October 1953 and 30 November 1955. Uttam played the lead role of Anil, though it was the ensemble cast that initially drew the crowds. Eventually, this role, enacted three nights every week, cemented Uttam's reputation as an actor of powerful stage presence, when otherwise he was still stuttering his way through cinema. Ironically, of all the veterans none other than Ahindra Chaudhuri stood awed by the talent of the young man, precisely when Uttam's performative style was signalling the demise of the hallowed generation of Chaudhuri.

The play's run came to an end because Uttam was a star by 1955 and could by no means appear on stage with any regularity. What is noteworthy is that despite its success, *Shyamali* could not keep Uttam affianced to the stage, unlike his predecessors Durgadas or Chhabi Biswas. Uttam's dispensation and style had that refreshing and notable un-theatricality about it. It was hence no small matter that the stage fortified his popularity in those early days and briefly made him contemplate the urgency and immediacy of theatrical heroics as against the protracted and belated returns of cinema. If only briefly. 1952 was still a year away from *Shyamali's* premiere at Star, but Uttam's later cogitation about acting as a quest draws us to the young man's searching questions and his initial efforts to bridge the acting styles. In fact, he also mentioned how he was stunned by Roland Colman's performance in

A Double Life, which was an unusual adaptation of Shakespeare's *Othello*. Incidentally, Dame Sybil Thorndike, the famous Shavian actress, and her husband, the renowned Old Vic director Sir Lewis Casson, were in the audience one night at Star. The English couple were thoroughly impressed with the play and were found inquiring about the actor who played Anil.

By the end of 1952, Uttam had some things to show for himself in the industry, now that he was, after all, a professional actor. In all the three films released that year, his performances were noted by the audience as well as the critics and the fact that he signed the next films of both Nirmal Dey and Sukumar Dasgupta was an indication that the directors too were rather pleased with his ways. And why wouldn't they? Uttam, for example, would visit Dey's one-room Bhawanipore apartment often when he was preparing for Sukhen's character, so that he could learn the intricacies of the craft outside the crowded space of the studio. He did this with most of his early directors, from Bidhuti Laha to Naresh Mitra, from Sukumar Dasgupta to Tapan Sinha. This way, he not only learnt way beyond the needs of his character, but established a personal rapport with most of his early directors, who in turn saw in Uttam the most diligent acting protégé that one could think of.

In fact, if there was one thing that Uttam never lacked it was his willingness to learn. Since he was conscious of his unremarkable background, Uttam always kept his eyes and ears open for further education. Many of the stalwarts of the industry, Naresh Chandra Mitra, for example, found new enthusiasm when they started working with the ever-eager-to-learn Uttam. In fact, it was Naresh Mitra, a revered classicist, who had coaxed him to break away from the contract with MP Productions for his much-hyped historical *Bou Thakuranir Haat*, which was adapted from Tagore's debut novel written in 1883. Mitra, who had introduced Durgadas to cinema three decades ago, was effusive about the promise he saw in Uttam and refused to proceed with the film unless he was on board. But MP Productions, of which Uttam was a staff artist, was reluctant. So, Mitra's producer Gobindo Roy paid MP Productions a full year's worth of Uttam's salary to let him become a freelance actor. *Bou Thakuraner Haat* (The Consort's Tale, 1953), based on the legendary anti-Mughal saber-rattler King Pratapaditya of Jessore, had an overdrawn style, punctuated by impressive night-time photography by Deojibhai. To Pratapaditya's fanatical, overarching egotism, his son Uday (Uttam) and uncle Basanta Roy are deeply pacifist counterparts. But they are helpless in the face of Pratap's brute bloodthirsty aggression that puts his estate in peril. In the end, the disconsolate widower Uday leaves the life of royalty, choosing to be a common man rather than the successor to a bloody regime. One must note the film's earnest efforts at adapting an expansive Tagore novel, especially within limited means; but that has not saved the film from not having dated since. At the same time, against the tenor of the film's overwrought theatricality, Uttam and Manju Dey (Uday's wife Suroma) were almost free of excess. Mitra helped boost Uttam's confidence by letting the actor's undeveloped style prevail over his own tried and trusted methods as a classicist. In fact, the film does carry the germinal promise of a naturalist that was to bloom later. Mitra had also told his friends that his seasoned eyes could foresee that Uttam, with some grooming, would become the hero that Bengal was waiting for. Interestingly, this is one of the early films to have introduced merchandising in Bengali cinema. A glass penholder with the title of the film embossed on the base could be bought for keeps.

ON THE CUSP OF STARDOM

In spite of these part successes, till *Agniporikha* (Trial by Fire), where he co-starred with Suchitra Sen, gave him mass approbation, Uttam had to contend with films where he was part of a larger cast rather than a leading character. Few wanted to bank singularly on his slender shoulders. Hence, New Theatres' *Nobin Jatra*, Shatabdi Chitra Pratishan's *Lakh Taka*, Aurora's *Shodanonder Mela*, SM Productions' *Ora Thake Odhare* were, in a sense, films 'without protagonists'. In *Nobin Jatra* (A New Journey) Uttam played the proud scientist Ashok who has to bow to the largesse of Nirmal, a talented young teacher, who forgoes a job abroad to create a new kind of education in a village that is unused and unwilling to change. He was one of the several clueless claimants in Niren Lahiri's *Lakh Taka* (Chasing a Bounty, 1953), a comic roller coaster about a surprise inheritance and how it tests the patience, honesty and loyalty of a set of misguided simpletons. These films were as much part of his quiescent pre-stardom phase as they were also germane to the evolution of the actor in him. The only film of that period with a similarly clustered structure but which was received with raucous applause was MP's *Sharey Chuattor*, to which we shall turn to later. It would be good to note here that Uttam had close to twenty releases before the breakthrough *Agniporikha* in 1954. And except *Bosu Poribar* and *Sharey Chuattor* none of the films were commercially redeemed. Clearly, Uttam had survived the early 1950s much less on audience support than on his rapport with veterans, colleagues and producers. In terms of critical acclaim, he was not ignored but he was not hailed as one who would bring any major transformation to the industry anytime soon.

Image 4.1: Early Uttam (with Shyam Laha and Sabitri Chatterjee). Publicity still of inheritance comedy *Lakh Taka* (Chasing a Bounty, 1953)

Source: Author.

That Uttam was an exemplar of diligence, hard work and fortitude is a common appraisal. From his heroines to his directors, everyone held Uttam in high regard for the way he battled his many deficiencies. Except having a voice and an ear for singing, Uttam wasn't born with any obvious talent. He followed a tough fitness regime in spite of his ready weakness for cigarettes, and at a later age, alcohol. A borderline stutter and a slightly warbled speech continued to haunt him till well into his professional years. He was advised to speak to the mirror, loudly recite poems with challenging phonetic sounds, and chew a betel-nut while talking to clear speech delivery. He did all of them. Later, he also home-tutored himself to speak Hindi, Urdu and English. But never did he train professionally or otherwise in acting, either in his younger days or later. What Uttam also had was a natural enthusiasm for learning on the go, which he retained till at least *Nayak*, by which time Uttam had attained, in Satyajit Ray's own words, the status of a legend of cinema. But that never came in the way of Uttam's eagerness to improve both his acting and his understanding of the craft of cinema. Even otherwise, when Uttam was designated as the 'flopmaster', seasoned hands and eyes had noticed the sincerity of this unassuming young man, who showed a keen interest in his art and stood out because of his natural felicity. They often advised him on further training and refinement of his skills. Uttam was only too willing to listen to anyone who had advice to offer.

Apart from the insatiable desire to learn, what helped Uttam survive was his other bounty, tenacity. Most others from his undistinguished background would have abandoned their fancy ambition at the opportune moment to embrace the safety of a government job.

But Uttam let his passion simmer through the difficult times as well as through his many failures. There was no way he could have immediately left his job; neither could he simply kill a longing that did not let him work during the day, or even after a hard day, let him sleep. At the same time, his tenacity and will to improve persisted because he had little to lose if he continued chasing the acting ambition for a while. Moreover, his countless absenteeism from work during his shooting stints were inexplicably overlooked; his wife Gauri provided steely support; and there were earnest industry veterans who were empathetic to a young man's efforts. So, it was not as much of a resolve but a series of supportive hands and recurrent opportunities that kept him from giving up on acting. Uttam survived in this quandary not for months but for years and even after he had let go of the job in 1952 and settled with a shaky acting career, the dilemma was far from over. At least for another two years. But the indecisive spell of wait for six years was showing clear signs of coming to an end.

Uttam's early life had the usual marks left by a stinging, stalking desire that refused to be throttled by either circumstance or untested talent. But till this far, his story is that of a struggler who refused to give up. There were many before him, and after. There was nothing prodigal or meteoric that discerned the ordinary, diffident, middle-class boy from the debonair, flamboyant, matinee-idol of the future. Neither did his life have the making of a fable. Yet.

NOTES

1. Uttamkumar Chattopadhyay, *Amar Ami*, Dey's Publishing, 1972.
2. Uttamkumar Chattopadhyay, *Hariye Jaoa Dinguli Mor*, edited by Abhik Chattopadhyay, Saptarshi Prokashon, 2013, p. 106.
3. 'Mahanayak Uttam Kumar', *Boisakhi* Journal, edited by Dhrubojyoti Mondol, 23 (2013–2014): 152.
4. Chattopadhyay, *Hariye Jaoa Dinguli Mor*, p. 81.

5

HOUR OF THE STAR

We are not figuratively, but literally stardust.
—Neil deGrasse Tyson

THE histories of modernity, urbanity and evolution of two principle colonial cities of Calcutta and Bombay cover a large portion of analogous and simultaneous ground. The entrepreneurial instinct of Bombay made it stand on surer footing economically; and it was closer to the western hemisphere. But Calcutta had not only been the colonial capital but had a significant stake in imperial geography. Even the loss of its status as the capital of British India in 1911 did not significantly diminish Calcutta's attraction as a cultural and commercial fulcrum, its spheres of influence facilitating its attraction for people of several tongues and nationalities. In cinema too—both in content and technology—Calcutta led the way. The tide started to shift during the 1940s and more specifically after Partition.

THE IN-BETWEEN YEARS

On the other side of the transitional tornado that accompanied India's decolonisation, it was clear that Bombay had gained substantially at the cost of Calcutta's troubles, not least in the significant flight of talent and finance from Bengal. Lahore's decline was Bombay's gain too. Bombay sequestered itself from its Marathi–Gujarati pulls and demarcated itself as the centre of Hindi-language mass entertainment, which substantially cleared the ground for its emergence as a cine capital. The talkies had since the 1930s made language the primary pivot of cinema's cultural economy; and since the 1950s the differences had matured into separate cohorts for language cinema. Being the receptor of Hindi language as against Bengali and Tamil, Bombay's gains were large and decisive. The studios had helped propel into public life the first national stardom in Bombay cinema, the temperament of those films being tied to the broader Nehruvian ideals and expectations (*Andaz*, 1949; or *Naya Daur*, 1957, for example). Bombay cinema was glossier, technological finesse being observably better than language cinema. Moreover, since it was not attached to any distinct template; 'Bombay films' could also employ routine requirements of mass entertainment, unencumbered by natural moorings in cultural landscapes, something the regional cinemas found difficult to negotiate. To top it all, a slew of attractive performers imported a sweep of quicksilver glamour that was missing from the screen before.

None of these was easily available to Bengali popular cinema. While the new-found idealism, aesthetic and imagination of art-house cinema drew intellectual weight, popular cinema, in Bengal, as we have seen, was reeling with problems much beyond its scope of correction. The once formidable pre-Partition economy and sphere of influence that constituted the base of this cinema were dissolved after Partition. Sharp and irreversible structural changes (in the studio economy and increase in cost of raw films) and influence and viewership (the gradual estrangement of East Pakistan from India-made cinema) precipitated a financial and territorial crisis. These factors had produced difficulties at every level, including the decline of safe anchors, something that the studios had provided in earlier decades. The dead weight of salaried actors and crew, controlled screens, studio-enabled scenography and culturally identifiable viewership—all of which the studios had stood for—had to go. It was evident that the idea of a gated studio, with a self-enclosed system of production was unsustainable in independent Bengal, where cinema was being seen as a mode of social change. A series of naive acting aspirants; the paucity of young talent; the inevitable ageing of a leading group of performers and makers; and that discernible sense of falling into a repetitive tedium further cloyed popular cinema.

No one was sure what could substitute the studio. The art-cinema movement was an esoteric intellectual diversion but was in no position to sustain an industry. All of this meant that Bengali popular cinema could neither be merged with the new art cinema, nor could it become the popular cinema of Bombay by morphing loosely into desirable forms of entertainers.

This historical shift had ensured that the decade between the death of Durgadas Banerji (early-1940s) and the rise of Uttam Kumar Chatterjee (mid-1950s)—which included the fading of the Pramathes Barua 'period of influence'—was a period of churn. In fact, since the end-1940s, Bengali popular cinema had swung between genres: studio socials and pansy romances merrily cohabited with realist films and adrenalin-pumping horror thrillers, travelogues, children's films and mythologicals. This intermediate period is indecisive and free-floating, a sort of *connecting link* as it were, between the last run of the studio era and the dawning of the star era; between the obdurate temperament of studio socials and the more synchronous prospect of *new* melodramas.

SIGNS OF STARDOM

Like every historical moment which has pressed itself forcefully upon human life, Bengal's moment of crisis also triggered the possibility of emancipation from prevailing conventions. So, the moment of despair gradually if inevitably proved to be also a moment of catharsis. Accordingly, since the early-1950s, finding itself at the cusp of a tall set of challenges, popular cinema started renegotiating its principles within the limited flexibility of form and aesthetic. And for that, it did not hesitate to look at the newfangled art cinema. Pegged by churns inside and outside, it too *turned* to the city—unfailingly Calcutta—as a locational particularity; while for form it found influence in IPTA and others radical forms of artistic engagement. The studios had wilted but thanks to WWII, speculative new money started to trickle into the industry and a new breed of producers emerged. This led to inevitable failed adventures but by the early 1950s there was an unmistakable boost in buoyancy. Bengali popular cinema also started to respond covertly to the conditions around: the trauma, the violence, the displacement, while embracing an overtly humanist ethos. As a result, instead of succumbing to the weight of its problems, popular cinema started to show signs of recovery.

Also, Bengali 'popular' and 'art' cinema were not trapped in their own, unyielding and exclusive domains. From the early days there was frequent exchange of personnel, not just to make a living but also to learn and appropriate lessons from each. A good example would be someone like Bijon Bhattacharya (remembered widely as the playwright of *Nabanna*) and his IPTA colleague Ritwik Ghatak, both of whom regularly wrote scripts and stories for mainstream films. They were part of an organic link between the radical nature of the more stringent realist school and those who found their calling in mainstream films. This link was not a fortuitous one, for there were any number of individuals, actors, screenwriters, technicians and authors, who constantly crossed between the 'two schools' of filmmaking. A quick recall would lead to writers Tarashankar Bandopadhyay, Premendra Mitra, Shankar; or actors Uttam, Soumitra, Madhabi Mukherjee, Chhabi Biswas and many others; musicians, poets and also technical crew. Rabindranath Tagore of course was that cantilever bridge that made the yawning gap between art and popular in Bengali culture, if ever there was one, somewhat narrow since very early. A certain divisive principle did emerge in later years but not in the 1950s. So, both forms of cinema kept their autonomy alive while also at the same time managing to find a degree of vigorous interdependence. This is not to argue that popular cinema gave away its fetishes but to insist that art cinema and the changing directions of popular cinema now seemed to converge from time to time. Apart from drawing into its fold a new set of talents, the *new* popular cinema could also tap into a vast body of powerful literary writing; a mellow, resonant cinema soundtrack; an identifiable cultural domain of middle-class belonging and everyday aspirations of a new republic.

What was lacking was a sense of cohesion that the by then defunct studios had once provided unfailingly. This time though, what Bengali cinema was missing was not a studio patriarch, but a convincing, credible, authentic but at the same time out of the reach figure of a star. While this search was on, Uttam was in a moderate ascent. Having seen, thanks to his father, a number of Hollywood stars from the stuffy projection room of Metro Cinema, Uttam, by the time he had gained public acceptability, brought in significant changes to the idea of the leading man. Uttam could, from his early films, solicit audience gaze, govern the camera's eye and regulate the movement of a scene. In other words, he was becoming an actor with a keen sensibility about the scope of screen drama, the limits of the cinematic form and the visual power of a star figure. By the mid-1950s, Uttam's stardom started to offer the much needed cohesion to the emerging new foci of Bengali popular cinema. His stardom helped bring a sense of urgency, a distinctive idiom, a safety of an anchor and an enterprise to go beyond the confines of earlier social dramas. And this stardom was insulated from any studio-enabled propulsion. In time, Uttam also imported a discernible contemporaneity to his cinema, an intelligence and insight that was of its own making. Coupled with its other new-found strengths, Uttam's rise acted as the desired catalyst. And together, the fledgling *new* Bengali cinema was firmly put on the road to unprecedented heights.

But when exactly did the anointed turn take place? Was it September of 1954 when *Agniporikha* (Trial by Fire) hit the theatres? Or was it *Shapmochon* (Breaking of a Curse) of May 1955? Or, do we have to wait till December 1955, when *Sobar Opore* (The Final Truth) signalled the definitive beginning of the star era? Even if the reel titles seem to carry an eerie happenstance in Uttam's rapidly changing fortunes, there is no easy answer to this question, because there is no clear-cut and conclusive trajectory of Uttam's rise to absolute fame.

Part of this conundrum was to do with the sheer power of numbers. In two years, 1955 and 1957, Uttam appeared in twelve films each, the maximum he had appeared in a single year ever in his career. 1954 and 1956 fell short by one each. This makes for a whopping forty-six films in just four years, between 1954 and 1957, by the other end of which he had become a star of great adulation. Though fewer, the numbers continued to dominate Uttam's calendar with him having appeared in another thirty-four films between 1958 and 1962. Thankfully, through the 1960s, Uttam, purportedly choosier, let his numbers decline considerably. In six years, between 1963 and 1968, he appeared in just twenty-eight films, a steep decrease since the mid-1950s.

Across these three phases and these 108 films, romantic melodramas are sprinkled generously on Uttam's body of work, even if they have a far thicker concentration between 1954 and 1961. They had a particular look and feel, having modelled themselves on the global popularity of black-and-white romances, often considered *art-de rigueur* of stardom in Hollywood. These romances not only epitomised the early part of Uttam's stardom but also helped in manufacturing a template of the middle-class, bhadralok star. Interestingly, *Pothe Holo Deri* (The Delayed Journey, 1957), a film that is often considered within this fold, was a bit of an exception, because it was, unknown to many, the first Bengali colour film, shot in Gevacolor. Satyajit Ray's *Kanchenjungha*, which enjoys the distinction (having been shot in Eastman Colour) in popular knowledge, was still five years in the future. In short, even if one could be unsure of the exact moment when Uttam attained stardom, one was in no doubt of having been under the glimmer of it.

Given his dominance, both in terms of fame and numbers, it is natural to comprehend the scale of Uttam Kumar's presence in Bengali cinema by seeing his oeuvre as *star-text*. Star-text(s) refer to a body of work that is primarily identified with (a) star. Star-texts, hence, parade a star's distinctive appeal for the public, letting other tools of storytelling—script, cinematography, editing, music—take a back seat. In Bengali cinema, even if there were several accomplishments to that effect, there was still the tendency to identify, annotate, archive and package tens of films as 'Uttam Kumar films', while the continuing appeal of these films were integral to the way Uttam had shaped his stardom. But star-texts do not explain what stardom is: that amorphous, intangible quotient of popular cinema, which is easy to gaze at, feel or even be touched but can barely be defined.

Given its slippery nature, there is a long history of probe into the idea of stardom in the United States, the spread of that stardom internationally, especially after WWII, and the role that stardom has played in the continual domination by American soft power of cultures as removed as Korean and Egyptian. What one can certainly glean from the scholarship on stardom is that there are as many routes to stardom as there are perhaps stars. The 'dream factory' of Hollywood, starting with MGM, *produced* a significant number of *stars* of many shapes and temperaments. There could have been a ready formula; but for an equally significant lot, their stardom managed to prevail beyond a studio, a period, a genre. We are not so much concerned here about the transnational portability of stardom as much as we are about its production, especially when our site of enquiry is Indian regional cinema, far removed from the monetary and cultural might of Hollywood.

So, can stardom be produced? Or, is it a fortuitous congregation of intangible whims and enigmatic coincidences? Many have taken their turn in defining the same. In *Stars*, a now classic study, Richard Dyer says that stardom is found in neither cinema as social phenomenon nor cinema as a carrier of signs. Dyer proposes a dialectic between the two, contending that the star is best found at the cusp of cinema as social value and cinema as a compendium of imagery. Christine Gledhill, in her introduction to *Stardom*, marks it out at the meeting point of apparent contradictions. She writes,

> The star challenges analysis in the way it crosses disciplinary boundaries: a product of mass culture, but retaining theatrical concerns with acting, performance and art; an industrial marketing device, but a signifying element in films; a social sign, carrying cultural meanings and ideological values, which expresses the intimacies of individual personality, inviting desire and identification; an emblem of national celebrity, founded on the body, fashion and personal style; a product of capitalism and the ideology of individualism, yet a site of contest by marginalised groups; a figure consumed for his or her personal life, who competes for allegiance with statesmen and politicians.[1]

Both definitions are befitting for a star like Uttam Kumar, whose continuing cultural appeal did not only dominate cinema during his time but seems to have created a template against which all popular undertakings about stardom are measured in his long afterlife. Satyajit Ray called Uttam the only Indian star in the Hollywood sense and wrote and directed an entire film addressed to this assertion. There are others too, who were keen to get under the skin of the kind of stratospheric stardom that Uttam enjoyed.

But this transformation in Uttam's screen persona did not come suddenly and unannounced. Rather, it crystallised over time, across a range of melodramatic figurations and with an assertive assortment of several factors. Hence, to understand the scale of this stardom we have to look at these layers of the phenomenon. Uttam's stardom, as we have noted, emerged in the vacuum that was left by the decline and then demise of the studio system. Was it a mere coincidence of history or was there a cycle of causalities that connected the demise of the studio with the rise of the star? To gauge at this question, we must look at the various types of melodramas between 1954 and 1968. To understand the temperamental differences within melodrama I have divided them into four parts: melodrama of *yesteryear*; melodrama of *excess*; melodrama *of custom*; and melodrama of *transformation*. They individually map the evolution of the actor and together constitute the making of the screen persona of Uttam. The rest of the films from this period (1954–1968) include commentaries on urban life, unorthodox plots or character studies. They hence find mention in subsequent chapters.

MELODRAMA OF YESTERYEAR

As we have seen, things were being shaken up in 1952 but the jury was still out on the direction Bengali popular cinema would take or if Uttam would be able to break free of his 'flopmaster' honorific. A fresh set of films—*Bosu Poribar*, *Sanjeebani* and *Kar Pape?*—were significantly attentive to the realist framework. There were important non-Uttam films too, such as the heart-wrenching refugee tragedy *Notun Ihudi* (The New Jew, 1953) and the slice-of-life saga *Keranir Jibon* (A Clerk's Life, 1953). But there was no definitive indication of any major shift. For example, 1952 also saw two important films from the thriller stable, *Hanabari* (The Haunted House, 1952) and *Kuhelika* (Fog, 1952). Among notable other films were comedies such as *Pasher Bari* (House of the Neighbour, 1952) and *Chikitsha Sonkot* (A Medical Mess, 1953); historicals such as *Moharaja Nondokumar* (Nandakumar the King, 1953); mythologicals such as *Mahishasur Bodh* (Killing of a Demon, 1952) and puranics such as *Dhrubo* (The Godly Son, 1953). Then, there was the trouble-in-marriage melodrama *Bastob* (A True Story, 1953), the science fantasy *Odrishya Manush* (The Invisible Man, 1953), social-upliftment drama *Notun Pathshala* (A New Schooling, 1952), Sarat Chandra Chattopadhyay-authored rural roaster *Pollisamaj* (A Village Life, 1952) and so on. The bilingual *Mohaprosthaner Pothe* (The Final Journey, 1952; *Yatrik* in Hindi) belonged to the spiritual travelogue variety, giving a final boost to New Theatres before its eventual and expected expiry in the mid-1950s. Performance-wise too, the primary set of actors seemed to have been caught in a theatrical code, except Chhabi Biswas.

The question is, were Uttam's films any different? *Bosu Poribar*, *Sanjeebani* and *Kar Pape?* certainly carried the marks of a new, bolder temperament but what about the other films? If you found yourself in

Calcutta in 1954 you would be perplexed to find several of Uttam's films that were devoutly old school, giving little sense of the period you were in. As for Uttam, after 1953's *Basu Poribar*, the next film that got the box office animated was *Agniporikha*, which came in the latter part of 1954. It is worth asking what films were there in the months in between. This is because even if the urge for a new kind of melodrama, attuned to the time, was felt, it was not readily available. Instead, studio-imported antiquarianism predominated for a while, ensuring that the bulk of Uttam's films during this phase were blind to cinema's changing self-perception in the post-War years. Film scholar Ravi Vasudevan has written that due to the availability of this kind of melodrama in the studio-produced talkie socials of the 1930s and 1940s, the term had a lower import, especially among the middle class.[2] He writes, "Central here is the persistence of a melodramatic engagement which has often, if not always, been invested with ambiguities, nostalgic tendencies, and 'backwardness' in response to the ideologies, if not the experience, of modernity."[3] Uttam's archaic melodramas fit perfectly into this description. These films, helmed mostly by veteran directors, hardly reveal any sense of the contemporary, betray little upheaval in form or content, or make no demands on the audience except soliciting for their most readily disposable sentiments. In other words, these films pretended as if the 1940s never happened in Bengal. This was the case as late as 1956. However, their quick succession and abrupt fading away indicate that they had over-lived their time. Since these films run well into Uttam's early stardom years, a quick look at them is imperative.

An English language review of *Bratacharini* (A Virtuous Woman, 1955) manages to put into context what was the common peeve in several films from this early phase of Uttam's rise. It says:

> Reduced to its essential concept the story sings the glory of the traditional goodness and lofty purity of Indian womanhood and the force of her silent devotion and love for the husband under all trying circumstances…. It being basically a story of the glorification of Indian womanhood with sacrifice as its burden of song. No one would call this a truly living story with prospects of any rich throw of dramatic suspense. Rather the ultimate aim is a foregone conclusion. Yet not many will deny its homely tenderness and its emotional warmth.

The possible reasons behind the plight of this feminine archetype could range from a pledge of loyalty (as in this film); or a commitment to a life of devotion as in *Montroshokti* (The Power of Prayer, 1954); or childlessness as in *Bidhilipi* (The Mark of Fortune, 1955); or a woebegone legend of a chaste wife as in *Kankabatir Ghat* (Bond of Purity, 1955). The actor Sondhyarani Chatterjee excelled in this sort of archaic, decorous portraits of miserable female martyrdom and so it is no wonder that she appears in all four of them. Even without her, the same theme continues in the caste-conflict drama *Moner Moyur* (The Singing Heart, 1954), or in the suffering-family outing *Debatra* (A Divine Will, 1955) with the venerable Kanan Debi in the lead in the latter. Not very different was the long-drawn village saga *Kalyani* (The Caregiver, 1954) where Manju Dey's titular figure was a similar prototype. The Vaishnav romance *Raikamal* (The Minstrel, 1955) had a new heroine in Kaberi Bose playing the character of the Krishna devotee who forgoes a long-awaited fulfilment of romance to choose a life of a wandering singer. In spite of New Theatres heavyweights Subosh Mitra (direction) and Pankaj Mullik (music), the verbose film barely manages to go beyond the pulls of mawkish drama. Set in a distant past of skewed caste barriers, *Lokhyoheera* (The Glitter of Good, 1956) champions the age-old theme of cursed or fallen women with pure souls who pull off impossible triumphs based on the strength of their faith. Three early films with Suchitra Sen too conform to this mould. In *Annapurnar Mondir* (Temple of Bounty, 1954), a young widow (Sen) sacrifices everything, even embracing death, to ensure that her equally righteous sister marries the man she loved. To ensure that there was not the slightest chance of error in their assessment, the sisters are named Sati and Savitri. Same goes for *Sanjher Prodip* (Light of the Dusk, 1955), except that here, the selfless young widow Rajlakshi must compete with Sumonto's devotion to the cause of India's national struggle. Not very far, in sentiment if not setting, was the life-after-death drama *Moroner Pore* (After Death, 1954), where Uttam's young psychiatrist Ashok is finally 'convinced' of the dubious theory of reincarnation, even though Suchitra does not play the vehicle of this trans-birth memory. This singular theme of a lofty woman protagonist who finds salvation only in being a wife and/or mother and is the carrier of traditional wisdom that stands as antidote to feminist agency made these films severely dated, even in the 1950s.

And they did not do much good to Uttam either. There are numerous testimonials to young Uttam's hard work as he tried to improve upon his acting. But one does not need to bank on them. A cursory look at these *archaic melodramas* is enough to show an ordinary actor more or less compliant with a predominantly theatrical style of performance, playing characters of stodgy subjugation to tradition. The above-mentioned films stand testimony to Uttam's rather mediocre early phase, he being stifled and nervous, even when he had much more substantive parts in them than those that came before. Naturally, these were not the sort of films which carried him into stardom. For that to happen, a different, in fact a new, kind of melodrama had to be sought. His transformation into maturity in films such as *Upohaar*, *Shapmochon*, *Sobar Opore* or *Shankar Narayan Bank*—all of which came at the same time as the films mentioned earlier—seems instantaneous. But it was as much a case of his own improvement as it was the changed configuration of the *new* melodramas, which managed to coax out the actor in him.

SUCHITRA SEN AND THE MELODRAMA OF EXCESS

What was this *new* melodrama? Was this *the* melodrama to whose métier some the biggest names in cinema, from Elia Kazan, Douglas Sirk, Vincente Minnelli, Billy Wilder and David Lean in Hollywood to Guru Dutt and Ritwik Ghatak in India, were attracted to? There is really no consensus about what it actually is because melodrama continues to be redefined again and again, making it also a notoriously shape-shifting idea.

In popular connotation, melodrama refers to cinema that makes use of formulaic narrative, script and craft to foreground voluble drama and emotion. In doing so, melodrama eschews the demands of realism, opting for a retinue of audience-pleasing plotting that proceeds to predictable resolutions. The academic definition is more intricate. The Melo-Drame (musical drama) came to the English stage from the French and since then, says Ben Singer,[4] most things between the "epistolary tale of sexual malice in *Clarissa* (1747) to the mystery-suspense film *Coma* (1978), via the turn-of-the century tied-to-the-tracks stage thriller and the classical Hollywood 'woman's weepie' claim to call itself a melodrama". In other words, as the family emerged into prominence in Western life, the theatre and the sentimental novel started mirroring signs of *being* a melodrama, where the 'home' became the organising principle of fictional narratives. By the time narrative cinema emerged, women were the decisive new consumer of entertainment, thereby putting melodrama at the heart of Hollywood's evolution into a movie-making factory. By that logic, a film that champions heterosexual, reproductive romance; provides unhindered emotional appeal; defends and reinforces the family as something inviolable and foundational to the real objective of human life cycle is, essentially, a melodrama.

This form of *melodrama*, which found powerful and popular iterations in post-WWII Hollywood is what took Bengali popular cinema by storm in the 1950s. Taking 1954 as a moment, it would be customary here to jump straight into the bandwagon of Uttam's ragingly successful romantic melodramas (most prominently with Suchitra Sen but not exclusively with her) that became the pivot of his rise. Countless accounts, both in popular press and in the roster of Bengali histories, have been dominated by this repertoire of romantic melodramas. Naturally, it is through these films that Uttam's fabular rise to stardom has been mapped and it is this standard narrative of these years that was credited to his becoming an unparalleled *matinee idol.*

But this 'standard narrative' refers to a problematic cultural trope because it consisted of films that fulfilled every platitude of an archetypal monochrome star vehicle. A rich, beautiful woman and a poor, educated man (or vice versa) would fall in love. Almost overnight, they would stake everything on each other. Then an implacable guardian of either would create outrageous hurdles. After which, a stupid rich suitor (male) or a pampered rich fiancé (female) would appear and make their half-baked claim. Then, our man and our woman would go through a prolonged period of separation, having been crossed either by parental proroguing or felled by fate. Our man is then rudderless and shaken; our woman is then depressed and suicidal. Following which they would meet and take months to sort out a petty dispute. Finally, the detractors and distractors would retreat, the season of love would commence and our man and our woman would be singing to the glory of the moon. This is all that there ever was in the monochrome megahit *Agniporikha* (Trial by Fire) or the box-office smasher *Trijama* (The Night River, 1956) or the Gevacolor blockbuster *Pothe Holo Deri* (The Delayed Journey), all of them directed by the ensemble directors' group Agradoot and all of them having Suchitra Sen as the female lead. The variations are minimal. Kiriti in *Agniporikha* is a rich dandy who rediscovers Tapasi years after their adolescent marriage was derailed by Tapasi's fashionable mother. In *Pothe Holo Deri,* poor doctor Jayanta pursues FRCS thanks to Mallika's deceased mother's jewellery, a transgression detested by the latter's wealthy grandfather. In *Trijama,* cocky Kushal and righteous Swarupa get in the way of each other thanks to a series of flimsy twists and another teary-eyed woman. Even the slightly developed romance *Bipasha* (The Tears of Beas, 1962), with the same director and pair was no improvement. The only difference was that the eponymous Bipasha is a Partition refugee and Dibyendu an engineer, both taking up causes of nation-building. But this reference pales as the flimsiness of the real plot, wasted in clichés, takes over.

One should add two more films to this grave list, both by the other director ensemble Agragami, both of them with Suchitra Sen and both of them stupendous successes. In *Sagorika* (The Call of the Sea), Sen's eponymous heroine refutes college mate Arunangshu's love for no apparent reason. A heartbroken Arunangshu accepts a would-be wife, in exchange for her father's offer to fund his foreign degree.

That would-be turns out to be Sagorika's distant cousin. While teaching that would-be to become worthy of an educated man, Sagorika finally falls in love, while news arrives that Arunangshu has lost his vision in a laboratory accident. After another set of hammy tribulations, they find union. Even more stagey was *Shilpi* (The Artiste, 1956), where star-crossed lovers are so crossed because they are from, ahem, different castes. And naturally, their union can't get the approval of the father of the rich, upper-caste woman, whose staunch refusal to accept the match pushes them towards a climactic union, if only in death.

The onus of these films was on the female protagonist (embodied in Suchitra), who was expected to embody patriarchal projections of agency, but who at the same time would never threaten the fantasy of control. In her critique of this contradiction, scholar Dulali Nag, in an essay focused on *Agniporikha*, writes,

> Desirability in a feminine image came to be defined by the image of Taposhi/Suchitra Sen. But one will miss the point of the meaning of the desirability if one focuses only on the end product of the narrative. For at that moment there is no difference between Suchitra Sen and earlier heroines like Chandrabati Debi or Padma Debi or Nibhanoni Debi. That the image of Suchitra Sen came to sweep the popular audience off its feet to rule over the market of Bengali cinema for about two decades is because Suchitra Sen *made a difference,* and that difference lay in the contradiction, expressed in a hysterical form in this film, inherent in the characters she played.[5]

Two Sarat Chandra Chattopadhyay literary romances also fall within this ambit. The need of a radiant damsel to be saved by the 'strong hands' of patriarchy is the theme of *Chondronath* (The Beautiful and the Damned, 1957), a 1916 novel, complete with all the cloying sentimentality that was staple of the author of *Devdas*. Here, Suchitra's Sarayu is both beautiful and damned, having to carry the shame of her mother's indiscretion of having eloped with a lover. Articulate aristocrat Chondronath marries her, abandons her for no fault of hers and then accepts her again after she has delivered his son; while she awaits her deliverance from misery all along. This film is to be remembered rather for being that famous one that was released in Calcutta's Metro cinema, signifying an end as well as a beginning and also marking a unique bond between a projectionist father and his star son. Ten years later came *Grihadaha* (A House on Fire, 1967), an adaptation of the same author's 1920 novel and again with Uttam and Suchitra in the lead. This was also the last film that Uttam bankrolled as a producer, roping in the veteran editor Subodh Mitra as director and Pradip Kumar as the third protagonist Suresh. Here, Suchitra's Ochola, thanks to her Brahmo upbringing, has a distinct voice. And yet, she cannot decide between poor and diligent Mahim (Uttam) and the wealthy and aggressive Suresh. She gets married to the former, runs away with the latter and in between causes a lot of heartburn till one of them dies and makes her job easy. Ochola's vacillations make the plot shift like a pendulum and the men go round and round. The problem is that unlike the novel's youthful fallacies and its early period, the film, in which the woman is above thirty-five and the men into their 40s, renders the plot an unbefitting prospect, their merry-go-round bordering on the mindless. The two films manage to carry some weight as literary classics, partially shielding them from living up to the call of the contemporary. But they are archetypal melodramas, fit only for literary readership of the early 20th century. On screen, they are vintage weepies.

Apart from this well-worn clichés and set-piece plots, what was also inevitable in these films was their being part of a sealed world. This world was not necessarily anti-modern but in it the business of the world seems to be nothing important unless they are to be found conspiring against or fostering a romantic pairing. Cloistered within that constricting world, these films are, in fact, models of the romance of excess. There is an excess of wealth, of showiness, of loyalty, of longing, of misunderstanding, of suffering, of remorse, of resolution. This is because unless the smallest of disputes, briefest of errors and tiniest of cracks are stretched to their limits, there would not be enough tugging at tear glands. Except for a series of tuneful and memorable compositions, these are actually pitiable films which managed to strike, without succumbing to studied orthodoxy, the sentimental chord with the public. But when was it, if ever, that a star's anointed life was only made of great romantic films? Can one ignore the unwatchable *An Affair to Remember* if one is poring over Cary Grant? In fact, we need not go all that far. Despite being of similar plotting, *Harano Sur* or *Indrani* manage to rise way above the stuffy, cosseted, self-same world of the girl-meets-boy-under-strenuous-circumstances romances. But the too-eager-to-be-satiated audience hardly made a difference between *Pothe Holo Deri* and *Indrani*. In fact, Suchitra's daintily worn nylon sarees rendered in colour, in spite of artificial eyebrows and over-waxed close-ups, became a rage in the former. So, it was not so much in the plot but how they were rendered on screen what shaped the artistic fate of the *melodramas of excess*.

And what did they leave the men with? Frankly, Uttam's parts in these films are either indecisive and vague; or irate and one-dimensional; or at best being an audience of his own misfortune. In fact, his characters seem to doggedly wait for the excess to play out for the crisis to find a resolution. However, the reception of these over-the-top melodramas gave Uttam's screen persona such a popular heft that it threatened to subsume his efforts at avoiding being imprisoned by an image. On the other hand, their spectacular success gave the on-screen partnership of Uttam and Suchitra an unassailable, indisputable standing; and their off-screen pairing the delectable palatability of an urban lore. So, the films bothered and pleased Uttam equally.

Despite the succession of mediocre films, Uttam and Suchitra had developed a temperament, sensibility and comfort that was increasingly transported, unforced, to the screen. 1956, 1957 and 1958 turned out to be the peak for their duet. Of the thirty films they had done together over twenty-two years, fourteen appeared in these three years, some of them much better than those mentioned here. And we will come to the better ones soon. But there was something more than the numbers or the varying quality. The stacking of these quickly succeeding romances deflates one of the founding myths of Bengali cinema: that an entire generation was wowed every Friday by a Uttam–Suchitra film. Three years do not make a generation and all reminiscences to that effect are foggy, mostly because the pair's stratospheric success merged with the entire range of romantic melodramas of this period. But there were several other screen pairs, there were several kinds of romances and there were also various other kinds of films. But good old memory hardly subscribes to the facts. And facts show that there was an overuse of this screen couple in hastily written films; and an over-mining of their commercial appeal, which together had produced a cinematic truism that continued to feed the public imagination. But facts also point out that after three hectic years, when it looked like another barrage of films of the screen couple were to clog the pipelines, there was a sudden and steep decline. The years 1959, 1961 and 1962 each saw just one film of them together, while 1960 did not have any release, making it the first such a case in eight years. Uttam in his memoirs have pointed to the obvious: that the pair was getting over-used within a limited framework, exposing both of them to exhaustion. Guessing the same, they pulled out of their partnership with mutual consent. In fact, the pair was virtually retired, with the exception of *Bipasha*, after the iconic blockbuster *Soptopodi*. In the next eighteen years—till Uttam passed away—they did just six films, none of them having come close to the aura or success of their peak romance films.

The collaborative success has, however, not concealed the fact that next to Uttam, Suchitra was much less of an actor. Born Roma Dasgupta in Pabna in undivided Bengal, she made her unpromising debut in 1952 and like Uttam had a long-unreleased film to contend with. By the time they came together in 1953, she had attained a degree of temperance on screen that was still elusive to Uttam. However, since then Suchitra got sucked into the image of a distant, diva-like figure with touch-me-not mannerisms that made her characters appear repetitive and predictable, which was more than apt for these melodramas. More than talent, what she had was a luminous and unstrained beauty, a radiant smile and that unmistakable celluloid magnetism, making her a figure of both adoration and desire. Much like the heady Joan Crawford in Hollywood. However, in films like *Harano Sur*, *Indrani*, *Surjotoron* and *Soptopodi*—armed with characters having a strong sense of will (and education) and with a good pair of directing hands behind—she could no doubt raise the bar. When her partnership with Uttam was withdrawn, she managed to find at least three films in which she could live up to the expectations of having screen autonomy and box-office appeal of her own. They were *Deep Jele Jai* (The Iridescent, 1959), *Saat Pake Bandha* (Marriage Trap, 1963) and *Uttor Phalguni* (A Parallel Life, 1963), the second of which got her a best actor's award at the Moscow Film Festival, the first for any Indian female actor. Incidentally, all the three were later made in Hindi as *Khamoshi* (1969), *Kora Kagaz* (1974) and *Mamta* (1966), the last with her in the lead.

Her talented peers were the free-spirited Manju Dey, the matured Arundhati Mukherjee and the sharp and dusky Kaberi Bose, none of whom could be 'accommodated' in the desired household of a Bengali middle-class family—well-meaning perhaps but no less patriarchal for that. Suchitra's persona on the other hand was the right blend of a beautiful, educated woman, who tended without threatening to appropriate full agency. This is the sort of female protagonist that these melodramas brought to the fore, as Nag has pointed out, through the mechanism of hysteric articulation of excess. The problem with Suchitra is that she too readily played into this stereotype, looking all the stagier next to Uttam's naturalist style. Her later films managed to sequester her talent to a degree from her being at the service of one kind of melodrama. But on the whole her onscreen mannerisms and an entrenched coquetry render her parts increasingly outmoded, redeemed, if at all, only in moments of onscreen quietude and gravitas.

From the mid-1960s Suchitra appeared sparsely, letting a younger generation take over, an indulgence that was denied forever to her famous on-screen partner and dear friend. Her Bombay soujourns were also the mirror opposite of Uttam. In fact, Suchitra was the only Bengali actor of her generation to have stayed put in her home language even after she found early success with Bimal Roy's *Devdas* (1955), preferring to appear in Hindi cinema sporadically, which climaxed memorably two decades later in Gulzar's *Aandhi* (1975). Her Garbo-like self-exile in 1979 has since been a steady focus of the voyeuristic mainstream press.

And her detractors saw that as another example of her sense of excess, from height of fame to height of seclusion, that she borrowed from her screen persona. But she was not remotely in the prime of her career when she retreated and neither was her seclusion an unthinking whim. It was always befitting of her person, who had managed to stay resolutely professional through her working years; had refused to be seduced by Bombay; and was undaunted on the face of collective male fixation that stalked her for over two decades. Years in this competitive industry also revealed to her the casual sexism and ageism of the trade she was part of; things she chose not to suffer after a point. So, she parted ways on her own terms, bequeathing to her substantive fandom the onus to remember her *only* as she wanted them to. She stayed unassailable till the end, even refusing the Dadasaheb Phalke Award in 2005, before she passed away in 2014, unseen in public for thirty-five years.

MELODRAMAS OF CUSTOM

The *melodrama of excess* was by no means limited to just one screen pair. In fact, the success of the pairing only emboldened the 'genre', even if it was clear that no one else could substitute the screen couple's collective reputation. Apart from Suchitra and beyond her, these melodramas, in fact, became a habit. So, long after Uttam found his feet as a star in the mid-1950s and after the onscreen pairing with Suchitra was withdrawn in the early-1960s, the spate of gratuitous melodramas continued to exist. This is because it is in the nature of both a popular industry and archetypal stardom that they keep partaking in movies which marshal faint artistic justification. At the same time, these other melodramas had an enlarged narrative scope, were not necessarily banking on the repeat value of a successful screen couple, and could sometimes even avoid the clichés. So, to separate them from the particular prototype of Uttam–Suchitra's over-the-top melodramas, I have called them *melodramas of custom*. They sometimes found passing audience appreciation; sometimes they silently passed into oblivion, but they kept coming with expected regularity every Friday. They had to.

This is why even some of the better filmmakers could not avoid the trap of making an inane romance, the formidable Debaki Bose being one. His village saga *Nabajonmo* (A New Birth, 1956) about a suspicious husband and high-pitched vows of wifely fidelity offered nothing new except Uttam's rendering of six, brief, musical couplets in his own voice. This film is close in setting and plot to *Chanpadangar Bou* (The Wronged Wife, 1954), which came two years before and was based on a popular novel by Tarashankar Bondopadhyay. What distinguished this Nirmal

Dey film was Uttam's Mohatap, the happy-go-lucky simpleton caught between a precocious wife, a protective sister-in-law and a cantankerous brother. Among his early films, this was a stand-out performance, but the film had little merit otherwise. These village-themed socials continued to dot Uttam's career, the roving romance *Sathihara* (Nomadic Love, 1961), being another. In spite of it having been directed by Sukumar Dasgupta and dealing with the pressing theme of capitalist aspiration luring carefree roamers, it was just as anodyne, even if it was bestowed with a terrific soundtrack. One exception could have been *Kuhok* (The Enchanter, 1960), the script having been adapted by the writer Samaresh Basu from the Robert Mitchum classic *The Night of the Hunter* (1955). What attracted Basu was the convoluted protagonist, who was both a killer and an entrancing singer of hymns, allowing Uttam to play in equal parts a lover and a murderer, something then out of sync with his image. Here, Mitchum's Harry Powell is Uttam's Sunondo. After his release from a brief incarceration, Sunondo rejoins a *jatra* group, a form of traditional travelling theatre. His travels bring him to his prison-friend Ganesh's village, where his mesmeric voice bewitches Ganesh's sister Sworno. The next night, Ganesh's final heist goes horribly wrong, when he is killed but his loot escapes the police. The prospect of that bounty being on the loose stops Sunondo from leaving with his troupe, while it takes him little work to convince the gullible Sworno about his false intentions. But gradually Sunondo gets enshrouded in two selves—one in love with Sworno and the other one craving for the money—till an old foe brings the tensions to a sudden and tragic resolution. The film could have been much more engaging, especially because of Sunondo's twisted clarity about his divided conscience. But the film narrowly depends on Uttam to deliver, investing only in music but neither in a psychological role-play nor in the language of a screen thriller. The other potential exception to the run of sentimental village saga was *Vibhas* (The Outcast, 1964), which had a political theme of exploited villagers unionising against a local bully under the leadership of an unthreatening outsider. Again, with great songs but little else.

Uttam sidestepped playing the lead in another long-drawn weepy *Mayamriga* (The Red Herring, 1960) about an adopted son who has to choose between his foster and real mother. Uttam's footloose cameo in Mahendra, who is unpaired, raised the hackles of his fans, who considered his choice unreasonable. But he is thankfully saved from being in the middle of another precocious family saga where the tenacity of the poor is tested to absurd lengths. Its only memory-worthy part is with Mahendra in it. Like this film, moments of quiet humour are also the takeaway for *Prithibi Amare Chai* (The World at Large, 1957), which had parallel stories involving two pairs of unmoored lovers, homeless and hurt. One of the pairs, Tapas and Meena, after a round of respective toil, head for the river to commit suicide. This scene, inspired from Frank Capra's *It's a Wonderful Life*, needs a re-visitation. Standing next to the Hooghly, Tapas (Uttam) persuades Meena (Mala Sinha) to rethink her decision. He starts describing the excruciating ordeal of choking to death in the depths of the cold river in the dead of the night, as if he had been there a few times. Then, he says, "That is precisely the moment when, like a movie, your whole life will emerge as a flashback—those who had ever smiled, those who had ever loved you, who had ever meant anything to you, you will see them with absolute clarity." Meena, listening intently, asks with all seriousness, "Is it? Will it be a silent one or a talkie?" To her absurd query, Tapas answers with all seriousness that it would be a talkie show down under, that past life will come back with the entire soundtrack attached to it! This is one of those scenes from such films where a possible sentimental overload is upturned to extract easy humour. They obviously retreat from the river and start living together in an abandoned house nearby. But love does not abate hunger. So, they go through another set of trials, this time jointly, before they find togetherness. All in all, a mildly likeable movie. Ditto for the 'joint family is a happy family' tale *Punormilon* (The Reunion, 1957) and the good-boy-in-bad-company stereotype *Goli Theke Rajpoth* (Rags to Riches, 1959). In the latter, Helen appears in a sprightly choreographed Hindi song 'Tere liye laya leke koi mera dil', this being her first appearance in a Bengali film. Asha Bhosle gave her voice to a tune set by Sudhin Dasgupta. A rarely heard Geeta Dutta gem 'Ke Go Tumi' compliments Bhosle.

In several of the films—*Nabajonmo, Chanpadangar Bou, Kuhok, Punormilon, Goli Theke Rajpoth*—Uttam is paired with Sabitri Chatterjee. She was the only possible alternative to Suchitra's screen persona, especially in the film set within a modest household, as all the films above are. Sabitri did not have or seek out the appeal or luminosity of Suchitra, even if she had more than enough of that Doris Day kind of girl-next-door currency. She was (in fact still is) a consummate actress who knew her limitations by heart and never tried to veer into cinematic territory where she might look out of place. No wonder, she is not found in the *melodramas of excess* but in a variety of other melodramas. She was Uttam's longest screen partner and their partnership, as I have stated earlier, was beyond any obvious pattern or affective formula, even if both had a delightful talent for refined comedy. A long life together on screen makes their filmography varied, showing their clear evolution on screen. But only a few films with them together will pass into the minority of the truly memorable. In Uttam's personal life, however, Sabitri was a confidant and a moral compass.

As Uttam became more comfortable in his stature as a star, she retreated, never making a claim to any exclusivity to his person, even though no one deserved it more than her. She was doubtlessly the best actress of the trio of Suchitra–Sabitri–Supriya, and surely one of the best ever in Bengali cinema. Age has taken its claim on her memory but she remains deeply committed to her esteem for Uttam, even if he was not always kind to her protestations about his choices.

If anyone actually took these Hollywood comparisons seriously it was Supriya, who tried hard to model herself on the erotic appeal of Sophia Loren. But she was an actor of unpredictable range, lacking either in Suchitra's grace or Sabitri's likeability. If pushed in the right direction, she could be unforgettable, as she was in a handful of films through her long career, including the iconic double-bill with Ritwik Ghatak. But otherwise, she re-plays herself endlessly, adorned with unbefitting make-up, inflated sexuality and thunderous acting, all of which looked even more amplified when paired with Uttam. But taking advantage of her real-life partnership with the star, she kept injecting herself into movies with him, only making her case even more excruciating.

So, Supriya Chowdhuri started to fill in for Suchitra, especially in movies campaigning for outsized romantic ambition. Her mannerisms, far more exasperating than Suchitra, only upped the impossibility index of the films. *Shuno Boronari* (An Unequal Romance, 1960) hammers on a typical template of romantic melodrama: a woman going to meet her fiancé falls for the travelling companion. Well, this woman is rich and the companion poor. That makes the film being made of two, most jaded of templates. The rest is predictable, because this film is similar to the predicaments of all such templates. *Uttarayan* (The Rising, 1963) is the only Uttam film whose Hindi adaptation—Dev Anand's *Hum Dono*— bettered the original. A commander crosses with his lookalike, an army chauffeur, at war, only to learn later that he has succumbed to injuries. The survivor opts to seclude the wife and mother of the poor driver from the news and impersonates him by becoming alien to his own lover. When she confronts him, he begs understanding. That leaves little hope for the wife of the poor driver, who commits suicide, paving the way for the commander's reintegration. As singularly preposterous as this plot is, it is accentuated by poor writing and listless acting. The Uttam-directed stylish romance *Sudhu Ekti Bochhor* (A Marriage Contract, 1966) carrying whiffs of Shakespeare's *Taming of the Shrew*, had car races, thrilling escapades and night-time serenades on the lake. But the film loses steam soon after it begins, thanks to the masochistic hemming-in of a freedom-loving woman, the predictable plot of foes turning into lovers during forced cohabitation and also Supriya's exaggerated Jaya, restless for release from the sham of her 'convicted' conjugality.

Image 5.1: Partnership on a piece of paper. Uttam directed the stylish romance with Supriya Chowdhuri. Lobby card of *Sudhu Ekti Bochhor* (A Marriage Contract, 1966)

Source: Parimal Ray.

In fact, sexism and masochism were nothing new or alien to these melodramas, even if they were couched in the saviour complex. Two films spread over a decade bring out this leaning. The directing hands of Ajoy Kar and the tall and striking Kaberi Bose's speech-and-hearing impaired titular character were major draws for *Shyamali* (A Woman in the Dark, 1956), the film version coming in the wake of the rousingly successful stage adaptation. But the plot, adapted from Nirupama Devi's 1919 novel, is problematic. The very virtuous gentleman Anil marries Shyamali under trying circumstances, but gets caught in the whirl of tensions, aggravated by Shyamali's adamant trust only in him and his mother's staunch dislike for her. The entry of Reba, doleful and caring, makes matters more maudlin, especially when she nurses her own affection for Anil while tending to the traumatised Shyamali. The conclusion is forgone because marriage is an inviolable 'matter' but even worse is the treatment of women who have no way out of their ordeal unless 'saved' by a good-as-angel man. This film is a good example that even though the social climate in Bengal had changed enormously between the 1920s and 1950s, there was a persistent denial to treat a plot like *Shyamali* as a period piece. Ditto for *Surjotopa* (Sun Prayer, 1965) which partly supplied the story to the Hindi superhit *Kati Patang*, both being also influenced by the 1950 noir drama *No Man of Her Own*. Kanak finds herself in charge of a newborn, having been foxed by his real mother. She raises the child as her own, ignorant of him being heir to a wealthy Calcutta family. When the family discovers them in Haridwar, she is mistaken as the widowed wife of their elder son, accused of abetting her husband's suicide. But they grudgingly take her in for the sake of the boy, the boy's uncle Dipendra (Uttam) being the most resentful. When Kanak's (Sondhya Roy) real identity is revealed, she shifts base and takes up work as a salesgirl, while the boy remains unaware of the revelations. When the pulls of motherhood keep bringing her back, Dipendra, betrothed to a shrewd woman, starts to take a liking for her capacity for selfless affection, hinting at her obvious rehabilitation. The sexism apart, both the films could well be credited to the formulaic populism that was entrenched in one kind of melodrama, under which unadventurous filmmakers found refuge from time to time.

But deviations from routine romances did not produce anything less middling either. For example, there was that rare road movie *Notun Tirtho* (A New Destination, 1964) where an ensemble set of characters get into a long-distance bus, each leaving behind something, each aiming for something new, before they get embroiled in an innocuous tale of mistaken identity. Though urbane and stylish, *Shohorer Itikotha* (Tales of the City, 1960), loosely adapted from Bernard Shaw's *Pygmalion* and mirroring class stratification, gets caught in a loop of romantic vacillation. Another similar adaptation was *Necklace* (The Necklace, 1961), scripted from the famous Guy de Maupassant story. Like the story, the film mocks the pomp and show of the aristocracy, questioning the fickleness of class ambitions. Uttam's first-class Supriyo is a treat, especially when the warring couple learns to belong to a cause together, labouring hard to pay for the expensive but fake adornment they had to replace. But compared to his act, newcomer Sunita Debi's Mallika is a serious lapse. A fake necklace is also at the heart of *Shokher Chor* (The Mischievous Thief, 1960), an impish comedy about a set of whimsical men who are not what they seem to be. Two late 1960s thrillers, *Jibonmrityu* (Life and Death, 1967) and *Kokhono Megh* (Shadows of the Cloud), involved murder, impersonation, theft, corporate rivalry, criminal gangs, police chase and such others. Uttam plays an intelligence officer in the latter. But it is in the former that he is memorable as an unsuspecting banker, who when severely checkmated by his colleagues, fakes his death and returns as a Sikh industrialist to heap misery on his foes. It was remade in Hindi with the same name. As thrillers, they are just about promising, but fall short of going all the way. Finally, there was the shoddy *Teen Odhyay* (Three Episodes, 1968), a half-baked relationship-quadrangle couching itself as a drama about company-intrigue and politics of labour welfare.

These films had a promising premise, which ultimately collapses into predictability, having been caught in their own lack of imagination and desire for populist approval. At the same time, these films do not carry the excesses of the Uttam–Suchitra melodramas and were also several notches below in popularity. But on a soft Saturday evening, some of them, like *Shokher Chor,* would pass the muster of being watchable, simply because they are easy on the senses and do not stretch credibility beyond the practicable. And there are always some likeable moments and some very hummable songs.

Others lacked even in those redeeming bits, failing to make any addition to the screen persona of Uttam. The colliery-set, mistaken-identity drama *Jatra Holo Shuru* (The Journey Begins, 1957), the lost-son tearjerker *Harjeet* (Toil and Triumph, 1957), the fugitive crime chronicle *Uttormegh* (Beyond the Cloud, 1960), the ambitious hunting drama *Shikaar* (The Hunt, 1958) and the crime-syndicate thriller *Sonar Harin* (The Golden Stag, 1959) seemed to have just kept the theatres occupied, if at all. These tacky films continued in the 1960s too with the Ritwik Ghatak-scripted insipid palace intrigue *Rajkonya* (Portrait of a Princess, 1965), the pot-boiler period drama *Rajdrohi* (The Royal Rebel, 1966) and the Mughal costume-drama *Garh Nasimpur* (The Fight for Nasimpur, 1968), the last two being unapologetically kitschy.

MELODRAMA OF TRANSFORMATION

None of the types of melodramas discussed in the previous sections, however, would direct us to the idea of performative stardom that Uttam's screen persona gradually pushed to the fore. For that, we need to look at a final set of films. These films were more than just romances. This is because popular cinema had to find means to mirror the world around; if not realistically, but at least symptomatically. Uttam began to shine in them, having found his forte and having surrendered himself to the more nuanced of directors and scripts bolstered by the coming to fore, in film after film, of a strong, exigent female counterpart.

The emergence of an *alternative* form of melodrama was by no means unique to Bengal, even if it came with local adjustments. In fact, scholars of cinema and mass culture have for long alerted us to the unpredictable directions that melodrama can move, its earlier import as a 'lowly', a-modern cinematic style notwithstanding. To start with, one tends to agree with the capacity of a melodrama to contest entrenched systems, including its own, especially if one remembers that the earliest import of Melo-Drame from French to the English stage involved radical Jacobins like Thomas Holcroft.[6] Peter Brooks influential *The Melodramatic Imagination* pointed decisively to the intricate relationship between melodrama and literature. In the 1995 preface to this book he summed up his thought: "(Melodrama) has the flexibility, the multifariousness, to dramatise and to explicate life in imaginative forms that transgress the traditional generic constraints, and the traditional demarcations of high culture from popular entertainment."[7] In another context Bill Nichols calls melodrama an imaginary form, which, in his introduction to a seminal essay by Thomas Elsaesser, he sums up as ambivalent and polyvalent, politically agnostic and internally elastic.[8] That essay by Elsaesser, on Hollywood melodrama, does try to address the continuation of the excessive melodramatic need for interiority even when divorced from its original impetus, the 18th-century sentimental novel. Following him Ben Singer offers a cluster concept theory of melodrama, insisting that a definitive and closed terminology is redundant. He writes:

> I propose a definitional scheme that analyzes melodrama as a "cluster concept" involving different combinations of at least five key constitutive elements: strong pathos; heightened emotionality; moral polarisation; non-classical narrative mechanics; and spectacular effects. Just a couple, and perhaps even just one, of these elements might prompt the designation of a play or film as a melodrama.[9]

There has even been further expansion of the idea of melodrama lately, where scholars have tried to see long historical time represented through it and not just a narrowly populist narrative form. Carla Marcantonio, for example, writes:

> At the turn of the nineteenth century, melodrama arose as a means to represent and help make sense of emerging democratic and industrial societies. Ever since, melodrama has retained an elastic ability to adapt to varying incarnations of modernity, becoming a form that can engage with and process cultural, social, technological, and political change.[10]

The best summation of what could be called the redemption of melodrama comes not from film but theatre scholar Matthew Buckley, though he by no means is talking about theatre exclusively. He writes:

> In the last few decades … critical interest in popular and mass culture has turned to melodrama as a central element of modern narrative culture, finding in it an essential mode of consciousness in the post-sacred world; a core rhetoric of emergent mass discourses of community and identity; a foundational aesthetic in the development of the novel, film, and television; a dominant language in the modern conduct of public life and politics; and a shaping force in the creation of modern conceptions of family, gender, race, and nation. No longer

exiled from cultural history, melodrama seems now central to it, an essential thread in the warp and weave of global modernity.[11]

These observations throw open the possibility of severe mutations in the melodramatic form, making it a protean and portentous project of modernity, rather than being opposed to it. No doubt, it gained further complexity when melodrama, among other imports, came to the independent post-colonies. We can infer that if in the studio era a certain kind of *old world* melodrama travelled this way, in the 1950s another kind did, even if the previous one had a long life in Bengali cinema. In Bengal, the coming of age melodrama was not simply a matter of cultural transportation but proved to be a unique and subliminal subcontinental imperative that was forced open by Partition. Given the elasticity of the form/genre and when coupled with a new scope and understanding of cinema, it was natural that Bengali cinema, between the early-1950s and the end-1960s, was evidently drawn towards this *new kind* of melodrama. In other words, the Partition and the newly independent Indian state opened new possibilities of dealing with modernity, space and the female subject and here is where the *new* melodramas of the 1950s made substantial gains, moving swiftly from old-school weepies to set-piece romances, and then, to the powerful *melodramas of transformation*. One must note though that given the tenacity, elasticity and variability inherent in it, melodramas do not exhaust themselves with romances, as we will see in the next chapters.

What is also comparatively unique to Bengal was that new romantic melodramas were a call to *comprehend* the limits and possibilities of life on an everyday basis, triggering a *new* cinematic language and a *new* aesthetic that was appreciative of the changed nature of life and culture in an independent province. Moreover, it is in these *romances* that we see a probing feminine authority who is propelled into being the embodiment of change and the embracer of modernity. Even if none of them declare war against institutions of marriage and motherhood, they question their casual and unproblematic acceptance. And in a major shift from archaic romances, where education is meant to have disturbed a woman's tenacity and distracted her from her traditional role, in these *alternate* melodramas, education is perceived as empowering and a marker of necessary individuality. And in all these cases, the men (plural in characters; but singular in most of them being *enacted* by Uttam) are either led by their partners or are willingly shouldering the commitment towards change. This is a crucial sign of the declared transformation that Bengali popular cinema undertook during that period. Not that strong female characters were absent in Bengali cinema before but they did not appear so regularly and so overtly as legislators of change as they did in these films. Neither popular acceptance nor the archetypal definition of melodrama is hence adequate to encompass these films. This is not to underestimate the popularity that Uttam's staple romances could command. But this is to situate Uttam's ascent within a much more complex and variable body of work than to gauge it through a simple, laudatory eulogy to blockbuster romances. To that end, this final set (and those what come in the next chapters) will most fruitfully reveal the emblematic cultural totem that Uttam became since the 1950s, both as a celluloid persona and as a figure of collective aspiration.

The surest marker of this change is that even the studios responded to it. One of New Theatres' last projects, *Bakul* (The Boy in the Middle, 1954), is a case in point. The film is about the rich heiress Jayanti, who is fiercely independent and aggrieved by the prospect of bearing children. Circumstances lead her to the widower Aparesh (Uttam), who having hidden his past life, ends up marrying Jayanti (Arundhati Mukherjee). But when a mishap renders Aparesh immobile and his life with Jayanti sours, it is upon Bakul, Aparesh's naughty, lovable son to surface as the catalyst of union. In the end Jayanti's independence is tamed, as she has a massive change of heart, deciding to adopt Bakul. But it is she who decides her life, throughout the film. If the man here had a chequered past, the woman has the same in Sushil Majumdar's *Pushpadhonu* (Bow of Flowers, 1959), which came five years later with the same pair of Uttam and Arundhati. Here, Uttam plays the vagabond Shantanu, befriended by the supremely confident danseuse Ishani, who had been forced to hide her unwed motherhood. As her young boy, growing up in a Christian orphanage, veers towards teenage and the father resurfaces after a decade, Ishani faces a crisis of trust and ownership, in which she finds the ungrudging companionship of Shantanu. Apart from Arundhati, who had a natural ownership of characters who were independent and mature, there was also Mala Sinha, who played the determinant woman quite aptly. For example, Mala Sinha's Sujata in Chitta Basu's *Bondhu* (Test of Friendship, 1958) is a warm but no-nonsense character. She finds herself at the receiving end of competitive attention of two dearest of friends, who had grown up to be inseparable. This film was in the mould of a classic romance triangle which finds resolution in the more go-getter of the two finally giving up his claim. But Sujata is no hand-me-down and she plays an active role in determining who she would like to be with. She plays a similar strong-willed character in the same director's *Surer Parashe* (The Touch of Melody, 1957), a musical-comedy involving a theatre actress and a writer, where a spate of moves to outwit each other lead to their falling head over heels in love. Here too, the actress Manisha is a proud ball of fire and does not settle for anything unless she is convinced that she should aim for it.

Mala Sinha, a Nepali Christian by origin and Calcuttan by residence, was fluent in Bengali. After her debut in 1952, she peaked in Bengali cinema between 1956 and 1961, when she appeared in about ten films, of which seven were with Uttam. She had a parallel life in Bombay at least since the mid-1950s, Guru Dutt's *Pyaasa* and Ramesh Saigal's Dostoevsky adaptation *Phir Subah Hogi* being two memorable films from that phase. Once she shifted base in the early 1960s, Mala Sinha not only had a long career in Hindi cinema but was a top heroine. Few actors have had an equally successful stint in two languages. And as far as Bengali cinema is concerned, the only other name that comes close is Sharmila Tagore. But unlike Tagore, Mala Sinha was not an actor of any distinguished sensitivity. In her Bengali films she does not stand out in any special way in spite of her hearty laughter and a passing resemblance to Suchitra. At the same time, hers is an unforced, natural presence, which did not lose its comportment, especially when repeatedly up against a co-actor of Uttam's range.

In two films, Sabitri Chatterjee played an assured woman who instructed the men. The lively comedy *Obhoyer Biye* (Education of a Simple Man, 1957) was a remake of an old classic about the talented scientist Abhoy, who having been fed John Stuart Blackies' Victorian tomb *On Self-Culture*, grows up a cloistered half-adolescent—innocuous, lonely and unused to the ways of the world. His 'real' edification, from monastic Victorianism to liberal modernity, is the theme of the film, which is secured through Maya, a wealthy lawyer's educated and self-assured daughter. Maya's provocations, taunts and life lessons help Abhoy outgrow a life lived vicariously through a borrowed book. Sabitri's tormented Deepa is also the one who aids the learning of psychoanalyst Surojit Sen in *Momer Alo* (The Light of Candle). Here, Dr Sen (Uttam) is summoned to a wealthy suburban gentleman's home to treat Deepa, who is suffering from a guilt-induced trauma for imagining herself to have been culpable in her fiancé's fatal accident. Dr Sen has to untie her knotted mind, prove her innocence and also help her find her being. But he finds himself emotionally drawn to his delicate client, something that professional psychoanalysis strictly prohibits. The film does not have the introspective arsenal of an art-house production or the emotional heft of *Deep Jwele Jai*, which had a similar theme. But it still manages to portray the psychoanalyst's turpitude with some finesse, making fine use of deep focus cinematography.

Three other films with different female actors manage to build persistent female characters. In *Joutuk* (The Dowry, 1958), Sudhira—only heir to her father's estate—makes her maiden voyage to her native land to save her property. On the way, she unknowingly falls in love with Viren (Uttam), who is accused of appropriating part of her estate.

She, however, tries to stick to her plan, repressing her feelings. Viren, too, nurses the same duality. The film follows a typical theme of enemies falling crazily in love, the call of duty, the nature of property, and so on. But the film stands out thanks to Sumitra Debi's (of *Saheb Bibi Golam*) Sudhira, who does not hesitate to upend gender roles and norms. It is not a heart-warming film, even if it was technically accomplished and had a fine soundtrack. A similar case is Agradoot's *Agnisonskar* (Fire Sermon), where Uttam plays the do-gooder engineer Rajat. His socialist conscience saves a family-owned factory, but he gets embroiled in a psychological play-off between a mother and son. The possessive son's suicide is taken for murder, implicating Rajat; but he is saved at the last moment by the tireless efforts of his love Sumita (Supriya). Like this film, a warm friendship saved *Sobar Opore*, their third blockbuster in a row, from collapsing into the set pattern of Uttam–Suchitra's *melodramas of excess*. *Sobar Opore* (The Final Truth), based on A.J. Cronin's novel *Beyond This Place* and the original of *Kala Pani* (1958), is eminently watchable because of its deft mix of quiet heartfelt romance and over-the-top courtroom drama. Shankar (Uttam) is a young lawyer who sets out to fight a case to reverse the order of life imprisonment of his father, who was accused in a concocted case of an insurance-related death. He is partnered in his quest by Rita (Suchitra), who offers her friendship and shelter, undeterred by the possibility of having herself embroiled in a scandal for having cohabited with a young man. Her perseverance, warmth and intelligence pulls Shankar out of gloom and sets him firmly on the difficult path of legal retribution.

Then, there were a series of curious commentaries on the pitfalls of conjugality, without trying to make any loud claims. They also manage to render the crisis as credible and determinant of the changing permutations of modern life. A good example is Chitta Basu's apparently prototypical mother vs wife romance *Putrobodhu* (The Daughter in Law, 1956), which had Mala Sinha playing Shukla, the wife. But unlike the predominant model of married womanhood on screen, she is not just educated and free from self-doubt, but also refuses to play the fawning wife to either her husband or her mother-in-law. More telling is Niren Lahiri's *Indrani* (The Egoist), where the marriage between Indrani (Suchitra) and Sudorshan (Uttam) starts to sour after the former gets a teaching job in a distant town. They shift out of their Calcutta dwelling hoping to start a new life. But Sudorshon, jobless and meandering in spite of a first-class degree, wallows in self-doubt and starts to resent the world of sufficiency that Indrani was able to create single-handedly. Unable to make his hollow existence useful to Indrani, he finally sets out on a mission to find worthy employment. The film is also notable for some astonishing music by Nachiketa Ghosh, including

Image 5.2: The restrained coquetry of romance. Uttam and Suchitra Sen. Poster of *Indrani* (The Egoist, 1958)

Source: Parimal Ray.

the quiet romantic song 'Sabhi Kuch Lutakar' by Mohammad Rafi, sung on screen by a walk-on troubadour while Uttam and Suchitra watch. Incidentally, Rafi was one of Uttam's very handful of friends in Bombay, who publicly mourned his passing and in fact passed away exactly a week after Uttam's death.

If the working wife is resented in *Indrani*, in Salil Dutta's *Surjosikha* (Flames of the Sun, 1963) it is the opposite. Here, Uttam's Dipto Roy, an obsessively dedicated surgeon at a provincial hospital, finds the right kind of working rapport with the talented nurse Achena (Supriya). They get married, Dipto hoping that her competence will make his dedication absolute. But Achena, an orphan who had never hoped for a married life, pines to escape work and find solace in being a dutiful wife. That irks Dipto no end. As their life's primary preoccupations start to diverge, they heap raging outbursts on each other till a pregnant Achena, unable to cope, walks away. Years later, the son, a promising doctor, reunites them in the autumn of their lives.

But marriage was not always a dispiriting prospect. For, there are three films—the best three of the whole range covered in this chapter— where couple-hood is seen through the prism of playful role-playing rather than as a complicated and contractual obligation. In Hemchandra Chandra's adorable comedy *Manmoyee Girls' School* (Scandal in a School, 1958), Uttam plays the queasy Manash, who simulates a conjugality with Niharika (Arundhati) to get a job as a teaching couple because only a couple could apply for it. They find themselves close to an exposure for not only faking their marriage but for also undertaking unmarried cohabitation. And to make matters worse, Manash is a Hindu and Niharika a Christian. But because both need a job and because they can rise well above the trifling fact of their faith, they manage to tie the loose ends amicably, never veering far from the overall climate of humour in the film. Couple-hood as play-acting and ceremonious gossip is also at the heart of directors' ensemble Jatrik's *Chawa Pawa* (Roads to Romance), adapted as it was from Frank Capra's racy *It Happened One Night* (1934). Cynical reporter Rajat (Uttam), unable to concoct a saleable story to his editor, takes a break. On his outbound journey, he is accosted by Manju (Suchitra), the runaway daughter of a wealthy gent, who in turn announces a prize to know her whereabouts. Rajat eyes the bounty, while Manju treats him as a support, all the while playing a couple so that any wagging tongue coming their way stays suspended. But the inevitable happens when they fall in love. Like *Manmoyee Girls' School*, the plot manages to avoid the familiar traps of soppy sensation, settling for a sunny and joyous appreciation of the little wonders of life. The third film, also with Uttam and Suchitra, had an even more interesting premise because it starts where most romances would end. The film is Chitta Basu's *Ekti Raat* (Story of a Night), a rollicking comedy about ex-friends, married to different spouses, who are forced to spend a night in one room of a dingy suburban hotel. Sushobhon (Uttam) and Shantona (Suchitra) decide to make an adventure out of their accidental rendezvous at a railway station, while their spouses get on their trail, all headed for the same destination. The adventure naturally provokes scandalous postulations from all quarters till it all comes to a good old laugh. What sets this film apart from it being a post-matrimony romance is that it also casually saunters into the no-go zone of adultery, making best use of Suchitra's coquetry and Uttam's heartthrob appeal. It never crosses the mark of gentility, naturally, but still manages to create memorable moments of frolic and laughter.

THE BENGAL HYPOTHESIS

This last group of films most fruitfully yoke together the fruits of romance, music, melodrama and marquee stardom into a convincing tapestry of everyday life and manners, and the small joys and sorrows of kinship, marriage, citizenship. They, in fact, make life a little more palatable, crisis a little more resolvable and loneliness a little more curable. In short, they keep magic in the realm of plausibility, rather than in the domain of fantasy; which is what is the surest mark of an enjoyable melodrama. A recent essay from writer Shankarlal Bhattacharjee makes this point eloquently. He writes:[12]

Jibananda Das died in 1954; a year later, Calcutta erupted to protest against increase of a penny in the tram fare; in 1958 Sisir Bhaduri had to bid adieu to both Srirangam and his acting life; but Bengal never forgot to laugh, to love or to discover new romances. It fell in love with Hemanta [Mukherjee], Manna [Dey], Sondhya [Mukherjee], Lata [Mangeshkar], Geeta [Dutt]; it yelled in support of Chuni [Goswami], PK [Banerjee], Balaram; it stayed the night awake for Ravishankar, Ali Akbar, Vilayet [Khan]; it crowded theatres in the evening for Shombhu [Mitra], Utpal [Dutt], Ajitesh [Bandopadhyay]; it lost itself in debates about Satyajit [Ray], Ritwik [Ghatak], Mrinal [Sen]; it read Tarashankar, Bibhutibhusan, Manik [all Bandopadhyay]. But all this while at the bottom of its heart it longed for the next Friday, when the adored pair will adorn the screen again—Uttam and Suchitra. One life is not enough for so much desire, for so much delight.

This is a sweeping act of assimilation of a time's cultural signposts rather than seeing the artistic and the popular as enjoying separate, mutually exclusive cohorts of admirers. This assimilation is also what the renowned intellectual historian Sudipta Kaviraj noted. In an essay[13] on the language of love, Kaviraj says that in the Uttam–Suchitra pairing, the ethical code of romance became an idealised norm, a norm whose literary imprint he traces in Bengal's literary giants Tagore and Bankim Chandra Chattopadhyay. This is to say that in the romantic pairings Uttam was a part of, an entire generation found an assertion; a liberty of aspiration and the legitimacy of seeking a space for couple-hood in the crowded habitation of the large Indian family. This was a crucial shift in the spectatorial reception of romances from the studio era to the star era.

Hence, this reconfiguration of melodrama was fundamental in how the star-system came into fruition in Bengal. This is because the acute crisis that befell Bengal just before and after Partition was unique, a crisis that cinemas elsewhere in India did not reflect in any meaningful way. Bengali cinema was expected to mirror or register the overarching climate of change. The portable form of melodrama had hence lent the right kind of aesthetic and narrative architecture that popular cinema was aspiring to encompass and iterate within the broader embrace of a new modernity and new kind of subjectivity.

Moreover, there was one idea where popular cinema differed substantially from the art-house counterpart: and that was in its desire for a specific kind of cinematic protagonist. Recent histories have tried to think through it. Bhaskar Sarkar writes,

Bengal's unique position in the evolution of modern Indian nationalism created strong regional aspirations … and because the events of the late 1940s ushered drastic changes that transformed the national film market, ending the primacy of the Calcutta industry. Once a vibrant proto-national formation, Bengal after 1947—in the west, as in the east—was reduced to its own spectral shadow.[14]

Echoing Sarkar, Sharmishta Gooptu[15] writes that the idea of an explicitly Bengali identity emerged most strongly at the moment when the idea of Bengal as a historical agent of nationalist aspiration was in rapid decline. What they are claiming is that as Bengal suffered a diminution of its national eminence, it reorganised its arts, especially cinema, into constituting a unique *sub*-nationality, with a particular set of expectations. It is this factor that explains the popular desire to hold strongly to an esteemed logic of *regionality* and a self-governing bhadralok sensibility, that could record, if not necessarily resolve, the sweeping changes in social and cultural life. In another essay, Subhajit Chatterjee hints at this context when he says, "The codification of a modern romantic persona that Uttam Kumar came to symbolize in the '50s may historically involve a reverse construction of prevalent star image in accordance to the new legal and social constraints placed on the masculine subject."[16] So whether as a constituent of a bhadralok social class or whether as a reconstructed masculine subject, Uttam's persona and the desire for a new kind of melodrama was historically necessitated and ascribed uniquely to Bengal's prospect.

So, Uttam's stardom, even if a textbook celluloid template otherwise, was equally, if not more, historically situated. Moreover, it managed to consolidate itself through multiple channels of appreciation and appropriation. But most importantly, his screen persona had assumed a renewable social adaptability and a recognisable cultural belonging very early in his stardom phase. And it is through it and with it that Bengali cinema decisively stepped into the era of Uttam Kumar.

NOTES

1. Christine Gledhill, *Stardom: Industry of Desire*, London: Routledge, 1991, p. XI.
2. Ravi Vasudevan, *The Melodramatic Public: Film Form and Spectatorship in Indian Cinema*, Ranikhet: Permanent Black, 2010, p. 31.
3. Vasudevan, *The Melodramatic Public*, p. 31.
4. Ben Singer, *Melodrama and Modernity: Early Sensational Cinema and Its Contexts*, New York: Columbia University Press, 2001, p. 6.
5. Dulali Nag, 'Love in the Time of Nationalism: Bengali Popular Films from 1950s', *Economic and Political Weekly* 33:14 (4–10 April 1998): 779–787.
6. S. Shepherd, 'Melodrama as Avant-Garde: Enacting a New Subjectivity', *Textual Practice* 10:3 (1996): 507–522.

7. Peter Brooks, *The Melodramatic Imagination: Balzac, Henry James, Melodrama, and the Mode of Excess*, New Haven: Yale University Press, 1995 [1976], p. 23.
8. Thomas Elsaesser, 'Tales of Sound and Fury: Observations on the Family Melodrama', reprinted in *Movies and Methods: An Anthology*, edited by B. Nichols, Vol. II, Oakland: University of California Press, 1976, pp. 165–189.
9. Singer, *Melodrama and Modernity*, p. 7.
10. Carla Marcantonio, *Global Melodrama: Nation, Body, and History in Contemporary Film*, London: Palgrave Macmillan, 2015, p. 2.
11. Matthew S. Buckley, 'Refugee Theatre: Melodrama and Modernity's Loss', *Theatre Journal* 61 (2009): 175–190.
12. Shankarlal Bhattacharya, *Anandabazar Patrika*, 2 March 2013.
13. Sudipta Kaviraj, 'Tagore and Transformations in the Ideals of Love', in *Love in South Asia*, edited by Francesca Orsini, Cambridge University Press, SA edition, 2007, pp. 161–182.
14. Bhaskar Sarkar, *Mourning the Nation: Indian Cinema in the Wake of Partition*, New Delhi: Orient Blackswan, 2010, p. 125.
15. Sharmistha Gooptu, *Bengali Cinema: The Other Nation*, Delhi: Roli Books, 2010, p. 21.
16. Subhajit Chatterjee, 'Bengali Popular Melodrama in the 50s', *South Asian Journal* 29 (July–September 2010): 12–25.

6

HARD TIMES IN A SOFT CITY

In thousands of eyes, in thousands of objects, the city is reflected.
—Walter Benjamin

WHAT is astonishing is not Uttam's absolute triumph but, in fact, its continuity for at least two more decades since the mid-1950s. If in the 1950s he sparingly moved in and out of formula, in the 1960s, he more regularly spiked romances with films that were offbeat or were not in sync with any purported image. And yet he continued to be an ever bigger star. In fact, by the early 1960s, Uttam, at the pinnacle of stardom, had managed to unchain himself from any set formula, insisting that he was tiring out as a greasepaint *matinee idol.* To that end, Uttam had caused serious insurrection in not only the assorted enthusiasm for a romantic hero but also to a singular pattern of stardom. So, having enquired into the rise, it is imperative that we concern ourselves equally with how Uttam managed to hold on to his successful star-making genus, even as he increasingly jettisoned any exclusive link with romance.

CINEMA AND THE CITY

Though not part of any planned aesthetic or narrative formula like the romances, one can locate, in one set of standout melodramas in the 1950s and the finer specimens of films in the 1960s, a deeply entrenched metropolitan consciousness. This idea, which gives the chapter its title, needs a modest explanation, because it is about a particular language of modernity that was employed by cinema in the appreciation of the space of the city. This is critical because our discernment of a significant part of Uttam's template of stardom in the 1960s hinges, apart from those specific to melodrama, on our ability to comprehend the interconnected nature of cinema, modernity and the metropolis.

Modernity is an intellectually contested term, for rarely have the definition and formulation of it settled into consensus. It would hence be capricious to try to explain modernity within the scope of a stardom that played out far from modernity's usual gallery of achievements in the West. I would rather go by the simple definition from the much loved work of Marshall Berman: "There is a mode of vital experience—experience of space and time, of the self and others, of life's possibilities and perils—that is shared by men and women all over the world today. I will call this body of experience 'modernity."[1] Through the 19th century, as the political and social climate in Europe became increasingly complex, the experience of modernity was heightened by the ever-changing nature of time and space. And it was one of the gains of modernity that the cultural technologies that were birthed by it seemed to have the power to explain modernity back to us. As literary scholar David Clarke puts it:

> The urbanization that accompanied the expansion of industrial capitalism was both a direct manifestation of, and itself served to shape, the historical transition towards a specifically *modern* mode of social living. Whilst both documenting and providing commentary on these developments, cultural forms such as the cinema and its various precursors were themselves implicated in such changes. Thus, the spectacle of the cinema both drew upon and contributed to the increased pace of modern city life, whilst also helping to normalize and cathect the frantic, disadjusted rhythms of the city.[2]

Hence, with the perpetually changing dynamic of encounter and mobility, the vigorous alteration of strangeness and familiarity, of imminence and transience, of utility and reflection, the modern metropolis became key to the understanding of modernity as phantasmagoric and fragmentary, as both Walter Benjamin and Siegfried Kracauer have noted. Referring to them, Brain Larkin says,

> The quotidian landscapes of life—posters on the walls, shop signs, dancing girls, bestsellers, panoramas, the shape, the style, the circulation of city buses—all are surface representations of the fantasy energy by which the collective perceives the social order. This structure creates an interpenetrated analysis of urban culture in modernity, one in which strikingly different phenomena are structurally linked.[3]

No wonder, a specific visual relationship developed between modernity and mobility in the metropolis and the narrative architecture of cinema. As scholars Mark Shiel and Tony Fitzmaurice explains:

> Cinema is a peculiarly spatial form of culture, of course, because (of all cultural forms) cinema operates and is best understood in terms of the organisation of space: both space in films—the space of the

shot, the space of the narrative setting; the geographical relationship of various settings in sequence of a film, the mapping of a lived environment on film; and films in space—the shaping of lived urban spaces by cinema as a cultural practice; the spatial organisation of its industry at the levels of production, distribution, and exhibition; the role of cinema in globalization.[4]

The second part of the excerpt is easy to comprehend. It is about how cinema makes use of and is part of actual urban topography. But the more complex part of this relationship is the first part: how cinema *imagines* the city or how is cityspace used inside a film. In other words, having been defined by modern urban space, cinema also re-*imagines* urbanity, producing an *in-cinema* urbanism, which is broadly referred to as the production of 'cinematic city'.

As modernity globalised the imperial colonies, the impetus of 'cinematic city' travelled with it. It was no wonder that Calcutta, whose fortunes were tied to the imperial economy, saw an emergent visual iconography of its urbanity too, in the very early years of pre-narrative cinema (those filmed by Hiralal Sen). But studio cinema, exceptions aside, barely found the language (and the technology) to accommodate the city as a thriving subject, a tendency that kept cinema sealed within a cloistered and stagey discernment of space. By the 1950s, as production apparatus and method advanced, and exposure to new kind of cinema gained currency, cinema in Bengal too found itself in a position to imbibe a language more natural to the medium. This was the moment— first brought to the fore in *art cinema*—where the haptic and tactile topography of the city could prospectively transform into visual sites of encounter, attraction and action. Popular cinema gradually started to participate in the historical need to reimagine the city in cinema. Hence, we need to rethink popular cinema and stardom within the framework of an urban culture that was forged by the convulsions of the 1940s, the Partition in particular.

STARDOM AND THE SOFT CITY

As we have seen, starting in the early 1950s, Calcutta became the *urbana prima* in art cinema. It emerged as the space where the anxieties of the years after Partition were played out. The city came across as both a provocateur and as a preserver of middle-class angst and hope. In Bengali cinema, in fact, it is not the *nation* but the *city* that emerged as the site of encounter between the *new* citizen and the *new* republic. Cinema from the art house—from *Chhinamul* to *Mahanagar* and later, from *Pratidwandi* to *Calcutta 71*—as recounted before, was an artistic repertoire that was largely built on a variation of this theme. This kind of cultural mirroring of the city is what Jonathan Raban famously termed as a *soft city*. "The city", he writes, "as we imagine it, the soft city of illusion, myth, aspiration, nightmare, is as real, may be more real, than the hard city one can locate in maps and statistics, in monographs on urban sociology and demography and architecture."[5]

Like art-house films, in popular cinema too, the many lives of a city—the intended and the unintended, the planned and the accidental, the formal and the informal—seemed to be emerging as a leitmotif. Several of them mirrored the crises in residency, anxieties of employment, class and spatial segregation, systemic exploitation of poor, dodgy state welfarism, failure of banks and institutional securities, the corroding undercurrent of corruption and the inevitable generational conflict that historical tremors push to the front. To that end, *Bosu Poribar* (The Basu Family) can be said to have propelled to prominence a series of films where archaic codes of honour, tradition and spatial norms were being challenged under a social climate of deficiency and displacement, particularly against the comparative plenitude of the pre-War, pre-Partition days. Perceptively, a sweeping change was putting the traditional self-sufficiency of the family under the aggressive weight of market, livelihood needs and disruptive commodification of daily life. So, Partition provided access to a cinematic material that was not 'specific' to art-house cinema but extended to and influenced popular cinema as well. In terms of visual language of space, however, popular cinema's format forced a more restrained use of *real* city space than art cinema, even if the city as a symptom of habitation and encounter was no less discernible. At the same time, in these Uttam films we get a palpable sense of the *real* city: trams and buses, roads and bungalows, streets and art-deco residences, stations and airports, luxury sedans and car audio systems, tape recorders and radios; cameras, photocopiers, air conditioners, shopping arcades, car races, gadgets, fashion and so on. So, if art-house cinema propagated a fictional Calcutta by 'cutting open' its hidden spaces, this *genre* of popular cinema provided a meaningful continuation of it, embossing their fictional Calcutta with all the power of the proverbial *soft city*. This chapter reveals how these films, spanning the decade and a half between 1953 and 1968, were a broader, if lambent, appreciation of the contemporary rather than being romantic routines or flights into escapist fantasies. To that end, these films not only went against the grain in the so-called high noon of melodramas and defied the law of convention but can also be understood as rudimentary carriers of a certain kind of 'cinematic city' that was not incongruous to them also being variations of the melodrama form. What actually distinguished them were their close alignment with the star figure of Uttam. These films also reflect the demands and functions of cinema within the cultural and cinematic life of Calcutta. Finally, given the long years of their unfolding within Uttam's body of work, one can notice a gradual evolution of both the cinematic imprint of the city as well as the screen persona of Uttam.

THE ENIGMA OF ARRIVAL

There is no better film to announce the 'arrival' to the city in Uttam's repertoire than Kartik Chattopadhyay's *Saheb Bibi Golam* (King, Queen and the Knave), the acclaimed adaptation of Bimal Mitra's expansive period novel. *Saheb Bibi Golam,* published in 1953, announces the 'arrival' of the 20th century into the life of Calcutta, putting the city's eccentric relationship with colonialism, modernity, feudalism and sexuality into the heart of a family's grandiloquent descent into obliteration. The attention that Guru Dutt's re-adaptation received six years later partially obscured the merits of the original, even though Dutt had repeatedly expressed his anxiety about not being able to better the source. The Bengali version was closer to the novel, adapted with a nuanced attention to detail and was enacted, compellingly, by an ensemble cast. It also underplays the grandeur of the affluent household to concentrate on the essential theme of a thriving metropolis at the crossroads of modernity.

Atulchandra alias Bhootnath (Uttam) arrives at the city of attractions and is sucked into the household of one of Calcutta's richest families. The family owns the splendid Borobari, which occupies half of the serpentine Banamali Sarkar Lane, squeezed between Bowbazar Street and Central Avenue. As he finds his feet he is also privy to the innards of the mansion. An awed and wide-eyed Bhootnath peeks, gingerly, into the household's indolent days and mercurial nights—complete with nautch girls, alcohol-fuelled soirees, bawdy card parties and assorted bacchanalia. His day job at a *sindoor* factory endears him to the wife of one of the three brothers of Borobari. She is Poteswari Bouthan, the lonely, neglected wife, who tries every trick in the book to keep her husband home at night. Mohini sindoor, 'with special ingredients', is expected to be one. But she is briskly brushed aside every time she tries to stop her husband from finding his way to the whorehouse. Bhootnath is smitten by her and in equal measure he becomes a confidant to her irrepressible desire, audacious for her time, for conjugal dignity. Poteswari Bouthan even takes to alcohol in a desperate bid to win over her husband; and it is Bhootnath who supplies her with the same.

Outside, the city is witnessing feverish change. The ways of the feudal families are at odds with the reformist zeal sweeping the young. The patriarchs of Borobari are undaunted by change, unaffected by newfangled prospects, untouched by financial sparring with a newer, more astute class of traders. The only one who reminds them of their fallibility is Ghoribabu, the man who keeps time on the hundreds of clocks in the humongous mansion. In due course, time catches up with Borobari: the brothers suffer huge losses and ill health, the supplicants part ways, Ghoribabu commits suicide and Poteswari Bouthan is declared untraceable after a night of escapade to find a final, promised totem to 'cure' her husband. In 1911, Calcutta Improvement Trust orders Bonomali Sarkar Lane to be bulldozed to make way for a wider road. Ironically, the older, memory-weary Bhootnath finds himself entrusted with the job of overseeing the project. As the labourers raze parts of the building and cut open the ground, a horrified, crestfallen Bhootnath is found staring at a female skeleton wearing two pairs of golden bangles, a telltale sign that Poteswari Bouthan was, after all, grounded unceremoniously. A new Calcutta is announced on the remains of the old. And the great Borobari of Bonomali Sarkar Lane is wiped off from history.

Saheb Bibi Golam was not only a deft adaptation but a fine specimen of a film managing to tick right all the boxes. Atulchandra is the archetypal emigrant who *discovers* both a city and himself, while being a *witness* to a period's passing into history. From the vantage of the 1950s, when Calcutta was adjusting to another cardinal shift in its life, this film came as a reminder of the time when modernity invaded the feudal household, most avidly through a woman demanding equality in conjugality, her doomed love brought to life with heartbreaking warmth by the beautiful Sumitra Debi.

INSIDE AND OUTSIDE THE BELEAGUERED CITY

We will jump ahead in time a bit and pick up the story of Calcutta in the films of its most enduring star about four decades after Borobari vanished. And we find ourselves in a teeming, partitioned city, truncated in stature, visibly poorer than before. Yet, it is ever more in the grip of change, ever more rapidly mourning the passing of its many pasts.

Uttam managed to sign a handful of films after *Bosu Poribar*. The film that became a major success next year was Nirmal Dey's *Sharey Chuattor* (The Secret Insignia). *Sharey Chuattor*, literally seventy-four-and-half, was a figure written on envelopes indicating that the contents inside were meant *only* for the addressee, and any violation of that command would bring the weight of misfortune. The number per se had folkloric references to war in the Rajputana region. But with time the origins were lost. What stayed was a mushy innuendo, the number being a sign of inviolable, secret and epistolary message of love.

At heart an ensemble film, *Sharey Chuattor* also launched the Uttam–Suchitra pair. In fact, if at all, Suchitra's Romola enjoyed a more central role in the film, which the actor legislated with more confidence than Uttam's Rampriti, who appears stiff. Also, the film is *not* about their romance, though its fulfilment provides the closure to the film.

The Bijon Bhattacharya-scripted *Sharey Chuattor* is set in the dingy Fariapukur Lane's Annapurna Boarding House, a mess for working, mostly bachelor, men. The film is without a narrative plot and is based on a series of connected incidents, mostly hilarious, that are animated when an elderly couple, with their beautiful young daughter, comes to stay in the working men's mess. Such messes or cheap boarding houses crowded Calcutta's central districts since the beginning of the 20th century. They mostly catered to lower middle-class bhadralok who had little provision but aspirations of respectability. They arrived in the city to explore opportunities, these houses being their first port of call.

In *Sharey Chuattor*, the family, we learn, has been dislodged abruptly and it takes shelter in the mess's extra room, where the manager, a distant relative, arranges for its temporary tenancy. The occupants of the *'mess-bari'* are initially astounded by the possibility of the young Romola moving in and out of this deeply gendered space. Moreover, Romola is educated, confident and unencumbered by her proximity to strangers. The men, while officially disinclined towards the family's stay are also, naturally, vying for the attention of the young woman. Much of the mirth of the film is triggered by these situations. Rampriti, a hot-headed, dashing bachelor, shows particular reluctance to accommodate the guests. Inevitably, he is the one who falls in love with Romola and his feelings do not remain nonreciprocal. Their secret romance through letters is intended to avoid the *gaze* of the crowd but creates considerably comic situations, something that the title refers to. Closure is found in the wedding of the lovers but also in the initiation of a more relaxed climate of acceptance in the *mess*. Apart from being a lively situational comedy, the Nirmal Dey film is remembered for the stellar performance of Tulsi Chakraborty as the nervous and gullible mess manager Rajanibabu, perpetually flummoxed by a loving but nagging wife (an equally brilliant Molina Debi) and their retinue of children.

Sharey Chuattor clearly, if covertly, simulates the multiple claimants to the city through the microcosm of the working men's mess. Like the city, the mess too is constantly in flux while the occupants live under the illusion of competitive ownership of space. At the end of the film hence, the occupants come home to the fact that restricted spaces, held tightly by conventional dogmas were no more possible in a city that was awash with newly unhoused thousands. Like the city, older rights and privileges had to be usurped in the boarding house too with the urgency that only an informed, gendered enlightenment can set free.

Three other Uttam films of the period are part of this canon, hoping to portray the city as a site of contest and conflict, even if from very different positions. None of them, however, had either the quirkiness of *Sharey Chuattor* or shared its box-office fate, and have largely vanished from further reckoning. Ajay Kar's light-hearted comedy *Grihaprabesh* (Housewarming Day, 1954), is a day-in-the-life kind of story of the close-knit Sarkar family whose members, having convened for a housewarming function, await its attendant excitement. They are joined by the young neighbour Surama, whom the younger Sarkar, Prithwish, was nervously courting. Soon it is learnt that an elderly gentleman, who had been initiated into the house as a distant kin, was but a famished trespasser who had mistakenly entered their domain. Expectantly, celebrations go haywire and the family hurriedly sits on judgement on the old man's indiscretion. It is Surama, the other 'outsider', who comes to his impassioned defence. The comic temper of the film does not obfuscate the play on the idea of family and outsider; and the meaning of home in a city of aliens. Agradoot's *Anupoma* (The Unequalled, 1955) is a trenchant realist saga of a household in deep distress and a working woman's relentless forfeiture of personal happiness to keep her badgered family, collapsing at the fringes, tightly together. The unsung film had parallels with Ghatak's *Meghe Dhaka Tara* and is equally bleak, even if Partition is not seen as the exclusive evil. But like it's famous peer, *Anupoma* is about a sad city that has been purged of all compassion and humour. Mrinal Sen's *Raatbhor* (Night's End) depicts the agonising days of a restless village lad on run from the sway of a rich, childless Calcutta couple. As is not unusual with early Sen, the film manages little dramatic effect, having frozen the plot into morbid shades of white and black. It is a poor film, even if the efforts of a young filmmaker to move beyond the confines of a hackneyed domestic drama are apparent.

ALLEGORIES OF PARTITION

A set of films with similar concerns to that of *Sharey Chuattor* came from veteran director Sukumar Dasgupta. Two of them, both with Suchitra Sen, were released in 1954, while the other one, after a gap, in 1960. One can perceive a thematic and stylistic continuity in these films and if seen together, there is an evident evolution of the actor in Uttam Kumar. But rather than projecting Uttam, Dasgupta preferred to deal, variously, with the theme of finding a *home*. A sophisticated taste in comedy and a set of well-drawn character types did the rest.

Ora Thake Odhare (They Live That Side) starts with *actual* footage of Calcutta with the camera panning over Sealdah Station and then moving through the busy streets for the time of the film's title sequence. The camera slows down at one of Calcutta's principal neighbourhoods, enters a building, walks up the stairs and halts at the landing between two face-to-face apartments. This is where the plot is to then unfold. The sequence has the effect of starting at the known site of happenstance (the station); and then having the actual city flow into the space of an apartment, hinting that the tensions without are to be played out within.

The plot concerns the day-to-day life of two families who come from differing Bengali *ethnicities*, though both belong to the broader bhadralok milieu. Of the two families, one has been displaced by Partition and forced to share quarters with another family, which was not 'displaced'. Hence one family was *bangal* (originating from East Pakistan) and the other a *ghoti* (those who have *belonged* to West Bengal). The financial and cultural standing of the two families are similar but they take pride in the variation of their petty, day-to-day customs. The displaced family carries with it the linguistic, culinary and other attendant habits that constantly threaten to disturb the peaceful coexistence with the other, *resident*, family, which is attached to its own ingrained practices. But they also share a broad range of interdependence. The middle-aged men share their insecurities around loans and employment; the younger share promises of friendship and romance; the women share their daily household chores—exchanging carrying-baskets, pressing-iron, sewing machines and other tools of daily utility. But peace is often threatened by this quirk or that, when one family wants to hold on too tightly to its intrusive identities. A range of hardships from time to time overwhelm them enough to make an obligatory, if fragile, peace, which is threatened the next moment. The so-called *ethnic* quibbles, however, never breach a self-imposed, public sense of civility.

Scholar Sibaji Bandyopadhyay has called *Ora Thake Odhare*, a 'romantic comedy that furnishes a light-hearted instance of displacement of the trauma attending the division of Bengal'. If at all a *romantic* comedy, the film underplays it, to foreground the hardship and the need to hold on to a sense of fellowship. The romance is part of the *need* to counter the trauma rather than escape from it. Bandyopadhyay also points out that the plot unfolds through incidents of 'provocative yet harmless laughter', rather than any major crisis. The laughter, indeed, arises from stern warnings about one-upmanship in one moment, to hapless dependency in the next, to desperate pulls of middle-class courtesy seconds after. When one family reaches the brink of calamity they plan to vacate the quarters. However, on the night they plan to quietly 'evacuate' (to avoid any lapse in decorum), the other family intervenes. Like a Shakespearean comedy, the misapprehensions are resolved, order is restored and coexistence is forged; with the realisation that there will still be uphill adversities. Evidently, the film *re-imagines* Partition within the living quarters of a Calcutta apartment, and divides a residential domain into two 'ethnic' spaces with full consciousness of the forced circumstances that have brought them together. But, unlike art cinema where hope is always on leave, in *Ora Thake Odhare*, it is stubbornly realised through the values of cohabitation.

But this was not the only film to obliquely refer to Partition that year. There was also *Shodanonder Mela* (The Occupants, 1954). The basic plot of the film was adapted from Roy Del Ruth's 1947 Christmas hit *It Happened on Fifth Avenue*, but it was indigenised fluently. The film's protagonist is Shodanondo (Chhabi Biswas), a bohemian violinist of uncompromising ethical bent. Shodanondo translates into Bengali as one who is of a perpetually joyous disposition. Shodanondo is rendered homeless when his dilapidated house is ruined on a night of squall. He befriends a roving kitten and through it a homeless family looking for respectable accommodation. Led by Shodanondo, the family reluctantly takes up refuge in an empty mansion that belongs to the millionaire industrialist Dakshniranjan. They are deeply mindful of entering the house *only* through the rear entrance and as a matter of principle, to not usurp the arrangements within. Clearly, Shodanondo's gang represents a group of 'ethical' refugees, who are both illegal tenants and at the same time dignified occupiers of someone else's excess space. A widowed mother, her youthful son Ajit (Uttam), his much younger sister and her kitten settle in the mansion, with assurance from Shodanondo that theirs is a temporary, if, 'rightful' occupation. The tensions around the curious occupancy are heightened by the entry of Sheela (Suchitra), the daughter of the industrialist, who, having announced her rebellion from her rapacious father, comes to stay at her own house. The occupants are ignorant of the purpose of her stay but accommodate her happily, thinking Sheela is one of them. Initially jolted, Sheela realises the intent of the occupiers and begins to wilfully cohabit with them, without revealing her identity. On coming to know about this arrangement, the father is naturally stupefied but pleaded by his daughter, he undertakes a similar assignment—to stay as a refugee in his own house. Here he is also united with his estranged wife, who like his daughter, had left him for his obsession with making money. A bout of romance (between

Ajit and Sheela), again fleetingly, is paid some service before the plot of both sets of occupiers is revealed. But, instead of the refugees being made homeless again, closure is found in a spirit of romantic pairing, togetherness and coexistence. Shodanondo, however, unchains himself from any certainty of a home and heads for the roads again.

Shodanonder Mela is a smartly scripted urban fantasy which, instead of sentimentalising homelessness, questions the class basis of spatial realignment and proposes a radical, if utopian, idea of spatial commons. The entering of the house from the rear and adjusting to new space without violence stand as a metaphor for desired realignments of Partition-divided spaces. The film's plea for a light-hearted closure to a historically enforced conflict is noteworthy, when placed in context of the sociology of dispossession and the enormous anxiety around legal residency in early 1950s Calcutta.

Shodanonder Mela and *Ora Thake Odhare*, both directed by Sukumar Dasgupta and both scripted by the author Premendra Mitra, made deft use of the metaphor of partitioned space, perhaps more compellingly than their 'weighty' art-house peers. The films continue to remain underappreciated films of Uttam's pre-stardom era, even though they were moderate box-office successes, just about preceded his imminent breakthrough and laid the foundations for his fabled future pairing with Suchitra Sen.

Sukumar Dasgupta made a return to mirth in *Haat Baralei Bondhu* (A Friend in Deed, 1960), a most gratifying comedy. Here, Uttam's Pratap is a smooth-talking caricaturist, who takes up tenancy in a house in Calcutta. He befriends the house-owner Trilochon Mitra and his nephew and niece, who have taken *shelter* with Trilochan, having run away from their uncle, the authoritarian Dr Ghosh. Trilochon runs a concern to rent houses which are mostly under the ownership of Dr Ghosh, his childhood friend. But Trilochon opposes Ghosh's bullying of his niece Nilu to get married, thereby losing the custody of the houses. On the verge of bankruptcy, Trilochon's survival is contingent upon finding a way to cajole Dr Ghosh, without abandoning Nilu (Sabitri). The entry of Pratap in this scenario, though initially resented, pushes the plot towards a possible resolution. The customary touch of romance between Pratap and Nilu is an expected outcome. And so is Dr Ghosh's self-realisation. Again, *Haat Baralei Bondhu* does not over-emphasise the crisis of finding housing but makes it the pivotal aspiration of respectability for the middle class. Like his early films, the script is based around adroit use of light-hearted situational manoeuvres among a group of warring but well-meaning stakeholders, till it reaches a chaotic but rib-tickling finale. By the time of this film, Uttam was at the top of the game, almost an equal with Chhabi Biswas, who plays Trilochon.

In all these films, there are the obligatory escapes into music and romance, though they never refute the overall climate of despondency, the plots being deeply conscious of their time. And yet the films doff a hat or two to the resolute nature of life itself, its essential plenitude, filling the gaps left by the daily business of hard survival.

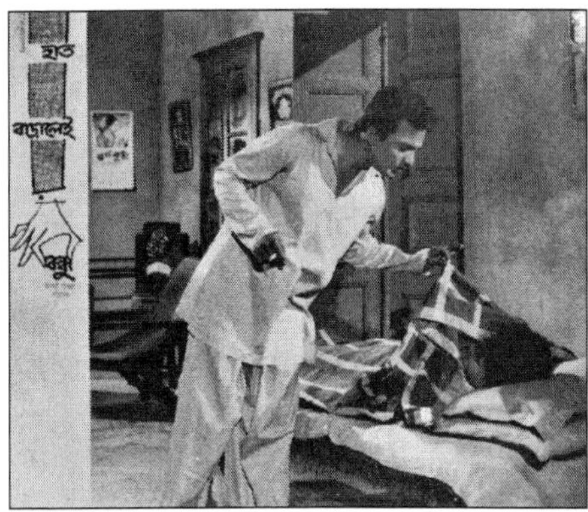

Image 6.1: Housing crisis couched in comic survivalism. Publicity booklet of *Haat Baralei Bondhu* (A Friend in Deed, 1960)

Source: Parimal Ray.

CITY OF EXCHANGE

The cinema of urban crisis was not found couched in sparkling humour always. But neither were they mawkish and sentimental. I have already referred to Tapan Sinha's *Upohar* (The Gift)—the film where Uttam's character Ashok refers, somewhat scornfully, to the 'star' Uttam Kumar. The fact that the script refers to Uttam Kumar's new-found craze hints that the film comes in the wake of it, but resolutely stays away from using either Uttam as a romantic hero or the film as a romance. It is, in fact, an unusually substantial document of middle-class aspirations and quibbles.

Ashok, the bespectacled young literature professor and his wife Neela (Manju Dey), shift to a rented floor in one of Calcutta's denser neighbourhoods. Urbane, without a child (yet) and sharing a deep bond, they settle down, along with their manservant Bhola. They also befriend the landlord's sprightly daughter Krishna and her admirer, the gifted student Sunil. But the better part of the film is not about them. It is about the house-owner Kangalibabu, a tightfisted, fanatical Brahmin with an acid tongue. He is so penny-cautious that he refuses to pay even for basic repairs, and is seen constantly undertaking various needless chores to save that one penny. In his initial meeting with Ashok, he calls himself the Robinson Crusoe of Bengal, a man who can 'survive' on his own. But he is not alone and at the receiving end of his obsessive parsimony is Krishna; so much so that he was willing to get her married to the 'lowest bidder'.

The film's main plot is about how Kangalibabu is constantly crossing paths with Ashok and Neela who get involved in Krishna's future, without any stake in it. Their generosity is resented by 'Mr Crusoe', who accuses them of nosing into his affairs. Tensions mount and the turn of events lead to Kangalibabu's cardiac arrest and death. Only after he passes away is it discovered that he had hoarded a roomful of valuable objects but never, even in his dire days, could he find the love within to open up his purse. Krishna receives a windfall while Ashok advises Sunil to look beyond a petty livelihood, pursue higher studies and to abandon thriftiness for a life lived generously. Apart from questions of home and dwelling, the film's essential tension is built around the ideas of 'family' and 'stranger' and their increasing interchangeability. This interchangeability finds an operative value in a growing, teeming city which is learning to question, if not also subvert, traditional forms of authority.

Upohar was appreciated on its release but got crowded out by wildly successful romances. But one must revisit the film not just because it is a Tapan Sinha work; or because it is a true-to-life portrait of middle-class quirks, sentiments and survival; but also because of Uttam and Manju Dey's delightful, delectable chemistry, rendering an authentic camaraderie in their couple-hood. Kanu Bandopadhyay, who is remembered widely as Harihar in Ray's *Apu Trilogy*, is apt as Kangalibabu.

It is unfortunate that two of Uttam's early co-stars, Manju Dey and Kaberi Bose, did not get to share enough screen space with him. Talented, intelligent, beautiful, tall and self-assured, both of them were a terrific contrast to their contemporaries. Their lives turned out to be very different though. Bose will be part of our story later but there is no better time to talk about Manju Dey.

Bengali film writer Rabi Basu begins a profile[6] on Manju Dey saying that had she been born in England, she would be Margaret Thatcher; in Israel she would be Golda Meir or in Philippines, Corazon Aquino. With anyone else, this would be preposterous hyperbole. But not for Manju Dey. Is there any woman in Indian cinema who had been a top-notch actor, an efficient co-producer, a gritty director, a feminist icon and a competitive motorist? Manju Dey was one and that too in the 1950s.

Born to a liberal family in 1926, Dey's debut came in 1945 but she found success in the early 1950s with films such as *Ratnadeep*, *Jighangsha* and *Beyallish*. She was married and doing her post-graduation when she entered films. The first was not a rarity, the second, by all means, was. What was even rarer for a Bengali woman was that she was a consummate motorist, taking part, in the mid-1950s, in amateur motor rallies, often finishing at the top. Through that decade she not only acted in some of Bengali cinema's signposts like *Kar Pape?*, *Kabuliwala*, *Neel Akasher Niche* and *Kancher Sworgo* but also assisted Tapan Sinha closely in most of his early films. She was rearing to go behind the camera. But breaking that glass ceiling, like everywhere else, was an exertion. It was only in 1967 that she managed to find the resources to adapt, act in, produce, and direct *Abhishapta Chambal* (The Cursed Valley of Chambal) based on the canonic Bengali novel by Jaya Bhaduri's father Tarun Bhaduri. Like her education, motoring, free-spirited characters in front of the camera, she managed to do be intrepid behind it too. The film was a roaring success and her Putli Bai remains one of the most memorable characters in Bengali cinema. By her mid-forties, the acting roles had dried up and she was losing confidence on her ability to direct another film. The last two decades of her life, which ended in 1989, was dedicated to home-grown spiritualism.

Had she not been born in the same year as Uttam, their pairing could possibly be explored far beyond the handful that exists. And among those that do, there is hardly another one where they play a modern couple. Uttam admired and revered her equally. However, in his early days, Manju Dey was already a mature performer, while the producers wanted someone vulnerable. Moreover, her spirit, personality and height made her ineligible for most roles, written as they were for a more modest depictions of femininity. Dey was not just a trailblazing feminist figure in every which way but was much ahead of her time even in then-progressive Bengal. It is difficult to imagine her in a rank of political icons. But had she been born in Hollywood, she could well have been a Katherine Hepburn.

Like *Upohar*, Niren Lahiri's *Shankar Narayan Bank* (A Banking Scandal, 1956) was also about financial security and the tightrope of middle-class aspiration, though, unlike it, it was couched as a sure-fire romance. Like *Upohar*, it too 'banked' on a set of mature character types, especially by putting Uttam together with Kaberi Bose.

The privately run Shankar Narayan Bank was founded on the creditworthiness of Harishankar and the hard work of his lieutenant Narayan. After the demise of Narayan, Harishankar adopts his children and oversees the budding romance between two sets of siblings. Harishankar's second wife, however, loathes the ambition of the lesser partner's kin. Humiliated, Narayan's children storm out. Five years later, Gautam, Narayan's son, re-emerges—flourishing, affluent and adroit—joining the city's industrial echelons. His once-beloved Meena returns to his life but falls short of expressing her longing. The other pair too resume their romance. But this time, Harishankar's younger son plays the devil, secretly betting the bank's shares to an unknown investor. Harishankar is decimated in the face of rising customer protest and threat of arrest as his long-cherished integrity comes under a cloud of suspicion. But Gautam (Uttam) comes to the rescue by cleverly playing his cards, manoeuvring shrewdly through the shadowy world of investors. He saves the bank, the family and reunites romantically with Meena (Kaberi Bose).

The film is a formulaic melodrama, complete with unsung romance, warring brothers and a rich patriarch's esteem at stake. It concludes as a melodrama too, where moral marksmanship triumphs over the steepest of ordeals. But the film's concealed onus is on the vagaries of the private banking system—the haggling for investment, the slipperiness of securities, the opportunism of the share market and such others, all of them giving the film a situatedness in the contemporary economy that was not usually found in average romantic melodramas.

ROMANCING THE CITY

The next two films are usually considered archetypal (and successful) Uttam–Suchitra romances. But I want to see them primarily as *city films*, because Sudhir Mukherjee's *Shapmochon* and Agradoot's *Surjotoron* are both about an unambiguous embrace of urban modernity. In *Shapmochon* (Breaking of a Curse, 1955), young Mohendra comes to Calcutta bearing the cross of a curse that had stalked his musician family for over three generations. Deeply bonded to his blind elder brother, Mohendra is determined to suppress his passion and choose an insignificant life in the city. He finds shelter in the house of the kind-hearted patrician Umesh, a friend of Mohendra's long-deceased father. Though ridiculed by others for being a gullible bumpkin, he finds a guardian in Umesh's young daughter Madhuri (Suchitra). Tutored more by her strict motherly reprimands than her easy affection, Mohendra prepares for the city life. And yet, he is conflicted by his dependence on her. In a huff, he leaves Madhuri's shadow but finds himself stranded in an alien city, without a job or home. Desperate to help a distressed family, he taps into the singer in him, discovering prompt adulation. Later, Madhuri finds him sequestered in a bachelor mess and their romance blooms. She also convinces Mohendra that the curse is nothing but an entrenched superstition and that he must rise above this unfair injunction against his natural call for music. Mohendra reluctantly obliges and soon attains success as a radio artist. In the distant, impoverished village home, his brother is shattered to discover Mohendra's rebellion and in a dramatic moment of trauma, meets his death. When Mohendra reaches his village, he is in a state of acute delirium, reproaching himself for having caused his brother's end. A string of coincidences brings Madhuri to his village too. Characteristically, Madhuri takes charge, beckons a doctor from the nearest city and ensures that Mohendra is brought back to health. Though the curse is broken, Madhuri decides to stay back with Mohendra.

Like *Sanjeebani* some years prior, *Shapmochon* puts the onus of both reform and tending to the woman protagonist, putting under her care the conflicted man. *Shapmochon* takes it a step further by making Madhuri question a supercilious provincial orthodoxy that is directly in contradiction to her urban disposition. At the same time, she also accepts the possibility of a provincial life unquestioningly. This figure of the women as both the reformer *and* the confirming feminine ideal, as I have said, was a popular motif. Rarely would Suchitra Sen's *character* bloom into a thorough rebel. One or two films memorably broke the mould.

An excellent example of breaking away from the mould was Agradoot's *Surjotoron* (Sun Tower), a nativisation of King Vidor's 1949 adaptation of Ayn Rand's *Fountainhead*. The plot is dominated by Somnath Mukherjee (Uttam), an arrogant and vocal campaigner for unconventional architecture. Somnath, our Howard Roark, an egoistic and exacting man, refuses to trade his architecture degree for a compromised livelihood and takes up apprentice with the neglected modernist Bipradas. Bipradas's old rival Chatterjee, who owns the successful but conventional architectural firm UN Chatterjee & Sons employs Mukherjee's classmate, the fraudulent nincompoop Subrata. Soon Subrata, Keeting of the novel, earns Chatterjee's favour and the hand of his daughter Anita (Dominique). Anita (played by Suchitra) is the rising star of Bengali letters and writes and lectures about the need for affordable urban housing. She is asked by her editor to follow the Left-wing intellectual legacy of Halldór Laxness and Upton Sinclair. When his mentor Bipradas dies of poverty, a hardened Somnath is forced to take up work with Chatterjee. But thanks to his devil-may-care arrogance Somnath falls foul and is rendered unemployable. He takes up work at a foundry away from the city. There, he meets Anita, vacationing. Somnath's dislike for Anita is instant because he suspects her socialism to be vacuous. He also breaks into her house one night to test her courage and to mock her pretences. The nocturnal break-in is referred to later in the film but unlike the novel, Anita never alleges rape.

From here the adaptation assumes a life of its own. Anita finishes her tomb *Surjotoron* (Sun Tower) laying down her dream of community housing. But Subrata betrays Chatterjee and dumps Anita. Somnath makes a triumphant return with award and recognition. Subrata's betrayal bankrupts Chatterjee and the latter is forced to sell his assets to Rajsekhar Mitra (Gail Wynand), a secretive, wealthy industrialist, who also proposes to Anita. He commissions Somnath to build the ultramodern, 30-floor Sun Tower (the Wynand Building), the grandest housing enterprise ever undertaken in Calcutta, which was to receive 'the first rays of the Sun when it falls on the city'. As an undercurrent of romance engulfs Somnath and Anita, Somnath abandons the project and leaves it with Subrata. Subrata, however, cheats his benefactor once more and Anita's dream is found to be a perversity. Enraged, Somnath dynamites it and in the ensuing trial, like Roark, gives an impassioned speech about human dignity. Since there is no casualty with Subrata finally owning up to his venality, Somnath is set free. That night, Somnath arrives in Rajsekhar's flat seconds after Anita to find Rajsekhar dead, his suicide note explaining his failure to 'buy' love and why he left his fortunes to build the *real* Sun Tower. Months later, Sun Tower is built as per Somnath's original plan, and becomes the spectacular new home for thousands of poor. The new inhabitants are ushered in by Anita and Somnath, a couple now finally at peace with each other.

Surjotoron heavily exploits the melodramatic bent of the expansive novel. But interestingly, it turns the ethic of individual triumph into a socialist campaign for better living. Moreover, the film argues for a productive *dialogue* between middle and elite classes to help engineer the future; rather than putting the weight of state-building on public institutions. To that end, the film belongs to Rand's plea for uber-individualism while also voicing a ubiquitous Leftist rhetoric familiar to the Bengali audience. Be it in Somnath's aggressive egotism, Anita's self-confidence, Subrata's rogue servility or Rajsekhar's grandiose self-sacrifice, *Surjotoron* was as melodramatic as it was a blazing, intense, contemporary city film.

CITY WITHOUT REST

In the next set of films, the city is not a direct participant in the film's narrative landscape but a quiet figuration. And yet the films are indeed that of the city and a quirky, often lonely, protagonist. A good example is Bishu Chakraborty's *Obak Prithibi* (Strange World). Chakraborty was the cinematographer of many of Uttam's films but directed him only once in this film, which was produced by Uttam's brother Tarun Kumar. The first part of the film was loosely adapted from O. Henry's short story *The Cop and the Anthem*. On his release from a brief stint in the prison, Arjun (Uttam), a good-natured pickpocket, finds it impossible to make an honest living. He meanders on the streets during the day and sleeps by the wayside at night. Then, like Soapy in O. Henry's story, the certitude of the penitentiary beckons him. He resorts to tricks such as dining at an expensive restaurant without paying or breaks the glass window of a clothing store unprovoked. But he is unable to convince his 'preys' to send him back to prison. By chance and without hiding his past, he gets absorbed in a Jesuit boy's school. But there too, the young boys initially give him a tough time before he finds admiration and respect. This part is much like E.R. Braithwaite's *To Sir with Love*, which was published the same year. While dropping a young ward at his home, Arjun is arrested on charges of kidnapping, the plot here making a return to O. Henry's story. But unlike the story, Arjun decides to fight to prove his innocence. And succeeds. The film has no romance, and instead, chronicles life on the city streets with adorable empathy. Like *Upohar*, *Obak Prithibi* must be retrieved from obscurity as much for the endearing humour as for Uttam's performance as a genteel crook who does not take life too seriously.

The next film under this rubric was also an adaptation and eschewed romance for class concerns. Mongol Chakraborty's *Tasher Ghar* (House of Cards, 1957) was indigenised from Mark Twain's *The Prince and the Pauper*. So, instead of 16th-century England, it has contemporary Calcutta as its setting. One night, persecuted, unhappy millionaire Ajay Mitra bumps into Benoy Dutta (both Uttam), an unemployed graduate. They look alike but beyond a point neither is keen to pursue the logic behind their likeness. Instead, on Ajay's persuasion, they decide to swap their lives. As the new day dawns, each of them settles into their 'other life', under the gaze of their kin, officers, sisters, lovers, and others. No one suspects them, except the aunt of Ajay, who is blind. She is taken into confidence while the plot progresses across two spaces. The millionaire is appalled at the way the poor lived, while the commerce graduate learns the tricks of the baron's trade. A series of incidents constantly test their oath of secrecy and both of them, naturally, fall in love. But the abject poverty of the adopted household prompts Ajay (as Benoy) to embezzle his *own* money, which eventually lays bare their game. In spite of the fable-like plot (reprised in the recent Netflix remake *The Princess Switch*), *Tasher Ghar* holds forth to a large extent. If the film does not make any major impression, it is because the plot of doppelgangers who interchange their stations in life and carry on their ideological surveys unhampered is in itself unreal. But the film otherwise is a nimble document of urban lives, social shelters and class moorings. There is that one scene which has stayed with me. On being asked by his fiancé Reba what ails him, Ajay (before he has met Benoy) causally says that his is a problem of excess, of being without a sense of want, of having lost the art of desiring anything anymore. 'My problem is even beyond Freud', he declares. The way he mentions Freud, casually by last name, is noteworthy. Clearly, the film expects the audience of a mainstream film not only to be familiar with the Viennese psychoanalyst but also comprehend why a loss of desire due to overbearing wealth is not an affliction he has dealt with at length. Impressive indeed.

Ajoy Kar, who shot his own films, had a knack of expressionist lighting. For *Khelaghor* (The Playhouse, 1959), he found inspiration in the Hollywood gangster noir. *Khelaghor* is set in the final years of British India, where a cat-and-mouse game is in progress between a group of nationalist youngsters and their bête noire, an Indian top cop. The noir temper of the film is set in the opening scene. News of a jailbreak triggers a series of jump-cut action sequences; the film's title starts rolling and the name *Khelaghor* appears on the top of four revolving spotlights of the prison house, announcing the escape of Gautam Chatterjee (Uttam). The chiaroscuro of lighted and dark space that the flashy spotlights create informs the entire film, because Gautam is a shadowy figure.

On the night of his breakout, Gautam unknowingly breaks into the house of his arch-enemy, the police boss R.C. Banerjee. He takes hostage his daughter Ruchira (Mala Sinha), changes into civilian clothes and leaves, without doing any harm to her. In the wonderfully filmed light and shadow of midnight chivalry, Ruchira is found aghast but does not see the silhouetted intruder. Gautam, chased by the police and warned by his group, shifts his base constantly, giving scope to Kar to exploit the city's unsavoury regions. Ruchira leaves home too, refusing to marry a dull fiancé. Expectantly, their ways meet. Gautam identifies Ruchira but Ruchira, naïve and gushy, remains ignorant of his past. The romance soon matures into a live-in where Ruchira's care and composure helps Gautam, injured in a chase, regain health. But soon they are intercepted. And here came the film's curious twist. Out of the blue, the *real* Gautam Chatterjee emerges and it is revealed that Uttam's character is Santanu Roy, a musician from a rich family who had aided the nationalist gang but was not involved in violence. Gautam's trial begins anew while Santanu is given a two-year sentence for abetting the 'enemies' of the colonial state. Ruchira decides to wait, realising the warped ways of the 'playhouse' that is the world around her. The film has many things going for it—the thriller pace, the taut editing, the unusual cinematography and the use of city's below-the-radar spaces such as graveyards, taverns and slums. But Kar fails to nail Gautam's character as an amoral anti-hero. The ending, instead of bolstering the plot, makes it forced, as the rash individualism of Santanu (as Gautam) succumbs to pulls of plangent romance.

Chronologically, the last film of this stock would be *Raja Saja* (A Royal Masquerade, 1960), which was not very unlike the theme of *Tasher Ghar*, except that the prince and the pauper are the same person. The film begins in a faraway village, where Rajat Subhra Banerjee (Uttam) is a simple schoolmaster who irks the local guardians with his mercurial habits. He is visited by a canny estate manager who announces, to the astonishment of everyone, that Rajat was not a poor wayward but the last surviving progeny of a wealthy estate. Rajat comes to Calcutta reluctantly and takes 'charge' of his new-found role in a humongous neo-Gothic mansion. Here, he finds out that silly traditions and elaborate protocols operate on a daily basis, extolling the silent servitude of hordes of kowtowing men. Rajat's maverick disposition soon starts to upset the long-held practices of what he calls a museum of dolls. His ingeniousness also unsettles the elaborate ploy of the manager to edge him out of his inheritance. When the conspiracy is revealed, Rajat sacks him and exits his masked role. But the manager plans a final coup. Rajat is summoned to the court where he is tried for being pathologically melancholic and unfit for assuming charge of his inheritance. Egged by his companion Malini, Rajat's final speech turns the tables.

Unlike *Tasher Ghar*, this film, directed by the actor Bikash Roy, has a comic tone and touch, thanks to Rajat's carefree whims, which Uttam brings to life with usual alacrity. But the real theme is the windfall of liberal sportsmanship that sweeps across the hoary, stuck-up, tradition-obsessed mansion in the heart of the city. What makes it interesting is that the house is unpeopled, except the soundless workers, letting Rajat develop an impulsive relation with statues and objets d'art that fill the gardens, stairs, halls, rooms and every corner of the ghostly mansion with a kind of pecuniary claustrophobia. So, it is not people so much as those objects, weighed down by custom, that he sets free. It is this interplay between a mansion's stately loneliness and its owner's jouissance that makes *Raja Saja* an enjoyable, piquant, light-footed parable.

THE 1960s

Unlike romances, where conventions ensure continuity, it would be an oversight to group the 1960s city films with those of the 1950s.

The historical anxieties of the decade after Partition had partially retreated in the early 1960s, while a new set of concerns emerged. The acute housing crisis, for example, and indeed the whole semantics of dispossession germane to city films of the 1950s had now abated. What occupied the new decade was an interrogation of citizenry itself, as they adjusted to the reordering of life and space. Uttam's cinema reflected the relative subsistence of civil and political stability, while his characters tried to live up to demands of a maturing viewership. The films of the 1960s, which cemented Uttam's stardom, hence underline a maturing performer, who was now aligning himself with a series of critiques of the melodrama mode, his stardom being his biggest guarantee to surpass any formulaic allegiance. If there was any time to confront the canons of popular cinema, this was it. And he did. Whether they were the genre-defining *Jhinder Bondi* and *Dui Bhai* (both from 1961), or the barely seen *Kanna* and *Shiulibari* (both from 1962), or the box-office favourites *Bhranti Bilash* and *Deya Neya* (both from 1963) or the elegant character studies *Jotugriha* and *Lal Pathor* (both from 1964) Uttam had put out one stellar performance after another; which spilled into 1965's *Thana Theke Aschi*, 1966's *Kal Tumi Aleya* and *Shonkhobela*, 1967's *Antony Firingee* and 1968's *Chowrongee*. He peaked, of course, with Satyajit Ray's *Nayak* and *Chiriyakhana*. Hardly any of these films are regular melodramas or carried the proclamations of a formula romance. But they all belonged to an imperishable star persona who also increasingly cemented his reputation as an actor par excellence.

More narrowly, the carefree 'Uttam persona'—a recurring thread in the roles he portrayed in the 1950s—was slowly being retired. The 'Uttam persona' as it advanced in age became more contentious and conscious of himself; with a more distinguished sense of belonging. His roles became more reflective, complex, ambivalent and grey, or one who could push the boundaries of social and moral acceptability. These characters partook in an increasingly commodified social economy and the shifting strands in metropolitan space; and are naturally conflicted and practical rather than being either an exemplar of godly virtues or a footloose drifter.

CITY NOCTURNE

After an extremely prolific seven years, 1961 was quieter for Uttam. He had just six releases but in every one of them his parts were varied. He played such roles as a magnanimous engineer; an artless prince and his canny doppelganger; a battle-hardened Jesuit doctor, an unrelenting elder brother. It is the last one, *Dui Bhai* (The Martinet, 1961), that concerns us here.

Having been cheated by their uncle, the young orphans Utpal and Kamal find themselves homeless and at the mercy of the elements on the streets of Calcutta. The narrative jumps two decades and we see Utpal as a hardworking overseer at a factory and Kamal as his darling young brother studying at the university. A series of short scenes establish their bond. Utpal has grown into a deeply caring if stern disciplinarian to the young Kamal and has forfeited the life of a family man to take better care of Kamal's aspirations. The brothers bond on everything but most eloquently through music. Their house, as per the disciplinarian Utpal's command, forbids entry of two essential seductions of the youth: women and politics. And predictably, that is where the tension starts to mount, as Kamal attains a voice of his own and shifts his affections to a comrade. Kamal's Leftist politics causes a labour uprising in the factory and Utpal, secretly sympathetic to the labourers but otherwise aghast at his brother, resigns. Jobless, alone and misunderstood, the maladroit Utpal feels increasingly powerless against the tide of the times. He leaves unannounced. For months, the brothers are separated before a spate of coincidences, rather amusing, brings them together. The film is uneven, the climax verges on the frivolous, though the performances are apt. But what stands out are two things. First is the lesson that the city, complete with its copious and formidable attractions, was bound to invade any carefully encoded space. The second takeaway is Uttam's Utpal, who is egoistic and concerned, irrational and practical, disdainful and sympathetic at the same time. Years of habit, a deep sense of responsibility and hard lessons of the past had made him aim for a righteous guardianship but no one more than him could comprehend the unsustainability of his moral project. It is a complex part that was rendered powerfully by Uttam.

The Bengali novelist Tarashankar Bandopadhyay was known for dramatic ups and downs in his plots. In 1961, his rousing drama *Soptopodi* became a blockbuster with Uttam and Suchitra in the lead. That success pegged the director ensemble Agragami to settle upon the author's *Kanna*, set in the community of 'native' Christians. It is this film that fortified Uttam's unmistakable shift from the lovable persona of his early romances to one who could be deviant and despondent.

Nathaniel Biswas is a musician torn between his commitment to the church and his obsessive love for his violin. He marries and gets divorced, settling down with daughter Launa and son John. But peace is short-lived. To a nightlong attack of cholera, he loses both his children. The inconsolable Nathaniel donates most of his assets to the church and leaves. After three years as a vagrant, he returns with a young girl he found abandoned. He calls her Launa. Years later he rescues a boy from a graveyard. He names him John. This is the backstory.

Kanna (The Cry) begins with Launa and John on the verge of coming of age. The handsome John (Uttam) grows up to be an exceptional violinist. But he is a tortured soul, respectful of his adoptive father but not of the church. John also struggles to come to terms with his rancorous past as a slumdog, a past that sits uneasy on his scriptural education. He soon realises that he loves Launa (Nandita Bose) but she is unable to commit herself. John, the unrepentant voluptuary that he is, starts to chase the charmed life in the city's volatile quarters, craving for sexual consummation. He eventually invites the wrath of an old foe. In a stroke of fate, Nathaniel is fatally shot and an attack on John leaves him without sight and song in his voice. The blinded violinist struggles with his disability, overcomes his erotic longings and finds peace with Launa, who decides to be with him instead of heading for the nunnery. The film ends on a promise of romantic fulfilment, which is different from the novel, the latter leaving John in desolate gloom.

The melodramatic twists notwithstanding, the film's music by Sudhin Dasgupta and camerawork by Ramananda Sengupta were notable. Given his long years, Sengupta had become a living archive of Bengali cinema. In an interview a year before he completed his centenary, Sengupta was effusive about *Kanna*. He remembered that a blind violinist in suit and a hat, who would saunter around Chowringhee was Tarashankar's model for John. Having learnt the same, Uttam would visit the area clandestinely to observe the violinist's ways of treading the ground, playing the violin and facing the streets without sight. Much of the film was set in Calcutta's nocturnes; and the tormented John would spend hours reflecting on his choices while strolling the mean streets of Calcutta's iridescent but lonesome after-hours. Since it would be impossible to shoot with Uttam on the streets before sunset, there were extended, nightlong shoots. "I have never seen an actor who was so assiduous. Uttam would surprise everyone with this patience, labour and dedication", Sengupta recounted to this author. *Kanna* had long scenes of the physical life, architecture and recognisable topography of the city, especially after sundown. The critics, however, considered the film's depiction of sexuality risqué and unbecoming of the directors' collective.

John was, however, *not* the only anti-hero Uttam played. In 1963's *Sesh Anka*, he played a murderer, in 1964's *Lal Pathor*, a shrewd patriarch and in 1966's *Kal Tumi Aleya*, an amoral survivor. *Kal Tumi Aleya* (The Survivor) was thought to be un-filmable, because of the non-structured, complex plot; non-formulaic, erotic complications; delicate corporate intrigues and a set of dark characters, none of which were staple stuff for a mainstream film. But Uttam was keen to have it adapted and his insistence finally convinced author Ashutosh Mukhopadhyay to adapt his novel for screen. Apart from the leading role Uttam, to the surprise of many, also scored the music for the film and passed muster with three admirably tuneful numbers. One of them was a light, flirty romp; the second a sensual, bordello-inspired *thumri*; and the third a mournful dirge, all three placed appropriately in the movie.

Dhirapada (Uttam), a man just past his youth, is a disenchanted, cynical freelancer who writes advertisement copies for a small firm. He keeps for himself a frugal room in Sultankuthi, a dingy cluster of dwellings for the poor. Unlike the usual stereotype of righteous poverty in mainstream films, Sultankuthi is an amoral space, filled with greasy neighbours constantly trying to play the dirty trick on the other. On the recommendation of a distant kin, a rich elderly lady, Dhirapada joins Ultra Pharmaceutical Company, a leading medical firm. Initially an outsider, he soon charms his way into the company's management, earning the trust of the company boss Mr Himanghsu Mitra, his nephew Dr Amitabha Ghosh and Dr Labonyo Sarkar, all of whom had a major stake in the company's well-being. Dhirapada is at odds with Himanghu's son Sitanghsu, the latter having found him an interloper. The film unfolds across the company's office and factory, the Mitra mansion, the medical shop, and the hospital. To the glitz of stiff-upper-lip, Westernised corporate manners, pestilential Sultankuthi provides the contrast.

Dhirapada, initially reticent, soon finds himself in a position of influence and more importantly, is sexually attracted to Labonyo (Supriya), a chic, smart, committed physician. Dhirapada also shares a relationship of reliance with Sonaboudi, his immediate neighbour at Sultankuthi. Sonaboudi is attracted to Dhirapada and never hides her admiration for him, though they never cross the social boundary that binds them. Wife to a nincompoop and degenerate wastrel, Sonaboudi (Sabitri) is a suffering spouse who hopes to steal a moment or two caring for Dhirapada from her otherwise excruciating domesticity.

Two parallel sets of crises are set into motion: one at the company, one at Sultankuthi. They range from threats of an exposé of the company's slimy deals, labour trouble, internal intrigue, sexual jealousy, unwed pregnancy; to problems typical of his poor neighbours—criminal sons, cavorting daughters with starry ambitions, enforced prostitution, shady pimps and nights spent in brothels. Unable to escape either, Dhirapada uses every weapon in his armoury to cajole, convince, threaten, persuade and entice the myriad characters in the unctuous worlds of his two contesting lives. In a tense moment, he also forces himself on Labanyo, which earns a belated consent. But in the quagmire, Dhirapada loses Sonaboudi to suicide; even if the pharma company is saved major embarrassment. Sequestered in his private grief, he adopts the orphaned young daughter of Sonaboudi and in the very end is joined by Labanyo.

This film was as contemporary as one could be and explores the sexual attraction between genders outside the socially sanctioned staple of romantic films. The city's nether attractions are also integral to the film's appreciation of the essential slipperiness of values and morals. Edited deftly, shot intelligently and scripted nattily, *Kal Tumi Aleya* broke conventions and attracted worthy performances from everyone. But Uttam reigned as ever, masterfully charting the choppy waters his character had to swim in and the unethical choices he had to make. Uttam was by then repeatedly indicating a realignment of his star image, an image no more at unease in a morally ambiguous world.

GOODBYE CALCUTTA

That the realignment was inevitable was signalled most vividly in the film that closes this chapter—*Chowrongee* (Chowringhee, 1968), adapted from Shankar's best-selling novel. With the exception of *Mayamriga*, it was in *Chowrongee* that Uttam played, for the first time since his stardom, a *spectator*. So, unlike *Kal Tumi Aleya*, *Chowrongee*'s significance is not about the indeterminacy of moral choices but about the star image being withdrawn from a position of authority.

Chowrongee offered Uttam a kind of role he had not played before: Syata Bose, the concierge-in-chief at Calcutta's famed (and not entirely fictional) Shahjahan Hotel. But even outside Uttam, *Chowrongee* had a memorable cast and a script that distributed its attention equally. Set in and outside the lavish luxury hotel in downtown Calcutta, *Chowrongee* is woven around a set of characters who animate the hotel's crepuscular coalition—the tuxedoed managers and vigilant staff, misfit musicians, itinerant guests, hawk-eyed lobbyists, shady businessmen, gossipers and hangers-on, secretive nightwalkers, inquisitive oddballs and wide-eyed foreigners. In other words, the hotel is the city and the city a hotel. The folks who walk in and out and those who work there form a chain of interdependence, of power and passion; while being observed by the narrator-receptionist Shankar, through the eyes of his colleague Syata Bose. Syata, on his part, is as much a participant in the hotel's gilded life as much as he is the detached observer of its entrails. Through a series of closely observed sketches hence, the yin and yang of the spectral city life are revealed, coupled with Syata's wry and wistful annotations. The film did not deviate from the source except keeping a few extra shots and a song or two for Syata (Uttam). And what a song Manna

Dey's 'Boro Eka Lage' (On a Lonely Night) is! For rarely has the solitude of a gentleman longing for unfound love on a stormy night been so mellifluously rendered.

Otherwise *Chowrongee* is a worthy adaptation and in fact betters the novel in some parts. Within a span of two-and-half hours, the film manages to get right the pace and temper of the glitzy life; without taking a moral position. The script also managed to get under the skin of the characters so effortlessly that Syata, Marco, Karabi, Sujata, Mrs Pakrashi, Fokla Chatterjee have become part of Bengali popular reference. The most interesting member of the assembly was the prickly Nyatahari (Nrityahari) Bhattacharya, the veteran laundry-in-charge. Nyatahari is one who keeps his Brahmin discriminations close to his chest and yet finds immense, fatherly fondness for the escort Karabi (Supriya). Bhanu Bandopadhyay, one of Uttam's most admired peers, played the role. It remains one of the finest portrayals of this kind, here matched only by Uttam's Syata.

Chowrongee is essentially a story of departures. Karabi, the kind-hearted escort to an opportunist businessman, having fallen in love with one of her hosts, is blackmailed to commit suicide; the mannerly manager Marco Polo (Utpal Dutt), mourning his wife's elopement, leaves for Africa; the Brahms-addicted cultured musician Gomez is asked to leave; Shankar loses his job and the hotel changes hands having been bought over by new, unscrupulous, upstart money. Syata, the weathercock of the hotel and the city, finds love in the autumn of his youth with the ebullient and caring airhostess Sujata and leaves Calcutta. But just before their wedding, Sujata is killed in a horrible accident during her final flight out of Bombay. Struck by the wretched tragedy, the ever-smiling, generous, genteel Satya—lonely, bereaved and devastated—decides to join Marco Polo in Africa.

Like *Saheb Bibi Golam* set three quarters of a century ago, *Chowrongee* was symptomatic of the end of a period in Calcutta's history. In the fragile days of the end 1960s, the last vestiges of the colonial city were noticeably in retreat, grace and civility were making way for vulgarism and cheap money. The film tapped into this vital moment of transformation in Calcutta's chequered history. After the relative calm of the 1950s and early 1960s, Calcutta was again thrust into abject street violence, visceral political unrest, militant trade unionism and ultra-Left-wing violence. Together, the years provincialised Calcutta further, expunging it of any residual cosmopolitanism, which was once germane to the city's imposing self-appraisal. *Chowrongee* mirrors a moment on the verge of this period's unfolding. It might remind one of the lines from poet Pritish Nandy's paean: "Calcutta if you must exile me, destroy my sanity before I go."

Chowrongee is hence a moment of reckoning in Bengali cinema and also in Uttam's ouvre.

There is Calcutta after *Chowrongee* but it is a different Calcutta. There is also stardom after 1968 but a different stardom. The dark Calcutta of the 1970s was to 're-emerge' in art cinema. A certain city continued to be part of Uttam Kumar's cinema too but popular cinema of a discernible urban provenance had bowed out by the end 1960s, *Chowrongee* being its climactic triumph. With it was gone not only the figure of the zealous protagonist but also the dogged everyman who had then metamorphosed into a complex, divided, greying star persona. Even otherwise, Uttam's cinema started to show unmistakable signs of fatigue. It is hence no exaggeration to claim that the picaresque, piquant cinema of early to middle Uttam—complete with its inimitable methods of mirroring Calcutta, through romance, humour, pathos and heroic discernment—was now gone forever.

NOTES

1. Marshall Berman, *All That Is Solid Melts into Air*, Penguin Books, 1982 [1988], p. 15.
2. David Clarke (ed.), *The Cinematic City*, London: Routledge, 1997.
3. Brian Larkin, 'Colonialism and the Build Space of Cinema', in *Empires of Vision: A Reader*, edited by Martin Jay and Sumathi Ramaswamy, Duke University Press, 2014.
4. Mark Shiel and Tony Fitzmaurice (eds), *Cinema and the City: Film and Urban Societies in a Global Context*, Oxford: Blackwell, 2011, p. 5.
5. Jonathan Raban, *Soft City*, London: Harvill, p. 10.
6. Rabi Basu, *Satrong*, Dey's Publishing, Vol. 1 and 2, 2013.

7

TO THE TOP, *TO THE* TOP, TO THE *TOP*

Acting is happy agony.

—Jean-Paul Sartre

ONE can call 'listicles' or 'best of this', or 'most famous of that' a digital-era truism, catering to an ever-widening shortfall of attentive reading time and a need for easy consumption of quickly rendered cultural commentary. Likewise, several of them on Uttam Kumar are floating on the worldwide web. Another list, under the rubric of his top films would not have hurt. But I have tried to avoid this fashion of consigning things to ranks. In this chapter are indeed ten films that can be considered Uttam's truly great work. But they are rendered neither chronologically or by merit. Rather they present themselves as pairs, because I felt that in this act of conscious coupling, the tensions within the performed characters reveal themselves most powerfully, mapping out Uttam's screen persona more profitably. Moreover, as films too they are exceptional in the Bengali canon, even if all of them are not of equal distinction. This way, those unfamiliar with Uttam's work, would have a sense of which films of his could be truly assigned to greatness. For the more familiar, this is a way of integrating the actor's best work with that of the star. And those who are in love with him and have thought many times about which films are actually his best, the following list could be something to argue with, because no two sets of preferences are likely to be similar.

ACT 1 | THE LOVER AND THE LONER

Random Harvest (1942), starring Ronald Colman and Greer Garson, piqued Uttam's interest when he saw it in the 1950s in Metro Cinema. So, for his first co-production *Harano Sur* (The Lost Tune) he decided to adapt the film. But he and his partner in Alochaya Films—director Ajoy Kar—did not think it fit to adapt the entire script, which had several twists. Neither was the Great War thought to be a fitting background.

They, instead, took the idea of trauma-induced memory loss, a haunting song sung next to a "low-hanging tree branch laden with blossoms" and two lost souls desperately trying to locate love in the foggy terrains of forgetful pasts.

In distant Polashpur, when Alok (Uttam) lands up as an amnesiac patient in a mental hospital, he has not just lost his memory but also his sense of himself. A train accident, we learn, had rendered him with a spotless mind. The senior doctors, having guessed his lineage as a Calcutta gent, try hard to bring his memory back. But that makes Alok recoil and harden further. It is only the young doctor Roma (Suchitra Sen) whom he finds judicious. On a stormy night, he manages to escape the asylum and having lost his way, lands up at the doors of Roma. Instead of handing him over, Roma takes him in. She explains to her father that Alok's case needs caution and care rather than blunt imposition of clinical methods. Her father happily obliges. What begins as a psychoanalytical case study soon turns into romance as Alok, now increasingly composed and cheerful, surrenders completely to Roma. They get married and sing an absolutely magical song ('Tumi Je Amar') under a Polash (Flames of Forest) tree heavily pregnant with blossoms. It is an idyllic union. Only if it lingered. For, no sooner had Alok set out for a job one day when he is almost run over by a car. Mildly hurt and lying in a roadside ditch, Alok is jolted out of his present, having suddenly recalled his past life. His immediate past months are wiped out. He buys a ticket and heads for Calcutta, Roma waiting, in vain, for his hour of return.

The narrative shifts to Calcutta and we find Alok, rehabilitated, as an authoritative figure running a successful business and cruising through life. He lives with his mother and young niece and is on the verge of getting married to his fiancé. Roma, having learnt about Alok's departure, comes to Calcutta and manages to trace him. She then takes up work as a governess for his niece. Her poise and wisdom appear out of place with her vocation but she avoids scrutiny. It is only in lonely unguarded moments that she tries to reach out to Alok, hoping for a blink of recognition in his eyes. But Alok remains distant and even rude, considering her a petulant distraction in his otherwise well-appointed life. She tries her final luck with the song that consecrated their union. For a moment it seems Alok is on the verge of a grand recall but he regains composure the next moment, stirred but not shaken by the tune. Roma, giving up hope, leaves. She hardly knows that she has stimulated a spasm in Alok, which incandescent, stalks him till he finds out about Polashpur, revisits their tree of bloom and runs to Roma's house. Here, a crestfallen Roma, having given up on him, is roused into a joyous embrace.

Harano Sur fulfils every obligation of a melodrama but it also takes them seriously. Ajoy Kar knew he was on slippery territory with the idea of loss and return of memory. If he traversed callously, the film was bound to collapse into another vacuous cinema of excess. But it does not. And that is because in Alok's guarded hesitation and in Roma's studied longing, the film does hint at the infeasibility of a project of extracting memory from forgetting. Hence the film plays with private and public space, with shadows, with echoes and murmurs, with instant and delayed time and so on. This style deftly distributes the *act* of remembrance across the mise en scène, instead of having the characters get weighed down under the demanding commission of the plot. Both Uttam and Suchitra manage to fuse Kar's style with their performative finesse, staying resolutely within the logic of the film rather than being superfluous to it. A deft management of soundtrack and a chiaroscuric use of light added to the appeal. No wonder Kar manages to construct a series of singular cinematic moments that instead of cloying sets free the exultations of a romance melodrama. The film was not just a record success but has since been a historic inscription on Bengali popular psyche, a testimony to the movie's magical conjuring of an improbable romance plot. Also, it was awarded a certificate of merit at the national awards that year.

So rewarding is the film as a romance that it would be enlightening to have it contrasted with a film that stood at the other end of the melodramatic measure. And if that film, like *Harano Sur,* also happens to be produced by Uttam, then there is surely an undeniable link. Uttam found commercial success with all his first four films as producer—*Harano Sur, Soptopodi, Bhranti Bilash* and *Uttor Phalguni.* Except the first, he produced the other three alone, under the banner of Uttam Kumar Films. All four had directors from the mainstream rank and it should have been *de rigueur* for Uttam to continue with them. But he headed for Tapan Sinha, who was by then known as a sincere practitioner of 'middle of the road' cinema. Sinha and Uttam had worked together twice before (*Upohar* and *Jhinder Bondi*) and both were keen to work with the other again. Betting on Uttam's eagerness, Sinha pitched a serious script based on a Subodh Ghosh story. The star-producer obliged, deciding to back *Jotugriha,* a film about the complex algebra of a marriage tiptoeing towards annulment. *Jotugriha* not only tossed aside the existing clichés of romance but, in fact, confronted the whole genre upfront, in the process also questioning Uttam's alleged umbrage under a purported image. So, in some ways, Uttam financed a film that challenged his own undisputed dominion.

Jotugriha (The House of Wax) opens with Shatadal Dutta, senior official of the archaeological department, contemplating divorce from his teacher-wife Madhuri (Arundhati Mukherjee). Satadal, an architect, is obsessed with the country's ancient built heritage and is a builder and preserver of homes, except, perhaps, his own. He is flanked, socially, by an acrimonious couple who noisily occupy the flat next to his and a pliant clerk who manages to find happiness in his sparse subsistence. The film moves to the past of Shatadal and Madhuri, where they are shown to share a deep bonding, socialise sparingly in their free evenings and are busy planning their future—a future shaping up, brick by brick, in the form of a two-storey house. But things start to falter once they learn the impossibility of having a child together. Initially they accept and agree to bear it out. But soon the walls come crumbling down when they are unable to work anymore on the emptiness of their attachment, which unattended, veers towards estrangement. Their marriage unravels behind a slick city life of parties and business deals, of nightclubs and live jazz music, or in the midst of neon signs and high-street apartments and the various grey lives within them. The acrimonious couple continue to live together next door with an overt sense of helpless doom, but Shatadal and Madhuri move on; quietly and without acrimony; abandoning their future apartment midway. They meet years later, accidentally, in a first-class waiting room in a railway station. After initial hesitation, they find comfort and spend some time together. Both realise that the other is single and has visibly aged in the years between. Perhaps both nurse a yearning to go back too. But they resist the temptation, knowing well that their marriage had no external instrument of damage but had hollowed on its own. They take their trains to respective destinations, never to meet again.

Jotugriha is an incisive and quiet study of a mature conjugality that slowly loses steam. What makes it even more poignant is that the usual traps of such circumstances—the 'other' woman, alcoholism, social or financial ruination, difficult in-laws, oppressive patriarchy or complaint gender playing—are shut out. The film, instead, penetrates into the architecture of contemporary conjugality and the slippery terrains of aspiration that it is built upon. Uttam is unsurpassable as Shatadal. He is both helpless and forceful, churlish and charitable, embittered and resilient; as one should be in a realistic portrayal of a failed marriage. Just like Madhuri is, whom Arundhati brings to life with flawless equanimity. There could not have been a better pair of actors to play them and there has never been a better film in Bengali about marital incompatibility. As a sensitive and progressive testament of big-city ennui and gendered modernity too, *Jotugriha* is unmatched. Satyajit Ray's *Mahanagar* (The Big City) called for a new role of women in a city charged with the flux of modernity. Coming a year after, *Jotugriha* furthered the force of this change beyond the role of the new working woman and towards a new realignment of spaces and desires within couple-hood. Gulzar's *Ijaazat* (1987) could barely touch the original's unobtrusive intelligence, deciding instead to surrender to the plangent conventions of a failed marriage.

ACT 2 | THE RADICAL AND THE ROMANTIC

Among a very substantial section of Bengali audiences, as we have learnt already, Uttam's 'image' or persona has been overwhelmingly overshadowed by a monolithic, somewhat vague idea of him being a *romantic hero* par excellence. Few have gone deeper into asking what being a *romantic hero* entails. Does it signify a male *hero* who *romances* a heterosexual partner onscreen? Does it mean a star whose films are mostly *romance* movies? Does it signify a definitive, identifiable disposition in the acting style and substance? Does it mean that this actor was capable of expressing a *romantic* temperament better than anything else more demanding and complex? In the case of Uttam, all of the above were true and untrue equally. True, because Uttam had an inimitable and irrefutable charm as a matinee heartthrob. Untrue, because Uttam himself punctured every protocol of that persona. The testimonials to the latter are spread across this book, including in *Jatugriha* mentioned earlier. The finest proof of the former, that is, Uttam as a romantic hero without parallel, lies with the two films we shall now discuss.

Soptopodi (The Seven Steps) was Uttam's first production since 1957's *Harano Sur*. This time he was the sole producer, though it was directed, again, by Ajoy Kar and proved to be even more unforgettable than the first. This film was the finest romantic film that one can imagine on a subcontinental soil, pitching the visual possibilities of romantic melodrama to such cinematic heights that there could hardly be any improvement upon it. The plot of *Soptopodi* concerns the epic exertions of star-crossed lovers from differing ethnic communities to attain union. But that is to say nothing about the film.

It is late 1930s Calcutta and Krishnendu (Uttam), a would-be doctor in Calcutta Medical College, has embraced the bequest of modernity, standing against the orthodoxy of his Hindu father. He is a jack of all trades and the sort of brilliant, restless young man who wants to change the world. He falls in love with Rina Brown (Suchitra Sen in one of her defining roles), a beautiful, self-assured Anglo-Indian lady who is studying with him. The film follows the pattern of them being at warring ends in the beginning, who, during a performance of Shakespeare's cross-race tragedy *Othello*, fall passionately in love. Krishnendu is asked to convert to Christianity by Rina's father. As a non-believer, he unhesitatingly accepts the proposition, brushing aside Rina's expressed remorse. But Krishnendu's father threatens, coaxes and finally pleads Rina to give up on the relationship. Rina relents. Spurned by her in a moment of dramatic turnaround, Krishnendu abandons his life as a rebel to settle down in a remote village as a Jesuit physician. Rina is undone further when it is revealed that she was born out of a wedlock between her English father and her native governess. Unable to cope with her traumatic losses, she loses herself to wanton self-destruction. As the WWII comes to South Asia, she joins the Red Cross.

One day in a faraway settlement, a washed-up, alcoholic nurse, in the middle of the war, is rescued and brought to Krishnendu, by then a reticent, wistful healer of the poor. To his shock, he sees that it is none other than Rina. Rina, broken and angry, discovers a born-again believer in Krishnendu but refuses to ascribe to his missionary pacifism. She accuses god of having betrayed her and the world at large. In an intense moment of confrontation, she also discovers her old portrait preserved behind a framed picture of Jesus, which she had just shot to pieces. Confused, hurt and weighed down in equal measure, she leaves in a huff, promising never to be found in the company of her old love. Months later, she is found again by Krishnendu, wounded and battered, but at peace with the news that Krishnendu's father had asked for her clemency for his foolhardy orthodoxy. She starts to soften. In the last scene, Krishnendu carries Rina in his arms to a silhouetted church to embrace a possible union.

Soptopodi is remarkable for its luminous cinematography; sharp editing; documentary use of war footage; minimalist soundtrack; an enlivened set design; and the consistent and unsurpassable chemistry of its lead pair. Be it in the tense scenes of one-upmanship between the settler whites and Indians, the deft use of *Othello*, a famous road song on the back of a motorcycle, the dramatic interplay of light and shadows, and that of the personal with the political, *Soptopodi* uses and subverts most set pieces of a melodrama. Instead, the first part of the film uses Calcutta's multicultural institutions and neighbourhoods for a spirited depiction of a protean modernity, which when challenged by orthodoxy, spills over into the lives of its two protagonists. The second part moves towards a humanist climax, in which the lovers eschew the catalogue of familiar dilemmas to embrace a trans-cultural autonomy. *Soptopodi* is larger than life and yet full of tender, endearing and lyrical moments. Whether it is because of the war background, the overall temperament of unattainable love, the charm of its actors or the range of cinematic possibilities it tries to encompass, *Soptopodi* was (and still is) *Casablanca* for the Bengali audience—an un-ageing and incomparable movie experience.

Antony Firingee (Poet from Another Land) shares an organic bond with *Soptopodi* for being a refined film involving another adorable pair of lovers from different faiths felled by a native orthodoxy that is incapable of rising above their prejudice. The major difference is the centrality of music in the latter. In fact, as I have recalled more than once, music was so integral to Bengali cinema of the period that many films can lay claim to being a sort of musical. But in no other Uttam film was its score so richly textured, was so constitutional to its plot and was so organic of the protagonist's person than in *Antony Firingee*. Thus, music is an equal stakeholder in the spell that the film manages to conjure.

Antony Firingee is loosely based on Hansman Antony, a Portuguese-origin, mixed-race poet and folk hero (late 18th to early 19th century) who made a name for himself in Forashdanga (now known as Chandannagar). The happy-go-lucky Antony grows up with music and goes around town looking for it. He embraces Bengali language, composes devotional songs and tests his luck with *kobigan*—an impromptu, freewheeling popular competition between poets involving banter and witty wordplay. Soon, with his humility, talent, compassion and silver voice he wins over everyone and every contest locally before he starts to break into the competitive Calcutta scene. And yet, he is never allowed to forget that he is, after all, a foreigner, a *firingee*.

In the meantime, Antony falls in love with the courtesan Nirupama, a woman abused and sold to the brothels for her beauty. They not only bond over music but in each other they find a companionship that could transcend the limits of provincial identity. They get married too, their individual faiths extraneous to their union. But local Hindu orthodoxy resents the happiness of people they consider foreign and fallen, and ostracises them. Nirupama insists on performing a Durga Puja at her home and awaits Antony's return after his big win in Calcutta. But the Brahmins are scandalised; and in Antony's absence, burn the house down. Niru stays put praying and dies, asphyxiated. The climactic scene of a disconsolate, broken-hearted Antony, carrying Niru's motionless body in his arms and asking the onlookers, "Why did you do this to us?", "Was this necessary?", "Did we ever hurt you?" whips, haunts and tugs at the heart.

The outline of the plot will not be able to render the film's great virtues, music being the first of them. The veteran composer Anil Bagchi surpassed himself with the magnificent score, so did Manna Dey as the voice of Antony (and Arati and Sondhya Mukherjee as the female equivalent). Sunil Banerjee's fabulous musical manages to go well beyond the artless pulls of historical accuracy. The film rather prefers to stay in the domain of fiction, elevating a folksy tale of an angelic bard and his trials in a land of wretched orthodoxy to a compelling cinematic tragedy. Tanuja is eminently likeable, making her affection for guileless Antony seamlessly discernible. But it was Uttam—with fuzzy whiskers, a beret on his head, a pair of tender eyes, a strapping liveliness and that instinctive capability to merge into the songs he lip-synced—who is, again, extraordinary.

Both films took the archetype of embattled lovers from different races/religions trying to find union at the other end of a world that was resolutely against it. But they leashed the excesses and lyrically avoided the clichés to weave two most rewarding specimens of romance in all of Indian cinema. Most importantly, both films were and are still a sort of memorial to an alternative emotional history of cosmopolitanism and interfaith love, both increasingly endangered ideas in a country tethered to xenophobia.

ACT 3 | THE MAGISTRATE AND THE MURDERER

Even if the germ of *Soptopodi* and *Antony Firingee* fitted into a pattern of melodramatic plotting, the next two films were barely so. In plot and narrative, they seemed to have little precedence, no one really expecting them from the cliché-ridden storehouse of popular cinema. In *Bicharok*, *judge* Gyanendranath—erudite, ethical, atheist—is forced to sit on judgement on his own past, having allegedly abetted his first wife's death from apathy. In *Sesh Anko* the much-vaunted Sudhanshu falls in love with a woman outside marriage and ends up killing his offending wife, laying himself open to an elaborate mousetrap. The judge and the criminal sit on two sides of the same arc of conjugal conscience, loveless commitment and natural justice. Also, of all accusations to that effect, they must, above all, confront themselves. Terrific plots rendered terrifically.

Image 7.1: The bhadralok as self-adjudicator. Uttam and Arundhati Mukherjee. Publicity still of *Bicharok* (The Judge, 1959)

Source: Author.

In *Bicharok* (The Judge), adapted from a Tarashankar Bandopadhyay novel, middle-aged Gyanendranath, judge at a district court in Bengal's provinces, is revered and feared in equal measure. He is considered morally incorruptible, ethically infallible and a man of deep insight into the philosophy of jurisprudence. He embraces atheism because he considers god an autocrat, who has to answer to no one. But as a human adjudicator, as he explains to his wife Suroma, he is answerable to the supreme authority of natural justice. A case involving two brothers is brought to Gyanendranath's attention, after one dies in a boat accident. The question that the case must ponder is, was it really an accident or did it involve an act of calculated homicide masked as coincidence, because both men were in love with the same woman. Reflecting on the case takes Gyanendranath away from the present to a time two decades past when as a naïve advocate, married to Sumati, he came to apprentice with a senior judge. The judge's sparkling daughter Suroma helps Gyanendranath socialise in the small town and a bond develops between them. Gyanendranath is evidently drawn towards the beautiful Suroma, unaffected, smart and warm, as he realises that his wife Sumati, suspicious and stubborn, is the opposite of Suroma. As tensions build up, Gyanendranath is unable to explicitly condemn his wife's allegations of having taken his attentions elsewhere, while her coarse meltdown in front of Suroma bares the fangs of their troubled marriage. As the present case mounts itself in public, the past case emerges with even more clarity in private. Finally, Gyanendranath finds himself recalling the events of a fateful night when their house caught fire and in a moment of turpitude Gyanendranath had freed himself from the frantic grasp of his gasping wife and escaped to safety. The world knew it as a tragic accident in which he had lost his first wife. Now, all these years later, Gyanendranath must face his only great moment of lapse in an otherwise unsoiled career. He finds himself confronting Suroma's cold and severe probing, and his own conscience. Could he have saved Sumati that night? Did he too mask a case of culpable homicide? Since he does not believe in any higher conscience, who can sit on judgement on his past but himself? And finally, can he anymore sit on judgement on others?

Rarely does popular cinema use a star to play a middle-aged character of such severe ethical persuasion, who paces up and down a thin line of moral redemption. Rarely does a crisis in couple-hood become a critique of existential solipsism. Director Prabhat Mukhopadhyay dared, managing to give Uttam his first truly breakaway role when the star was just thirty-three years old.

And Uttam is exemplary as the fumbling young advocate who morphs into an introverted, insightful and tormented judge who has to live up to his own exacting standards. Mukhopadhyay's then wife Arundhati flawlessly played Suroma, the best possible counterpoint in a film like this. She was also the producer. In its minimalism, in its scripting and in creating moments of formidable philosophical tension, *Bicharok* was not just ahead of its time but also a remarkable testimony to Bengali cinema's distinctive and daring sensibility.

In *Sesh Anko* (The Final Act), widower Sudhangshu, handsome and successful, is, in fact, a dreamboat. The eminent Sir Haraprasad and his daughter Soma accept him into their midst. It is certain that a happy life awaits Sudhangshu. But during a ceremony, an advocate arrives and declares a woman in tow to be Kalpana, Sudhangshu's deceased wife. She also presents telltale proof in support of her claim. Everyone is shocked, not least Sudhangshu. He pleads that Kalpana was long suffering from trauma and after an embittered married life, had killed herself in a moment of acute depression. Though he manages to wriggle out of the quagmire for the time being, there is a whiff of suspicion that lingers among the witnesses, not least Soma (Sharmila). Soon, the advocate and the woman are joined by a suspicious oddball. As they start to stalk Sudhanshu, he finds himself increasingly isolated from the warm affections of Soma and Haraprasad. And the more he tries to distance himself from his past, the more he seems to get embroiled in it. Unable to release himself from the claimant 'wife' and watching his world crumble slowly, Sudhanshu agrees to a legal resolution. And almost immediately, all evidence starts to go against him. Desperate, Sudhanshu's barrister telegrams Deben, Kalpana's brother, hoping that the arrival of the merchant officer would clinch the case on behalf of Sudhanshu. Deben arrives the night before the hearing at Sudhanshu's house; and to the latter's utter disbelief, also identifies the second woman as Kalpana. Sudhanshu is appalled; and in a moment of demented rage shouts out that Kalpana could not have been alive by any means because she was, after all, murdered by him, even if it was an act of accidental manslaughter. That was it! The cornered, crestfallen Sudhanshu realises that he had become part of an elaborate plot, largely devised by Deben, to coax out his confession, which was the only evidence of his culpability.

Everything about *Sesh Anko* carries the marker of a great film; the tight writing and the shadowy cinematography complimenting the subtle performances. And it would be an injury to the film's near-

Image 7.2: The homicidal hero. Publicity booklet of *Sesh Anko* (The Final Act, 1963)

Source: Jadavpur University.

originality if we recall that it was very loosely adapted from British crime drama *Chase a Crooked Shadow*. But what is striking is that director Haridas Bhattacharya, known for mellow adaptations of literary classics, performed an act of heresy by casting Uttam as Sudhanshu. Even if Uttam was already breaking free of any dominant image, to cast him as a murdering anti-hero was audacious. Uttam gave him full aid. And we have a most striking standout thriller in Bengali cinema.

Both the films must also point towards their leading female actors, Arundhati Mukherjee and Sharmila Tagore. The fact of them sharing two films each (Arundhati in *Bicharok* and *Jotugriha*, Sharmila in *Sesh Anko* and *Nayak*) in this league of crowning films—as many as Suchitra Sen (*Harano Sur* and *Soptopodi*)—hints at the extent of their participation in Uttam's anointed body of work. Both came from enlightened families with links to either Tagore's family or his university at Santiniketan. Both of them brought a reserved sentience and sophisticated finesse to their parts on screen. Both could provide a compelling counterpart to Uttam's ample talent. Apart from the two here, Arundhati had several other notable films with Uttam, Sharmila had much less, but that handful demand close attention. Sharmila, of course, had that impressive range of being a favourite of both Satyajit Ray and Shakti Samanta, a feat unequalled otherwise. She was also a top Bombay heroine. Arundhati was a more accomplished actor, a singer of repute (though she never sang in films), a producer early in her life and an intellectual companion to both her husbands—Prabhat Mukhopadhyay and Tapan Sinha. She also evolved into a director of three much loved films in Bengali and was, in fact, slated to cast Uttam in an unmade film which was abandoned after the latter's death. Both actors earned the high admiration of Uttam and returned it equally. Sharmila continues to do so even today. Between them and Uttam, they gave Bengali cinema much to cherish.

Between *Bicharok, Sesh Anka* and *Jotugriha* Uttam ruptured the romantic melodrama from within. Unless romances were now crafted with finesse (like *Deya Neya, Antony Firingee* or *Nayika Songbad*), they were deemed unworthy of Uttam. The hurly-burly of a conventional romance—the ups and downs, the star-crossed lovers meeting at the other end of a world conspiring against their coming together—or, the excesses of familial sentimentality were now to be considered pansy and dated, even though they did keep coming in some form or the other. But introspective films like *Bicharok, Sesh Anka* and *Jotugriha* (along with *Thana Theke Aschi, Shonkhobela* and *Kal Tumi Aleya*), not only raised ethical and existential questions but also dealt with them with gravitas and discernment, making their way into Bengali cinema's hall of fame. They also displayed Uttam's increasing confidence in his ability to push the boundaries of the actor in him, who no longer longed to be just liked and adored. The next two films consolidate this fact further.

ACT 4 | THE SLEUTH AND THE SLAIN

Justice is the song of burden in the next two films too. If the first two saw Uttam as the judge and the criminal, here he plays the detective and the victim respectively, the third and final arm of the quadrangle that is law. And like the previous set, the two films here were character studies mounted on two very different plots; and neither was made for the marquee audience. Also, like the other pair of *Bicharok* and *Sesh Anka*, these two also sit on two sides of an arc. On one side of the arc is the dashing and daring Byomkesh Bakshi and on the other side is the subjugated and slaughtered Gana-da. The films are Satyajit Ray's *Chiriyakhana* and Parthapratim Chowdhury's *Jodubongsho*.

Chiriyakhana (The Zoo) has an interesting backstory. While the shooting for Ray's *Nayak* was underway, few of his assistants mentioned to Uttam their plan to make a movie with him that would be scripted by Ray. Forever obliging to such requests, Uttam gave his consent. Ray agreed to adapt a Sharadindu Bandopadhyay novel about ace sleuth Byomkesh Bakshi. And because they were on board, Ray's producer R.D. Bansal was keen too. But after the release of *Nayak*, a strange incident happened. The Bansals got caught in legal trouble when the fake banknotes made for the film were suspected to be actual bootlegged currency. Till the matter was sorted the Bansals had to keep away from any new commitment. For months no other producer was found. They either wanted a heroine opposite Byomkesh or a popular story to piggyback on Uttam. Finally, one producer agreed but on the condition that Ray must direct.

This well-known backstory has prompted many critics to take the film lightly, imagining that Ray was a reluctant participant in the film's fate or that as a detective film, the project was below the weight of his name. But the film carries every Ray signature; and even if Ray has testified to having taken it up reluctantly, he never said he took it up casually. He, in fact, made advance payments for the film when finances got stalled, the money having come from the Magsaysay Award he received in 1967. But the best proof of his involvement is in how he re-imagined the character of Byomkesh, which was played, needless to mention, by Uttam.

One rainy morning Byomkesh and his sidekick Ajit receive their client, the retired judge Nishanath Sen. Sen runs the Golap (Rose) Colony, a horticultural project on the outskirts of the city. Here he had rehabilitated a bunch of criminals who had served their sentence. They work in the colony and Nishanath arranges to sell the produce. Nishanath had come to meet the sleuth because he was under the impression that a forgotten singer might be hiding in his colony. Byomkesh senses more than a trifle of a song and agrees to take up the case. It is decided that he would visit the colony as a Japanese horticulturist. In the meantime Byomkesh and Ajit schedule a meeting with Ramen Mullick, a noted bon vivant and connoisseur of cinema. Mullick gives them hush-hush information about a one-film heroine who vanished after a brutal murder, her major claim being a song she had sung in the film. The visit to the colony reveals that Sen's was a virtual menagerie with a weird set of outlaws of both sexes, each with shadowy pasts. That same night, Sen is killed while on phone with Byomkesh when he was indicating of being subjected to an act of blackmail. The case draws the attention of local police. Before long there is a second murder of a speech-impaired attendant in the colony, who is suspected to have had clues about the first murder. Two murders, a truant song, several instances of blackmailing and Nishanath's own chequered past as a judge tie up the case in knots. Byomkesh chases the criminal at large, trying to outsmart his moves with a series of manoeuvres. Unlike most cases, he must pluck a criminal from a collective of criminals, which needs a full play of his detection methods. He finally calls for an exposition at the colony and in the presence of all stakeholders, the case is resolved in a dramatic climax.

Ray employed the full force of his imagination in the script, managing to create all the necessary pulls of a screen mystery. For that he made effective changes to the original story, including a bravura shift in the unveiling of the climax. There are also those customary touches of intelligence, humour, deft editing and great detailing, all of which carried the Ray stamp. But nothing was as striking as how Ray had re-booted Byomkesh. Sharadindu Bandopadhyay's best-selling detective had built his reputation on a template of moral cynicism and social conservatism. Ray frees Byomkesh from those chains and brings him up to date with the liberal ethos of the 1960s. Against a married, judgemental and too-full-of-himself Byomkesh of Sharadindu, we have a charismatic and daring bachelor sleuth who drinks and smokes, takes little interest in moral positions and lets his intelligence rest lightly on his shoulders. This was a radical departure and expectedly not to the liking of the author. To make it more meaningful, Ray deliberately projects Uttam's natural charm offensive, not least in the scene where Byomkesh mildly seduces a young woman in an Anglo-Indian neighbourhood. And that he had let Uttam re-imagine Byomkesh is most evidently found in the film's publicity. In a colourful, calligraphy-heavy poster, Ray stacks the keywords of a sleuth film along with the film's title against each other on a vertical plane. But on the place where there should have been, expectedly, the mention of Byomkesh, Ray mentions Uttam in bold beige lettering. Byomkesh is absent. Nowhere in Ray does the performer supersede the character on a poster. This is the first and only exception, carrying Ray's obvious proclamation of having the real star prevail over the fictional Byomkesh. Uttam more than lived up to Ray's confidence. He is uniformly brilliant. But in at least three scenes—one with Ramen Mullick, one with Ajit where they ponder over the women suspects and in the exposition scene—Uttam's is a masterclass of performance.

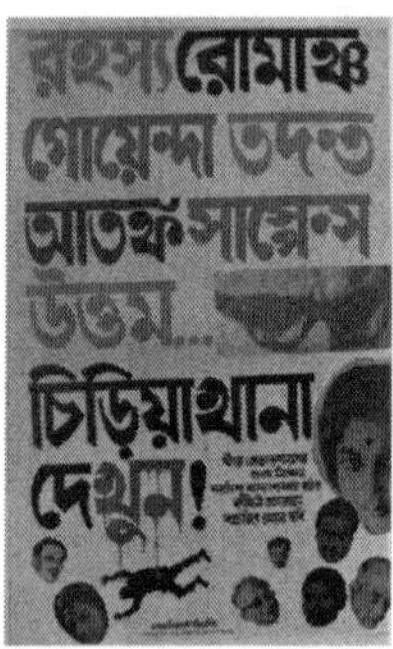

Image 7.3: In this Satyajit Ray-designed poster, the name of Uttam substituted that of the fictional detective Byomkesh Bakshi. *Chiriyakhana* (The Zoo, 1967)

Source: Ray archives.

In this case, Uttam was also rewarded with the first ever national award for the best actor. In fact, he was awarded for two films. Uttam Kumar of *Antony Firingee* shared the award with Uttam Kumar of *Chiriyakhana*.

One can hardly imagine *Jodubongsho* (The Parricide) next to *Chiriyakhana*. The films are chalk and cheese and common sense militates against this juxtaposition. Against the lyricism, style, humour and elan of Ray's mystery comes this angry, grim and unrelenting arty film that wears its non-conformism as a badge of honour. But the two films are bound by an actor's triumphant trajectory of letting go of all popular clichés he had accrued over the years.

If one considers its time, *Jodubongsho* is not as distinctive as it seems. This is because 1970s art cinema in Bengal, coming in the wake of abject political violence and vendetta, was uniformly bleak, including that of Ray, who had also relatively suppressed his habitual wit in his Calcutta trilogy. Parthapratim Chowdhury had always had a knack of walking against the grain, but by the time he made *Jodubongsho*, he decided to abandon several norms of conventional narrative cinema. Even then, his cinema as montage resembled Mrinal Sen's fiery films of the decade, like *Chorus*. What actually made *Jodubongsho* an exception, if at all, was Uttam playing Gana-da. If he was ever clinging to any image, here he shed it as determinedly as a reptile abandons its skin, shedding it with delight.

Gana-da is the man who purportedly had the central role in the film. I say purportedly because Gana-da is so vulnerable, so discomfited, so defeated that it is impossible to consider him as claiming any worth whatsoever. Also, there is hardly a plot in *Jodubongsho*, so there is hardly any flow of narrative. It is rather about a few faces and a few recurring images in a dingy suburban neighbourhood (*para*) trampled by vacant eyes and sterile agitation. Why this angst? Against whom is the vendetta? To what end? That is not what the film set out to explain. Rather, in *Jodubongsho*, anger is oxygen, agitation is survival, humiliation and assault the natural order of things. Here, four adrift jobless young men spend their days having tea, counting their pennies, cycling around purposelessly and howling at the world. The young men, scarred like mongrels and bamboozled by a cynical political hoodlum, find in defenceless Gana-da a man they can relieve their torment on. On the pretext of extorting a paltry sum of fifty rupees which he owes them, they taunt Gana-da from time to time. Gananath or Gana-da, once a local do-gooder and the Man Friday of the *para*, is the archetype of the failed man—without bearing, shelter or resources to run even his run-down store of household supplies. Shabby and wretched that he is, the camera repeatedly closes in on his pair of pained eyes looking for a spot of empathy in a world without kindness. He is taken in by two sisters (both Aparna Sen), the older of them finding in bespectacled Gana-da a mirror of her own helplessness. An ageing prostitute (Sharmila Tagore in a cameo) is the only other person with any residual compassion for the abandoned man who means no harm to anyone. But it all comes to an abrupt end when the young men storm into Gana-da's shelter one day, accuse him of petty theft and in a moment of heated exchange, beat him up mercilessly. Gana-da succumbs to his injuries. The film ends with Gana-da being carried away for cremation when, after a brief hesitation, the four men decide to join the small group of ragtag mourners.

Image 7.4: The defeated hero. Lobby card of *Jodubongsho*
(The Parricide, 1974)

Source: Parimal Ray.

The title of this film, adapted from a Bimal Kar novel of the same name, very aptly refers to the clan of Krishna in *Mahabharata* who were cursed to be wiped out by their own kin. But even without this reference, the film leaves one with a deep sense of dread, hinting at a world restless with rage. The film had no box office impact to speak of and is largely forgotten even as a Uttam film. But that is a grave mistake. The pitiless bleakness of the film still lingers, but it is Uttam's astonishing Gana-da—discoloured, weather-beaten, wrinkled—which haunts. Also, the cinema of the 1970s is full of the pain of the young but rarely did it turn to older men who were abandoned to the cruelty of the times and relegated to history overnight. To that end, in spite of the film's overbearing gloominess, it is a very crucial one.

ACT 5 | THE SCOUNDREL AND THE STAR

The Good-Joe Uttam persona, as we have seen, underwent a series of mutations and showed varying degrees of what we call dark shades. If it had a shadow of an unjust inclination in *Bicharok*'s ethical slippage or in the simplistic binary of *Kuhok*; in *Sesh Anko*, *Lalpathar* (1964), *Kal Tumi Aleya*, and later in *Stree*, *Jibon Jigyasha* (1971) and *Bonhisikha* (1976) they were considerably tilted towards being grey and grotty. But nothing came close to the degenerate Machiavellianism of Bhabesh Banerji in Pijush Bose's *Baghbondi Khela* (The Hunting Game), which is a study of an ambitious, assertive and scheming scoundrel.

When Rajesh is summoned by his father Bhabesh to dusty Ranipur, he has little clue what awaits him. He had grown up with uncles on his deceased mother's side far away from his influential father's domain. Rajesh has a foggy memory of his father, whom he knew vaguely as Ranipur's *nouveau riche* jouster with significant local clout. His first impressions, however, conflict with his memory. From what little he remembered, Bhabesh was a vulgar and bare-knuckle local thug who had taken to every possible venality—alcohol, women, smuggling in bootlegged goods and assorted illegality. But the greying Bhabesh Rajesh meets had attained respectability, owned a palatial house and legal businesses, had an army of ingratiating servants and had the local authority eating out of his hands. Bhabesh presents himself as a reformed do-gooder. He also informs that now, having attained all gains that money can buy, he wants to forego all of it so that he can dedicate his life to public service. He wanted Rajesh to claim his rightful place as the sole inheritor of the estate of Bhabesh Banerji so he could pursue his political programme with unswerving attention.

Rajesh is initially swayed, his inexperience getting the better of his suspicion. But a string of encounters reveals the extent of his father's shady affairs. A chance meeting with his father's estranged second wife Bibha (Supriya), a school teacher, partially reveals the nature of Bhabesh's plan. By bringing Rajesh into his fold, Bhabesh is trying to create an elaborate appearance of sagely philanthropy. But he had willed his property in such a way that he would trick Rajesh out of it on the other side of his electoral success. More and more revelations pile up till one day, sheltered at a brothel during heavy rains, Rajesh witnesses his father in a state of kinky succor. He was not just a customer but owned the place of trade. Rajesh sees the young Bhabesh emerging again from the creepy skin of the old and gets a hint of the depths of evil that his father was capable of. He decides to break rank, teams up with other local dissenters and files a police complaint. Bhabesh is found calmly sitting on his chair when the police arrive. Equally calmly he excuses himself to get dressed, goes inside and shoots himself.

What is striking about Bhabesh Banerji is that he is without scruples, has nothing to redeem his evil and till the end, stays resolutely unassailable. But what sets him really apart is that he would trick even his own son for the lust of power, without blinking his eyes. That makes him a sort of a remarkable rascal, who unsettled one of the most treasured tropes of the average melodrama of the family. Uttam, like a myriad of other characters, owned Bhabesh Banerji too. Whether as a vulgarian in his younger days or a charlatan in his older years; whether in his assertive thuggery or his contrived demagoguery; whether in his agitated insensitivity or his composed manipulation, Uttam regaled in the disrepute of his part, making Bhabesh Banerji an outstanding study of power and depravity. His transformation from the lovable hero of his early years was now total and indelible.

One can recall an amusing incident to highlight the extent of success that Uttam garnered. After one of the opening houseful shows, an actor of the film spotted a young viewer crying copiously, standing next to a shop. All he could say was, "Guru, you too have become bad?", perhaps convinced that Bhabesh Banerji was in actuality a transformed Uttam himself. The 1970s was a terrible time for Bengal's youth. And this man could hardly be faulted to have taken seriously the horrifying possibility that his hero—one of the last surviving monuments of decency in his volatile world—had gone rogue too.

This brings us around to asking what made our hero *the* hero; who he was and why; and what that young man mourned after all. And there is no one better to turn to for the answers than Satyajit Ray, who pondered over similar questions in one of his most famous films.

Satyajit Ray was not a man to go after cults. He had a recondite logic of understanding his world. Like other so-called cultural truisms to whom he rarely bowed, he did not share the general cynicism of the art-film fraternity about the plastic charms of a popular hero. Even if he did, in some cases, he was unwilling to reach the final verdict unless he tried them. In the case of Uttam, it was the latter. In fact, he had for long watched Uttam from a distance, often wondering if this man, who clearly oozed talent, would want to step out of the comfort zone of greasepaint stardom. Ray wrote later:

> I was not a film-maker yet when I first saw Uttam on the screen.
> I had heard of the emergence of the new hero and was curious to see
> what he was like. The heroes that one saw on the Bengali screen those
> days—Durgadas Banerjee, Pramathes Barua, K.L. Saigal, Dhiraj
> Bhattacharya—were hardly in the same league with the Hollywood

heroes one admired. I saw three of Uttam's films in a row, all made by one of our ablest directors, Nirmal Dey. First impressions were certainly good. Uttam had good looks, a certain presence, an ease of manner, and no trace of the theatre in his performance. He, obviously, had a future.[1]

That future, as a star and a marquee matinee idol, was much more in excess of any prediction that Ray and others could have made. So, with time, Ray became even more intrigued with the phenomenon of Uttam Kumar, but did not have the chance to work with him. Ray wrote:

> The opportunity to work with him came much later. By the time, Uttam Kumar had already become something of a legend. Every other Bengali film had him in the lead, usually paired with Suchitra Sen. This was a romantic team which for durability and width of acceptance had few equals in world cinema. Uttam was certainly a star in the true Hollywood sense of the term. The question was: was he also an actor?[2]

Ray's intention to probe Uttam's talent has been a matter of deliberation. This is because before he started to shoot with Uttam, his opinion of popular actors was far from glowing, as Andrew Robinson recalls in his book on Ray.[3] But Ray was not one to write a film based on untested talent, nor was he doing it with Uttam, even if he had to face accusations of selling out. Ray chose Uttam because he intrigued him and because he considered Uttam's talent capacious. Ray had hence resolved to work with Uttam for sometime, while for Uttam, anything that came from Ray would be an enticement. In the mid-1960s, Ray was at the peak of his powers and a much admired global cinema auteur, so an invitation from him was a mark of distinction far beyond the limits of Bengali cinema. But little did Uttam know that Ray had bigger plans.

> I was anxious to work with Uttam and wrote a part with him in mind. It was a part I thought he would find easy to identify with, being that of an ordinary middle-class youth who gets a break in films and quickly rises to the top. In fact, a rags-to-riches story which bears some resemblance to Uttam's own life. Uttam liked the part and accepted to do it although he could see that it meant shedding—at least for the time being—some of his glamour boy mannerisms. He also agreed to use no make-up although a recent attack of chickenpox had left its mark on his face.[4]

This was as big as it could get for Uttam. He did not hesitate to sign. For Ray, the stripping of greasepaint glamour was part of his plan to chip away at the facile exterior of a star and extracting the person within. But it still required a star. As Robinson writes:

> Here, though, a star was doubly appropriate since he was being asked to play a matinée idol and, according to Ray, he had read somewhere that "if you are showing a matinée idol, then you have to cast a star. Nobody else would do; people wouldn't accept the fact. So I thought that I was doing the only possible thing." On the other hand, he "always believed Uttam had it in him to give good performances."[5]

So was born *Nayak* (The Hero), which portrayed, in a span of a train journey, the loneliness of a phenomenally popular, always-on-the-verge-of-being-mobbed cine-star. As Pico Iyer writes in a recent *New York Times* article:

> Ray sends a handsome star of the silver screen from Calcutta to Delhi to receive a prize. As soon as he boards the train, the professional heartthrob, named Arindam Mukherjee (Uttam Kumar), finds himself, by turns, released from his public role and obliged to play it constantly. Everyone recognizes him, sighing over his legend, yet as soon as he's alone, he's overcome by memories and dreams that move him to ask himself whether he made the right choice in deciding to become a commercial icon.[6]

In fact, the closed space of the train works as a precise co-relative of Arindam's claustrophobia—offering him little escape from himself or from a set of passengers who get down to creating transactional value out of the time they spend on the journey; including evaluating their famous co-commuter. Arindam had prepared to spend the journey sleeping but was perturbed by a recent case of having lost his cool, an incident that had warmed the newspapers that morning. So, when a journalist (Sharmila) casually approaches for an impromptu interview, Arindam expresses a sense of resigned dismay. But he also finds in her a safe haven, because she remains somewhat dismissive of his public persona. Slowly, she manages to coax out of the star a frank and unguarded appraisal of his own life, revealing his inner torment, his acute isolation, moments of severe dilemma and his incessant fear of failure. As he goes back in time, either in conversations with her or by himself, Arindam hunts for signs in his incredible rags-to-riches story; while also looking for redemption in the counsel and conscience of an intelligent woman.

Outside, his life showed little signs of fracture. As Iyer writes:

> The Philips electric shaver in the opening scene—a novelty, surely, in the mid-1960s—tells us something about the cosmopolitan world

that its central figure, the larger-than-life movie star, inhabits. Very soon, we're in a thicket of *Mad Men* details, from a BOAC bag in the background to a reference to cocaine. Echoes of Federico Fellini's 8½ are everywhere—Uttam Kumar even looks like an Indian Marcello Mastroianni with his blend of debonair, sulky good looks and rumpled vulnerability.

Arindam's confessions lead him to two impressionist dream sequences and an alcohol-fuelled moment of forbearing self-loathing; but next morning he emerges into light with his habitual self-assured persona restored. Aditi, the journalist, decides to discard the interview. As the train arrives in Delhi, she walks away stoically, while the star vanishes into an ecstatic cry of assembled adulation.

So, what was on paper a rags-to-riches story was in actuality a psychologically loaded, demanding and layered script. And how did Uttam respond to it? Ray's peek into the crepuscular solitude of a matinee idol's inner life gave Uttam what he needed: an author-backed role, and Uttam rose to the challenge with "considerable intelligence and sophistication", to quote the hard-to-please critic Chidananda Dasgupta. Agrees Iyer.

> The film is anchored at every moment in Kumar's performance, and to me it's an astonishment. Everything about his soft hands as the film begins, his designer socks in two-tone shoes, his baby-faced insouciance, gives us a sense of spoiled entitlement; here is a man who thinks nothing of decorating his home with large, framed glossies of himself. Yet the beauty of Kumar's Arindam Mukherjee is that he has the capacity to surprise us, again and again. He can be witty and charming and kind. As Ray and Kumar push beneath the leading man's smooth surfaces, we expect, perhaps, demons and sleepless nights; but we may not be prepared for such grace. The professional hero, after boarding the train, helps an old man open a bottle and is patient with an elderly scold who dislikes all "talkies"; he even uses a glossy picture of himself as an instrument of compassion to heal an ailing child. Maybe because she's the rare soul who doesn't need him to be anything other than what he is.[7]

And what he *is* told in a momentous scene in the film, where Arindam is starting to taste the blood of cinema. In the scene, he is found severely discontented with his debut screen performance. Closeted in a small, near-dark room with just a window to peek out into the late night, Arindam, in vest and trousers, struts restlessly while taking his first sip of alcohol, egged on by his friend Jyoti. Jyoti wants to convince him that his debut has been a noticeable act, but Arindam remains disconsolate.

For him, it has been a failure, because he could not live up to his natural ways, bullied as he was by a senior actor to succumb to populist styles. He considered it a moment of defeat, a miscarriage of the potential of cinema against the tried-and-tested doctrine of the stage. "You cannot overact in front of camera. Everything on camera gets exaggerated ten times over, even the slightest deviation", he reasons. Then, he says, "I sense a missed chance, a vacuum, a lack. You won't get it, because you are biased." Jyoti relents, admiring Arindam's nagging sense of perfection. "This discontent of yours is a great gift. You will go far", Jyoti predicts. Arindam, with the camera closing in and the stark beam of a table-lamp radiating his eyes, replies with his fists thumping on the table in front: "Of course I will. I will go to the top, to the top, to the top." This is where Arindam and Uttam merge and become one. Iyer concurs.

> In almost every shot, Ray picks away at our easy assumptions, and Kumar embodies just what a star should be, as Ray would put it in 1971: "a person on the screen who continues to be expressive and interesting even after he or she has stopped doing anything".[8]

But one must note that as a film where Uttam *was* the subject, it made very atypical demands from him. It, of course, dared him to step into the more stringent territory of screen realism and paint-free close-ups. It also touched upon his ordinary origins, his passing compromises, his attendant vulnerabilities and his overwhelming *aura*. But most importantly, the film, rather than boasting the idea of *a hero*, probed against the phenomenon itself; putting under a harsh scanner the very nature of Uttam's formidable and forbidding stardom. And it was Uttam who had to do the surgery.

But few people then saw it that way. In fact, Iyer's appreciation of Uttam is a far-cry from the time of the film, even if it was liked, among others, by Pier Paolo Passolini, a member of the jury at the Berlin Film Festival, where *Nayak* won the Critics' Prize in 1966. Marie Seton's book on Ray[9] gives an idea of the Indian critical reception, which was unhappy because not only had Ray allegedly bowed to the charms of commercial cinema, but more so because the film was anything but a sordid expose of that cinema's corrupt workings. In fact, the quietness and sophistication of Ray's interrogation of mainstream stardom baffled them more than it irked them. This is a typical mistake because critics only managed to see *Nayak* as a Ray film. It is also, equally, an Uttam film. I would hence rather see *Nayak* as a virtuoso specimen of movie-making where two titans of Bengali cinema meet and interpret *the idea* of stardom, putting under investigation the furtive tensions between art and populism, camera and stage, person and persona and the reality and plasticity of fame. It is also a crowning testament of a top actor in top form. Needless to claim that this was always Uttam's best work and perhaps one of the finest by any leading actor anywhere in the world. It would not be precocious to claim that Uttam's stardom, having secured the rite of passage through Ray's censorious homage, was now ensconced in history.

NOTES

1. Sandip Ray (ed.), *Satyajit Ray on Cinema*, New York: Columbia University Press, 2013, pp. 107–108.
2. Ray, *Satyajit Ray on Cinema*, pp. 107–108.
3. Andrew Robinson, *Satyajit Ray: The Inner Eye*, IB Taurus, 1989.
4. Ray, *Satyajit Ray on Cinema*, pp. 107–108.
5. Robinson, *Satyajit Ray*, p. 177.
6. See Pico Iyer, 'Satyajit Ray's "The Hero" Revisited', NYRB, 27 February 2018, available at https://www.nybooks.com/daily/2018/02/27/satyajit-rays-the-hero-revisited/.
7. Iyer, 'Satyajit Ray's "The Hero" Revisited'.
8. Iyer, 'Satyajit Ray's "The Hero" Revisited'.
9. Marie Seton, *Satyajit Ray: Portrait of a Director*, Penguin 2003 [1971], pp. 161–182.

8

A GALLERY OF PORTRAITS

And one man in his time plays many parts.
—William Shakespeare

HOWEVER loudly one might proclaim otherwise, a career as rich as Uttam's cannot be boxed into a list of only ten films, even if they are, arguably, his most accomplished. There are more movies which stand out. These films, of various hues and shades, stand in a diverse and differential relation to the star, while they also bring to fore the vitality of the performer. As films, they carry inconsistencies but are key signposts in the busy and buoyant calendar of Uttam. Only a handful here are from the romance genre; while several are those that got eclipsed by the selfsame romances. But they need not be. Also, the films discussed in this chapter are distributed across the 1950s, 1960s and early 1970s, substantiating that Uttam had been committed to a range of characterisations throughout his career, whatever be the source of the massive untruth that was in popular circulation of his taking umbrage at romantic roles. So, to draw out his versatility as well as to reclaim what was lost to box-office fame, several of these films need to be restored to public appreciation. Needless to add, a number of other films across Uttam's career could have been included in this list. But I have placed them elsewhere for need of context and for them to be best revealed accordingly.

I have submitted the twenty films here to the conventions of genre, which I have avoided elsewhere in the book. This is to highlight both Uttam's range as well as the richness of Bengali cinema. Most of the genres below are commonly found in studies on cinema, or have been mentioned in literary scholarship. A few terms have been coined here for clarity.

PSYCHOLOGICAL DRAMA

Mental health has always been a slippery territory for narrative cinema, because of the anxiety that cinema, in trying too hard to *visualise* psychic tension, would simplify it to the point of a caricature. *Hrod* (The Lake) almost squanders itself on similar grounds, portraying inmates of an asylum as lunatics given to habitual exaggeration. But thankfully, the film's focus is not them but Banibroto (Uttam), a delicate young man thrown into the deep end of the psychic pool as he is tormented by a failed romantic pursuit. He is also found to be on the run for alleged manslaughter. Banibroto reveals signs of psychic trouble when he is unable to write 'I' and is deposited in a private asylum where the learned Dr Dasgupta takes up his case. Parallel to the investigation into his deep-seated psychosis, the criminal interrogation into an act of murder also begins, at the site of which Banibroto had left telltale clues of his involvement. Haunted by childhood trauma, guilt of matricide and trust deficit, Banibroto manages to reveal a recurrent dream of a lake, a connecting bridge and an aggressive dog. Dr Dasgupta starts to abandon the harsh and tried-and-tested methods to try newer, more mercurial ways of treatment in trying to find ways into Banibroto's erased memories of a disturbed past. When nurse Dora, infatuated with Banibroto, tries to elope with him, the crisis starts to unravel. The shocking repeat of a repressed event brings Banibroto out of his state of delirium and he starts responding to Dr Dasgupta's investigations. His confessions to that effect also extricates him from allegations of murder.

Hrod is rarely seen, though it fetched Uttam, deservingly so, the first of six BFJA awards. The film's existing print is in bad shape but what is decipherable is that the film's craft is terribly amateurish, the writing is uneven and the narrative jittery. But no one can fault it for being an audacious attempt (from young novelist Bimal Kar and the young director Ardhendu Sen) to tap into the mid-20th century zeitgeist of psychoanalytic care before medicinal psychiatry took over. The film also makes admirable use of a young actor's talent, even if one wishes that the film came to a more seasoned Uttam.

LITERARY COMEDY

Chirokumar Sobha (Bachelor's Club, 1956) was adapted from Rabindranath Tagore's 1904 popular comedy about a collective of avowed celibates among Calcutta's turn-of-the century gentry. The gap of half a century had not caused any dent in the play's charm. The strict rules of the club that absent-minded Professor Chandra runs from his home precludes women and also any scrumptious humour about them. The members, reluctantly committed to lifelong celibacy, resent the latter more, for a life without women is dry enough and is insufferable without the droll humour. Young and bashful Purno joins the committed fray, but to his dismay, his heart starts beating faster for Chandrababu's unmarried niece Nirmala (Jamuna Sinha). A previous member Akkhoy, now 'fallen' to conjugality, requests entry of new members and a change in the club's location. Nirmala declares her intention to join the club. The new premises are abuzz with talks of social service and nation-building but all young members secretly pine for the attention of educated, intelligent women hovering 'behind the scenes'. A series of chances and factors are set in motion simultaneously to build a climate of romantic longing for both genders. Finally, it is upon the tireless Rasik-da to bring the pining pairs together. The young men and women are in the end suitably rewarded as per their pertinent pairing, while the ghost of lifelong bachelorhood is purged. Only Purno continues to wallow in his unspoken love for Nirmala, which finally earns her consent.

Staying true to the original with a spate of Tagore songs that add to the climate of romantic yearning, Debaki Bose's lively film was, for its time, as feel-good a literary comedy as there were any and as memorable a Tagore adaptation as any other. Bose did not peddle Uttam's stardom, which, after 1954, was a temptation. Uttam, intense as the hesitant Purno, also chose to be part of a larger, meaningfully engaging cast, the chemistry between whom was essential for a film like this. That this film cannot be seen anymore is a very great pity.

OEDIPAL TRAGEDY

Sarat Chandra Chattopadhyay's maudlin fiction continued to hold forth past the studio era, Ajoy Kar's *Bordidi* (Elder Sister) being a good specimen. With a spherical face, elongated eyes, slight portliness and an overall air of melancholy, actor Sondharani Chatterjee had a natural ownership of Sarat Chandra's female leads. She plays the eponymous elder sister, the widowed Madhobi, who discharges the responsibilities of an aristocratic household in Calcutta. But the appointment of bespectacled, absent-minded, buttoned-up Suren as home tutor upsets her poise. A postgraduate in mathematics, the geeky Suren, obsessed with calculus, had planned to pursue higher education in England. But when his overprotective stepmother jinxes his ambition, Suren flees hometown Allahabad for Calcutta. But overprotection had turned Suren into an atrophied adult. He gets fixated with the sensitive Madhobi in lieu of his obsessive mother, even if they do not get to meet. Instead, from her widowed isolation Madhobi keeps a keen eye for Suren's childlike demands, and is drawn to his neglect of everything worldly for his obsession with books. Her long-frozen femininity is jolted. Realising that she was on the verge of an impossible prospect, Madhobi forces Suren to leave. Lumbering as ever, he meets with an accident and is rehabilitated in Allahabad with an unhealed injury at the bottom of his ribs. Years later, a married Suren, still withdrawn and sallow, is at the helm of his grandfather's estate in Pabna. He discovers that his wily manager had usurped the land of a widow and banished her, who turns out to be none other than Madhobi. An aggrieved Suren sets out on a horse to stop Madhobi from going away. But the ill-advised equestrian misadventure renders him breathless, sick and bruised, as his old wound oozes blood. Even though he manages to meet Madhobi for the first time, he succumbs to his injuries, dying on her lap.

The obvious sentimental overload of the story is neutralised by Ajoy Kar's sprightly direction and low-key drama, which imports a rare smartness to an overwrought tragedy. In this act of updating, however, historical specificity is a casualty; and the Oedipal theme remains uncharted. What stands out is Uttam's copybook Suren. His is a captivating study of how to bring to life a character who lacks animus, is visibly absent-minded and has little agency.

ROMANTIC MELODRAMA

Director Asit Sen was known to have done wonders to the genre of melodrama, his lyrical triumphs *Mamta*, *Khamoshi* and *Safar* (1970)—remade from the Bengali originals *Uttor Falguni*, *Deep Jwele Jai* and *Chalachal* in that order—standing testament to his control over the medium. So was *Jibontrishna* (Thirst for Life, 1957)—his only film with Uttam—it being a fine example of the elasticity of a romantic melodrama. *Jibontrishna* is structured like a cube, for there are six entry points to the plot, each a primary character. Rajnath (Uttam), handsome heir to Dr Haranath's wealth, is modest and gentlemanly. But he fails to convince the painter Shakuntala (Suchitra), one of his tenants, that he is a genuine suitor. Sakuntala's foster brother Debkamal, desperate to raise funds for his orphanage, wants Shakuntala to rethink. Shakuntala's neighbour Sabita, the comely widowed mother and a lonely soul, takes a liking for bleeding-heart Debkamal. Dr Samanta's will reveals his chequered past, for he had abandoned a wife and child to bond with Suprabha. Rajnath learns that his aunt Suprabha is actually his mother, while the abandoned son is the long-orphaned Debkamal.

Haranath's will, in an act of atonement, promises half of the wealth to Debkamal. But Debkamal demands the whole, threatening to muddy Haranath's good name otherwise. Sabita is unable to halt Debkamal's rapacity. Rajnath forfeits all of his inheritance and takes shelter with his 'new-found' mother. Sulekha's aversion to Rajnath melts away and she sets out, on a night when the city is lit with firecrackers, towards Rajnath's home. At the same time, Debkamal enters the house of Haranath to take possession. In the mesmeric climax scene, as a flurry of lights and shadows intermingle, Rajnath and Sulekha find togetherness; while Debkamal is possessed by the large, uninhabited mansion whose walls seem to press themselves on him. Under the chiaroscuro of overarching statues, portraits, lampshades and mirrors, he faces himself and is devastated at his gratuitous heartlessness.

The power of the last scene heightens the film's overall effect but even otherwise, Asit Sen's deft directorial hands elevate the potentially incredulous plot into a sharp, synchronous movie experience.

SOCIALIST MELODRAMA

Bijon Bhattacharya's story about a brilliant doctor who forfeits prosperity and abandons the city to provide free consultation and medicines to poor villagers carried within it a dewy-eyed socialist ethos. This is particularly so because the individual assigned with this weighty commission is sure to become an unreal messiah. Suren in Bishu Dasgupta's *Dactarbabu* (The Physician, 1958) is precisely that. By dedicating himself entirely to the villagers, he dries up any source of income for himself and his wife Kamala. His pharmacy is free for all. He also takes charge of his brother Ranen's education, walking into the traps of debt from local loan shark Narahari. Ranen comes back happily married, carefree and untethered, while Suren continues to toil, managing to hoard only veneration from his co-habitants but no material securities. Later, Ranen leaves with his ill-adjusted wife, while Narahari makes a claim to his house to recover debts. On the day his house is set to go up for grabs, Suren fails to show up at the court to attend to a case of a complicated delivery. Though unhoused and broke, the undeterred Suren stays steadfast in his mission to provide healthcare to the villagers. His dedication is such that when Narahari's son is detected with stomach perforation, Suren performs a major surgery and transmits his own blood to save him. He is taken severely ill. It is then that Ranen, his wife and the debtor realises the value of Suren's sacrifice, find words of remorse and a happy concourse is ensured in the climax.

This Cane and Abel inspired lost film of Uttam would have been another sloppy and teary melodrama and Suren Roy would have been noble to the level of absurdity. But like all such personas that he played, Uttam, with another fabulous turn, not only rescued the film from its ham-handed premise but managed to leash the excesses of Suren with his innate naturalism, making the doctor seem faintly possible. In some ways, *Dactarbabu* pre-empts Uttam's late-career hurrah *Agniswor* (The Lord of Fire) for the characters, similar in their zealous idealism, create an arc of how Uttam had matured over the years.

LITERARY ROMANCE

Sarat Chandra Chattopadhyay's four-part novel series *Srikanto* is considered his masterpiece. The film adaptations of the first three parts were all directed by Haridas Bhattacharya with his wife, the iconic yesteryear star Kanan Debi, being the producer. All three had a different cast. But the best among them was *Rajlakshi O Srikanto* (The Deviant and the Demimonde, 1958). Srikanto is the perennial vagabond, orphaned, daredevil and unchained from worldly gains. On an invitation from an aristocrat friend, he sets out for a hunting expedition where he meets Pyari Baiji, who was accompanying his spoiled companion. She turns out to be none other than Srikanto's childhood mate Rajlakshi, who had hopelessly been in love with him. She renews her deep affection and stands vigil on his reckless adventures, especially to the crematorium to disprove the existence of ghosts. Later, Srikanto, habitually daring, joins a traveling squad of sages but finds himself felled by a smallpox epidemic near Patna. The abandoned Srikanto is rescued by Rajlakshi and brought home. It is while recuperating that he hears her horrific tale of having her poverty and beauty preyed upon by Hindu patriarchy and its fecund agents, both male and female. Their long familiarity with each other is now cemented for them having been outcasts, one by force, the other by choice. And there is a real possibility that both would finally find the elusive romantic fulfilment with the other. Yet, Srikanto is unable to commit himself to a life of certitude and sets out for another gamble, this time in faraway Burma.

Although technically under-accomplished, the film's heart is in the right place, complemented by Gyan Prakash Ghosh's refined score. Suchitra is luminous as the conscientious courtesan, her affectations merging with the film's appeal as a period romance. Uttam is comparatively underused as Srikanto, who is habitually non-committal and withdrawn. But there are several fine moments in the film. In a spate of classical literary romances in that period, this is the most delicate—sensitively drawing out an elemental romance between two luckless people without making them look pitiable or abrasive.

SPIRITUAL TRAVELOGUE

To adapt spiritualist Avadhoot's dense 1953 travelogue into *Morutirtho Hinglaj* (Desert Pilgrimage) was an act of daring from debutant producer and director Bikash Roy. Hinglaj is considered the most perilous undertaking in the Hindu pilgrimage circuit, being on the remote end of the Makran Desert stretch, next to river Hingol and close to the coast in Pakistan's Balochistan province. Avadhoot (Roy) leads the pilgrims from Karachi, where the trip commences. A day later, the group rescues an injured and traumatised couple found unconscious on a barren stretch of the desert. They become part of the travelling pilgrims. Gradually, the debilitating physical and psychological demands of the grueling 150-kilometre journey start to test the forbearance of each. The scalding sun cuts open the strange life histories of the salvation-seekers, some of whom fall on the way. But others reach the sanctum, overcoming days of hunger, toil and thirst. But more than the harrowing journey, it is the momentous tragedy of the lovelorn pair which lingers. The rootless Thirumal eloped with the married Kunti (Sabitri). Hounded and bedevilled since, they escaped to the desert, where Kunti was raped and Thirumal injured. A bruised and battered Kunti embraces the mission of her rescuers, looking to find penance at Hinglaj. But the guileless, clear-sighted Thirumal remains adamant and insolent, hurt and mad that the world was conspiring against his union with Kunti. Unable to convince Kunti and on the verge of a complete breakdown, he kills himself by jumping into a geothermal eruption. Pulverised to silence for the rest of the journey, Kunti later walks away into the bleak, barren oblivion in a state of acute trauma. In an otherworldly, inexorable setting, the fate of the star-crossed pair attains the weight of a folk tragedy. Also, in spite of its professed air of spirituality, the film (like the novel) is devoutly humanist; Avadhoot takes little moral position while binding his comrades in copious sympathy.

Image 8.1: Obsessive, tragic hero. Uttam and Sabitri Chaterjee. Shooting still of *Morutirtho Hinglaj* (The Desert Pilgrimage, 1959)

Source: Author.

This was a starkly different film, emboldened by an unforgettable soundtrack and moving performances from Bikash Roy and Sabitri among others. But Uttam's Thirumal was unsurpassed. Whether in passion, fury or rebellion, rarely have the nervous obsessions of a lover, cornered into a bundle of rage by an unforgiving world, been so hauntingly authored.

LITERARY TRAGEDY

The director collective Agradoot's earliest gesture of moving away from textbook populism was *Khokababur Protyabartan* (Return of the Prodigal Son). A celebrated Tagore story, *Khokababur Protyabartan* plays with German philosopher Friedrich Hegel's master–slave dialectic, knowingly or not. Raicharan's capacious loyalty, an inheritance from his father, makes him the *slavish* figure, whose tender devotion to his *master* Anukulchandra is absolute. They also get married at the same time. But nothing pulls Raicharan away from his obsessive sense of duty, it being most pervasively directed towards Anukulchandra's newborn or *khokababu*. But a moment's lapse causes a catastrophe— the toddler is washed into a ravaging monsoon river. Raicharan's sense of devastation barely touches the bereaved master, while his wife pleads him to 'return her son'. Raicharan's own son is born soon after and his long-neglected wife dies at childbirth. Raicharan, increasingly penitent under a cloud of severe guilt, gets gradually infatuated with the idea that his own child was but the return of the master's departed one. He keeps his fatherhood a secret from his son, relocates to Calcutta, and undertakes a life of severe drudgery to raise his son in the likeness of his master. On hearing that Anukulchandra was planning to marry again to secure an heir, Raicharan decides to reveal *khokababu*, groomed enough to be comfortable in the skin of the affluent. He spins a false tale of having kidnapped the toddler for his adornments, which the couple buys readily, taking little time to own up to the 'new' *khokababu*. When Anukulchandra also takes little time to formally dismiss Raicharan from service, the latter dithers. But when his young boy lectures that Raicharan be given a monthly stipend for having looked after him, Raicharan is assured that the slave had effectively metamorphosed into the master. He takes one look at his son, leaves the house and evaporates into thin air.

The film's cast had initially caused a flutter, as few could imagine that the thirty-four-year-old Uttam could play the effete and compulsive manservant, who grows into an old and haggard vagrant. As a proclaimed deviation from his image, the film stayed in debate for years after. In the end, Uttam does see Raicharan through, managing to live up to the emotional tug of the story. But his efforts at *playing* Raicharan are only too visible, which is not considered a mark of an exceptional performance; and even less so for an unforced naturalist like Uttam.

HISTORICAL FICTION

"A kingdom at stake, a princess in peril and the most daring impersonation of all time" was how Anthony Hope's 1894 classic *The Prisoner of Zenda* was advertised. Tapan Sinha's palace-intrigue drama *Jhinder Bondi* (Prisoner of Jhind), though, had the novelist Sharadindu Bandopadhyay's Bengali trans-creation (of the same title) as the source. Fauzi Sardar, trusted lieutenant of the state of Jhind, travels to late colonial Calcutta in search of Shankar Singh, his prince, missing for the third time before his coronation. In the two instances before he was entrapped by his brother Udit (Tarun Kumar) and his aide Mayurvahan. If found missing for the third time, Udit, as per the law of the land, would usurp the throne, which Sardar wants to prevent at any cost. Sardar chances upon Gauri Shankar Rai, a spitting image of Shankar Singh. On Sardar's request Gauri Shankar arrives in Jhind to impersonate his doppelganger. Udit, who had kidnapped the king-elect, is found floundering, as he could neither acknowledge nor disobey his 'brother'. Even the estate doctor and Shankar's betrothed Rani Kasturi fail to detect the impersonation. Astute and sharp, Gauri Shankar manages to dodge nagging anxieties and palace gossip to set the stage for a climatic invasion of Udit's fort. After a series of horse races, sword fights, shadowy movements in hushed passages and hand-to-hand duels, the conspirators are killed, the would-be king is found and Gauri Shankar abandons a budding romance with Kasturi (Arundhati Mukherjee) to return to Calcutta.

The attractions of this film are manifold: the thrilling theme of impersonation, the rustic landscape of Udaipur, Sinha's able direction, the ambient soundtrack of Ali Akbar Khan, the eloquent outdoor photography of Bimal Mukhopadhyay and the confident turn of Soumitra Chatterjee as the wily Mayurvahan. The film suffers from a collective inexperience of shooting convincing action sequences but the coup, to cast Uttam and Soumitra together for the first time and that too as rivals in a game of royal succession, still remains an attraction. Soumitra's Mayurvahan is as craftily convincing as Uttam's double, the amorous, timid Shankar as well as intelligent and gallant Gauri. In spite of the film's explicit and avoidable technical faults, Sinha deserves credit for having given Bengali cinema its finest (and only) swashbuckler, without falling into the traps of stagey, noisy histrionics.

THE NEHRUVIAN SOCIAL

Tapan Sinha had scripted *Shiulibari* (The Townmaker) from a Subodh Ghosh story (like *Jotugriha*) but invited his assistant Pijush Bose to direct this slender, sensitive film.

When Bijon loses his doting father, he also learns that he is an 'illegitimate' son. Angry and hurt, the young Bijon escapes and settles in a quiet tribal hamlet, watered by the Damodar and nestled within the scenic Chhota Nagpur plateau. Over the years, his tireless toil, unwavering resolve and unfailing commitment help develop the hamlet into a programmatic Nehruvian idyll: complete with a colliery, a wood factory, new roads and markets, a railway station and extensive settlements. When we meet the adult Bijon (Uttam), he is the adored, ever-smiling 'mittibabu' (man of the soil). In the meantime, Bijon had also persuaded Niru (Arundhati) to abandon her miserable life as a widow and join him as his companion. Niru becomes a dependable partner in Bijon's epic pursuit to transform the town. The town is also named after Bijon's house (or *bari*) under an October Jasmine (or *Shiuli*) tree. As the narrative voice says: two wounded souls abandoned by the ruthless ways of the Bengali society start afresh and bring well-being to everyone around. But a final reckoning is only a visitor away. This happens as their only daughter grows up and at a wedding, an elderly man identifies Bijon and humiliates him publicly. Challenged, Bijon opens up about his and Niru's past, expressing no remorse and asking for no consolation. The townspeople side with him. It takes a while though to convince their daughter. It is only then that Bijon manages to pass on to her his father's motto: that work and not lineage is the hallmark of reputation.

Bijon's story is a textbook Nehruvian case-study, epitomising the self-made new Indian man cut from feudal ties, uncaring of pedigree and usurping of handed-down orthodoxy. Niru compliments him with her courage. It is as much for its progressive plot as for being a sensitive drama that *Shiulibari* must be recovered from obscurity and rehabilitated as a fine specimen of social realism that sought a fertile pollination with the promise of Nehruvian welfarism.

COMEDY OF SITUATIONS

In 1963, Uttam produced *Bhrantibilash* (Comedy of Errors, 1963), based on an 1869 story by Bengal's epochal reformer and educator Ishwarchandra Vidyasagar. The story was, in fact, a fine early case of naturalising Shakespeare for the subcontinent. Chiranjib and Chiranjit, estranged twins, get trapped in the same locale when one—a timbre merchant—ventures out of Calcutta for a new contract (with his manservant in tow). It brings him to the territory of his doppelganger, setting off a chain of identity thefts. Everything about them is the same, except that one is a bachelor while the other is married; one a smoker while the other takes a nose-puff; one is of an irate kind while the other of milder temperament. Over a day and a night, the resident brother finds himself sleeping on the station platform, is locked out of his own residence and is seen spending the night at his female friend's house. The fate of his double is no better. He gets locked up with the wife of his mislaid brother, finds himself attracted to the sister-in-law Bilashini and gets pushed around for having lost his mind. The manservants Bhakti and Shakti Kinkar, also twins, keep bumping into the wrong 'master', complicating matters insanely. Only in the morning after does it comes to light that there are actually two brothers (and their servants) of the same visage, and also, vintage.

Bhrantibilash is an archetypal situational comedy with fine interludes of music and mirth. Uttam's gift as a comic actor is on full display and so is that of Bhanu Bandopadhyay, who plays the Kinkars. Sabitri as the testy wife and Sondhya Roy as the bubbly Bilashini add to the merriment. The theatrical conventions of the Shakespearean play and the adapted story seemed to have merged seamlessly into the believable tropes of narrative realism that were staple to Bengali cinema. This Manu Sen-directed film is neither overly dramatic nor forcefully comic, letting the laughter emit from the unenforced confusion that a set of lookalikes trigger unwittingly. It is much more satisfying than Gulzar's scene-by-scene Hindi re-adaptation *Angoor* (1982) might be able to reveal.

ROMANTIC COMEDY

It would be an understatement to say that Sunil Banerjee's *Deya Neya* (A Romantic Exchange) fulfils all the felicity of a romantic comedy. It would be rather apt to say that it employs them so successfully that it has since become an archetype of a specimen that could not be bettered in Bengali cinema. Prashanta (Uttam) leaves home in Lucknow after an altercation with his pragmatic, industrialist father, the latter being opposed to his pursuing a career in music. He comes to Calcutta at the invitation of the Gramophone Company, putting up at his friend Asim's house. He also finds chance employment as a chauffeur with the wealthy Mr Majumdar and is immediately drawn to his niece, the beautiful and proud Sucharita (Tanuja). Prashanta's music career blooms under the pseudonym Abhijit but he remains invisible to the public. While hassled to sustain two lives, Prashanta finds out, to his disbelief, that Sucharita swoons over the radio-voice of his alter ego. Soon, Sucharita starts to chase the disembodied Abhijit, making it difficult for Prashanta to keep his disguise under wraps. In the meantime, his close friend, the socialist poet Sukanta is taken severely ill while Prashanta receives news that his truancy has taken a toll on his mother's health. To raise funds for Sukanta, Prashanta reluctantly decides to appear in public, convinced that the end of his anonymity would also mean an end to his calling. On the day of the function, his father arrives on the scene chasing the missing son, while Sucharita buys tickets to the front row. The raised curtain reveals to a shocked Sucharita that her missing driver Hridoyharan is after all, the man of her heart, while Prashanta's father is astonished by the popularity of his son. Prashanta's appearance breaks records and Sukanta's treatment is ensured. The culprit chauffeur/son is taken hostage and brought to Mr Majumdar's house, who turns out to be his father's childhood friend. The riddles of identity are resolved, father and son make peace and romance is ensured.

The film's high point was the music score by Shyamal Mitra, which merged seamlessly with the atmosphere of harmless tensions, fraternal frolic and buoyant humour, making this set-piece romance an utter treat to both hear and watch. Uttam's jollity and Tanuja's effervescence added dollops of charm to the film's appeal, ensuring its reception as a magical romantic comedy. The Hindi remake *Anurodh* turned out to be dismal.

SUPERNATURAL FICTION

After a spate of loud, syrupy romances in the 1950s, directors' ensemble Agragami increasingly challenged themselves with complex scripts. But they kept coming back to Uttam, daring the actor in him to break free of the prison-house of his popular image. *Nisithe* inaugurated their trilogy on contentious conjugality, followed by *Shonkhobela* and *Bilombito Loi*. All three had Uttam as the tangled male figure, who threatens to overwhelm the already stretched contours of couple-hood. *Nisithe* (At the Dead of Night, 1963) was adapted from a Rabindranath Tagore story written in 1894, which has an unmissable similarity with Daphne du Maurier's bestseller *Rebecca*, published forty-four years later. The tale of two wives, the suspicious death and hovering spectre of the former, an overbearing mansion and its eerie atmospherics are all there in Tagore's story. There are two exceptions. One, the narrator in *Nisithe* is the man himself, Dakshinacharan, a wealthy landlord who is also a lover and an aesthete. This gives the story the temper of a confession, making it more difficult for the reader to abandon him to his faults than in *Rebecca*. Second, the younger wife is no plain woman, but an intelligent and talented lady of letters. Dakshinacharan does not kill his first wife Nirupama, and no one even suspects the same. But he did let his wife, whom he had promised eternal remembrance, wither away in a state of permanent sickness, till she committed suicide. And all this while he shifted his attention to the promised companionship of the young Monoroma. Dakshina (Uttam) becomes increasingly agitated with his surroundings, being persecuted by Nirupama's spirit, whom he imagines of accussing him of erasing her too easily. But Monoroma resists succumbing to the hostility of the ghostly mansion, and it is her poise that saves Dakshina from falling into raving, guilt-ridden insanity.

Supported by able performances, the film renders Tagore's powerful psychological tale of repressed guilt and redemption faithfully on screen, keeping the pace lingering, to let the atmosphere play its part. Unlike several films which lose their generic characteristics to popular appeal, this one stays close to being a slow-burning supernatural drama that is also tantalisingly close to being a Freudian study. Not to forget that the original story not only predated du Maurier, but Freud's breakout theories too, by at least a decade.

REVENGE TRAGEDY

The bare-bones plot of Sushil Majumdar's *Lal Pathor* (The Red Stone), made later in Hindi with the same title, is three-bits neurotic and one-bit obtuse. Kumar Bahadur, the rich, charismatic, game-loving heir to an estate, rescues a poor woman from local outlaws. He takes a liking for the dainty but low-born beauty Saudamini but does not marry her. Instead, he changes her name to Madhuri and unveils an elaborate plan to change her person, tutoring her in music and literature and the ways of the nobility. Though obsessed with him, Madhuri is resistant to change. After ten long years, Kumar realises that her shallowness and prejudice is beyond correction. Disgusted, Kumar takes to the much younger Sumita and marries her, having bribed her father. But young Sumita had a soulmate in Ambor, who on his return from England, finds her married. Kumar, never one to take the straight route, invites Ambor home to test the loyalty of his wife. He is egged on by Madhuri's jealousy too, who feeds him with suspicion of Sumita having taken a paramour. The fear of being cuckolded stalks Kumar as he invites everyone to Fatehpur Sikri, where in a dramatic and bizarre decoy, he kills his wife and her friend. But Sumita's dying words reveal her love for Kumar and her being pregnant with his son. An insane Kumar abandons everything to wait eternally for penance, turning into an old, senile reconteur to tourists visiting the landmark on ceremonious nights, giving them a breathless tour of his distorted past.

This plot would be apt as a period work; but the fact that Kumar has an master's degree in psychology, quotes from Bernard Shaw when he tutors Madhuri, is fearfully well-read and remarkably sharp, gives the film a dissident bent. Masochistic and pathological but also observant and refined, Kumar savours every bit of his ability to control others. A weak actor would have messed up such a role, but the script and Uttam's pitch-perfect performance made this a very persuasive study of ambivalent masculinity in all of Bengali cinema.

ALLEGORY

Thana Theke Aschi (An Inspector Calls, 1965) was artfully localised from English playwright J.B. Priestley's famed play. It is a drawing-room thriller, exposing an elaborate network of power and social privilege, which casually, if inadvertently, pushes a poor woman, struggling stoically, to take her life. Like the play, the film spans an evening in the living room of the respectable and rich Chandra Madhab Sen's house. At the fag end of a family celebration, Sen has a visitation from a local sub-inspector. He reveals that a refugee woman called Sondhya Chakraborty (Madhabi) has taken her life, having consumed carbolic acid. Sen remains unmoved and so does wife Roma, daughter Sheela and son-in-law Amio. Only Sen's son Tapas, on hearing the news, becomes fidgety. The inspector starts to first nudge, then push, then implore the family, referring to the diary of the deceased woman. And the more they try to distance themselves, the more they reveal their dirty part and culpability in abetting Sondhya's suicide. Sen sacked her from work for leading a demand for wage increase; Sheela spited her spirit as a salesgirl; Amio pretended to have an affair with her; Roma rejected her application for formal aid; and Tapas, in-spite of his good intentions, failed to protect her quiet dignity. The visiting cop does not arrest anyone but leaves the family in a state of shocked convulsion, naked to their bones. Only after he leaves is it known that the local police had not sent any inspector, but was only beginning to enquire on a case of suicide by a refugee woman.

This Hiren Nag film barely deviates from the play's single-set setting except with flashbacks. This creates an atmosphere of tense anticipation as the venality of the Bengali bhadralok is slowly unmasked under the insistent probing and stony watch of sub-inspector Tinkori Halder. Uttam's titular inspector and his method of adjudication—a deft mix of courtesy, sarcasm and severity—is piercing. Even otherwise, this is a thoughtful and trenchant moral allegory about class and feminine labour, with touching performances, an incisive script, crisp dialogue and long, uninterrupted scenes of daunting interrogation.

CONJUGAL DRAMA

Agragami's *Shonkhobela* (Hour of Return, 1966) brought the tensions of *Nisithe* forward by a few decades into the heart of 20th century's urban bane—the insatiability of middle-class aspiration. Sunil and Tripti, like most urban couples of their class, have a quick romance before they get hitched. Soon after, Sunil, already aspirational and competitive, receives a promotion at work, bringing him a step closer to the murky world of corporate one-upmanship. As Sunil acquires the tricks to further gratify the powerful, he finds himself distanced from Tripti, who is loathing of Sunil's obsessive pursual of good living. The birth of a son bridges the gap a bit before Sunil's lust sees him float further away from Tripti's modest needs. But the corporate ladder proves to be more slippery than Sunil had made allowance for. As he finds himself at the receiving end of his boss's shifting temperament, he starts bringing his resentment home. One day, when a badgered, drunk Sunil returns home to take it out on his son, Tripti protests and decisively ejects herself from Sunil's life, carrying away the child with her. Months later, as the boy battles appendicitis in a hospital, a caring doctor, drawn to Tripti's motherly dedication, coaxes her to open up. He then arranges for Sunil's return

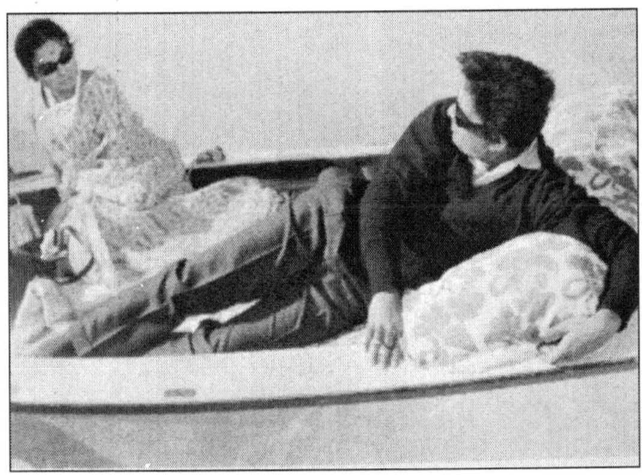

Image 8.2: Seduction of aspiration. Uttam and Madhabi Mukherjee. Lobby card of *Shonkhobela* (The Hour of Return, 1966)

Source: Parimal Ray.

to the fold, reproaching him for his negligence. Under his watch, the couple find a way to rise above their differences.

Shonkhobela is an unsentimental study of urban couple-hood, buttressed by marvellous songs, a pertinent script and competent performance from Madhabi Mukherjee in the lead. As an actor Madhabi's arsenal was not varied but she was incomparable in characters who expressed quiet but resolute rebellion; which Ray (*Mahanagar, Charulata, Kapurush*), Ghatak (*Subarnarekha*), Mrinal Sen (*Baishe Shrabon*), Tapan Sinha (*Tonsil*) and even Harisadhan Dasgupta (*Eki Onge Eto Roop*) and Purnendu Patri (*Streer Potro*) used adroitly. Between the mid-1950s and early 1970s, she has had a most distinguished and critically acclaimed life on screen (*Joradighir Chowdhury Poribar, Ghum Bhangar Gan, Thana Theke Aschi, Chhoddobeshi* being some of the other memorable ones) never trying to be part of either any star system or any schooling. She has also managed to age gracefully, making a quiet shift to playing roles suiting her age, both on television and cinema.

With Uttam, her work is limited to a handful, *Shonkhobela* being her best with the star. There should have been more, at least in the 1960s, which were the peak years for both. Uttam is not particularly challenged in *Shonkhobela*, because he had already been exceptional in similar, but more stimulating, studies in *Bicharok* and *Jotugriha*. But unlike the earlier, where the disputes bordered on the ethical, here his character is clumsy, which makes it difficult to like him. But he makes a fine job of his waywardness and is an equal stakeholder in the film's reception as an observant conjugal drama.

SCREWBALL COMEDY

A screwball comedy in Bengali? Yes. And the premises are not far from Frank Capra, even if *Nayika Sombad* (Runaway Star, 1967) is more *Roman Holiday* than *It Happened One Night*. After her first hit, Urmila (Anjana Bhowmik) becomes a star, though she refuses to forfeit the simple middle-class pleasures she grew up with. When her curiosity gets the better of her on an outbound journey, she finds herself stranded in a nondescript station on a rainy evening. That is how she lands up at stationmaster Alok's quarters. The bachelor Alok (Uttam) is a bit uneasy in the beginning because he has no extra room while the kitchen is full of a 'battalion of bugs'. But as the ice breaks and a rudimentary friendship stirs, she settles in. What was supposed to be a night's surreptitious settlement, assumes a comic crisis when Alok's manservant concludes the next morning that Alok has gotten married. To save either from saucy gossip, Alok does not talk him out of it. On the other hand, reports reach Alok that Urmila was in reality a star gone missing, something he keeps to himself. So, when he and Urmila are invited by an elderly, affectionate neighbour, they are forced to cover up their situation. And it becomes all the more exigent as neither of them want to harm the other's standing. Naturally, romance silently blooms between the commoner and the star, while the difficulty of it becomes all the more apparent. As a professional protocol, Alok finally alerts the film crew and they arrive to take Urmila back. A visibly gloomy Alok flags the signal for the train to start pulling out, moments into which Urmila pulls the chain, stumbles out of the train and to the surprise of all, runs straight into Alok's bosom.

The fantasy that *Nayika Sombad* after all is, is tempered with fluid storytelling, tender moments, a quiet intelligence and a series of witty repartee between Urmila and Alok. It is a fine and competent comedy by any standard of cinema. Also, Bengali cinema in the 1960s had no more capable young female co-star of Uttam than the carefree and mannerism-free Bhowmik. She deserves equal credit for this very memorable Agradoot-directed film.

SOCIAL REALISM

Ekhane Pinjor (The Prisonhouse, 1971) begins with celebrated author Amol Basu accosting the criminal Nabendu in a police lock-up while visiting an old friend, who is a cop. Months later Nabendu visits him and asks for a job, to enable him to crawl out of his deplorable life. As a writer, Amol is interested in Nabendu because he is no run-of-the-mill crook.

But no sooner does Amol promise him a way out, Nabendu is killed in a shoot-out. Shaken, Amol decides to visit Nabendu's family in a faraway Bengal town rather than send a cold telegram. On arrival, however, he is shocked by the dire poverty and destitution of the family, which seemed to be living on the brink. A sickly father, an expectant mother, a jobless brother and a comely sister aside, Nabendu also had elderly sister, Lila, who made a living by assisting a local gang in cross-border smuggling. What was supposed to be a brief, officious visit becomes an experiential journey for Amol as he starts to acknowledge the severity of the world outside his fiction. He is not only unable to break the shattering news to the family, but is sucked into their unremitting cycle of suffering. He decides to intervene, letting go of his writerly detachment. Finally, on Amol's insistence, Lila deserts the gang but is kidnapped as punishment. Amol helps the police find her but Lila is sent for a brief penal service. Amol decides to wait.

Ekhane Pinjor is a stark film, bringing to the fore a grim world that lies outside the purview of the Calcutta bhadralok. The film also shares a clear likeness with *Nogor Dorpone*, having been directed by the same directorial ensemble Jatrik. But it is Uttam again who made the film his own (well-advised in this case by Prafulla Roy, the author of the source novel). He legislates, with flawless authority, a non-partisan author caught in the vortex of an amoral world. In a *kurta–dhoti* and thick-rimmed glasses, Uttam, with his studied elegance and his hands in his pockets to display detachment, is impeccable.

COMEDY OF MANNERS

The best comedy of manners in Bengali cinema is Agradoot's *Chhoddobeshi* (The Trickster, 1971), the original of *Chhupke Chhupke* (1975). Like most remakes, the Hindi version manages to reveal nothing of the original's sparkling wit and language play, which together with another of Uttam's immaculate acts, forms the cornerstone of this film. Edinburgh University doctorate and botany professor Abonish (Uttam), recently married to Sulekha, plans a vacation. At the same time, they are invited to visit Allahabad by Sulekha's sister and brother-in-law Labonyo and Prosanto (a superb Bikash Roy). Learning that Prosanto was also looking for a knowledgeable chauffeur from Calcutta, the playful Abonish decides to present himself as the chauffeur. It is decided that Sulekha would join her hosts alone, insisting that her husband will follow later. As Abonish joins work as a uniformed chauffeur, he realises that Labanyo and Prosanto have bitten the innocuous bait too eagerly. As the new chauffeur Gaurhari, Abonish tests their patience at every step with his innocent but taunting questions, play on words and small acts of disobedience. They are humoured and appalled in turn. When Sulekha arrives, Gaurhari starts to flirt with her, to the wide-eyed consternation of her relatives. Since they show no signs of seeing through this hoax, Abonish's friend Subimal arrives as Abonish. But this is not before the chauffeur and the lady has eloped. A physics professor, the bachelor Subimal faces considerable trouble with a young woman who wants to 'learn biology from Abonish'; before they fall in love. As tongues in the town start to waggle and a set of marital scandals threaten to overwhelm Labonyo and Prosanto, Abonish and Sulekha resurface. They confess the masterplan, Subimal confirms his bachelorhood, and it ends with lots of laughter and Subimal getting hitched.

The film's laugh-out-loud comic overtone is underpinned with light-footed mockery of class barriers that fence the geography of the otherwise well-healed bhadralok. Of course, it is all an elaborate facade and the restoration of 'order' liquidates the possibility of any actual transformation in social mobility. But a glimpse of a carnivalesque subversion, reminiscent of *Midsummer Night's Dream*, stays in the realm of the possible. And that makes *Chhoddobeshi* a most worthy and memorable comedy.

MÉNAGE À TROIS

Of all the dictionary meanings of *ménage à trois,* artistic cinema has mostly been fond of one—when three people form a mutually loving unit. François Truffaut's *Jules et Jim* (1962) is a glorious illustration of it. The French connotations, bordering on the risqué, may be a little too alien for a mainstream Bengali film but *Ami, She O Shokha* which translates into 'me, him and my friend' does doff its hat to polyandry rather than to a romantic triangle.

Inseparable friends and fellow physicians Sudhir and Prosanto fall in love with Chandrani at the same time. But Sudhir overrides Chandrani's preference for him to let his friend marry her. It had always been the case: Sudhir (Uttam), beholden to Prosanto's father for having sheltered him since childhood, never came in the way of Prosanto's yearnings. But Chandrani (Kaberi Bose), a brainy and sensitive author, retains an inviolable love for and a deep bonding with Sudhir, without hiding anything from Prosanto (Anil Chatterjee). Their unusual bonding raises a few obstacles but Sudhir's uprightness and charm wins over the gossip. The two friends set up a nursing home, moving up the social ladder. Sudhir's appetite for risk also makes him go in search of his brother, locked in an asylum after a breakdown. Sudhir traces his naïve brother's troubles to a society lady, whom he seduces and abandons, for her having wrongly implicated him. Later, Prosanto's greed gets the better of him and he gets involved in a case of illegal abortion. Again, it is Sudhir who takes the blame, undaunted by the possibility of his name being muddied. Before he leaves for his penal punishment, Sudhir makes a grieving Chandrani promise that she would start a family. The film ends on the day Sudhir is to be released, while Chandrani finishes her novel about their life, beseeching her young son to grow up to be like Sudhir.

Mangal Chakraborty's *Ami, She O Shokha* (Inverted Triangle, 1975), remade in Hindi as *Bemisal* (1982), is, in spite of its distinct flaws, a significant film. It not only draws mature performances from all three but also taps into the complexities of urban affiliations and shifting sexual patterns. But it is the uncommon friendship that is the highlight, marking Bengali cinema's evolution way beyond the safety latches of a romance formula. The film also brought closure to Uttam's last great year as an actor.

9

AUTUMN OF THE PATRIARCH

For me, cinema is a vice. I love it intimately.

—Fritz Lang

SAHEB Bibi Golam's Ghoribabu, the keeper of time, was also a keeper of conscience in the indolent, decadent zamindari mansion. As a custodian of clocks, the eccentric veteran keeps reminding everyone that time spares no one, however indestructible, however abiding. Countries vaporise, civilisations collapse, empires fall, stars get snuffed; we humans, thus spake Hamlet, are but a "quintessence of dust". There was no reason why the great Uttam Kumar would be any different. History was bound to catch up with him, and by the late 1960s, it was as if Ghoribabu's forecasts had started to come true.

TIME'S WINGED CHARIOT HURRYING NEAR

Till this time, Uttam Kumar the person (individual), the performer (actor) and the persona (star) seemed to have been aligned with each other's axis of progression, seamlessly diverging and effortlessly collaborating. In other words, the extraordinary trajectory of Uttam's stardom barely found itself contradicting the performer and the person in him. This is not evident till we look at the latter part of his story of stardom, when three separate identities seem to have emerged out of one. Increasingly since the late 1960s, it seemed that the person, the performer and the persona were each going their own way, pulling away from the core. Uttam the individual—burdened with two families and an industry to look after—played the conformist; Uttam the actor, ever eager to explore, found himself stranded, waiting as if for redemption. And the star? With slow, imperceptive but inevitable regularity the star was exhausting its supply of helium, burning every day, supplying energy to a solar system that had little to extract from elsewhere.

On the surface Uttam still seemed to be quite in demand; the melodramas—now mostly reduced to pansy patchworks—continued to find an audience; his box-office showed signs of strain, but no major depletion; and his attraction as a 'matinee idol' was secured in a cult that was beyond the vagaries of commerce. History had been kind to him. He had worked with the worthiest in the industry, had toiled tirelessly for twenty years; after the early years, barely would the box office disappoint him and he had turned into a living icon who was well beyond the conventional algorithm of success and failure. In fact, Uttam's fame eluded adjectives. If one discounted his failure in Hindi cinema, Uttam had no more heights to conquer in Bengali cinema. But that is not necessarily a state of comfort, because what is worse than having nothing to lose is having nothing to look forward to. For Uttam, this professional dead-end assumed the shape of an existential quagmire.

So, if there was ever a moment in which the blazing midday sun of stardom took a decisive tilt towards a mellower afternoon, it was in 1970 or thereabout. To that end, the years mark a departure in Uttam Kumar's incredible saga. Why 1970? And how? Were there any obvious portents? Any observable interventions? Telltale signs? The answer is yes, there was a discernible change in the tempo and tenor of Bengali cinema in general and the saga of Uttam's stardom in particular. Part of it was signalled by Uttam himself, who at forty-four was increasingly restless to play roles that suited his age. At the same time, no one was willing to let him leave the limelight midway and Uttam was not in a position to not oblige the greed of the industry. Also, the period after 1968 was of that peculiar decline that comes after the ultimate triumph of having reached the summit. This natural trajectory, however, was complicated by other contributions to the process of decline—some of his own volition and others beyond his means of redressal. So, it is not difficult to see why there was a fissure in the figuration of the star persona.

One of the factors that led to Uttam's willing participation in his own decline was what can be called *the tormented soul* of the star, which we must trace to Uttam's diehard desire to make a mark in Bombay. In the mid-1960s, bolstered by unctuous biddings of some of his lackeys, Uttam committed himself to producing *Chhoti Si Mulakat* (1967). I have already discussed the issues around the film. But it is worth reinforcing that Uttam was largely egged on by bad counsel that made him greedy for national fame rather than any intention to lend his name to good cinema. And he was reprimanded, heart-breakingly for him, adequately. His Bombay debut was a humiliation; he was undone financially and was forced to sell part of his assets in Calcutta. Most importantly, his cardiac muscles started to misbehave, leading in 1967, to the first of several attacks. In other words, the Uttam Kumar who survived the debacle of his maiden Hindi venture was less than himself in whichever way. On the other hand, the mid-1960s also saw him reach stratospheric heights in popularity, receive a key national honour, and a dream role in a Ray film that brought him fame internationally.

Since then, Uttam's life could have gone in one of either directions: He could have cut down heavily on his acting commitments; taken on only substantively diverse roles; backed films with directors of repute; challenged the status quo; pushed the boundaries of local cinema; and created a body of work for posterity. But the actor and the star pulled away in different directions. And the person of Uttam, always cagey, preferred the safer, showy road. Instead of cutting down on roles, he took whatever came his way; he stopped producing films; while signing films shunned the better directors for second-rate studio-hands; kept wretched company; capitulated to mindless alcoholism; and saw himself as the sacrificing big brother of a large joint family in distress. It would, however, still be half a decade before Uttam's fatigue as a leading actor would show, while the poverty of an insatiable industry, used to abusing its golden goose, would become increasingly unmanageable. Hence, in the first half of the 1970s, Uttam was still offered a handful of films where he could live up to the kind of performances he eagerly waited for. He was more than willing to rave and rage on his walk to the sunset; to a kind of performative immortality that could have become a suitable culmination to his already stratospheric stature as a star. But his poor decisions, coupled with a despairing industry, seemed to have eventually engulfed him. Hence, after that brief but powerful burst of unforgettable performances, came the dive into abject darkness. Not one film from his last five years (1976–1980) was worth his endowments. They were not just bad films, they were, mostly, abominable kitsch—raffish, ludicrous potboilers. No wonder, what was left of the great Uttam Kumar after 1975 was the disquiet of slow decimation; till death rescued him from the further ignominy of a great actor in a free fall. There were undoubtedly cultural and political reasons extraneous to the man, but at a more personal level, Uttam's unexceptional surrender—first to mediocrity and then to misery—can be blamed perhaps to one thing: his lack of reflection, or at least his unwillingness to act on what he reflected upon. A man so full of tenacity, so attentive to training and so teeming with talent could have done wonders with good counsel, focus and insight. But he abdicated the first two and could not muster the benediction of the third.

"I HAVE SEEN SO MUCH, HEARD SO MUCH THAT I AM REALLY FED UP"

But then, Uttam, despite his omnipotent stardom, was not above the forces of his place and time. A piece of dialogue from a film called *Jibon*

Jigyasha (The Atoner), excerpted in the heading, seemed to have slipped out of the film's moody protagonist to become a truism in Uttam's life. After 1967, Bengal was plunged into a series of political crises which, as has always been the case in Bengal, viciously affected every aspect of life. The warring political parties—the Indian National Congress and the Communist Party of India—suffered mutations in the early 1960s, giving birth to the Bangla Congress and the CPI(M). The breakaway parties joined hands to form the government twice in those years and were twice toppled, causing the state to succumb to President's Rule three times between 1967 and 1972. This led to widespread political uncertainty, street violence and institutional disorder. And this was just one crisis. Another was the widespread anti-capital sentiments blowing through the land, upsetting employment, labour relations and industrial output while severely affecting flights of finance. Moreover, a group of radical communists, vowing to keep the class struggle alive and refusing to court the 'compromised' parliamentarism of mainstream Leftists, broke away to activate the ultra-Left-wing Naxalbari movement. They were joined across Bengal's towns by young students who merged their inspiration of Mao Zedong's radical mobilisations in China with the audacious Vietnamese resistance under Ho Chi Minh. The events of May 1968 in France further bolstered their belief in a student-led revolution. The result was a total breakdown of law and order across the state and a Calcutta that got sucked into an abyss of anger, mistrust, secret associations, social turmoil, bloody confrontations and furtive violence. In 1971, Bangladesh declared war against Pakistan. India's open and vociferous support pressed into Bengal another stream of refugees, fewer in number than in 1947 but as the state was crippled by political uncertainty dealing with the newcomers was no less daunting than before. Bengali cultural life in general and cinema in particular reflected the turmoil more directly than it had found itself equipped to do so in the 1940s. But our concern here is not the reel but how things on the ground were jolted. It was inevitable that Uttam and the industry he cared deeply for were pulled into the vortex of widespread chaos. But it unsettled Uttam with much more force than he had prepared for.

By the late 1960s, the Obhinetro Songho, the union of cinema artists and technicians, already under the shadow of the toxic political climate, entered a divisive phase. Uttam was at the helm of the body, which had a justified goodwill as a custodian of industry's working class. The industry was hardly organised and unless a modicum of security were provided, the low-ranking technicians ran the risk of being exploited ad nauseum. So, the organisation, founded by Chhabi Biswas, was always found planning fundraisers and charities that would create a pool of funds for needy workers. For some years by then, the Left and centrist 'lobbies' in the otherwise fraternal collective were sensing a greater divide than ever before, not so much about the cinema industry itself but the nature of politics in the day-to-day running of the organisation.

Sometime in 1968, armed with key members, the Leftist lobby, powerful and potent, came to Uttam asking for a show to raise funds for Vietcong comrades. Uttam refused, pleading that Vietnam was a global issue, there were hundreds of ways in which funds were being raised for Vietnam. But not so for local technicians. So, if there had to be another fundraiser, it might as well be about the film industry and not Vietnam. The Leftist lobby, which has always been internationalist in an obstinate way, dissented. They accused Uttam of being a reactionary; against interests of the people and also socialism. Soon, a series of rumours were pressed into circulation, alleging that Uttam was sabotaging the name and character of the actors' union by safeguarding the interests of the Congress Party. The Congress Party's political appeal in Bengal was on serious wane in those years (and since). It was still, in a way, the incumbent power in Bengal and the most obvious target for its failures. But it was also because the statist Congress could never disassociate itself from the interests of the landed gentry and well-to-do middle class, something that was against the winds of socialist disposition blowing across the cultural spectrum. Uttam had never vouched for Congress but neither did he try to distance himself from what was considered his 'natural' affinity for it. So, being labelled as a broker of the Congress in the industry, even if it was a falsehood, affected Uttam deeply. There were graffiti too, proclaiming 'Uttam Kumar is a thief'.

The crisis at Obhinetro Songho, hence, was escalated. It was no more about raising funds but taking political positions. A disgruntled and distraught Uttam, along with other non-Left industry veterans exited the Songho and formed, in November 1968, the Shilpi Sansad (Artistes' Fraternity). The mandate of the latter was no different from the former but Uttam's presence gave it weight, attracting the numbers. Obhinetro Songho continued to exist under its shadow, exclusively Left and short of influence. The Leftists, who were increasingly used to prominence in cultural fronts, did not take this defeat lightly. Uttam became a steady target of their taunts. On its part, Shilpi Sansad backed a plan to ban Leftist factions from finding work, bringing things to a bitter conflagration.

Another vital incident in this period was Uttam's accidental witnessing of Saroj Dutta's murder in a police encounter in 1971, which I have already recalled. Uttam could neither forget his being a spectator to this grievous crime nor could he easily stake a claim in its legal ramifications. Eventually, one afternoon, a group of young Naxal men, armed with guns and hearsay, confronted Uttam in the studio, asking for his statement. They vouched not to leave the precincts without the star as their chief witness. With the help of friends, Uttam fled through the studio's secret exit and not risking another scare, left for Bombay straightaway. As advised, mostly by senior police officers, he did not return for three whole months. In the early 1970s, Uttam's unannounced and cowardly escapade cost the industry dearly: sets had to be pulled down, finances juggled, money was lost and dates were wasted. Suddenly, his famed discipline and dyed-in-the-wool commitment to his work came under the scanner and this small chink in the armour of trust soon became inexorable. He then shifted base to Allahabad, not having found much support in Bombay. Several films in the early 1970s were hence shot in Allahabad. On his return, Uttam overworked to make up for his absence. But overwork eventually affected his health and also the kind of work he signed on. Both proved counterproductive.

In the early 1970s, Uttam was reportedly offered support from the Congress Party (for the prestigious Chowringhee seat) if he contested the 1972 elections on an independent ticket. It was a secret deal that Congress considered its potential pocket of triumph in the face of massive public outrage. But Uttam declined—even the independent ticket—blaming it on his lack of interest in organised politics. Uttam, in fact, was uncharacteristically and openly condescending of organised politics, considering it as a refuge of only the rogue and the corrupt. His refusal lost him even the residual support he might have had in the Congress.

So, between 1968 and 1972, Uttam had made himself vulnerable to the kind of corrosive politics he had always shunned. It was inevitable that his phenomenal fame would be the target of the derisive dispensation of organised politics. But it was equally calamitous that Uttam, who had few enemies, was dragged into the political amphitheatre not so much as an individual but as a colossus of the industry. It was the star who had to be leashed with a political carrot and stick, not unlike a similar and potent scene in *Nayak*. Timorous at heart, his lack of political nous and any streak of opportunism doomed him to take further shelter in his work. Only if that work could provide him peace.

Uttam's roster in the 1970s is, therefore, full of the disposable. From his first films till the end 1960s, one has to pick the mediocre and the bad from a career suffused with an astonishing bounty of memorable works. Starting in the 1970s, it is the other way round, as truly notable films waned significantly. One can, at best, pick a dozen odd films that deserve serious attention from a number that touches almost eighty.

"THE NIGHT IS STILL YOUNG BUT I AM GETTING OLD"

Between 1969 and 1975 Uttam appeared in forty-four films, which translates into a new release every two months. The numbers are startling; particularly because Uttam was getting no younger. And hence, the lines as in the heading here uttered by Uttam's character in a mediocre late romance assumes a weight beyond the movie. The thin drape of shallow greasepaint could not hide his deepening wrinkles; the collared, rolled-sleeve shirts could not cover up for the folds on his neck and accumulation of subcutaneous adipose; while the reclining hairline indicated a wearing and weathering star. It would still be a while before age appeared undaunted on him but the signs were doubtlessly there. In 1969, he was still exceptionally good-looking, charismatic and by the standards of a Bengali man, healthy and fit. By 1975, when he was 49, obviously less so. But few understood that.

Some films took note of his advancing age. Some of the better films also tried to correspond to the contemporary, trying to participate in the tensions of the period. The lead characters in these films are often limpid and stray, trying to find meaning in a hostile and unprincipled world. These films were testimonials to an ageing actor's efforts to choose 'un'-heroic and grotty roles over romantic or virtuous ones. Of these kinds of films, he was good in the late romances, to which I will turn soon; and exceptional in a few others, of which *Chhoddobeshi, Jodubongsho, Baghbondi Khela* and *Ami, She O Shokha* have already found mention. In fact, 1975 was unusual in being a year that gave Uttam not one or two but five memorable roles, including *Sonyashi Raja, Agniswor* and *Nogor Dorpone*. These roles substantiated that Uttam was dressed for his next part, where he could be stripped of facile glamour, perform his age, carry his gait and weight through characterisations that suited him, and converse with his eyes than volubility. One can also count *Jibon Jigyasha* and *Jodi Jantem* (1974) as those extolling the actor in him. These films attest to a decisive shift in his screen persona.

1969 proved to be Uttam's most unremarkable year since at least 1951, because for the first time in eighteen years there was not a single movie which stood out. Given that this year was preceded by three memorable years of outstanding performances in *Nayak, Shonkhobela, Kal Tumi Aleya* (in 1966), *Nayika Songbad, Chiriyakhana, Antony Firingee* (in 1967) and *Chowrongee* (in 1968) makes it all the starker. This pale year hence is the apt moment to recognise the beginning of the shift in Uttam's screen persona and in the overall tenor of Bengali cinema. That this year contained the surest sign of fatigue was indicated by all the six films being romances, revealing a tenuous desperation on part of the industry to cling to (or return to) the apparently safe habit. In them and those that followed, Uttam is found visibly trying to repress the ageing, greying, tiring person in him, asking his character to taste the fruits of romance while asking the audience for a heightened suspension of cognitive identification.

It is hence no wonder that in *Chirodiner* (The Call of the Eternal, 1969) and *Shukh-Sari* (The Love Birds, 1969)—both being dramatic calls of return to nature from the allures of plastic modernity—Uttam looks hopelessly forged, playing a bohemian musician in the former and a wandering flutist in the latter. Equally bloodless was both *Komollota* (A Noble Woman, 1969)—the fourth and final episode of Sarat Chandra's Srikanto saga—and *Sobormoti* (The Confluence, 1969), a film set among Ahmedabad's textile manufacturing entrepreneurs. Suchitra Sen's eponymous Kamallata, another of Sarat Chandra's selfless sacrificial women, is a stale shadow of her Rajlakshi, the much more gratifying Srikanto romance she had starred in with Uttam twelve years ago. By *Sobormoti*, Supriya Chowdhuri had internalised her apparent resemblance to Sophia Loren to the extent of her having become a caricature. This false preoccupation is further augmented by the self-same story of a rich girl on the run from a strict father, who 'discovers' the life of the poor when she is sheltered by a travelling companion. The film that had promise but mired itself within the confines of populism was *Mon Niye* (A Forked Mind, 1969), which sought to tackle murderous schizophrenia in a story involving an author, his possessive sister, his wife and her twin. There is an underlying darkness about this romance, which could have given it an edgy, gray temper, but which was wasted on Supriya's persistent overacting and usual set pieces of an overdone melodrama. Uttam's Amitabha tries hard and fails to hold the film together, except in a final heartfelt act in the court after his late wife's deadly persecutions are laid open. It was a brief moment of archetypal Uttam. That brief outburst of great acting is also the only takeaway from Salil Dutta's *Aporichito* (The Stranger, 1969), a meek adaptation of Fyodor Dostoevsky's magisterial *The Idiot*. Dostoevsky's existential inquisitions have always been a tough act to render on screen. That a Bengali mainstream film even tried it is commendable, aided primarily by writer Samaresh Basu's script. But the film is a sad under-accomplishment. Sujit (Soumitra Chatterjee) is released from the asylum under the impression that he was finally able to live a functional life; but circumstances lead him to a reprobate world of easy money, high-society scandals, hushed deals and obsessive lovers. His honest and artless simplicity earns him the affection of two women, Dola and Sunita. While Dola is simple and giving, Sunita, heiress to an ambitious, amoral entrepreneur, is complicated, disjointed and vulnerable. Sujit falls in love with the 'sadness in her eyes', promising her a life of dignity. His rival in love is Ranjan (Uttam), a charming rogue, who bets his life and fortunes on Sunita, pursuing her adamantly. Sunita keeps running

Image 9.1: A Dostoevskian romance triangle with Uttam, Soumitra
Chatterjee and Aparna Sen. Lobby card of *Aporichito*
(The Stranger, 1969)

Source: Parimal Ray

from Ranjan to Sujit and back, unable to surrender either to Sujit's
sincerity or to Ranjan's ruthless possessiveness. Having failed to either
possess her or get over his obsession, Ranjan finally kills Sunita and the
trauma revives Sujit's dementia, sending him back to the asylum. Ranjan
meets him one last time in prison, deranged and disconsolate, enquiring
if he, like Sujit, could also erase his memories. The rare combination
of Uttam and Soumitra playing rivals in a Dostoevskian triangle is
severely under-utilised, aggravated by Aparna Sen's thoroughly artificial
Sunita. The film suffers under its oversized ambition, unable to decide
if it should be an existential tragedy or if it should cater to the middlebrow predictability of a mainstream Bengali romance. It ends up being
a worse kind of the latter, except Uttam's piteous climactic confession.

The next years brought little joy, three purported adaptations
continuing with the propensity to fall back on half-baked romances.
Rajkumari (The Princess, 1970) was a modernised version of the Brothers
Grimm's *Rapunzel*, but the predictable plot is further undermined by
a silty script and ordinary performances failing to cash in on the hit
pairing of Uttam and Tanuja, who had starred in two magical romances
before. Of similar import was *Joy Joyonti* (The Governess, 1971), which
was localised from the landmark Rodgers and Hammerstein musical
The Sound of Music. The iconic film was a tall order to live up to anyway
and neither Uttam nor Aparna Sen could salvage the tawdry writing.
Rater Rajanigandha (The Fragrance of Night, 1973), about a runaway
heiress to a fortune who is abetted by a smart journalist, has a bit of
Roman Holiday (1953) thrown in. But two Uttam films had already

been fabulous adaptations of the runaway-bride plot. Even the fact of this one being a romance between people of differing ages did not add anything to the film. Only the superficial affectations of the spoilt heiress Anuradha (Aparna) stick out like a sore thumb in the film. And no one knows why the film was named as it was.

Of these middling romances, *Memsaheb* (The Beloved, 1972), deserves mention because the plot is potentially absorbing though the final film is a half-hearted effort. It is about the laid-back, out-of-work stringer Amit, whose life changes dramatically when he finds romance with Kajal (Aparna), who is called Memsaheb, a pun on her dark complexion. Kajal is a sort of 'complete woman' Bengali fiction would turn out with unblushing regularity. No wonder, she brings joy, acceptance and success in Amit's life, in that order. Almost overnight, Amit not only becomes a leading journalist but is sent to Delhi to report the most sought-after of assignments—war with Pakistan in 1971. Kajal joins teaching. On completing his assignment, Amit is set to return to Calcutta, eager to secure his partnership with Kajal. But he arrives at the disconsolate news that a spate of political violence in her college had claimed Kajal's life days before, as she eagerly awaited Amit's return. The film walked away from the regular formula by having the woman killed and was a popular tragedy in its time. But compared to better works in Bengali cinema, it remains underwhelming, even if it tapped into the unrest and easy violence of that period. Moreover, Aparna's Kajal is as unconvincing as Uttam's Amit is uninspired.

In any case, Aparna Sen was not the one to save a mediocre film because she was one of the weakest of actors in Bengali cinema to have had a long career. And no one has attested to it more than she has. But that did not stop her being the one with whom Uttam had the maximum number of appearances (twelve) after the trinity of Suchitra–Supriya–Sabitri. Of them, two films, *Ekhane Pinjor* and *Jodubongsho*, stand out thanks to several constituent felicities but Aparna is hardly one of them. In all other films together, she is less than average.

After *Komollota*, suddenly, there were four films with Suchitra, a flurry, considering that in the whole of the 1960s, Uttam and Suchitra had appeared in just three films together. Clearly, there was an effort to invoke and exploit the pair's past fame. But their films from the 1970s had no claim to anything that came before. The conjugal drama *Nabarag* (The New Scale, 1971) and the love-cures-all melodrama *Alo Amar Alo* (The Light Within, 1972) proved to be stale do-overs. Uttam is quite watchable as Binu-da in *Har Mana Har* (A Victory in Defeat, 1972), which is otherwise a mawkish triangle involving a painter with a bohemian bent. The plot about Binu-da's long-drawn encounter with a schizophrenic patient, which almost ruins him, drags needlessly under the weight of flimsy misunderstandings. What could have been an introspective study of a mistreated woman's mental anguish is rendered ineffective by having her compete with a devoutly selfless woman, played by a stodgy Suchitra. Both characters are unreal and so is the film. The final film of the once infallible screen pair is *Priyo Bandhobi* (Dear Friend, 1975), a remake of the Durgadas Banerjee classic, but it was a conspicuous washout. The charm of the leading pair was long gone but the scale of failure of these films reinforced the obvious fact that every good thing comes with a date of expiry.

The fact of Aparna's repeated casting against Uttam, or the flagrant effort to rekindle the Suchitra–Uttam pairing, bares one of the fundamental impairments of Bengali cinema in the 1970s—that of not having a female lead of any new gift to be cast along with Uttam. Of all the things that plagued him on screen in his graying years, this remained the most unrecognised, while also being the most obvious. We shall have the chance to look at this lack closely.

The romances were adding nothing to either Uttam's body of work or that of Bengali cinema's coffers. But they came nevertheless. In fact, in terms of percentage, Uttam played more 'romantic roles' in the period between the end 1960s and mid-1970s than he did all through the 1960s. This was as abysmal a signal of collective myopia engulfing Bengali cinema as any other. And nowhere was this felt more lamentably than in the unmistakable sign of Uttam's losing his sheen. In *Kolonkito Nayok* (The Disgraced Hero, 1970), *Andho Ateet* (The Blind Past, 1972), *Chhinnopotro* (The Torn Letter, 1972), *Duti Mon* (Two Souls, 1970), *Roudrochaya* (Shadows of the Sun, 1973) and *Alor Thikana* (The Site of Light, 1974) Uttam's performance is jaded and strained—his spontaneity lacking, his scene-stealing charm missing substantially. There have been any number of films which were undistinguished otherwise, except for Uttam's part in it. These films suffer not only because they are of a poorer lot but also because Uttam looks dispirited, discoloured, disjointed; sheepishly going through the motions of a walk-on part. It is not difficult to guess that he was tiring out, was severely distracted, and was unable to commit to his natural genius for unforced characterisation. There were others films that were even worse: *Manjari Opera, Biraj Bou, Sonar Khancha, Rakta Tilak, Kajallata* and *Mouchak*. The slipshod football drama *Dhonyi Meye* (The Restless Bride, 1971) and the Uttam-directed, overlong saga *Bonpolashir Podaboli* (Song of the Wildflower, 1973) have remained unduly popular in spite of their inferior drollery and pathos respectively. None deserve to be. *Bonpalishir Podaboli* had a declared duty of raising funds for Shilpi Shansad. But the other films were unofficially a work of charity too. What I mean is that Uttam signed most of these films—nondescript, slapdash, disingenuous—to keep the industry from the inevitable meltdown that was to come if he had withdrawn into being selective.

This is why his personal choices, however problematic, cannot be held singularly responsible because Uttam did not operate on his own, nor were his decisions independent of the fate of the industry he had come to rule. It is hence doubtful that even if Uttam had the benefit of good advice and insight, he could still be able to make a resilient shift towards a kind of rarefied isolation and concentrate on rarer, meatier roles. This is because of all the 'roles' Uttam took seriously in those years, the one he took to heart was being the patriarch of an increasingly parochial industry. If at all, this can be blamed only on Uttam's essential good nature. Post the political calamity and his own financial miseries, Uttam decided to not test the nerves of his disconsolate, inoperable beneficiaries any further. He committed himself to these cheaply made, gratuitous, redundant films to keep the industry on a supply of wages. He also led a retinue of charities and fundraisers, directed plays and also a *jatra* performance to that end; took part in nightlong functions and led petitions—many of them—to improve the conditions of cinema infrastructure and commerce, including for something as basic as uninterrupted power supply to the studio floors. Films became less of a concern. As I have pointed out, a handful of them managed to escape the erosion. Otherwise, it was an inevitable saga of decline.

LOVES IN THE AFTERNOON

A handful of films in this period can be brought under the rubric of being interesting 'late romances', films which base their appeal on non-formulaic, atypical couple-hoods. These films begin where robust, archetypal romances end. They are records of a visibly ageing Uttam on screen and there is a perceptible tension in his persona, testing the limits of the residual 'romantic hero' that the public still wanted to anchor on his persona. Rather than succumbing to this expectation, these films were 'using' Uttam's age and his less charismatic look to create atypical partnerships or contestable monogamy or something more nuanced than the set-piece romances of his younger days. The best two films of this kind, *Ekhane Pinjor* (The Prisonhouse) and *Ami, She O Shokha* (The Inverted Triangle, 1975), have already found a mention elsewhere. But there were a few others.

If there was a turning point for Uttam's romantic 'persona' on screen then it has to be Arobindu Mukhopadhyay's *Nishipodmo* (The Night Flower) based on the short story *Hinger Kochuri* by his brother, the gifted storyteller Balaichand Mukhopadhyay. The film was also the original of Shakti Samanta's *Amar Prem* (1972). But those who have seen the Hindi film would not be able to gauge the original. This is not only because Rajesh Khanna was no comparison for Uttam but also because Uttam's Anangababu is not remotely like Khanna's Anandababu, who turns himself into a self-pitying, alcohol-drenched, 19th-century dandy. The Bengali film is essentially about Pushpo (Sabitri)—an archetype of the kind-hearted prostitute. The plot is woven around her sad backstory of poverty, her being ejected from her in-laws, her being thrust into a Calcutta brothel tricked by an uncle-like felon and her guardianship of a young boy who surrogates for her unborn child. None of this was terribly new in popular cinema. What was unusual was the character of Anangababu, who appears after almost an hour into the film. The film makes no effort to 'explain' Anangababu's visits to the brothel or offers a 'backstory'. All we know is that the otherwise jovial, undemanding and unsentimental Anangababu's marriage had left him cold and lonely. So, when freed from his day's commitments, he came looking for some comfort in the company of a tenderly harlot, away from the glare and noise of parties, clubs and dinners. As it is, Ananga's affection for Pushpo is that of an itinerant companion who will indulge, counsel, condole with but not want to possess. Just as he had come, he leaves too, on Pushpo's slightest insistence. Pushpo's life, however, continues to be bleak, even at the boarding house where she takes up work as a maid as she grows older. And it is Anangababu who brings Pushpo's grown-up doctor 'boy' back to his 'lost' mother. After a life of being pushed around, Pushpo finally finds a 'family'. Anangababu sees them off. Clearly, Anangababu is more of a cameo, is not 'paired' with Pushpo and *Nishipodmo* is not anything close to a conventional romance. It is rightly remembered as one of Sabitri's most touching performances. And Uttam? He shows a confident maturity, indicating a clear sense of relish in playing a character close to his vintage—moody, genteel and one who has allowed the wisdom of age to settle amicably. Even by the standards of his numerous good performances, Anangababu, especially the older version with streaks of white hair, thick black-rimmed glasses and that gentlest of smiles, is a memorable one. No wonder, it proved to be way beyond Khanna's best efforts.

Bilombito Loy (The Delayed Rhythm, 1970) is a serious, unwavering film about conjugal misapprehension, carrying the deft touches of the directing ensemble Agragami. It was also one of the sources of Hrishikesh Mukherjee's *Abhimaan* (1973), except that in the Bengali version the husband is a painter. Otherwise, there are unmistakable similarities, including that of a key role played by the husband's diehard friend.

A failed artist, Mriganko finds himself isolated by his singer wife Aditi's fame, as the marriage heads for a bitter split. As her laurels pile up, Mriganko takes shelter under alcohol and then commits to a life of a vagabond. But his art keeps failing him as his debts increase. He is retrieved from sinking further by Edith, Aditi's old accomplice. Aditi prefers to live alone, savouring the life of a single woman. Unlike Aditi, Edith offers herself fully to Mriganko, assuaging both his ego and his 'artistic' wants while also keeping the kitchen running. And yet, as a good Christian, she stays anxious for having earned Aditi's disfavour. Edith falls ill when a stillborn baby takes its toll on her and she dies thereafter, not able to find either Mriganko's dedication or Aditi's 'pardon'. At her grave, the dishevelled Mriganko, down in the dumps in every which way, confronts Aditi. The film ends on an open-ended note when outside the gates of the cemetery Aditi reminds Mriganko that his age has still not equipped him to manage his life on his own.

Unlike *Abhimaan*'s dramatic turnaround of the couple, *Bilombito Loy* is every bit realistic, realisable and relatable. It is also unforgiving of entrenched male egotism, offering Mriganko no reprieve from his contemptible selfishness, both as a man and as an artist. Perhaps that is why Uttam's Mriganko appears forged and unidimensional, lacking vitality even at the height of his chauvinistic rashness. As Aditi, however, Supriya is befitting and it is perhaps her best performance in a film with Uttam Kumar. The musical score is catchy though Deepa Chatterjee's Edith is rather stiff. *Bilombito Loy* could have been a much more memorable study of competitive conjugality had it not faced a crisis of legacy. This is because Uttam had appeared in more sophisticated chronicles of otherwise agreeable couple-hoods torn apart under the weight of guilt (*Bicharok*), the vacuity of childlessness (*Jotugriha*) or careerism (*Shonkhobela*). And in all of them, he was almost flawless, which is not the case with *Bilombito Loy*. To that end, ten years earlier, *Bilombito Loy* could have been a forthright study of male vanity, but in 1970, in Bengali cinema, this was not new anymore. But it is still a very good film.

The author Samaresh Basu was asked to adapt Billy Wilder's *Love in the Afternoon* (1957). He wrote *Bikele Bhorer Phool* (Love in Autumn) with Uttam in mind. In keeping with the broad bhadralok agenda of his films, he transformed the playboy of the original into a writer of repute, who is also a scholar of music and carries a degree in engineering from a university abroad. In other words, Anish Mitra is a master of all trades as much as he is also wealthy, refined and a bachelor. Thankfully, he is not young and has reached an age when he is beyond the traps of casual romance. Anish escapes to the seaside town of Digha in south Bengal to deflect a spate of meetings, lectures and another reluctant engagement with a prospective wife. Happily single and enjoying his vacation, he is soon accosted by a group of camping college girls. One of them, Tuku, becomes obsessed with him. A difficult daughter of a dysfunctional family, Tuku is restless, sassy and impulsive. She stalks Anish, slowly drawing him out of his shell. But never one to mess up his life, Anish has a moment of turpitude on the beach but then leaves for Calcutta, ejecting himself out of Tuku's life forever. The unusual plot apart, *Bikele Bhorer Phool* is unabashedly Western in its look and feel, except Sumitra Mukherjee, who is intolerable as Tuku. With his white sideburns, square glasses, self-driven Cadillac and bathing suit, Uttam resembles the older Marcello Mastroianni, carrying the film entirely on his own. And it is mostly thanks to his reticence, civility and quiet rebellion that the film manages to come close to being a credulous study of a May–December romance.

Image 9.2: Convulsions of a May–December romance with Uttam and Sumitra Mukherjee. Poster of *Bikele Bhorer Phool* (Love in Autumn, 1974)

Source: Parimal Ray.

Two films, *Stree* and *Sonyashi Raja* have, at their helm, a comparable character-prototype and hence the first half of the films are strikingly similar. In both the films, Uttam plays a frolicking feudal lord, moody and dismissive, oblivious to the intrigues of his underlings, contemptuous of change, and devoted to cavalier spells of merriment and music as well as to the submission of sycophants. In short, they wallow in their decadence. In both cases, their wives, denied the dignity of companionship, are driven to retaliation. The comparisons, however, end here.

Written by the same Bimal Mitra of *Saheb Bibi Golam*, *Stree* (The Wife) is the alter-ego of that great novel. Here, in the year 1930, jobless lensman Shitapati finds shelter in Babu Madhab Dutta's (Uttam) vast mansion as his personal photographer. As Dutta's romps continue, Sitapati (Soumitra Chatterjee) discovers that Dutta's dejected wife Mrinmoyee is his former fiancé. Mrinmoyee leans towards him, asking for a chance to escape her life of neglect, which Sitapati is unable to oblige. Like *Saheb Bibi Golam*, Shitapati is the outsider who peeks (this time literally, as a lensman) into the innards of a decadent aristocracy but unlike it, is drawn into a saucy scandal. Sitapati leaves his shelter in a huff only to let his condition worsen further. After his wife's death at childbirth, Madhab detects the apparent affair. Furious, he chases Sitapati's footprints only to find him on the verge of death. Madhab lets go of him, and instead, shoots himself dead. Another feudal patrician falls to decay and dust.

Between the two films made from Mitra's works, that is, between 1956 and 1972, Uttam's persona moved from being the young, wide-eyed spectator of the grandiose spectacle of babudom to being the archetype of that decline itself, a totem of the fading aristocracy and their habitual, congenital excesses. This connection seems to complete a circle, tracing Uttam's trajectory from the younger self to the older one, from being an outsider to being the sovereign. Whether conscious of this connection or not, Uttam had repeatedly mentioned another. He confessed that he had imitated Chhabi Biswas's Biswambhor Roy in Ray's *Jalsaghar* as his 'preparation' for Madhab Dutta. Few believed him, because he was awarded the BFJA award for best male actor for *Stree*. But for me, it is the former connection, between *Saheb Bibi*'s Bhootnath and *Stree*'s Madhab Dutta, which I find more compelling than the one with *Jalsaghar*; and also the fact that between Bhootnath and Madhab, Ghoribabu's time was catching up, thick and fast, with Uttam.

Sonyashi Raja (The Sagely King, 1975) was loosely based on the famous Kumar of Bhawal case about which the world now knows, thanks to historian Partha Chatterjee's magisterial *The Princely Impostor: The Strange and Universal History of the Kumar of Bhawal* (2002). The makers of the film obviously did not have access to the book's remarkable insights into colonial lawmaking and the politics of identity, which contributed to this being the longest case under colonial jurisprudence. The film's scale is hence much smaller, the main cast of characters largely limited to the controversial Kumar Surjo Kishore Nag Chowdhury, his comely wife and a resident doctor. As I said, the first half is all about Surjo Kishore's frolics with women, wine and music. And chess. In fact, Surjo Kishore playing chess (with one or the other of his toadies) is a leitmotif in the plot, a move in the game hints at an impending twist in the tale.

Unlike Madhab, Surjo Kishore is more romantic and caring about his subjects but like him, he is neglectful of his wife. The details of the actual case are much more complex but in the film, a resident doctor sheltered by Surjo Kishore emerges as an arch-villain. He seduces Kumar's wife, uses his medical skills to slow-poison his patron and after his death at a seaside resort, prepares to take over the estate. Unlike the actual case where Kumar's widow had a role to play, here she is blackmailed into silence. Months later, a monk appears in the vicinity of the estate with an unmistakable similarity to Kumar. Prodded by others, he makes his claim to the estate. A legal case is summoned. As the case progresses, and the jury gets increasingly convinced of Kumar's claim, the accused doctor makes a final attempt to conceal his role by gunning the wife down. But Kumar's subjects rampage his mansion and lynch the doctor. Kumar, however, relinquishes everything, hands over the estate to a council of his subjects and walks away as a monk.

The film, like *Stree*, created persuasive melodramatic moments and is an intimate character study, creating a indelible portrait of a vexed and ambivalent individual. Both films are also essentially about modernity encroaching upon the feudal household and causing a commotion: law, medicine, photography, new claims of conjugality being the instruments of this intervention. Also, in both, Uttam plays his age, dominates the screen and makes the characters completely his own. He is aided by some great music with Manna Dey as the vocal counterpart of both the characters. Both the films are also memorable for having richly portrayed a feudal past that had just passed into oblivion, having left its many traces in the postcolonial life of Bengal. The factoring of these facets ensured that the films could rise above others of their time. But above all, there is a chilling presence of Uttam's own person in these two screen figures—of the adamant chieftain who stubbornly stands as guarantee of a time which has otherwise, just outside his sphere of influence, long vanished. There was no better sign that the autumn of the patriarch had arrived.

"THE OLD MAN IS BUT A PALTRY THING"

Among other mentionable films of that period, one should include the bilingual film that gave Uttam his first and last national audience: *Amanush* (The Savage, 1974). It was a blockbuster success in Hindi and also, surprisingly, in Bengali. But is it worth its name?

This is what was said about it in the column 'Blast from the Past' in *The Hindu* in August 2013.

One only needs to watch Shakti Samantha's *Amanush* (made simultaneously in Bengali and Hindi) to marvel at the scope of the man's (Uttam) histrionic capabilities. Kumar shines as Madhusudan Roy Chaudhary, or Madhu, a straightforward scion of a zamindar family settled in a fishing village in the Sunderbans. He reflects angst and anger with understated ease after his life is ripped asunder by the machinations of the family *munim*, Maheem Ghosal (a superlative performance by veteran Utpal Dutt). Reduced to a penniless drunkard, he is condemned to live the life of an amanush—half human, and half beast. As a debauched vagabond, he raises his voice on behalf of the downtrodden who suffer under the highhanded and corrupt Ghosal.[1]

In spite of the glowing appraisal, the *re*-view fails to grasp, predictably, the range and reach of Uttam, given the scant exposure to his cinema outside Hindi. This is revealed in the judgement about the film, because *Amanush* is a vapid, over-the-top and high-octane melodrama, and Uttam's performance (or that of Dutt) is nothing to rave about, compared to their work in Bengali. Also, the script is naive and stereotypical, thick with predictable binaries of good and evil, rich and poor, 'chaste' and 'fallen' femininity and so on. The only memorable take-away was the soundtrack. This movie, celebrated as Uttam's licence to national visibility and one that gave him a brief taste of national fame on the verge of turning 50 is to be otherwise rated rather low in Uttam's roster. At the same time, however middling the film might be, it was still better than the other Hindi films Uttam starred in in his sunset years—*Ananda Ashram, Bandi, Nishan, Desh Premee*—all of which deserve to be trashed. *Kitab, Dooriyan* and *Plot No 5* were better even if they could in no way retrieve Uttam from the general disgrace of being declared a failed actor in Hindi.

What is more compelling was that *Amanush*'s Madhu was one of the two major prototypes in which the Uttam persona appeared in those years, except in the late romances. Madhu is the prototype of the wronged man, innocent to the core and with a heart of gold, who is then exploited, tortured, blighted, till the very end, when the wheel starts to turn and moral order is restored. In several Bengali films before or after *Amanush*, this idea is repeated with similar lack of discernment and without much recourse to realism. Films such as *Bonpalishir Podaboli, Rodonobhora Bosonto* (Tears of Spring, 1974), *Chander Kachakachi* (Closer to the Moon, 1976), *Osadharon* (The Extraordinary, 1977), *Anondo Ashram* (A Doctor's Tale, 1977), *Dui Prithibi* (Two Worlds, 1980) are different in context but at the core they harbour a variation of the male figure who is at the receiving end of the debased moral order of the time. So do films like *Chhinnopotro* (The Torn Letter) and *Duti Mon* (Two Souls), where Uttam has double roles, one being the good guy and the other the vile one. Same goes for the Ajoy Kar-directed supernatural thriller *Kayahiner Kahini* (The Tale of the Disembodied, 1973), where the do-gooder Uttam accosts the ghost of the murdered beloved of the repugnant one. These films were hardly bothered with the plot: once Uttam came on board (in cases, 'twice' over) they tried to piggyback on the impunity that Uttam's box office guaranteed against mediocre films. But till the mid-1970s, even if there was a degree of commercial cushion that the poor films enjoyed, there was none thereafter.

But what a good script and a directing hand could extract from the motif of the defeated Uttam persona can be found in two films. They were dark, cynical, distraught and extracted fine performances generally, though the onus was on Uttam. I have already discussed the discomfited, fallen Gana-da of *Jodubongsho* (The Parricide). But there is that other film which many would argue should find a place among Uttam's tallest. And it is indeed one of the great performances in a leading role by any actor in all of Bengali cinema. More importantly, that it came in the last of his laudable years, 1975, underlines the depressing fact that just as he was getting under his autumnal skin with cracking grace and spirit, it all came to a naught. The film I am talking about is *Nogor Dorpone* (In the Mirror of the City). Anupam Chakraborty, the flailing, misunderstood, maladjusted writer at the heart of *Nogor Dorpone*, is the sort of author-backed character-study that Uttam usually shone in. It is not surprising that Parthapratim Chowdhury, who directed *Jodubongsho*, collaborated closely on this script with the Yatrik group, who directed the film. In some ways Anupam is a variation of Gana-da; and they end up not very differently.

Fatherless as an adolescent, Anupam grew up self-made, under the gaze of his principled mother, inheriting her unforgiving sense of good and bad. As an adult, we see him as a copywriter who also finds success as a writer of fiction. But the world Anupam grows up into is not only different from his mother's, but is also in a state of feverish transformation—old certainties are gone, values have shifted ground and crude transaction is the primary mode of social exchange. Anupam is not a Luddite, for he works in the notoriously frothy world of advertising. But a part of him is an old-school, value-laden adult male, who is not comfortable with the ways of the young. At the same time, he is not an irksome old-guard either. He simply expects others to live by a code of honesty. But that was a tall order, especially in those days of spontaneous ferocity of the besieged streets, which seemed to be testing the culpability of each and every individual.

Apart from his mother, the fulcrum of Anupam's moral compass, he is close to his wife Sreelekha (Kaberi Bose) and brother Ajitesh. As the world around him, in the grip of violence, seems to spin out of control, Anupam starts to lose the thread that had bound it all together. His mother passes away, a spate of dirty tactics in his office forces him to resign and soon after, the publishers turn him down for writing unpalatable, moralistic fiction. Anupam sits at home or wanders around the streets, pained by the apathy and guile of the world which no more flinches from walking over the dying. He confides in Sreelekha without solace, while Ajitesh, a police officer, seems to be the waning link to a world over which he had long kept a brotherly watch. His son is sent to a boarding school, away from the mercurial authority of his father. The third brother, whom he had sent to study abroad spending his last resources, returns without a degree or a semblance of sensibility. Lonely, dejected and cantankerous, Anupam finds himself at odds with everyone, including his wife, whom he accuses of being too tolerant of the casual malady of everyday life. One night, driven to despondency, Anupam asks Sreelekha: "Can you tell me why I cannot comprehend anything anymore?"

Anupam's collapse into maladjusted solipsism is lost to everyone around. Rather, he becomes an embarrassment for the ambitious Ajit; a distant force of intimidating morality for Ajit's wife and his younger brother; and for Sreelekha, a noble failure of a man. One night, tensions mount into a conflict and Ajit, unable to tolerate Anupam's rage, makes the call that he was long waiting for. The asylum attendants troop in and remove Anupam for treatment, against his severe protests and in front of the grudging but tearful acceptance of Sreelekha.

As the night deepens, Anupam's family faces up to what they had done, realising that Anupam after all, never strayed from what was essentially human. They feel aggrieved at their own haste and capacity for hostility to their own brother. Next morning, a despairing and repentant Sreelekha rushes to get him back from the asylum. In a mid-long shot, Anupam is shown sitting with his back to the camera, facing a large, open window in a prison-like cell. "I have come to take you back. Do you hear me? I have come. I have realised my mistake", Sreelakha says, as she softly touches Anupam's back. The camera closes in as Anupam turns around, and we see a dishevelled man, hair ruffled, stubble on his cheek, and strong dark circles around a pair of vacant, forlorn eyes. A shocked Sreelekha hastily retreats while Anupam sits with the same blank stare. The camera starts to pan out. The gates are locked, Anupam turns back to the window, unperturbed; and Sreelekha is held by Ajit from falling apart. Anupam, over that one long and tortuous night, did, after all, become entirely unhinged from reality, having been coerced into madness.

If anybody could have imported to screen Sreelekha's warmth and studied posture in equal measure it had to be Kaberi Bose. After a promising beginning in the mid-1950s—two of her films had Uttam as her co-actor—Bose suddenly retired young from cinema and chose a family life away from the arc-lights. In the mid-1960s, she suffered a terrible tragedy when her husband and daughter were lost to a ghastly car accident. She fought a bout of severe depression to make a surprising comeback as the lonely Jaya in Ray's *Aranyer Dinratri* (Days and Nights in the Forest, 1969). Yet, she denied herself a full-time acting career and appeared sporadically since, *Je Jekhane Dariye* (1974) being one of her notable films. But her best was kept for two of her last films, both made in 1975 and both with Uttam. The other film, as we saw, was *Ami, She O Shokha*. In 1977, a year short of being forty, she passed away. Bose brought to the screen a rare combination of grace, intelligence and tenderness. One only wishes that she had a longer and fuller life in front of the camera both for her sake and the sake of her cinema. But we still have Sreelekha. Thanks to her and Anupam, *Nogor Dorpone* is a thoughtful, grim and timely film. One cannot emphasise enough the superlative turn of Uttam in this film, aided as he was by the film's demanding plot and Kaberi Bose's first-class performance. This film is also the climax of the flailing, vanquished persona of Uttam—a far cry from the sprightly, bonhomous romantic characters of yore. Nothing better could come or indeed came his way after this film, making *Nogor Dorpone* one of the swansongs of his last great year.

In a recent essay, scholar Smita Banerjee expands on the idea of the elder brother figure in Uttam's domestic melodramas of the 1970s, culminating in Anupam. Banerjee writes:

> In these films, Uttam undergoes a significant transformation; he becomes old and seems unable to cope with the varied shifts of values confronting the young, a brooding, and melancholic presence, often in confrontation with the younger generation. I argue that it is this confrontation that lets us glimpse the changing dynamics of the bhadralok and the transformations within its ranks where the elder dada figure is confronted by generational differences and seems unable to come to terms with his space and the increasingly antagonistic familial/social situations. As the dada he is held responsible for the whole predicament facing the younger generation, and he fails to have any dialogue or conversation that he so desperately seeks, or he remains silent not least because he has begun to recognise his own hand in the destruction of the youth.[2]

This is indeed a deft observation about the *hero* figure's gradual decimation into maladroit defeatism since at least the mid-1970s.

Anupam's helpless degeneration in the face of systemic entropy recalls Lear's famous lines "Who can tell me who I am", while there is something distinctly Learean in his collapse into madness, pushed against the wall as he is by an unforgiving world. Lear is echoed by Irish poet W.B. Yeats when he wrote, "An old man is but a paltry thing", which gives this section its name. As the films attest, our hero was no doubt imploring his viewers to feel his advancing age in a changed and excruciating world he was increasingly unable to find his feet in. But very few among the viewers had the eyes to see it.

"RAGE, RAGE AGAINST THE DYING OF THE LIGHT"

If one of the two prototypes was the figure of 'the vanquished', the other was exactly the opposite: the figure of the larger-than-life messiah. So, if one part of an ageing Uttam was Yeats's old man, the other part was that of Dylan Thomas. And under this rubric, the films on the whole are more interesting than the other set of films. In fact, they gave Uttam a chance to revel in roles that had a strong sense of the central figure. Of the best two films of this temperament, we have looked at Bhabesh Banerji in *Baghbondi Khela*. The other is *Agniswor* (The Lord of Fire). As characters, they are chalk and cheese—as we will soon see in the latter—but both carry the unassailable weight of a magisterial figure who towers way above the rest. But there are others, much less impressive than either of these two films, but nevertheless part of this leitmotif, at least four of which actually overdid this larger-than-life figure. *Bonhisikha* (The Renegade) is the story of a spurned lover who morphs into an undercover mafia boss to avenge his humiliation. The film was inspired by the gaudy overkill of early James Bond villainy: full of garish sets, staccato mafiosi lingo, set-piece technological gobbledygook and a brash antagonist. The twist is that Uttam is both the much-revered barrister Barin Ghosh in the morning and the shadowy, dreaded ringleader Mr Sinha at night, running an extensive racket of illegal services for an international coterie of outlaws. There is also an English cabaret song that goes like: "Life is a gamble/Love is a game/Heart you are heartless/Traitor is your name". All this is deliciously outrageous and a promising premise for unadulterated kitsch, which was not just oddly funny but also a serious exception to the dogged sanctimony of Bengali cinema. But the film's fantastic setting and over-the-top plot was wasted, thanks to the phoney message that bad men are actually good souls driven to evil by lack of love. As was often germane to his bad films, Uttam is surprisingly credible and kind of holds the rakish plot together, the cheesy make-up and the corny dialogues notwithstanding. He also received his last BFJA award for this film. *Nidhiram Sardar* (The Vigilante, 1976) is another example of a fantasy plot wasted. The eponymous Nidhiram (Uttam) refers to the double life of a masked vigilante, who Robinhood-like redistributes wealth and takes to task a cohort of creepy characters. Modelled loosely on popular comics, this film, directed by the actor Rabi Ghosh, could have been, like *Bonhisikha*, an entertaining potboiler. But the writing was poor, the filming poorer. Uttam's dark character, unlike that of Mr Sinha, is shallow, leaving him hardly with anything to do except appear in a strange mask and white wig in odd places. Ditto for *Brojobuli* (A Man Made of Words, 1978), which is about an innocuous clerk who lives a parallel life of bizarre heroics and stunning absurdity. The germinal comic fantasy needed a buoyant imagination but instead got a hackneyed, over-the-top, lousy treatment. Not much far is *Sabyasachi* (The Revolutionary, 1977), it being inspired by Sarat Chandra Chattopadhyay's late novel *Pather Dabi* (1926). If the other three films were guilty of trying to find reason in freaky surroundings, this one went the other way. It glamorises, much like the novel, the toil and muck of a die-hard anti-colonial crusader, turning it into the thrilling adventure of a bespoke, shape-shifting globetrotter. Historian Tanika Sarkar has described Sabyasachi Mullick, the ambidextrous hero of the novel, as one "capable, literally of everything, [Sabyasachi] is the first superman in serious Bengali fiction, always a million times larger than life".[3] By signing the fifty-one-year-old Uttam for the role of a young and daredevil firebrand, the film indicated its lack of interest in finding an equivalent of the figure on screen. Instead, the script hoped to embellish the already overblown protagonist's case with a dose of glamour that Uttam would import in a role of this nature. The result? Another pathetic film. On days when nothing better is available to watch, these films are still watchable specimens of populist film-making among the barrage of terrible films of the period, providing some quirky amusement without always intending to do so.

On the more familiar end of the larger-than-life prototype there is recurrence of the figure of the advocate, or the advocator. *Jibon Jigyasha* (The Atoner) starts with the impending return to Calcutta of Indraneel (Uttam), a dashing and debonair barrister with a colourful past. His arrival sets aflutter the tongues in the city's high society. He soon storms Calcutta's legal world, as expected, and is appointed a senior standing counsel, well on his way to becoming the advocate-general. His fiancé, painter Rina, is as footloose as he is. Indraneel's libertine past has left him cold towards women and in Rina he looks for companionship rather than romance. In fact, the early scenes reveal Indraneel as a world-weary but perceptive misanthrope, who is rich, cocksure and having tasted life to the lees, now wants to relish it from a distance.

A case involving the murder of a cloth merchant with links to a prostitute is brought to Indraneel's attention. But in court Indraneel recognises the accused Shefali (Supriya) as none other than Radha, a woman he had seduced long ago in the solitude of his ancestral property. He had then moved on, pursuing his barrister-ship abroad while Radha was left to rot, pregnant, homeless and dirt poor. She had never revealed his name though and was refused any refuge. Poverty killed her son and a half-crazed Radha was brought to the brothel by a kind, elderly lady. Since then, the brothel had helped her survive. Shefali recognises Indraneel in the court but stops short of acknowledging, instead announcing herself guilty. Unconvinced, Indraneel starts to investigate and is increasingly convinced of Radha's innocence. As Radha's dismal life after their tryst unravels through flashbacks and old witnesses, Indraneel finds himself standing on judgement on his own life. If he admitted to his past, he risked everything, and if he didn't, he risked being a prisoner to his own conscience. Soon, hence, a professional dilemma assumes an existential tone. Against the warning of his friends, Indraneel decides to atone. In the climactic court scene, he not only wins the case on behalf of Radha but also announces that she was his wife and that he should stand accused of murdering their son. Later, Radha succumbs to alcoholism and Indraneel, leaving everything behind, walks into the unknown. The playboy chooses penitence.

This sort of plot walks the tightrope between realism and the sentimental fantasy of retrieving masculine agency. This film contains every trope to fall squarely on the side of the latter. But it does not, thanks largely to Uttam's Indraneel. From the flippancy of his debonair parties to his mature bonding with Rina, from the debauchery of his early days to his mellowing into a man of judgement, from his vague remembrances about Radha to his saddened eyes owning up to his own venality, Uttam is incomparably good. The film is tightly scripted too, staying to the plot, giving Indraneel's dilemma enough screen-time to pan out. Most performances are apt in the film except Supriya's. Even some admirable close-ups from cinematographer Dilipranjan Mukherjee could not save her performance from her pesky mannerisms. But as in many cases, it is Uttam's bravura part that not only saves the film from cracking under the weight of its moral posture but makes his atonement almost tragic to experience.

Jatrik's *Jodi Jantem* (A Secret Formula) is a thriller, adapted from Bengali author Narayan Sanyal's *Nagchampa*. Sanyal had explicitly localised the plot from one of Eric Stanley Gardner's early mysteries from the Perry Mason series. The first half of the film concerns Kaushik

Mitra (Soumitra Chatterjee) an engineer who for lack of jobs, takes up driving a taxi in Calcutta. He is discovered by the intelligence bureau and is sent on a secret mission to set up surveillance on a prominent businessman (Basanta Chowdhury) at a border town. The incognito 'informant' soon learns that the entrepreneur, among his other crimes, is also coaxing Sujata (Supriya), the daughter of a deceased scientist, to part with a secret formula. As expected, Sujata and Kaushik start to take an interest in the other without Sujata's knowledge of the mission. But much to Kaushik's dismay, the businessman, a chillingly astute sophisticate, manages to avoid any lapses that would reveal his plans. He closes his net on Sujata for a final showdown but on a fateful night, is gunned down in his bungalow. Sujata and Kaushik, found on the scene of murder, get embroiled. Till this part, the film, like most thrillers in Bengali, is anodyne. Then, P.K. Basu arrives on the scene.

It is more than an hour into the film that P.K. Basu appears, initially sporadically. He is a gray-haired, bespectacled, pipe-smoking retired advocate who is deeply attached to his paraplegic wife Roma (Ruma Guhathakurta), living a quiet life in a sprawling mansion after the death of their only daughter. He is revered locally, stays aloof and is known as a man of few words and fewer friends. Sujata had solicited his brief acquaintance before the troubles had overwhelmed her. It is only in the third quarter of the film that the retired advocate takes up the case and begins his inquiry. When Basu decides to reveal the real murderer to an unofficial jury at the site of the crime, the fate and form of the film makes a radical turnaround.

As P.K. Basu, Uttam is dazzling in the long, climactic scene. Every bit of this scene is as riveting as any good thriller, focused as it is on Basu's compelling and brainy set of probes, witticisms and the confident unravelling of a night's portentous events. His lighting the tall lamps in the spacious room with his smoldering pipe with purposeful pauses between his revelations is perhaps one of the most gorgeous exposition acts one can see on screen. Basu's arguments prevail and the real culprit confesses, releasing Sujata and Kaushik from their impending incarceration. It is not Basu who prevails however, but Uttam, who once again seemed to have transfixed into insignificance his formidable co-actors, including Soumitra.

All these enactments, however, pale in comparison to the figure of the eponymous Agnishwar Mukherjee in Aurobindo Mukhopadhyay's *Agniswor* (The Lord of Fire). Based again on a novel by the director's brother Balaichand, the film—about an idealistic doctor in late colonial Bengal—towered over all others when it came to a larger-than-life figure in Bengali cinema. Banbihari Mukherjee, the brother of iconic muralist Binod Bihari Mukherjee, was a polyglot physician and a radical humanist, a man of severe principles and endless generosity. He was called 'an Indian Voltaire' by the scholar and author Syed Mujtaba Ali for his searching criticism of the entrenched bigotry and fanaticism of Bengali life and manners. Banbihari had left a considerable mark among a young group of progressives, Balaichand being one of them. He is the film's Agnishwar Mukherjee.

Agnishwar Mukherjee's name preceded him wherever he was posted. A brilliant student and an equally brilliant doctor, he had a reputation for being difficult, undaunted and unbending. He showed submission to no one, not even the British officials. At the same time, he was a benevolent freethinker, a political radical and a consecrated soul, who stopped at nothing to save a human life from being wasted at the altars of poverty, malnutrition and disenfranchisement. He is hence, constantly, crossing paths with the powers that be, while emerging as a messiah to the ill and the poor.

The script shifts between Agniswar the doctor and the person, each an extension of the other; chronicling his lonely crusade against the suffering submission of a nation in distress and the vain middle class, waiting to take over the spoils after the impending independence. His incendiary caricatures, which he draws in spare time, targets the complicit and the cowardly; while he also helps the secret cause of an intrepid group of nationalists. He gets his widowed sister remarried and then marries a quiet, god-fearing woman who, unknown to him, gets crushed under the weight of his nonconforming demands. In later years, he quits his medical practice to settle down in a sparse house in Calcutta, preferring to live on his meagre pension. Having given up on his meat-eating extravagance, he seeks to live frugally, atoning for having caused his wife's silent embrace of death. Yet, the fire in him refuses to die, as his son, who decides to marry into a rich family, learns the hard way. Concerned that his presence might smother his son's life too, Agniswar leaves Calcutta and makes a journey across the country, meeting odd fellows in a wide nation finally free of its colonial chains. Ageing and tired, he settles down in a remote tribal hamlet, where the long arm of the nation was yet to reach in any meaningful way. Having pinned him down after a long search to bestow an award on him, the Bengal government sends a team, with his son, looking for him. As they arrive, the old, weakened, weather-beaten, white-haired Agniswar, having just given blood to save a local boy, rushes out to receive his son. But he stumbles at the doorway and falls. Lying there, he exhausts himself of his last breath, refusing one more time, and this time finally, to be courted by the embrace of the establishment.

The last scene, set against the rousing tune of a Bengali anthem about India's greatness, risks sabotaging the film's otherwise sentient setting.

Also, throughout, the film director Arobindu Mukhopadhyay tries to turn *Agniswor* into a hagiography. But he is undercut by the script and (as expected) by Uttam's singularly competent embrace of the character as a living and credible entity; not only helping the defiant doctor morph into a heroic iconoclast but also giving him a life that has outstayed the film. In fact, whenever one sees an enlightened, radical physician, one thinks of Agniswar; whenever one sees an exponent of anti-colonial pride and a messianic healer, one thinks of Agniswar; whenever one sees a graying doctor with spectacles hanging from the bridge of his nose, exposing a pair of inquisitive, sarcastic eyes, one thinks of Agniswar.

THE SENSE OF AN ENDING

Agniswor was a fitting swansong for Uttam, as there are obvious parallels between the two. The defeated Gana-da, the lonesome Anish Mitra, the romping Madhab Dutta, the diminished Anupam had all carried a germinal extension of the star's persona in them. But none was closer to it than Agniswar, who seemed to have been carrying the weight of the beleaguered nation on his chest as much as Uttam was carrying that of the cinema commons in Bengal. It was not the moral uprightness that is the link here, but the severity of a commitment that is beyond the scope of any human being, even one a few sizes larger than others. Hence, however agitated one might feel at his slow decline, one cannot particularly blame Uttam for thinking beyond himself. How can one be damned, whose weakened heart missed one more beat, again and again, for lowly technicians, production hands and studio operators? After all, those who stand at the gates during war, fall first. Uttam's greatness is perhaps that he was both the commander at the gate and the patriarch in the parlour.

Thus, post 1975, there was no stopping the rot from taking deep root. As Uttam's films became increasingly unwatchable, they also failed miserably at the box office. Whatever good intentions may have been driving Uttam in those years, the audience was unequivocal in rejecting the films; sending a clear signal that movies made to fortify the industry may not please the viewer. So, this whole munificence about being the grand patriarch of the industry turned out to be a tragic farce in the end. Uttam had more than forty releases after 1975, including those in Hindi and those that released after his death, two of them having to make use of a dummy actor. Films like *Shei Chokh* (The Eyes, 1976), *Jal Sonyashi* (The False Monk, 1977), *Bondi* (The Convict, 1978), *Dhanraj Tamang* (Revenge in the Hills, 1978) and *Nobodigonto* (A New Horizon, 1979) were so tormenting that they seemed to have come from another land, while competing with each other to reach for the bottom. Others do not even merit a mention. Even his most ardent admirers are unlikely to remember any of these films. The posthumous release *Ogo Bodhu Sundori* (My Beautiful Wife, 1981) was an exception to the routine failures, while it is also an excellent example of the state of malady that had engulfed Bengali cinema. The film was completed with a dummy actor after Uttam's death which came after he suffered the fatal cardiac arrest on its sets. Based on *My Fair Lady* (1964), the film is a fatuous adaptation full of tired humour, overacting and bad direction. But it was a huge hit as scores of his fans went to see it, as it turned out to be the last of the star's films to be released on time. Other incomplete films took years.

Among his last films was *Devdas* (Devdas, 1979), yet another Bengali adaptation of Sarat Chandra's seemingly undying classic. The film is dreadful but an incident during the shoot is telling. The director Dilip Roy recounted how during the filming of a key indoor song sequence (*Shawono rate jodi*, 'On a rainy night') with Uttam, the lights went out, as was common those days. The crew went out to air themselves, only to realise that Uttam was missing. After a frantic search they hurried back to the dark, airless set to find Uttam sitting there, motionless, since when the lights had gone. Uttam told Roy that he did not want to get distracted, so he was sitting there, waiting for the shoot to start the moment power was restored, he assured. For Roy, this was a measure of Uttam's unstinting dedication. But it is more than that. It is an allegory of the time—a star drowned in darkness, sitting hapless and outcast in a posture of readiness, waiting for lights and make-up, to perform yet another unremarkable scene in yet another horrendous film. What better way can there be to expose the hollowness of his efforts to ensure bread for others? In fact, if some of the more avaricious producers had their way, they would probably be content to have the deceased Uttam, taxidermied, propped straight up on screen to make their junk work at the box office. Rarely, if ever, has generosity turned itself into such scorn, and a sense of resigned profligacy been so embarrassingly close to schlock horror. Uttam's last days, hence, have all the hallmarks of a well-wrought and catastrophic tragedy.

Uttam was once the totem of postcolonial Bengal's romance with cinema. After two decades, Uttam's persona once again became a titular, figurative entity that carried the profound ambivalence of the period—the unrest, the mistrust and the thrusting into public life of the 'brutish and the short', to remember Hobbes. Having *become* the industry, Uttam bore the cross of his fame too heavily, making his fall inevitable in a time of irrevocable change. To that end, Uttam did not have the luxury of fading out gradually. His stardom was one that had to exhaust itself while at work. And that is exactly what happened.

NOTES

1. Available at https://www.thehindu.com/features/friday-review/amanush-1975/article5049063.ece#!.
2. Smita Banerjee, 'Evolution of *Dada* Uttam Kumar: Performing Masculinity and the Disillusioned Bhadralok Maha Nayok in the 1970s' Popular Melodramas', *BioScope* 10:1 (2019), pp. 52–74.
3. Tanika Sarkar, *Bengal 1928–1934: The Politics of Protest*, Oxford University Press, 1987, p. 24.

10

AFTERLIFE OF THE BHADRALOK

Outside the window, the darkness. After me, the deluge.
                              —Osip Mandelstam

ON the night of 24 July 1980, Uttam Kumar was declared dead after he failed to recover from what was, by an account, his fifth cardiac arrest. After his last attack in 1978, he was diagnosed with cardiac asthma. In fact, for much longer, his heart had been a problem. He always carried a sorbitrate for any abnormal spasm of the chest. There were also several restrictions. Uttam listened to some but the restrictions on overwork and alcohol—usual collaterals of fame—were not among them. Barely could he cut down on work, barely could find any repose in his personal life; and barely could he minister to himself. And because he could not, he overruled the moratorium on alcohol.

A favourite tape recorder having been stolen from his car parked near his home on the morning of 23 July is often taken as a portent for the unruly day that was to come. Sometime later, he found his make-up room at Technician Studio occupied by a young female actor, which had never happened before, and which prompted a stormy visit to New Theatres 1, a few buildings away. On returning, he had to shoot a scene involving a flight of stairs. It was a nominal scene by Uttam's measure but somehow he considered it faulty each time and went for seven retakes. The director Salil Dutta had to whisper to others to clap forcefully to stop Uttam from retaking it any more. By the end of it, Uttam was sweating, tired and in a bitter mood. After all, unbeknown, he had already suffered a sting on his heart. None of the toils of the morning, however, deterred Uttam from heading to a boisterous party that evening which continued well into the night. On return, he felt severely ill. This time, suspecting an attack, he drove himself to Belle Vue, the city's pre-eminent hospital, which was a five-minute drive from his Moira Street residence. When he was admitted, his doctor Lalmohan Mukherjee considered his case, helplessly, to be par for the course. He had for long cautioned Uttam about his failing cardiac condition, and had explained how with each new attack, the chances of recovery diminished further. But on that midnight, none of that really mattered. Dr Mukherjee and his team tried their utmost to revive Uttam the rest of that night and the whole of the next day with less and less hope. For a brief while the following evening, he was doing better and had convinced his brother Tarun that he should not skip a scheduled stage performance. But things started to deteriorate a couple of hours later and his heart bled itself to death a little after 9 in the evening of Thursday, 24 July. Tarun was the first one to be given a call.

The thousands who thronged the streets the next day and brought to stop the whole of south Calcutta came to witness a sight they did not think would arrive so early; or with such numbing unpreparedness. What they saw were a sea of people surrounding a single, open-air truck that was converted into a hearse and filled with mounds of white wreaths and funeral flowers. At the centre of that flowery bed, lying prostrate, on a makeshift wooden plank was Uttam Kumar, robed in white, the portals of his nose and ears plugged with cotton and with a pair of closed eyes as if in deep and restful slumber. Those who could see more, saw that the man was sleeping peacefully, having finally found liberation from the gruelling labour of being Uttam Kumar.

On the same day, 25 July, the Bengali daily *Anandabazar Patrika* carried—on the front page of course—two reports of Uttam's passing away. The headline of one was brief: "*Cholochitre Indrapatan*", which translates to 'Cinema Loses Its Titan'. No phrase could be more apt. There was a palpable sense of emptiness that his death left behind; not just among his family and friends but also, naturally, in the industry—co-workers, colleagues, veterans, thespians. A no less profound sense of bereavement seemed to have pervaded the viewers and fans too, many of them unable to come to terms with his absence. Uttam's departure was a collective sigh.

BEREAVEMENT

Whether immediately after his death or since, there has been no dearth of homages that were addressed to him. These voices grieved not only Uttam the actor but also Uttam the guardian; not only Uttam the star, but also Uttam the person, and not just Uttam the professional, but also Uttam the altruist. Collectively, the reminiscences cover a very wide personal and professional orbit where Uttam's talent, tenacity and warmth were natural referents of remembrance. Since Uttam died early, several of his precursors and peers were still alive at the time, including the veteran actress Kanan Devi. Almost all of them left a testimonial in homage to Uttam after his death. His directors—Satyajit Ray, Tapan Sinha, Chitta Basu, Pinaki Mukhopadhyay, Kartick Chattopadhyay, Gulzar and several others—talked about his dedication and effortless performances. Sinha also observed, correctly, that Uttam freed cinema from the stranglehold of theatre, bringing in a new freshness to his screen persona. Ray was even more precise. He recalled how Uttam's instinctive style was unmatched, how he broke his dialogues with meaningful pauses, and how he made use of his characters' silence on screen. But what Ray was also particularly impressed by was Uttam's strong sense of involvement. "I never saw him fooling around on the sets. He either prepared himself for the scene or sat isolated and read books. This is a rare discipline among actors in India."[1] The list of homages, interestingly, involved those who never worked with him but always wanted to, Hrishikesh Mukherjee, for example. He recalled having congratulated Ray about how valuable a film *Nayak* was. In reply, Ray had said, "Thank you, but I won't have risked the film if Uttam did not come on board. It is actually his film, more than mine. He is the first and last hero of Bengali cinema."[2]

Then there were poignant reminiscences from all his co-stars, from Suchitra Sen to Arundhati Mukherjee, Tanuja, Madhabi Mukherjee, Aparna Sen, Sabitri Chatterjee to Sondhyarani Chatterjee. For them, what stood out was Uttam's charisma, gentility and geniality rather than a strict professional code of conduct. So echoed his co-actors too: Bhanu Bandopadhyay to Bikas Roy, Subhendu Chatterjee to Anup Kumar, many of whom considered Uttam the only friend they had in the industry. No less warm memories surfaced from notable people unconnected to cinema: footballers, singers, sports commentators, doctors, barristers, chiefs of corporations, bureaucrats and others. Their case fell in between those who worked with Uttam in a close capacity and the average fan who saw him only from a distance. What they mostly remembered, apart from his screen persona, was Uttam's homegrown civility. Among the most insightful was the one from the outspoken journalist and editor Santoshkumar Ghosh. He had concurred that intensive romantic acting somehow involved a level of stupidity, and concluded that only Uttam could disturb his conviction to that effect. Soumitra Chatterjee held a grudge, one that we have encountered before: that Uttam the actor was muzzled, at least partially, by Uttam the star. He was echoing Saroj De of the director's group Agragami who had years ago said something similar. The critical and commercial failure of their 1962 film *Kanna* made De reflect on this. Saroj De considered Uttam's stardom, which he did not take at face value, as the real reason for the film's cold reception. "Uttam could have become a far better actor had he not succumbed to the pitfalls of stardom, secured in his romantic portrayals and barely making an effort to leave his comfort zone", he had said.[3] De insisted that *Kanna*, where John was the archetype of an anti-hero, was a rare case which dared the actor hiding behind the star. He thought that the film failed because Uttam's audience could not appreciate him playing a weakling at the mercy of his hormones. This assessment is only partially true because Uttam did break away from the prison-house of the image repeatedly. But what De said next was prophetic: "There was barely a meeting point between Uttam the person, who was rather ordinary and Uttam the actor, who was superlative. Whenever the actor rebelled, the cautious man in him leashed the actor, pulling him back into playing set-piece, anodyne characters."[4] This is an astute and a rare insight into Uttam from his peer, which is otherwise filled with salutary verdicts. In fact, more than the 1960s, this assessment did assume a note of foretelling in the 1970s, when, as we have seen, the tension between the man and the actor had torn Uttam apart. But De never lost his admiration for Uttam the actor and Agragami continued to tease the actor in him throughout the 1960s, often with manifest success.

Litterateurs Premendra Mitra, Ashutosh Mukhopadhyay, Buddhadeb Bose and Ramapada Chowdhury were long-time admirers, as much of his talent as of his manners. Bose also wrote a novel fictionalising an ageing heartthrob who had been grounded by cancer. Uttam had read it and dreaded the possibility of rotting away with age. Whatever other wishes of his may or may not have been granted, he surely did not resent not having to watch himself fade into sickness and irrelevance.

Image 10.1: An ageing Uttam staring at the fading light
(Photographer unknown)

Source: Parimal Ray.

Equally telling tributes came from the relatively unknown industry technicians: make-up artistes Debi Halder and Bashir Ahmed; sound recordists Subir Ghosh and J.D. Irani; film laboratory owner R.B. Mehta; producer Ardhendu Mukherjee; dresser Kanailal Das; art directors Gour Poddar and Satyen Roychowdhury; photographers Sukumar Roy and Prabhakar Prabhu and many others. They revealed Uttam's stewardship of the industry, his unfailing efforts to elevate cinema's environs: studios, film laboratories, cinema halls. What is striking is how Uttam had a personal and touching rapport with all of the industry's 'invisible' crew. They shared precious moments of calling on him in person and expressed their delight at being asked by Uttam about a scene here and a take there. They also felt gratified when Uttam, in the early 1960s, sided with them against the distributors and sat in protest against the running of his own film. They felt part of a larger communion of artists and saw Uttam as their natural guardian. He also led their union. We are accustomed to the so-called popular wisdom about how stardom, by sucking the light all by itself, forces others around to merge with the darkness. And yet here was a star who made sure his colleagues went along as he progressed from strength to strength, especially those who toiled behind the scenes. His death, no wonder, was seen by the industry's insiders as an intimate, filial loss, as well as the end of their belonging to a community. Many of them grieved for days. The director Salil Sen said,[5] "Uttam received steady disregard from institutions, so-called film buffs, a section of the intelligentsia and those who contribute to public discourse about cinema.… But he got unconditional love and admiration from the studio-hands, technicians, crew, daily-wagers." Perhaps only one act of remembering, from Bashir Ahmed,[6] will suffice.

> On July 22, I was doing my usual job of putting make-up on his face. He looked distraught. When I asked, why don't you rest a little, why do you torture yourself with work, Uttam*da* said, "I have been around a long time, Bashir. I think my need is over. It is time to go." I heard he said this to other colleagues too. And in two days he was actually gone. It was really all over. To say I was devastated is to say little. Allah, God, Kali, whoever is up there, I pray that you bring peace to the soul of this very precious human being.

Uttam's wife Gauri, son Gautam and his family; brother Tarun and actress wife Subrata; another brother Barun; and mother Chapala Debi were inconsolable. They had the right to grieve in public. But they were not his only family. In 1967, Uttam had legally adopted Shoma Chowdhury, daughter of Supriya Chowdhury. Soma and Supriya grieved Uttam in a different way than his family, away from cameras and onlookers, having been denied access to Uttam after his demise. There was hardly a meeting point between the two 'families' of Uttam once he was gone. They even went to court when Shoma, as legal successor, sued them for rights to his estate, a case that was fought bitterly in the end-1980s. This is perhaps as persuasive a reason as any other about why Uttam may not have found old age a prospect to look forward to.

THREE REVERBERATIONS

The barrage of outpouring that Uttam's departure triggered brought to the surface the bare fact that this was not an exit of just another popular star. No one found the courage to proclaim that the show must go on, because after all, Uttam *was* the show. The ground shook on his death, leaving far-reaching reverberations, a natural legacy after the passing of a behemoth. But it was much more than that. How do we understand the effects? Well, when a small star loses the nitrogen steam, it's called a white dwarf; when a moderate star suffers breakdown, it's called a supernova; but when a star which is many times bigger than the others collapses, it sucks everything into a black hole. The question is not *if* Uttam was a humongous star, or if his demise caused the collapse of Bengali cinema into a black-hole, because they have been proved indisputable. The question is, *how*.

A Cinematic Partition

Uttam's late career, as we have seen, was a copybook of poor decisions, bad publicity and a despondent effort to save a dwindling industry from decimation. It became clear that he stood alone, especially after 1975, between a past of spectacular riches and a future of terrible infamy. His death closed the gap irretrievably. But the story is bigger than that.

On coming to power in 1977 in Bengal, the Left Front [led by Communist Party of India (Marxist)] had put its weight, if not money, behind the so-called serious cinema. Doing so, it thought, would not only help cement its image as a custodian of high culture but in the years to come, would reinforce the Party's vanguardism. But the effect was crushing. Those wanting to work in cinema outside the confines of Tollygunge had to cozy up to the CPI(M)'s cultural apparatchiks, which inevitably meant censorship on more than one level and a stifling definition of what constituted meaningful cinema. Throughout the 1980s and early 1990s, therefore, 'good cinema' was all about poorly lit, sadly textured, brooding cinema that in no time lost all its artistic value.

By this time the original art-house masters—Ray, Sen, Ghatak and Sinha—had either passed away or were scarcely productive. There was hardly any breakthrough cinema; on the contrary, the 'serious films', piggybacking on government patronage, focused on family and gender, petty crime in cities, the changing moral landscape of the middle classes, and other issues that added little to the rich thematic repertory of Bengali cinema of yore. Beyond its own definition of cinema and cultural field of vision, the Left had left everything to rot, inevitably hurting the prospects of popular cinema, once the touchstone of Bengali cultural taste. Having lost both public and institutional backing, mainstream cinema was now abandoned culturally and waylaid financially. It naturally started to seek out the lowest denominator by cutting costs and looking for desperate patronage in the farthest of places, distant from the judgement of the city and its dominant classes.

So, from the mid-1970s and more glaringly after Uttam's death, Bengali cinema was left deeply divided into two watertight categories: the gaudy, loud, retrograde potboilers; and morbid 'art-house' cinema, both unwatchable in their own way. Uttam, whose arrival after Partition closed the schism between the material and the affective in popular cinema, on his death left behind another kind of split.

In fact, it was more than a partition. Because this elemental split had coupled with other grave matters: a sinking economy, a derivative aspirationalism, outbound migration, and a general overtaking of crudity and conformity in daily life. Slowly but inevitably, cinema movements came to a halt; the physical space of the single theatres started to wind up; pirated, private video broadcasting cannibalised the meagre profits; and the substantial patronage of the middle class dried up. Bengali cinema's historical coupling with metropolitan space and spectatorship evaporated. Effectively, over two generations grew up faced with the possibility of not having seen even a single specimen of Bengali cinema in the theatres, destroying an entire economy, history and sociology that grew around the public culture of cinema since at least the 1930s.

A Televised Reincarnation

This continued well past the mid-1990s. By then, not only had popular cinema become invisible to the urban middle class, but the art films too, despite the patronage of the Left, turned out to be a washout. The first ripple of change was felt with the arrival of liberalisation. Though Calcutta, owing to the gate-keeping of its communist bosses, was slow to wake up to a new economy, liberalisation still managed to bring in far-reaching changes. Among significant developments was the broadening of the market, easy loans and access to consumer goods, a heightened global exposure through a liberal media economy and new possibilities thrown up by telecommunication and the later the worldwide web. Soon, the middle class swelled in size and purchasing power, a young crop of actors and technicians arrived, new money came to the industry and a new kind of corporatised entertainment started to sprout. The most prominent Bengali filmmaker to emerge from this new market was Rituparno Ghosh. He has since become an early pioneer of a market-friendly cultural creed.[7] Naturally, since his time, the propensity to think against the grain and to work against the tide has further eroded. Bengali cinema of the last two decades is noticeably better than the 1980s and is adventurous in technology and production design. But at heart, it is entrenched in casual elitism, political escapism, familial trifling and wanton self-indulgence. As I write this, it continues to wallow in its facile embarrassments.

What concerns us here is not so much cinema but its cousin, the television. Since the late 1970s, television—as a public broadcasting engine—dished out family entertainers and cinema of yore. In fact, whatever was left of Bengal's historic cinema culture was to be perceived through television. The story of Uttam too takes an interesting turn since when his cinema experienced a major revival through television, it being an essential part of Calcutta Doordarshan's commitment to the middle-class drawing room. For years since the mid-1980s, Sunday evenings on television were dedicated to old Bengali cinema, which captivated an entire generation, including that of this author. We watched, with awe and wonder, the sheer diversity, intelligence and cinematic sense that Bengali cinema could muster again and again. These decades cemented the Left's hold over Bengal's politics and reinforced the class divide between Bengal's burgeoning urban middle class and its huge rural population. This division was marked, among other crucial things, by privileged access to technological and cultural resources, which amplified many times over after liberalisation. Over a period of time, hence, Uttam's cinema, which had once managed to close class and social boundaries, was co-opted by the middle class, leaving a once participatory spectatorship in the provinces at the mercy of the conservative kitsch in skeletal cinema halls. In some ways, the cinematic partition that Uttam had left on his death now seemed to have snowballed into a cultural apartheid. It has not been bridged since.

A Political Resurrection

What coincided with television's reach was the mass outbound migration of Bengal's substantial cultural intelligentsia. They carried with them significant fragments of Bengali culture, Uttam being a much cherished component of this portable pool. His name and fame helped the burgeoning diaspora preserve a tenuous link with its past, underlining his repertoire with the heavy tinge of nostalgia. In the decades since, newer diaspora generations have learned to see Uttam through the prism of memory, largely inherited from their parents. For many of them, Uttam's individual films are less of a concern. Instead, Uttam is a sign, a talisman, of everything that was great about Bengali cinema of the past. The case of the home-bred urban millennials is not too different. They are less effusive about Bengaliness than their predecessors and more appreciative of various global cultural forms. But when it comes to boasting of legends closer home, Uttam is often a natural selection. In short, Uttam's status has remained largely undiminished since his death, though increasingly as a middle-class icon, reinforced again and again through professional and now social media.

This continuity of Uttam's posthumous fame has also led to his political 'resurrection'. The Left's enormous cultural assets had left the kitty of its rivals, the Trinamool Congress, without a saleable figure of any prominence. But given the legacy of culture's fellowship with politics in Bengal, the Trinamool desperately needed figures of repute. Uttam's distance from the Left during his lifetime, his continuing appeal, and his increasingly exclusive cult status among the middle class, made him a secure choice for Mamata Banerjee. So, to please the middle class and to showcase their 'cultural' leaning, Trinamool marshalled Uttam—a staunch political non-partisan—back into political prominence. There is also an intriguing fact to note here. The very last film that Uttam was in talks to be part of was to be called *Ma Mati Manush*, the title giving away the film's premise as one banking on puerile kitsch, as was the norm those days. Three decades later, exactly the same phrasing became the political slogan of Trinamool when it challenged the incumbent Goliath CPM in 2011, the latter having found itself severely depreciated in its commitment to all 'three of these categories' in the aftermath of the Singur–Nandigram debacle.

Hence, in the first year of coming to power in 2011, Mamata announced a slew of measures in Uttam's name. And since then, Bengal's favourite golden goose continues to be an important weapon of middle-class mobilisation for a party that is otherwise little concerned with the art and craft of cinema. No wonder then that none of what was promised—a museum to Bengali cinema or an institutional will to save the rotting public cinema infrastructure or a digitisation of cinema materials—has materialised. The only consolation was having Moira Street renamed Uttam Kumar Sarani. This was the easiest thing to do. Otherwise, like the Left, the Trinamool too has left Bengali cinema's most gifted period to the mercy of the climate, to the vagaries of changing taste and to the whims of memory.

As we have seen, to be a puppet of competing electoral one-upmanship was a prospect that haunted Uttam throughout his late stardom years. Which is why he considered any inclination for pulpit popularity miles beyond his felicity—as actor, a star or just human being. Incidentally, when asked about politics in Bengal, Uttam commented that to him both the Left and the Congress were two faces of the same coin. "Both are as distasteful as the other. They are like popular cinema and art cinema; both so abysmal that people are turning away from them and watching Hindi films sitting in Calcutta."[8] Uttam, from his vantage of having seen it all closely and suffered equally, made this comparison, which was both unusually cynical and unusually prescient in the politically charged Bengal of the 1970s. In fact, not just politics, Uttam pre-empted even the cinematic devastation his vacating the scene was likely to cause. But then, the silence of the departed is usually taken as consent. Thus, as in life so in death, Uttam continues to remain a popular magnate and focal point of mass frenzy. And also a political object.

MOURNING

If the days after death were about bereavement, the reflections shifted tenor as decades passed. In fact, as time deposited more and more years between Uttam's death and the present, the appraisals have moved away from the person to the *figure*. And more the present has distanced itself from the fact of Uttam's lived life, the more the acts of bereavement have attained an element of epic mourning.

Cinema historians, critics and a new generation of writers seemed to have moved on from measuring Uttam by his love for homemade food, his sartorial choices or his largesse as a family man, which crowded earlier acts of assessment. The latter have been typical stuff of remembrance for years and carried the onus of unnecessary mythification. Good epicureans, evolved stylists or benevolent fathers-in-law are, hopefully, galore in Bengal. So are actors of talent. But none of them are Uttam Kumar. So, what he ate, what he wore, how he functioned at family reunions is a frippery matter, if at all worthy of note; and surely no measure for a life lived much larger than what most Bengalis can even fathom. In fact, about four generations that have grown up since Uttam's death, have witnessed to him having emerged increasingly as more insurmountable as a screen icon. The informed among them are also less patient with trivial homages. Hence, more perceptive appraisals have emerged in recent years, including an overwhelming recognition that *in* Uttam resided a figure of supreme confidence and an actor of endless talent. But there is more.

In September 2010, to commemorate thirty years of Uttam's departure, Rituparno Ghosh published a special issue of *Robibar*, the Sunday supplement he edited. "Rabindranath Tagore was Bengali's 'Gurudeb'. And then there is the unmistakable 'Guru'—Uttam Kumar. No one else can be crowned with either of the titles", Ghosh mused in his editorial,[9] reflecting on Uttam's longevity and the expanding geography of yearning that keeps him in warm custody of memory. A year later, the popular author Suchitra Bhattacharya wrote,[10]

> Why can't I still move away when the television plays a movie with Uttam? He was not really handsome. We have seen better-looking and better-voiced actors even in Bengal cinema. What was it then? Was it because he had that very fine, uncluttered, archetypal Bengali look? But he was also a westernized sophisticate on screen. Then? Is it that smile? That beatific, hypnotic smile?

An editorial in a special issue of a journal referred to the same.[11]

> Can Uttam Kumar really die? He is the Bengali *super*-hero. Not just on screen, his being as if mirrored the social economy of a people. Of a period. From *Sare Chuattor* to *Chawa Pawa*, from *Pothe Holo Deri* to *Harano Sur*, from *Shilpi* to *Shapmochon*, he was the face of the Bengali male. From the consummate lover of *Chawa Pawa* to the revolutionary of *Sabyasachi*, from the physician of *Agniswor* to the vile politician of *Baghbondi Khela*, his roles embodied a cross-section from across the social spectrum.

This is a sign of a distinct shift in Uttam's assessment. More recently, Swapan Mullick wrote in his book *Mahanayak Revisited*,

> Even from the critical and emotional distance where the present generation stands more than three decades after the sudden turn of events on the night of 24 July 1980, he remains the *Mahanayak*. There is a persistent reluctance to rob Bengal of the thrill of worshipping the only star whose memories can extend from the grassroots in a remote village to the classy ambience of an American city where the Bengali diaspora cannot forget the childhood images of the man they still consider to be one of them.

Clearly, Uttam's appraisals have moved way beyond the gushing homages of him being a heartthrob and a romantic idol.

What is even more striking is Uttam's partial rehabilitation in the world of the Bengali intelligentsia. In the 1960s and 1970s, the bona fide intellectuals did not care for Uttam nor did Uttam seek their approval. As we have seen, there were hints of silent hostility, which the cultural press projected on Uttam and Soumitra as representing the warring camps on two sides of the cinema divide. They could have looked at *Nayak* with more attention. There is a key scene in which the young Arindam and Jyoti wait for the funeral fires of their mentor Shombhu-da to subside. Jyoti asks Arindam if he would still want to give cinema a chance, something that Shombhu-da loathed. When Arindam is hesitant, Jyoti argues, "This is the age of Marx and Freud, no providence, no rebirth." He wants to convince Arindam that he has one life and he should exorcise Shombhu-da's ghost and make a dive for the arc-lights. Arindam ponders and then throws his cigarette at the pyre as a sign of him having made his mind. This is an epiphanic moment of embrace of cinema as the new visual modern; this scene resonating with Uttam's world where the faculties of intellect, talent and hard work were meant to be the passage to an intelligible world of liberal values and politics. This scene should have stimulated those who were cynical of Uttam's cinema. But it didn't.

Four decades later, it will be useless to fall into the same trap. This is not only because the intellectual ownership of art cinema has vaporised or because Uttam's long afterlife has stunned the sceptics. This is also because the definition of what constitutes good cinema itself has changed. So even among the critical or cynical circles, popular cinema of that time is not dismissed anymore as an airy assortment of transient clichés. This way, both the afterlife of Uttam and the world-weary intellectual has somewhat moved towards each other, the latter now making it known that they failed to watch Uttam with any attention when it was his time. There are several testimonials to this effect, with some being from critics, academics, movers of cinema movement. These assessments have more or less agreed that Uttam managed to retain a unique, bhadralok individuality and a stoic civility even in the face of the comparative decline of his name and fame in the mid-1970s. Evaluations also range from identifying Uttam as having visibilised aspiration in popular psyche; to him playing into the masquerade of pantomimic populism; or seeing him as an objectified fetish; a tradeable commodity of desire; an ombudsman of a vainglorious industrial purpose; as symptom of an emasculated romantic malady and so on. In short, film scholarship has followed the usual practice of projecting on to Uttam their particular propositions (and prejudices) about popular cinema.[12] Only the more insightful have managed to look beyond the painted face of stardom and the semiology of cinema into the cultural fascination that a figure like Uttam provokes. But there is still very little discussion about Uttam's persona being a complex carrier of modernity; or him being at the cusp of great historical and cultural convulsions; or his ecumenical stature as a peerless cinematic sovereign.

Nevertheless, Uttam, if he had lived, would have been surprised at this scale of engagement, despite them not always being appreciative. One only wishes that there was more traffic between the world of the cinephile and that of Uttam when he lived. Maybe, the master of the matinee could have saved himself from the dive into the disquiet of his last years. Maybe their companionship could have helped Uttam acquire one thing he increasingly lacked: discernment.

THREE POST-MORTEMS

Is this shift in appraisal enough for Uttam to still hold on forty years later? Why does the enormity of his departure still speak to us? To what extent did he dominate Bengali cinema in his lifetime, that his legacy continues to haunt? How does a charisma and screen persona frozen for forty years include new generations removed from the original time and cultural clime? I have tried to reflect on this question throughout the book, but there are at least three interconnected symptoms that a thorough postmortem should bring to light.

The Singularity of a Screen Stardom

Uttam's deep suspicion for pulpit politics should be seen as an oddity because the story is different elsewhere. Stars in India have gained mythic popularity by riding on popular political platforms or embodying likenesses of mythical figures of majoritarian aspiration. This was common among Uttam's peers in south India. For example, Tamil cinema's M.G. Ramachandran found his first major success in 1954 with *Malaikkalan*, the same year that Uttam found his first major success. MGR almost immediately joined Annadurai, finding himself at the centre of a fierce battle for Dravidian identity. Cinema, for MGR, became a platform to exploit and sustain the popularity that had propelled him to politics, a lesson he had learned from his mentor. Between Annadurai and MGR were born the two most influential Tamil political parties and he also was the first actor to have become the chief minister of a constituent Indian state. Likewise, cinema and politics have been inseparable in Tamil Nadu since the 1950s, at one point sucking in even the politically sceptical Shivaji Ganesan. If MGR leveraged Tamil identity, Andhra's biggest star NTR was the great benefactor of the grandiose mythological throughout his film career. And on retirement from movies, he spent his energies in strengthening Telugu identity with Telugu Desam Party (TDP), which joined other Dravidian movements to create a broader non-Congress base in southern politics.

The case of Hindi cinema was different but there too stars received their own kind of traction: the Bombay Talkies-propelled Nehruvianism of Dilip Kumar being an obvious case study. On the other hand, Dev Anand and Raj Kapoor came from families already invested in cinema and received generous studio backing. In fact, as early as his debut in the 1940s, Raj Kapoor was already a second generation entrant of a seemingly endless dynastic chain. And yet, none of them had a career as a *leading actor* for three long decades. Except Guru Dutt, who was beyond the mathematics of regular stardom, all other leading men of Bollywood were either from film families or had short shelf lives, the most prominent being Rajesh Khanna. The only exception to the rule of longevity is Amitabh Bachchan. But Bachchan has made use of his proximity to various political dispensations since the early 1980s and except a brief half decade, was not obliged to bear the cross of the film industry alone.

Uttam did not come from a film or prominent family. As we have seen, in his early days, he was constantly compared to Pramathesh Barua and Durgadas Banerji, to whose pedigreed background, Uttam's own despondently middle class upbringing would fade incomparably. The backing he received from MP Productions in the early years was a professional gamble rather than parental shepherding. But after the mid-1950s there was no old-style studio to speak of, making his long stardom unchained from any studio-enabled plutocracy. Since then, it was just Uttam. There was every provocation for the star to enhance his cinematic appeal through sources outside cinema. But Uttam was never sustained by a mass movement, nor did he play a mythological character. Ever. This must be noted. Except in one case of a biscuit brand, Uttam never appeared for any print advertisement either. Politically, too, he was agnostic. As we have noted already.

Imagine a career that dawned with Dev Anand and Dilip Kumar, passed through Raj Kapoor, Guru Dutt, Rajendra Kumar, Shammi and Shashi Kapoor, Rajesh Khanna, Amitabh Bachchan, even Amol Palekar and sets only with the rise of Mithun Chakraborty. Imagine a career which, by one trade estimate, had forty super hits, fifty hits and about sixty films that did more than average business. Only about forty were serious duds, of which the chunk came either in the early days or at the very end. This means that between 1955 and 1975, the peak years of his stardom, Uttam had, on average, an annual 'turnover' of two blockbusters and five films with healthy returns, a whopping number to have sustained for twenty years. This entire range, duration and extraordinary mass appeal was based on a singular platform of a screen stardom, and not from extra-cinematic buffers, whether as a fresher looking for supportive shoulders or as a declining star looking for sanctuary. One can take recourse to hyperbole and claim that Uttam was in fact the mythology and the movement. *All by himself.* He hence needed neither.

Even without the hyperbole, the case was no less than exceptional. Hence, to understand Uttam's story is to rethink the idea of the *icon*, the methods of representation of that icon and how cinema manages to keep an iconic figure in perpetual circulation. To that end, Uttam's case tests and teases the fascination with cinema itself—its powers of projection, articulation and dissemination. It is beyond doubt, therefore, that Uttam is not just a fascinating study in middle-class cultural iconography but also a unique study of stardom in India. The fact of this singularity elevates Uttam into a cultural phenomenon. Any great actor would want his *act*, his art, to extend beyond the screen into the continuum, into the great open, into the giant unknown that coalesces into collective memory. Uttam not only managed that but stands like a prodigious figure whose shadow seems to grow bigger and bigger over the industry he had once embodied. There is thus no surprise that with the exception of Tagore and Ray, Uttam enjoys the readiest recall among Bengal's cultural colossi. The picture-framing vendors on Calcutta's streets, after all, had understood this intuitive connection long before hard-boiled cultural observers did.

The Loneliness of a Screen Stardom

To come to the next thesis, some recollection is necessary.

We have learnt that Uttam arrived in Bengali cinema at a momentous historical period, which was also a culturally critical one. For years before, the public life of cinema was complex: it induced loathing and anxiety as much it triggered curiosity and wonder. Some feared cinema, some abhorred it, some called it mass hypnosis, some a grandiose falsity. So, when in the 1950s, cinema started to become an intrinsic part of the newly independent nation's crucible of mass contact, it demanded a figuration that was unique to it. It is on the doors of this restless and charged time that Uttam knocked for opportunity. Soon, Uttam was launched into a stardom that made him the lifeblood of an industry. He could bring to this cinema a delectable finesse, anchored as it was to the changed circumstances in Bengali cultural life and the emergence of a new kind of citizen. Further, Uttam's appeal was built not only on an edifice of feel-good, gratifying romances but also on a great variation in the temperament and ethical code of the male protagonist. Fundamental to the Uttam story is hence how he managed to resolve this dichotomy between the market demands of an unrivalled screen persona and a deep-seated craving for artistic and performative autonomy. Finally, we have learnt that as early as the end 1950s, Uttam was getting tired of the selfsame romances and indicating that a meaty, credible, intelligent part was enough for him to be engaged. Whether he managed it as well as he wanted to is debatable but what is beyond doubt is that very few star-actors have been able to fulfil, for so long, the role of a commercial star, a cultural mascot and a cinematic sovereign at the same time. This part we know.

But what is equally true is that inside this exceptionalism resides a deep-seated isolation. So, what the more seasoned Uttam reveals is not a star enjoying a seemingly endless run at the box office but being reckoned as having colonised the industry, which puzzled, troubled and saddened Uttam in equal measure. And it remained unabated till his death. Indeed, this lonely exceptionality of Uttam's screen persona is to be measured not only with respect to the body of work that was contemporary to it but also as it emerges in stark contrast to Bengali cinema's free-fall into poverty in the post-Uttam phase.

Let's turn to *Nayak* again. Arindam's face is not revealed for the first few minutes of the movie. Rather, the narrative tries to build the idea of the movie star from objects strewn around—the posh room, the hanging glossies, the travelling bag, the swank cabinet, the electric shaver, the bottle of scotch. Moments later, Jyoti walks in with the day's paper, which carries a mention of a drunk Arindam having heckled a man the previous evening. For Jyoti, the news would further dampen Arindam's new release, which was not doing much business anyway. Arindam, while fixing his shoes enquires why. Jyoti says, 'Why would it? Except you, what is there in the film anyway?' Here, Arindam looks up and the camera pans close to his face for the first time. Arindam asks, 'Why? I am there. Isn't that enough?' Clearly, the film wanted Arindam's face to surface exactly at the moment when his singularity is both obvious and under threat. Jyoti reasons that Arindam is not enough anymore, the times were testing and people were reluctant to pay for poor films. Arindam becomes dismissive. 'The idiotic public', he rants, 'they should be bulldozed!'

Having raised this moment of tension between a star and his public early in the film, Ray lets it rest there, letting it find resolution in the film itself. But in real life, Uttam was stalked time and again by the fact of him being the *only* box office wager for all the long years of his working life; and an industry that too narrowly banked on him. More than once he wrote and mused that the fact of no one having come to replace him in all the years was an absolutely deplorable deficiency in Bengali cinema. "I have been forced to play a match without an opponent", he had said. "How can an actor continue to do any good work if there is no one to compete with, no one to look up to?" he had pondered.[13]

In fact, the 'opponent' here is not only a male actor of any promise or prominence but also a female figure, the latter case relevant from at least 1970. By 1970, most of the memorable heterosexual screen partnerships Uttam had been part of showed signs of having exhausted themselves. As early as the mid-1950s, Uttam was forced to bid adieu to an under-realised partnership with Manju Dey and an overwrought one with Sondharani. By 1962, he had to see off both Suchitra Sen and Mala Sinha, the latter permanently. Ditto for Arundhati Mukherjee in 1964. There were gleaming moments with Tanuja, Sharmila, Madhabi and Anjana Bhowmik through the 1960s. But by 1970, the screen pairing with Tanuja, Anjana and Sharmila (except in one case) ended resoundingly and only carried wearily with Madhabi. Even the fabulous and motley partnership with Sabitri (that began in early 1950s) came to a waste after 1970. There are films with her but hardly anything of any substance. The only exception was Supriya, who continued to find her way into movies with Uttam but with increasingly painful results. Her best with Uttam, anyway meagre, was also over by 1970. The efforts of young Aparna Sen to clock the numbers or those at reviving the pairing with Suchitra, as we have seen, bombed. Same for Arati Bhattacharjee in later years. Except a memorable two-film partnership with Kaberi Bose in 1975, very few Uttam films solicited a female lead of any lasting impression. Like all vicious cycles, there is an unresolved one here too. It is not clear if the industry's surrender to Uttam's stardom was responsible for drying up the roles of the female actors; or if the lack of comparative talent forced makers to opt for films where Uttam had a larger-than-life role. Either way, the films, even the better ones, were all about Uttam. And from 1976 and after; the less one counts, the better. It was, hence, a loneliness both on and off the screen.

The loneliness of being all alone and larger-than-life got the better of Uttam's usual affability and adjustability too. In his very last year, to his co-actor Sondhya Roy he complained, "They have made me into a money-making machine. I simply cannot go on this way."[14] When Kanan Debi said at Uttam's memorial gathering that the star may have had a massive following but never had one genuine friend, she was not exaggerating. The Goan lensman Prabhakar Prabhu, who was from the renowned photography concern Edna Lorenz and had shot Uttam on many assignments, said, "I saw Uttam closely in his later years. When he was not posing and if one could catch his eyes on a close frame, they would betray a deep vacuum, a severe loneliness and stark sense of helplessness."[15]

The saying 'it is lonely at the top' not only realised itself with full force, but for Uttam had clearly assumed the shape of a metaphysical deadlock, one which only his death could undo.

The Starkness of a Screen Stardom

But this deadlock, in retrospect, hints at a far more disturbing possibility. All the accolades and awards, the tributes and testimonials notwithstanding, the singularity and loneliness of Uttam's stardom had a blunt and brute script of domination accompanying it. Inside and outside the screen, his presence was so overwhelming, so colossal, so omnipotent, that every bit of the tangled, multifarious circuit of popular cinema eventually led to him. This tendency started in the mid-1950s, when Bengali cinema found a bankable agency in Uttam. Soon, trust became a habit of security and gradually it meant relinquishing of other, potent possibilities of popular expression in cinema. This meant that over the years the industry became habitually addicted to Uttam, sapping itself off all other sources of nutriment. Uttam's stardom had plateaued at the very summit, concealing this sorry submission to the phenomenon he had become. So, till the mid-1970s, the industry did not manage to grow beyond what was just about necessary to uphold a figure like Uttam. It eventually and inevitably started to buckle under that very weight. The way the industry collapsed after Uttam's exit clearly hints at the possibility that in effect, Uttam's long and terrific stardom was much in excess of the industry that pillared him. Or rather, Bengali cinema consumed itself trying to reinforce the unbearable heaviness of Uttam's stardom.

But this is just one part of the problem. The second is about what happened to the screen persona. Because there, another kind of mining went on unabated. Uttam's filmography—so fulsome, so versatile and so generous—was ultimately based on a variation of the bhadralok figuration. Uttam's appeal was transcendental and his cult all-encompassing. But his cinema was doggedly middle class and his screen persona an assorted collection of it. His death made two things tangible. First, that the celebrated bhadralok figuration had reached its bankruptcy on screen, exhausting it of all possibility of any further enunciation. No one could embody it better than Uttam; so with his death, the figure itself had to be exterminated. Second, that Bengali popular cinema had developed no other voice, no other vantage, no other optics to look at the world unless it did so through that of the middle-class bhadralok.

The most remarkable part of Uttam's stardom as well as Bengali cinema's distinction was its close and collateral participation in the project middle-class modernity. But with time Bengali popular cinema did not develop the means to operate outside the stardom of Uttam and outside the provinces of bhadralok dominion. For three decades it stayed awed by and chained to these safeguards, both inside and outside the screen, even risking the possibility that the on-screen bhadralok figuration was in denial of Bengal's changing social mores. Then, Bengali cinema lost the on-creen and off-screen figure together—abruptly, unprepared and unequipped. All kinds of superstardom saps at the foundation of a structure. Uttam's was no exception. So, what happened after his death bared a simple fact: that in three decades, Bengali cinema's biggest asset had *also* come to be its most arduous burden. In brief, Uttam's life and work came to be an exemplar of both the seduction and the severe limits of messianism.

Hence the void Uttam left behind started to bleed like a gaping wound, searing the heart of Bengali cinema, a wound from which that cinema has not managed to emerge in the four decades since. In effect then, Uttam virtually overworked himself to death for an industry that had long forgotten how to look beyond him. At the same time and unknown to him, Uttam took with him the Madelaine of his cinema, leaving it sapped, brittle, hollowed out. An era surely came to an end with Uttam. But Uttam took away too much of that era with him. No wonder, cinema after him had nowhere to go, nothing to hold on to, nothing to be beholden to. After Uttam, thus, came the deluge.

A FINAL ODE TO INFINITY

This kind of miraculous stardom is not an easy phenomenon to gauge. Perhaps Freud might offer some help. Since Uttam has played both a psychoanalyst and an object of enquiry, and his character(s) refers directly to Freud at least twice, it won't be out of place to end this book with the revered, controversial, psychoanalyst.

In 1928, Sigmund Freud wrote an essay titled *Dostoevsky and Parricide*, his only one on a writer and his last one on literature. Freud begins the essay saying:

> Four facets may be distinguished in the rich personality of Dostoevsky: the creative artist, the neurotic, the moralist and the sinner. How is one to find one's way in this bewildering complexity? The creative artist is the least doubtful: Dostoevsky's place is not far behind Shakespeare. *The Brothers Karamazov* is the most magnificent novel ever written; the episode of the Grand Inquisitor, one of the peaks in the literature of the world, can hardly be valued too highly. Before the problem of the creative artist analysis must, alas, lay down its arms.[16]

What Freud insists here is quite extraordinary: that even the best tools of psychoanalysis cannot probe the genius of a writer.

And an actor? Let us recall a memorable exchange about this. During the shoot of *Nayak*, two train cars became a case of curiosity. Rarely were such detailing accommodated in a Bengali film. Ray usually shot on location after extensive preparations. But for *Nayak*, he got an exquisitely designed set made, where the locomotive principles were also strictly adhered to. The man behind it, as usual, was Ray's noted art director Bangshi Chandragupta. When Uttam first saw the set, his jaws fell. He walked up to his Bangshi-da and said, "How did you manage to make such an eye-popping set? What thinking goes into it, tell me."[17] Bangshi-da thought for a minute and replied, "If you can explain to me how you bring that unforced, uncanny, unscripted naturalism to your performances, I will tell you how I go about my work."[18] Uttam smiled. And fell silent.

This conundrum of the uncodifiable genius of an artist was not just a problem facing Freud or Bangshi-da. Genius is generally impenetrable even to the most astute intelligence. Or so we learn from Satyajit Ray, who made an entire film for a glimpse into the genius of Uttam. *Nayak* carries all the markers of Ray's brilliant cinematic sense but what is less explicit is Uttam's bravura confidence. We certainly know that whether in his public poise or in his private agony, whether in his charismatic finesse or in his alcoholic stupor, Uttam's Arindam is matchless and marvellous. But Arindam is *none other* than Uttam Kumar. What Ray's script was doing was daring the actor in Uttam to deconstruct the star. In other words, the better Uttam played the troubled hero, the more the fictional star (and *the* real star*)* would find himself belittled and diminished. What confidence it must have taken for Uttam to perform a clinical surgery on his own stardom, unperturbed by the possibility of perforating the carefully constructed mythos that surrounds a star figure. So, do we have a deconstructed hero at the end of *Nayak*? By all means, no. *Nayak* upped the ante for him as an actor but did not cause a dent in his stardom nor a penny of discount on his appeal. This confidence is not the make of Uttam the actor or the person. It is the constituent of the genius of the star. And it is this genius which ensured that even after the *actor's* relentless self-examination and self-loathing, and the probing eyes of Ray's script, the *star* would emerge unscathed into sunlight; a realisation that has repeatedly sent Ray into acknowledging, wholeheartedly, the enormity of Uttam's singular greatness; a realisation that Ray had laid open in one of the film's posters. It modestly said, "Satyajit Ray's observance of the hero."

Freud, Bangshi-da or Ray, in their own way, and in spite of their individual brilliance, never managed to get beyond the skin of genius. This book, naturally, makes no such claim. So, after all the interrogations, the deliberations and the affirmations that have gone to make this book, if you have not been able, dear reader, to still put your finger on the extraordinary screen genius of a mediocre man, into the incomprehensible brilliance of his singular stardom, or into the epic ruin that he left behind, then let it be known, let it be acknowledged, that genius, in the final count, is unknowable. So, after all the efforts of containment and confinement that a vernacular film culture imposes on a transcendental, titanic stardom, let it be known, let it be acknowledged, that everything about Uttam's cinema runs the risk of getting dated one day; except Uttam himself.

He is such stuff as dreams are made of.

NOTES

1. Satyajit Ray, *Probondho Songroho* (Collection of Essays), edited by Sandip Ray, Kolkata: Ananda Publishers, 2015, p. 335.
2. Asishtoru Mukhopadhyay, *Ojana Uttam*, Dey's Publishing, 2006, p. 118.
3. 'Mahanayak Uttam Kumar', *Boisakhi* Journal, edited by Dhrubojyoti Mondol, 23 (2013–2014), p. 157.
4. 'Mahanayak Uttam Kumar', p. 157.
5. *Chalachitra Purbabharati* Journal, Uttam Kumar Memorial Issue (December 1980), pp. 49–50.
6. *Chalachitra Purbabharati* Journal, p. 44.
7. Sayandeb Chowdhury, 'The Endangered City in Rituparno Ghosh's Early Cinema of Confinement', *South Asian History and Culture*, 6:2 (2015), pp. 277–289.
8. 'Ontorongo Uttam', *Boisakhi* Journal, edited by Dhrubojyoti Mondol, 23 (2013–2014), p. 80.
9. Rituparno Ghosh, *Robibar* Magazine, 5 September 2010.
10. Suchitra Bhattacharya, 'Rabibashorio', *Anandabazar Patrika*, 24 July 2011.
11. *Chitrabhash* Journal, Uttam Kumar Special Issue 36:1–4 (2001).
12. See several such works of critique in *Tehai* Journal, Uttam Kumar Special Issue, edited by Saptarshi Bhattacharya, 2:1 (January 2010).
13. 'Ontorongo Uttam', p. 82.
14. Mukhopadhyay, *Ojana Uttam*, p. 69.
15. *Chalachitra Purbabharati*, p. 34.
16. Sigmund Freud, 'Dostoevsky and Parricide', in *The Standard Edition of the Complete Psychological Works of Sigmund Freud*, edited by James Strachey et al., Vol. 21, London: Hogarth Press, pp. 177–194.
17. Amio Sanyal (ed.), *Uttom Sorbottomo*, Ritwick Publication, 2008, pp. 175–176.
18. Sanyal, *Uttom Sorbottomo*, pp. 175–176.

BIBLIOGRAPHY

ENGLISH LANGUAGE SOURCES

Bandyopadhyay, Sibaji. *Sibaji Bandyopadhyay Reader.* New Delhi: Worldview Publications, 2012.

Berman, Marshall. *All That Is Solid Melts into Air.* Penguin Books, 1982 [1988].

Bhaumik, Kaushik. 'The Emergence of the Bombay Film Industry'. Unpublished PhD thesis, Oxford University, 2011.

Biswas, Moinak (ed.). *Apu and After, Re-visiting Ray's Cinema.* Calcutta: Seagull Books, 2005.

———. 'Rich Tradition'. *Frontline* 30:20, 18 October 2013: 81–94.

———. 'From Space to Location'. *Positions: East-Asia Cultures Critique* 25:1, 2017: 9–28.

Brooks, Peter. *The Melodramatic Imagination: Balzac, Henry James, Melodrama, and the Mode of Excess.* New Haven: Yale University Press, 1995 [1976].

Chatterjee, Ranita. 'Journeys in and beyond the City: Cinema in Calcutta 1897–1939'. Unpublished PhD thesis, University of Westminster, 2011.

Chatterjee, Shoma A. *Suchitra Sen, the Legend and the Enigma.* HarperCollins India, 2015.

Chatterjee, Subhajit. 'Remapping Transitions of Bengali Cinema into the 50s'. *Journal of the Moving Image* 9, 2010: 117–146.

Chaudhuri, Sukanta. *Calcutta: The Living City,* Vols 1 and 2. Oxford University Press, 2013 [1990].

Chowdhury, Maitreyee. *Bengali Cinema's First Couple.* Om Books, 2013.

Chowdhury, Sayandeb. 'A Postcolonial Iconi-City: Re-Reading Uttam Kumar's Cinema as Metropolar Melodrama'. *Journal of South Asian History and Culture* (Bengali Cinema: Star Texts, Genre, Tropes) 8:2, 2017: 171–185.

———. 'Power to the Bourgeoisie: How the Left Bengali Cinema'. *Caravan Magazine* 12, 2011: 20–21.

———. 'Stardust Memories: The Cosmopolitanism of Uttam Kumar and His Era-Defining Cinema'. *TheWire.in,* published online, 24 July 2017. Available at https://thewire.in/film/uttam-kumar-bengali-cinema.

———. 'The Heroic Laughter of Modernity: The Life, Cinema and Afterlife of Bengali Matinee Idol Uttam Kumar'. *Film International* 10:04/05, 2012: 82–91.

———. 'The Indian Partition and the Making of New Scopic Regime in Bengali Cinema'. *European Journal of English Studies* (Special Issue: Poetics and Partition) 19:3, 2016: 255–270.

Clarke, David (ed.). *The Cinematic City.* London: Routledge, 1997.

Dasgupta, Susmita. *Amitabh Bachchan: Reflections on a Star Image.* Bloomsbury, 2018.

Dass, Manishita. *Outside the Lettered City: Cinema, Modernity, and the Public Sphere in Late Colonial India.* Oxford: Oxford University Press, 2016.

Desai, Meghnad. *Nehru's Hero Dilip Kumar: In the Life of India.* Roli Books, 2017.

Dyer, Richard. *Stars.* London: British Film Institute, 1998.

Eliot, Marc. *Cary Grant: A Biography.* Three Rivers Press, 2005.

Freud, Sigmund. 'Dostoevsky and Parricide'. *The Standard Edition of the Complete Psychological Works of Sigmund Freud,* edited by James Strachey and others, Vol. 21, pp. 177–194. London: Hogarth Press.

Ghosh, Nipabithi. *Uttam Kumar: The Ultimate Hero.* Rupa, 2002.

Ghosh, Parimal. *What Happened to Bhadralok.* Primus, 2016.

Gledhill, Christine. *Stardom: Industry of Desire.* London: Routledge, 1991.

Gokulsing, K. Moti and Wimal Dissanayoke (eds). *Routledge Handbook of Indian Cinemas.* Routledge T&F, 2013.

Gooptu, Sharmistha. *Bengali Cinema: The Other Nation.* Delhi: Roli Books, 2010.

Harding, D. *Writing the City: Urban Visions and Literary Modernism.* London: Routledge, 2003.

Iyer, Pico. 'Satyajit Ray's "The Hero" Revisited'. NYRB, 27 February 2018. Available at https://www.nybooks.com/daily/2018/02/27/satyajit-rays-the-hero-revisited/.

Jacobson, Brian R. *Studios before the System: Architecture, Technology, and the Emergence of Cinematic Space.* Columbia University Press, 2015.

Jay, Martin and Sumathi Ramaswamy (eds). *Empires of Vision: A Reader.* Duke University Press, 2014.

Kaarsholm, Preben (ed.). *City Flicks: Indian Cinema and the Urban Experience.* Calcutta: Seagull Books, 2007.

Kanfer, Stefan. *Somebody: The Reckless Life and Remarkable Career of Marlon Brando.* Faber, 2011.

Majumdar, Ranjani. *Bombay Cinema: An Archive of the City.* Minneapolis: University of Minnesota Press, 2007.

Marcantonio, Carla. *Global Melodrama: Nation, Body, and History in Contemporary Film.* London: Palgrave Macmillan, 2015.

Mukherjee, Madhuja (ed.). *Aural films, Oral Cultures: Essays on Cinema the Early Sound Era.* Kolkata: Jadavpur University Press, 2012.

———. 'Inside a Dark Hall: Space, Place, and Accounts of Some Single-Theatres in Kolkata'. *South Asian History and Culture,* T&F, 8:2, 2017: 269–282.

———. 'Rethinking Popular Cinema in Bengal (1930s–1950s): Of Literariness, Comic Mode, Mythological and Other Avatars'. *South Asian History and Culture* 8:2, 2017: 122–142.

———. 'The Story of Arri: Imagined Landscapes, Emergent Technologies and Bengali Cinema'. *Journal of the Moving Image* 2011: 61–80.

Mullick, Swapan. *Maha Nayok Revisited.* Westland, 2013.

Nandy, Ashish. *The Ambiguous Journey to The City: The Village and Other Odd Ruins of the Self in the Indian Imagination.* Oxford University Press, 2001.

Pal, Pratapaditya (ed.). *Calcutta: Changing Visions, Lasting Images.* Mumbai: Marg Publications, 1990.

Pandian, M.S.S. *Image-Trap: MG Ramachandran's Film and Politics.* Sage Publications, 2015.

Pinney, Christopher. *The Coming of Photography in India.* New Delhi: Oxford University Press, 2008.

Prasad, M. Madhava. *Cine-Politics: Film Stars and Political Existence in South India.* New Delhi: Orient Blackswan, 2014.

Raban, Jonathan. *Soft City.* Picador/Pan Macmillan, 2017.

Ray, Sandip (ed.). *Satyajit Ray on Cinema.* New York: Columbia University Press, 2013.

Robinson, Andrew. *Satyajit Ray: The Inner Eye.* IB Taurus, 1989.

Sarkar, Bhaskar. *Mourning the Nation: Indian Cinema in the Wake of Partition.* New Delhi: Orient Blackswan, 2010.

Sarkar, Tanika and Sekhar Bandyopadhyay (eds). *Calcutta: The Stormy Decades.* Delhi: Social Science Press, 2015.

Sengoopta, Chandak. *The Rays before Satyajit: Creativity and Modernity in Colonial India.* Oxford University Press, 2016.

———. 'Satyajit Ray: Liberalism and Its Vicissitudes'. *Cinéaste* 34:4, 2009.

Seton, Marie. *Satyajit Ray: Portrait of a Director.* Penguin Books, 2003 [1971].

Shiel, Mark and Tony Fitzmaurice (eds). *Cinema and the City: Film and Urban Societies in a Global Context.* Oxford: Blackwell, 2011.

Singer, Ben. *Melodrama and Modernity: Early Sensational Cinema and Its Contexts.* New York: Columbia University Press, 2001.

Vasudevan, Ravi. *Meaning-Making in Indian Cinema.* Oxford University Press, 2000.

———. *The Melodramatic Public: Film Form and Spectatorship in Indian Cinema.* Ranikhet: Permanent Black, 2010.

Virdi, Jyotika. *The Cinematic Imagination: Indian Popular Films as Social History.* Ranikhet: Permanent Black, 2003.

Ziegler, Philip. *Olivier.* Quercus, 2014.

BENGALI LANGUAGE SOURCES

Basu, Ashok. *Mahanayok.* Kriti, 2016.

Basu, Robi. *Satrong*, Vols 1 and 2. Dey's Publishing, 2013.

Bhattacharjee, Jayanta. *Mahanayok Uttamkumar: Ami, Somoi ebong Smriti.* Sutonu Prokashoni, 2005.

Bhowmik, Someswar. *Cinema Ebong Koekjon.* Ebong Mushaira, 2014.

Boisakhi Journal. 'Mahanayak Uttam Kumar', edited by Dhrubojyoti Mondol, Vol. 23, 2013–2014.

Chalachitra Purbabharati Journal, Uttam Kumar Memorial Issue, December 1980.

Chattopadhyay, Himansu. *Tollywooder Mahanayok.* Urvi, 2010.

Chattopadhyay, Tarunkumar. *Amar Dada Uttamkumar.* Sahityam, 2000.

Das, Sachin. *Swoyong Kondorpo Durgadas.* Protibhash, 2012.

Ghosh, Jayanta Kumar. *Bratyojoner Bioscope.* Dey's Publishing, 2008.

Ghosh, Jayanta Kumar. *Matinee Idol Uttamkumar*. Dey's Publishing, 2105.

Mukhopadhyay, Arabindo. *Alochhayar Dinguli*, edited by Sarbajit Mukhopadhyay and Gopal Das. Dey's Publishing, 2018.

Mukhopadhyay, Asishtoru. *Ojana Uttam*. Dey's Publishing, 2006.

Mukhopadhyay, Chandi. *Bangla Cholochitrer Itihash*. Gangchil, 2015.

———. *Ochena Uttam*. Pratibhash, 2016.

Palit, Dibyendu and Nirmalya Acharjya. *Sotoborshe Cholochitra*, Vols 1 and 2. Ananda Publishers, 1996.

Ray, Satyajit. *Probontho Songroho*. Ananda Publishers, 2015.

Roy, Sukumar and Shaibal Biswas. *Uttom Chobi*. Sutradhar, 2014.

Sanyal, Amio (ed.). *Uttom Sorbottomo*. Ritwick Publication, 2008.

Sen, Prithwiraj. *Alo Andhare Mahanayok Utam Kumar*. Priya Book House, 2016.

Sengupta, Ramananda. *Ajo Mone Pore*. North Calcutta Film Society, 2016.

Sinha, Tapan. *Chalachitra Ajibon*. Dey's Publishing, 2009.

Tehai Journal, Uttam Kumar Special Issue, edited by Saptarshi Bhattacharya, 2:1, January 2010.

BOOKS BY UTTAM KUMAR

Chattopadhyay, Uttamkumar. *Amar Ami* (An unfinished autobiography). Dey's Publishing, 1972.

———. *Hariye Jaoa Dinguli Mor* (A memoir of early days), edited by Abhik Chattopadhyay. Saptarshi Prokashon, 2013.

———. *Nayoker Kolome* (A collection of writings by Uttam). Saptarshi Prokashon, 2015.

SELECT FILMOGRAPHY

1948
1. *Drishtidan* (The Gift of Sight)

1949
2. *Kamona* (A Plea)

1950
3. *Morjada* (The Honourable)

1951
4. *Ore Jatri* (Listen, Traveller)
5. *Sohojatri* (The Fellow Traveller)
6. *Nostonir* (The Poisoned Nest)

1952
7. *Sanjeebani* (The Healing Tree)
8. *Bosu Poribar* (The Basu Family)
9. *Kar Pape?* (The Sinner)

1953
10. *Sharey Chuattor* (The Secret Insignia)
11. *Lakh Taka* (Chasing a Bounty)
12. *Nobin Jatra* (A New Journey)
13. *Bou Thakuranir Haat* (The Consort's Tale)

1954
14. *Moner Moyur* (The Singing Heart)
15. *Ora Thake Odhare* (They Live That Side)
16. *Chanpadangar Bou* (The Wronged Wife)
17. *Kalyani* (The Caregiver)
18. *Shodanonder Mela* (The Occupants)
19. *Annapurnar Mondir* (Temple of Bounty)
20. *Agniporikha* (Trial by Fire)
21. *Bakul* (The Boy in the Middle)
22. *Grihaprabesh* (Housewarming Day)
23. *Montroshokti* (The Power of Prayer)
24. *Moroner Pore* (After Death)

1955

25. *Sanjher Prodip* (Light of the Dusk)
26. *Anupoma* (The Unequalled)
27. *Raikamal* (The Minstrel)
28. *Debatra* (A Divine Will)
29. *Shapmochon* (Breaking of a Curse)
30. *Bidhilipi* (The Mark of Fortune)
31. *Hrod* (The Lake)
32. *Upohar* (The Gift)
33. *Kankabatir Ghat* (Bond of Purity)
34. *Raatbhor* (Night's End)
35. *Bratacharini* (A Virtuous Woman)
36. *Sobar Opore* (The Final Truth)

1956

37. *Sagorika* (The Call of the Sea)
38. *Saheb Bibi Golam* (The King, the Queen and the Knave)
39. *Lokhyoheera* (The Glitter of Good)
40. *Chirokumar Sobha* (Bachelor's Club)
41. *Ekti Raat* (Story of a Night)
42. *Shankar Narayan Bank* (A Banking Scandal)
43. *Shyamali* (A Woman in the Dark)
44. *Trijama* (The Night River)
45. *Putrobodhu* (The Daughter in Law)
46. *Shilpi* (The Artiste)
47. *Nabajonmo* (A New Birth)

1957

48. *Harjeet* (Toil and Triumph)
49. *Bordidi* (Elder Sister)
50. *Jatra Holo Shuru* (The Journey Begins)
51. *Prithibi Amare Chai* (The World at Large)
52. *Tasher Ghar* (House of Cards)
53. *Surer Parashe* (The Touch of Melody)
54. *Punormilon* (The Reunion)
55. *Harano Sur* (The Lost Tune)
56. *Obhoyer Biye* (Education of a Simple Man)
57. *Chondronath* (The Beautiful and the Damned)
58. *Pothe Holo Deri* (The Delayed Journey)
59. *Jibontrishna* (Thirst for Life)

1958

60. *Rajlakshi O Srikanto* (The Deviant and the Demimonde)
61. *Bondhu* (Test of Friendship)
62. *Manmoyee Girls' School* (Scandal in a School)
63. *Dactarbabu* (The Physician)
64. *Shikaar* (The Hunt)
65. *Indrani* (The Egoist)
66. *Joutuk* (The Dowry)
67. *Surjotoron* (Sun Tower)

1959

68. *Morutirtho Hinglaj* (Desert Pilgrimage)
69. *Chawa Pawa* (Roads to Romance)
70. *Bicharok* (The Judge)
71. *Pushpadhonu* (Bow of Flowers)
72. *Goli Theke Rajpoth* (Rags to Riches)
73. *Khelaghor* (The Playhouse)
74. *Sonar Harin* (The Golden Stag)
75. *Obak Prithibi* (Strange World)

1960

76. *Mayamriga* (The Red Herring)
77. *Raja Saja* (A Royal Masquerade)
78. *Kuhok* (The Enchanter)
79. *Uttormegh* (Beyond the Cloud)
80. *Hat Baralei Bondhu* (A Friend in Deed)
81. *Khokababur Protyabartan* (Return of the Prodigal Son)
82. *Shokher Chor* (The Mischievous Thief)
83. *Shohorer Itikotha* (Tales of the City)
84. *Shuno Boronari* (An Unequal Romance)

1961

85. *Sathihara* (Nomadic Love)
86. *Agnisonskar* (Fire Sermon)
87. *Jhinder Bondi* (Prisoner of Jhind)
88. *Necklace* (The Necklace)
89. *Soptopodi* (The Seven Steps)
90. *Dui Bhai* (The Martinet)

1962

91. *Bipasha* (The Tears of Beas)
92. *Shiulibari* (The Townmaker)
93. *Kanna* (The Cry)

1963

94. *Sesh Anko* (The Final Act)
95. *Nisithe* (At the Dead of Night)
96. *Uttarayan* (The Rising)
97. *Bhrantibilash* (Comedy of Errors)
98. *Surjosikha* (Flames of the Sun)
99. *Deya Neya* (A Romantic Exchange)

1964

100. *Vibhas* (The Outcast)
101. *Jotugriha* (The House of Wax)
102. *Notun Tirtho* (A New Destination)
103. *Momer Alo* (The Light of Candle)
104. *Lal Pathor* (The Red Stone)

1965

105. *Thana Theke Aschi* (An Inspector Calls)
106. *Rajkonya* (Portrait of a Princess)
107. *Surjotopa* (Sun Prayer)

1966

108. *Rajdrohi* (The Royal Rebel)
109. *Sudhu Ekti Bochhor* (A Marriage Contract)
110. *Nayak* (The Hero)
111. *Shonkhobela* (Hour of Return)
112. *Kal Tumi Aleya* (The Survivor)

1967

113. *Nayika Sombad* (Runaway Star)
114. *Jibonmrityu* (Life and Death)
115. *Grihadaha* (A House on Fire)
116. *Chiriyakhana* (The Zoo)
117. *Antony Firingee* (Poet from Another Land)

1968

118. *Chowrongee* (Chowringhee)
119. *Teen Odhyay* (Three Episodes)
120. *Garh Nasimpur* (The Fight for Nasimpur)
121. *Kokhono Megh* (Shadows of the Cloud)

1969

122. *Sobormoti* (The Confluence)
123. *Chirodiner* (The Call of the Eternal)

124. *Shukh-Sari* (The Love Birds)
125. *Komollota* (A Noble Woman)
126. *Mon Niye* (A Forked Mind)
127. *Aporichito* (The Stranger)

1970

128. *Kolonkito Nayok* (The Disgraced Hero)
129. *Duti Mon* (Two Souls)
130. *Rajkumari* (The Princess)
131. *Nishipodmo* (The Night Flower)
132. *Bilombito Loy* (The Delayed Rhythm)

1971

133. *Ekhane Pinjor* (The Prisonhouse)
134. *Joy Joyonti* (The Governess)
135. *Nabarag* (The New Scale)
136. *Chhoddobeshi* (The Trickster)
137. *Dhonyi Meye* (The Restless Bride)
138. *Jibon Jigyasha* (The Atoner)

1972

139. *Alo Amar Alo* (The Light Within)
140. *Andho Ateet* (The Blind Past)
141. *Stree* (The Wife)
142. *Chhinnopotro* (The Torn Letter)
143. *Memsaheb* (The Beloved)
144. *Har Mana Har* (A Victory in Defeat)

1973

145. *Bonpolashir Podaboli* (Song of the Wildflower)
146. *Kayahiner Kahini* (The Tale of the Disembodied)
147. *Rater Rajanigandha* (The Fragrance of Night)
148. *Roudrochaya* (Shadows of the Sun)

1974

149. *Alor Thikana* (The Site of Light)
150. *Jodi Jantem* (A Secret Formula)
151. *Jodubongsho* (The Parricide)
152. *Rodonobhora Bosonto* (Tears of Spring)
153. *Nokol Shona* (False Glitter)
154. *Bikele Bhorer Phool* (Love in Autumn)
155. *Amanush* (The Savage)

1975

156. *Agniswor* (The Lord of Fire)
157. *Nogor Dorpone* (In the Mirror of the City)
158. *Ami, She O Shokha* (Inverted Triangle)
159. *Baghbondi Khela* (The Hunting Game)
160. *Sonyashi Raja* (The Sagely King)
161. *Priyo Bandhobi* (Dear Friend)

1976

162. *Shei Chokh* (The Eyes)
163. *Nidhiram Sardar* (The Vigilante)
164. *Bonhisikha* (The Renegade)
165. *Chander Kachakachi* (Closer to the Moon)

1977

166. *Osadharon* (The Extraordinary)
167. *Anondo Ashram* (A Doctor's Tale)
168. *Sabyasachi* (The Revolutionary)
169. *Jal Sonyashi* (The False Monk)

1978

170. *Bondi* (The Convict)
171. *Dhanraj Tamang* (Revenge in the Hills)
172. *Brojobuli* (A Man Made of Words)

1979

173. *Devdas* (Devdas)
174. *Nobodigonto* (A New Horizon)

1980

175. *Dui Prithibi* (Two Worlds)

1981

176. *Ogo Bodhu Sundori* (My Beautiful Wife)

ABOUT THE AUTHOR

Sayandeb Chowdhury teaches in the School of Letters at Ambedkar University Delhi and is a doctoral fellow in the Department of Film Studies, Jadavpur University, Kolkata. His research and teaching interests are in colonial and postcolonial visual modernisms, cinema and photography studies, adaptation studies and city studies. His essays have been published in *Film International, Journal of South Asian History and Culture, South Asia Review, European Journal of English Studies, Economic and Political Weekly* (*EPW*), and scholarly collections *Rituparno Ghosh: Cinema, Gender and Art* (2016), *Sea Narratives: Cultural Responses to the Sea 1600–Present* (2016), *L'entrée en ville: Aménager, Expérimenter, Représenter* (2017), *Mistrust: Developmental, Cultural, and Clinical Realms* (2017), *On the Politics of Ugliness* (2018) and *Ideas of the City in Asian Settings* (2019). He was a UKNA Fellow at the International Institute of Asian Studies, Leiden, in 2015, and a Charles Wallace Fellow in 2016. He has written on art, books, politics and cinema for *Huffington Post, The Monthly Review, Art India, Caravan Magazine, Café Dissensus, Outlook, Biblio, Indian Express, Critical Collective, The Wire, Scroll, Business Standard, The Hindu, Anandabazar Patrika* and others. More about his work and interests can be found at www.sayandeb.in.